The Open University

A206
The Enlightenment

Texts, II

Edited by Simon Eliot and Keith Whitlock

First published in 1992 by
The Open University
Walton Hall
Milton Keynes
United Kingdom
MK7 6AA

ISBN 0 7492 1103 2

Edited, designed and typeset by The Open University.

This book forms part of an Open University course A206 *The Enlightenment.*

Printed and bound in Great Britain by The Bath Press, Bath
1.5

Contents

Part D
Religion and humanity

Contents

David Hume
Dialogues concerning Natural Religion

Prepared for the Course Team by
Rosalind Hursthouse

Contents

David Hume
Dialogues concerning Natural Religion

These Dialogues *were completed some time during the decade before 1761, but were not published until three years after Hume's death in 1776 because of their controversial nature. His friends advised against their publication during his lifetime, and he himself expressed the wish to 'live quietly and remote from all Clamour' for his remaining years. Even after his death, his great friend, Adam Smith, refused to sponsor their publication, despite Hume's known wishes, and they were eventually brought out by his favourite nephew and heir.*

The Dialogues *are ostensibly a written record made by a young man, Pamphilus, of a conversation between three characters, Cleanthes, Demea and Philo. Pamphilus, whose education is being supervised by Cleanthes, sends the account, with an introductory section and occasional interposed remarks of his own, to a friend Hermippus. The conversation is about the argument for the existence of God as the Designer of the Universe. Hume exploits the dialogue form to explore various objections to, and defences of, it.*

The Dialogues *are modelled on a classical source,* Cicero's[1] *dialogues* On The Nature of the Gods, *as Johnson imitated Juvenal, and Gibbon, Tacitus; and like Cicero, Hume uses the device of a narrator who introduces the discussion, and who draws conclusions at the end about whose arguments have prevailed.*

The three protagonists in Cicero's dialogue are Cotta the Academic or Sceptic, Balbus the Stoic, representative of orthodoxy, and Velleius the Epicurean. Philo, in Hume's Dialogues, *corresponds to Cotta, and Cleanthes to Balbus. Hume's choice of names was probably determined by the circumstance that Philo was the name of Cotta's teacher, and that Cleanthes was one of Balbus' masters in philosophy. However, Cicero's narrator is himself, whereas Hume's is fictitious, thus it is left unspoken which protagonist, if any, Hume himself favoured. So skilfully are the* Dialogues *written that this remains an open question, and there is extensive disagreement amongst commentators as to whether it is Philo or Cleanthes (the two main disputants) who is really the victor in Hume's own view.*

Pamphilus to Hermippus

IT has been remarked, my Hermippus, that though the ancient philosophers conveyed most of their instruction in the form of dialogue, this method of composition has been little practised in later ages, and has seldom succeeded in the hands of those who have attempted it. Accurate and regular argument, indeed, such as is now expected of philosophical inquirers, naturally throws a man into the methodical and didactic manner; where he can immediately, without preparation, explain the point at which he aims; and thence proceed, without interruption, to deduce the proofs on which it is established. To deliver a SYSTEM in conversation, scarcely appears natural; and while the dialogue-writer desires, by departing from the direct style of composition, to give a freer air to his performance, and avoid the appearance of *Author* and *Reader,* he is apt to run into a worse inconvenience, and convey the image of *Pedagogue* and *Pupil.* Or, if he carries on the dispute in the natural spirit of good company, by throwing in a variety of topics, and preserving a proper balance among the speakers, he often loses so much time in preparations and transitions, that the reader will scarcely think himself compensated, by all the graces of dialogue, for the order, brevity, and precision, which are sacrificed to them.

There are some subjects, however, to which dialogue-writing is peculiarly adapted, and where it is still preferable to the direct and simple method of composition.

Any point of doctrine, which is so *obvious* that it scarcely admits of dispute, but at the same time so *important* that it cannot be too often inculcated, seems to require some such method of handling it; where the novelty of the manner may compensate the triteness of the subject; where the vivacity of conversation may enforce the precept; and where the variety of lights, presented by various personages and characters, may appear neither tedious nor redundant.

---

[1] Marcus Tullius Cicero (106–43 BC), sometimes referred to in English literature as Tully, was a lawyer and politician as well as a philosopher. [eds]

Any question of philosophy, on the other hand, which is so *obscure* and *uncertain,* that human reason can reach no fixed determination with regard to it; if it should be treated at all, seems to lead us naturally into the style of dialogue and conversation. Reasonable men may be allowed to differ, where no one can reasonably be positive. Opposite sentiments, even without any decision, afford an agreeable amusement; and if the subject be curious and interesting, the book carries us, in a manner, into company; and unites the two greatest and purest pleasures of human life, study and society.

Happily, these circumstances are all to be found in the subject of NATURAL RELIGION. What truth so obvious, so certain, as the being of a God, which the most ignorant ages have acknowledged, for which the most refined geniuses have ambitiously striven to produce new proofs and arguments? What truth so important as this, which is the ground of all our hopes, the surest foundation of morality, the firmest support of society, and the only principle which ought never to be a moment absent from our thoughts and meditations? But, in treating of this obvious and important truth, what obscure questions occur concerning the nature of that Divine Being, his attributes, his decrees, his plan of providence? These have been always subjected to the disputations of men; concerning these human reason has not reached any certain determination. But these are topics so interesting, that we cannot restrain our restless enquiry with regard to them; though nothing but doubt, uncertainty, and contradiction, have as yet been the result of our most accurate researches.

This I had lately occasion to observe, while I passed, as usual, part of the summer season with Cleanthes,[2] and was present at those conversations of his with Philo and Demea, of which I gave you lately some imperfect account. Your curiosity, you then told me, was so excited, that I must, of necessity, enter into a more exact detail of their reasonings, and display those various systems which they advanced with regard to so delicate a subject as that of natural religion. The

remarkable contrast in their characters still further raised your expectations; while you opposed the accurate philosophical turn of Cleanthes to the careless scepticism of Philo, or compared either of their dispositions with the rigid inflexible orthodoxy of Demea. My youth rendered me a mere auditor of their disputes; and that curiosity, natural to the early season of life, has so deeply imprinted in my memory the whole chain and connection of their arguments, that, I hope, I shall not omit or confound any considerable part of them in the recital.

Part I

AFTER I joined the company, whom I found sitting in Cleanthes's library, Demea paid Cleanthes some compliments on the great care which he took of my education, and on his unwearied perseverance and constancy in all his friendships. The father of Pamphilus, said he, was your intimate friend: The son is your pupil; and may indeed be regarded as your adopted son, were we to judge by the pains which you bestow in conveying to him every useful branch of literature and science. You are no more wanting, I am persuaded, in prudence, than in industry. I shall, therefore, communicate to you a maxim, which I have observed with regard to my own children, that I may learn how far it agrees with your practice. The method I follow in their education is founded on the saying of an ancient, 'That students of philosophy ought first to learn logics, then ethics, next physics, last of all of the nature of the gods.'[3] This science of natural theology, according to him, being the most profound and abstruse of any, required the maturest judgement in its students; and none but a mind enriched with all the other sciences, can safely be intrusted with it.

Are you so late, says Philo, in teaching your children the principles of religion? Is there no danger of their neglecting or rejecting altogether those opinions of which they have heard so little during the whole course of their education? It is only as a science, replied Demea,

---

[2] Cleanthes was Pamphilus' tutor. [eds]

[3] The reference is to Plutarch's *Moralia* 'On Stoic Self-Contradictions': 'Chrysippus thinks that young men should hear lectures on logic first, on ethics next, and after that on physics, and should get theology last as the termination for these studies' (trans. H. Chermiss, Loeb, 1976, p.429). [eds]

subjected to human reasoning and disputation, that I postpone the study of Natural Theology. To season their minds with early piety is my chief care; and by continual precept and instruction, and I hope too by example, I imprint deeply on their tender minds an habitual reverence for all the principles of religion. While they pass through every other science, I still remark the uncertainty of each part; the eternal disputations of men; the obscurity of all philosophy; and the strange, ridiculous conclusions, which some of the greatest geniuses have derived from the principles of mere human reason. Having thus tamed their mind to a proper submission and self-diffidence, I have no longer any scruple of opening to them the greatest mysteries of religion; nor apprehend any danger from that assuming arrogance of philosophy, which may lead them to reject the most established doctrines and opinions.

Your precaution, says Philo, of seasoning your children's minds early with piety, is certainly very reasonable; and no more than is requisite, in this profane and irreligious age. But what I chiefly admire in your plan of education, is your method of drawing advantage from the very principles of philosophy and learning, which, by inspiring pride and self-sufficiency, have commonly, in all ages, been found so destructive to the principles of religion. The vulgar,[4] indeed, we may remark, who are unacquainted with science and profound inquiry, observing the endless disputes of the learned, have commonly a thorough contempt for philosophy; and rivet themselves the faster, by that means, in the great points of theology, which have been taught them. Those who enter a little into study and inquiry, finding many appearances of evidence in doctrines the newest and most extraordinary, think nothing too difficult for human reason; and presumptuously breaking through all fences, profane the inmost sanctuaries of the temple. But Cleanthes will, I hope, agree with me, that, after we have abandoned ignorance, the surest remedy, there is still one expedient left to prevent this profane liberty. Let Demea's principles be improved and cultivated: let us become thoroughly sensible of the weakness, blindness, and narrow limits of human reason: let us duly

consider its uncertainty and endless contrarieties, even in subjects of common life and practice: let the errors and deceits of our very senses be set before us; the insuperable difficulties which attend first principles in all systems; the contradictions which adhere to the very ideas of matter, cause and effect, extension, space, time, motion; and in a word, quantity of all kinds, the object of the only science that can fairly pretend to any certainty or evidence. When these topics are displayed in their full light, as they are by some philosophers and almost all divines; who can retain such confidence in this frail faculty of reason as to pay any regard to its determinations in points so sublime, so abstruse, so remote from common life and experience? When the coherence of the parts of a stone, or even that composition of parts which renders it extended; when these familiar objects, I say, are so inexplicable, and contain circumstances so repugnant and contradictory; with what assurance can we decide concerning the origin of worlds, or trace their history from eternity to eternity?

While Philo pronounced these words, I could observe a smile in the countenances both of Demea and Cleanthes. That of Demea seemed to imply an unreserved satisfaction in the doctrines delivered: but, in Cleanthes's features, I could distinguish an air of finesse; as if he perceived some raillery or artificial malice in the reasonings of Philo.

You propose then, Philo, said Cleanthes, to erect religious faith on philosophical scepticism; and you think that if certainty or evidence be expelled from every other subject of inquiry, it will all retire to these theological doctrines, and there acquire a superior force and authority. Whether your scepticism be as absolute and sincere as you pretend, we shall learn by and by, when the company breaks up: we shall then see, whether you go out at the door or the window; and whether you really doubt if your body has gravity, or can be injured by its fall; according to popular opinion, derived from our fallacious senses and more fallacious experience. And this consideration, Demea, may, I think, fairly serve to abate our illwill to this humourous sect of the sceptics. If they be thoroughly in earnest, they will not long trouble the world with their doubts, cavils, and

[4] i.e. the mass of ordinary people. [eds]

disputes: if they be only in jest, they are, perhaps, bad railers; but can never be very dangerous, either to the state, to philosophy, or to religion.

In reality, Philo, continued he, it seems certain, that though a man, in a flush of humour, after intense reflection on the many contradictions and imperfections of human reason, may entirely renounce all belief and opinion; it is impossible for him to persevere in this total scepticism, or make it appear in his conduct for a few hours. External objects press in upon him; passions solicit him; his philosophical melancholy dissipates; and even the utmost violence upon his own temper will not be able, during any time, to preserve the poor appearance of scepticism. And for what reason impose on himself such a violence? This is a point in which it will be impossible for him ever to satisfy himself, consistently with his sceptical principles. So that, upon the whole, nothing could be more ridiculous than the principles of the ancient Pyrrhonians;[5] if in reality they endeavoured, as is pretended, to extend, throughout, the same scepticism which they had learned from the declamations of their schools, and which they ought to have confined to them.

In this view, there appears a great resemblance between the sects of the Stoics[6] and Pyrrhonians, though perpetual antagonists; and both of them seem founded on this erroneous maxim, That what a man can perform sometimes, and in some dispositions, he can perform always, and in every disposition. When the mind, by Stoical reflections, is elevated into a sublime enthusiasm of virtue, and strongly smit with any *species* of honour or public good, the utmost bodily pain and sufferings will not prevail over such a high sense of duty; and it is possible, perhaps, by its means, even to smile and exult in the midst of tortures. If this sometimes may be the case in fact and reality, much more may a philosopher, in his school, or even in his closet, work

himself up to such an enthusiasm, and support in imagination the acutest pain or most calamitous event which he can possibly conceive. But how shall he support this enthusiasm itself? The bent of his mind relaxes, and cannot be recalled at pleasure; avocations lead him astray; misfortunes attack him unawares; and the *philosopher* sinks by degrees into the *plebeian*.

I allow of your comparison between the Stoics and Sceptics, replied Philo. But you may observe, at the same time, that though the mind cannot, in Stoicism, support the highest flights of philosophy, yet, even when it sinks lower, it still retains somewhat of its former disposition; and the effects of the Stoic's reasoning will appear in his conduct in common life, and through the whole tenor of his actions. The ancient schools, particularly that of Zeno, produced examples of virtue and constancy which seem astonishing to present times.

> Vain Wisdom all and false Philosophy.
> Yet with a pleasing sorcery could charm
> Pain, for awhile, or anguish; and excite
> Fallacious Hope, or arm the obdurate breast
> With stubborn Patience, as with triple steel.[7]

In like manner, if a man has accustomed himself to sceptical considerations on the uncertainty and narrow limits of reason, he will not entirely forget them when he turns his reflection on other subjects; but in all his philosophical principles and reasoning, I dare not say in his common conduct, he will be found different from those, who either never formed any opinions in the case, or have entertained sentiments more favourable to human reason.

To whatever length any one may push his speculative principles of scepticism, he must act, I own, and live, and converse, like other men; and for this conduct he is not obliged to give any

---

[5] Pyrrho lived in the time of Alexander the Great, 356–323 BC; he founded the Sceptical or Pyrrhonian school of philosophy, and maintained that certain knowledge on any matter was unattainable, and that suspension of judgement was true wisdom and the source of happiness. [eds]

[6] Stoicism was a school of philosophy founded by Zeno of Citium (344–262 BC) whose successor as head of the school was Cleanthes (died *c.*232 BC). Rivalry between Stoics and Sceptics was a feature of Hellenistic philosophy. Stoics believed that knowledge, of a kind needed for us to lead a rational and happy life, is achievable, while Sceptics doubted that a criterion of knowledge can be given. Cicero (see below) studied Stoicism. [eds]

[7] John Milton, *Paradise Lost*, Book II, ll. 565–9. Hume quotes a modernized text. [eds]

other reason, than the absolute necessity he lies under of so doing. If he ever carries his speculations farther than this necessity constrains him, and philosophizes, either on natural or moral subjects, he is allured by a certain pleasure and satisfaction which he finds in employing himself after that manner. He considers besides, that every one, even in common life, is constrained to have more or less of this philosophy; that from our earliest infancy we make continual advances in forming more general principles of conduct and reasoning; that the larger experience we acquire, and the stronger reason we are endowed with, we always render our principles the more general and comprehensive; and that what we call *philosophy* is nothing but a more regular and methodical operation of the same kind. To philosophize on such subjects, is nothing essentially different from reasoning on common life; and we may only expect greater stability, if not greater truth, from our philosophy, on account of its exacter and more scrupulous method of proceeding.

But when we look beyond human affairs and the properties of the surrounding bodies: when we carry our speculations into the two eternities, before and after the present state of things; into the creation and formation of the universe; the existence and properties of spirits; the powers and operations of one universal Spirit existing without beginning and without end; omnipotent, omniscient, immutable, infinite, and incomprehensible: we must be far removed from the smallest tendency to scepticism not to be apprehensive, that we have here got quite beyond the reach of our faculties. So long as we confine our speculations to trade, or morals, or politics, or criticism, we make appeals, every moment, to common sense and experience, which strengthen our philosophical conclusions, and remove, at least in part, the suspicion, which we so justly entertain with regard to every reasoning that is very subtile and refined. But, in theological reasonings, we have

not this advantage; while, at the same time, we are employed upon objects, which, we must be sensible, are too large for our grasp, and of all others, require most to be familiarized to our apprehension. We are like foreigners in a strange country, to whom everything must seem suspicious, and who are in danger every moment of transgressing against the laws and customs of the people with whom they live and converse. We know not how far we ought to trust our vulgar[8] methods of reasoning in such a subject; since, even in common life, and in that province which is peculiarly appropriated to them, we cannot account for them, and are entirely guided by a kind of instinct or necessity in employing them.

All sceptics pretend,[9] that, if reason be considered in an abstract view, it furnishes invincible arguments against itself; and that we could never retain any conviction or assurance, on any subject, were not the sceptical reasonings so refined and subtile, that they are not able to counterpoise the more solid and more natural arguments derived from the senses and experience. But it is evident, whenever our arguments lose this advantage, and run wide of common life, that the most refined scepticism comes to be upon a footing with them, and is able to oppose and counterbalance them. The one has no more weight than the other. The mind must remain in suspense between them; and it is that very suspense or balance, which is the triumph of scepticism.

But I observe, says Cleanthes, with regard to you, Philo, and all speculative sceptics, that your doctrine and practice are as much at variance in the most abstruse points of theory as in the conduct of common life. Wherever evidence discovers[10] itself, you adhere to it, notwithstanding your pretended scepticism; and I can observe, too, some of your sect to be as decisive as those who make greater professions of certainty and assurance. In reality, would not a man be ridiculous, who pretended to reject Newton's[11] explication of the wonderful phenomenon of the

---

[8] i.e ordinary, common. [eds]

[9] i.e. claim. [eds]

[10] i.e. reveals. [eds]

[11] Sir Isaac Newton (1642–1717), whose *Optics: or, a treatise of the refractions, inflections and colours of light* was published in 1704. [eds]

rainbow, because that explication gives a minute anatomy of the rays of light; a subject, forsooth, too refined for human comprehension? And what would you say to one, who, having nothing particular to object to the arguments of Copernicus[12] and Galilæo[13] for the motion of the earth, should withhold his assent, on that general principle, that these subjects were too magnificent and remote to be explained by the narrow and fallacious reason of mankind?

There is indeed a kind of brutish and ignorant scepticism, as you well observed, which gives the vulgar a general prejudice against what they do not easily understand, and makes them reject every principle which requires elaborate reasoning to prove and establish it. This species of scepticism is fatal to knowledge, not to religion; since we find, that those who make greatest profession of it, give often their assent, not only to the great truths of Theism and natural theology, but even to the most absurd tenets which a traditional superstition has recommended to them. They firmly believe in witches, though they will not believe nor attend to the most simple proposition of Euclid.[14] But the refined and philosophical sceptics fall into an inconsistence of an opposite nature. They push their researches into the most abstruse corners of science; and their assent attends them in every step, proportioned to the evidence which they meet with. They are even obliged to acknowledge, that the most abstruse and remote objects are those which are best explained by philosophy. Light is in reality anatomized. The true system of the heavenly bodies is discovered and ascertained. But the nourishment of bodies by food is still an inexplicable mystery. The cohesion of the parts of matter is still incomprehensible. These sceptics, therefore, are obliged, in every question, to consider each particular evidence apart, and proportion their assent to

the precise degree of evidence which occurs. This is their practice in all natural, mathematical, moral, and political science. And why not the same, I ask, in the theological and religious? Why must conclusions of this nature be alone rejected on the general presumption of the insufficiency of human reason, without any particular discussion of the evidence? Is not such an unequal conduct a plain proof of prejudice and passion?

Our senses, you say, are fallacious; our understanding erroneous, our ideas, even of the most familiar objects, extension, duration, motion, full of absurdities and contradictions. You defy me to solve the difficulties, or reconcile the repugnancies which you discover in them. I have not capacity for so great an undertaking: I have not leisure for it: I perceive it to be superfluous. Your own conduct, in every circumstance, refutes your principles, and shows the firmest reliance on all the received maxims of science, morals, prudence, and behaviour.

I shall never assent to so harsh an opinion as that of a celebrated writer,[15] who says, that the Sceptics are not a sect of philosophers: they are only a sect of liars. I may, however, affirm (I hope without offence), that they are a sect of jesters or railers. But for my part, whenever I find myself disposed to mirth and amusement, I shall certainly choose my entertainment of a less perplexing and abstruse nature. A comedy, a novel, or at most a history, seems a more natural recreation than such metaphysical subtileties and abstractions.

In vain would the sceptic make a distinction between science and common life, or between one science and another. The arguments employed in all, if just, are of a similar nature, and contain the same force and evidence. Or if there be any difference among them, the advantage lies entirely on the side of

---

[12] Nicholas Copernicus (1473–1543), whose *On the revolutions of the heavenly spheres* (1543) proposed that the sun is stationary at the centre of the universe with the planets revolving round it. This theory replaced the ancient theory associated with Ptolemy that the earth was the stationary centre of the universe. [eds]

[13] Galileo Galilei (1564–1642) compared the Ptolemaic and Copernican systems in his *Dialogue concerning the two chief world systems* (1632). [eds]

[14] Euclides, celebrated geometrician, lived in Alexandria, Egypt (323–283 BC). [eds]

[15] Cleanthes refers to *The Art of Thinking* or *Port-Royal Logic*, published in 1662 and written by Antoine Arnauld (1612–94) and Pierre Nichol (1625–95). [eds]

theology and natural religion. Many principles of mechanics are founded on very abstruse reasoning; yet no man who has any pretensions to science, even no speculative sceptic, pretends to entertain the least doubt with regard to them. The Copernican system contains the most surprising paradox,[16] and the most contrary to our natural conceptions, to appearances, and to our very senses: yet even monks and inquisitors are now constrained to withdraw their opposition to it. And shall Philo, a man of so liberal a genius and extensive knowledge, entertain any general undistinguished scruples with regard to the religious hypothesis, which is founded on the simplest and most obvious arguments, and, unless it meet with artificial obstacles, has such easy access and admission into the mind of man?

And here we may observe, continued he, turning himself towards Demea, a pretty curious circumstance in the history of the sciences. After the union of philosophy with the popular religion, upon the first establishment of Christianity, nothing was more usual, among all religious teachers, than declamations against reason, against the senses, against every principle derived merely from human research and inquiry. All the topics of the ancient academies were adopted by the fathers; and thence propagated for several ages in every school and pulpit throughout Christendom. The Reformers[17] embraced the same principles of reasoning, or rather declamation; and all panegyrics[18] on the excellency of faith, were sure to be interlarded with some severe strokes of satire

against natural reason. A celebrated prelate[19] too, of the Romish communion, a man of the most extensive learning, who wrote a demonstration of Christianity, has also composed a treatise, which contains all the cavils of the boldest and most determined Pyrrhonism. Locke[20] seems to have been the first Christian who ventured openly to assert, that *faith* was nothing but a species of *reason*; that religion was only a branch of philosophy; and that a chain of arguments, similar to that which established any truth in morals, politics, or physics, was always employed in discovering all the principles of theology, natural and revealed. The ill use which Bayle[21] and other libertines made of the philosophical scepticism of the fathers and first reformers, still further propagated the judicious sentiment of Mr Locke: and it is now in a manner avowed, by all pretenders to reasoning and philosophy, that Atheist and Sceptic are almost synonymous. And as it is certain that no man is in earnest when he professes the latter principle, I would fain hope that there are as few who seriously maintain the former.

Don't you remember, said Philo, the excellent saying of Lord Bacon[22] on this head? That a little philosophy, replied Cleanthes, makes a man an Atheist: a great deal converts him to religion. That is a very judicious remark too, said Philo. But what I have in my eye is another passage, where, having mentioned David's fool, who said in his heart there is no God,[23] this great philosopher observes, that the Atheists nowadays have a double share of folly; for they are not

---

[16] i.e., that the earth moves, and the sun is stationary, not the other way around. [eds]

[17] i.e. Protestant reformers, such as Luther and Calvin. [eds]

[18] i.e. statements, writings, etc, in formal praise. [eds]

[19] Cleanthes refers to Pierre-Daniel Huet, Bishop of Avranches (1630–1721), whose book *A Philosophical Treatise on the Weakness of Human Understanding* was published in 1723. [eds]

[20] John Locke (1632–1704) published *The Reasonableness of Christianity* anonymously in 1695. [eds]

[21] Pierre Bayle (1674–1706), an outstanding sceptic. His *Historical and Critical Dictionary*, published in 1697, is full of sceptical arguments. [eds]

[22] Francis Bacon, Lord Verulam (1561–1626), in an essay 'Of Atheism' (1597), wrote: 'A little philosophy makes men atheists: A great deal reconciles them to religion.' [eds]

[23] Psalms XIV:I. [eds]

contented to say in their hearts there is no God, but they also utter that impiety with their lips, and are thereby guilty of multiplied indiscretion and imprudence. Such people, though they were ever so much in earnest, cannot, methinks, be very formidable.

But though you should rank me in this class of fools, I cannot forbear communicating a remark that occurs to me, from the history of the religious and irreligious scepticism with which you have entertained us. It appears to me, that there are strong symptoms of priestcraft in the whole progress of this affair. During ignorant ages, such as those which followed the dissolution of the ancient schools,[24] the priests perceived, that Atheism, Deism, or heresy of any kind, could only proceed from the presumptuous questioning of received opinions, and from a belief that human reason was equal to every thing. Education had then a mighty influence over the minds of men, and was almost equal in force to those suggestions of the senses and common understanding, by which the most determined sceptic must allow himself to be governed. But at present, when the influence of education is much diminished, and men, from a more open commerce of the world, have learned to compare the popular principles of different nations and ages, our sagacious divines have changed their whole system of philosophy, and talk the language of Stoics, Platonists,[25] and Peripatetics,[26] not that of Pyrrhonians and Academics.[27] If we distrust human reason, we have now no other principle to lead us into religion. Thus, sceptics in one age, dogmatists in another; whichever system best suits the purpose of these reverend gentlemen, in giving them an ascendant over mankind, they are sure to make it their favourite principle, and established tenet.

It is very natural, said Cleanthes, for men to embrace those principles, by which they find they can best defend their doctrines; nor need we have any recourse to priestcraft to account for so reasonable an expedient. And, surely nothing can afford a stronger presumption, that any set of principles are true, and ought to be embraced, than to observe that they tend to the confirmation of true religion, and serve to confound the cavils of Atheists, Libertines, and Freethinkers of all denominations.

Part II

I MUST own, Cleanthes, said Demea, that nothing can more surprise me, than the light in which you have all along put this argument. By the whole tenor of your discourse, one would imagine that you were maintaining the Being of a God, against the cavils of Atheists and Infidels; and were necessitated to become a champion for that fundamental principle of all religion. But this, I hope, is not by any means a question among us. No man, no man at least of common sense, I am persuaded, ever entertained a serious doubt with regard to a truth so certain and self-evident. The question is not concerning the BEING, but the NATURE of GOD. This, I affirm, from the infirmities of human understanding, to be altogether incomprehensible and unknown to us. The essence of that supreme Mind, his attributes, the manner of his existence, the very nature of his duration; these, and every particular which regards so divine a Being, are mysterious to men. Finite, weak, and blind creatures, we ought to humble ourselves in his august presence; and, conscious of our frailties, adore in silence his infinite perfections, which eye hath not seen, ear hath not heard, neither hath it entered into the heart of man to conceive.[28]

---

[24] i.e. the schools of philosophy summarized a few lines later. [eds]

[25] Platonists were followers of Plato (*c.*427–348 BC). [eds]

[26] Peripatetics were followers of Aristotle (384–322 BC). [eds]

[27] Stoics (note 5 above, p.10), Platonists and Peripatetics were not total sceptics. Pyrrhonians (note above) and Academics (another school of ancient Greek sceptics) were. [eds]

[28] I Corinthians 2:9. [eds]

They are covered in a deep cloud from human curiosity. It is profaneness to attempt penetrating through these sacred obscurities. And, next to the impiety of denying his existence, is the temerity of prying into his nature and essence, decrees and attributes.

But lest you should think that my *piety* has here got the better of my *philosophy*, I shall support my opinion, if it needs any support, by a very great authority. I might cite all the divines, almost, from the foundation of Christianity, who have ever treated of this or any other theological subject: but I shall confine myself, at present, to one equally celebrated for piety and philosophy. It is Father Malebranche,[29] who, I remember, thus expresses himself. 'One ought not so much,' says he, 'to call God a spirit, in order to express positively what he is, as in order to signify that he is not matter. He is a Being infinitely perfect: of this we cannot doubt. But in the same manner as we ought not to imagine, even supposing him corporeal, that he is clothed with a human body, as the Anthropomorphites asserted, under colour that that figure was the most perfect of any; so, neither ought we to imagine that the spirit of God has human ideas, or bears any resemblance to our spirit, under colour that we know nothing more perfect than a human mind. We ought rather to believe, that as he comprehends the perfections of matter without being material... he comprehends also the perfections of created spirits without being spirit, in the manner we conceive spirit: that his true name is, *He that is*;[30] or, in other words, Being without restriction, All Being, the Being infinite and universal.'

After so great an authority, Demea, replied Philo, as that which you have produced, and a thousand more which you might produce, it would appear ridiculous in me to add my sentiment, or express my approbation of your doctrine. But surely, where reasonable men treat these subjects, the question can never be concerning the *Being*, but only the *Nature* of the Deity. The former truth, as you well observe, is

unquestionable and self-evident. Nothing exists without a cause; and the original cause of this universe (whatever it be) we call God; and piously ascribe to him every species of perfection. Whoever scruples this fundamental truth, deserves every punishment which can be inflicted among philosophers, to wit, the greatest ridicule, contempt, and disapprobation. But as all perfection is entirely relative, we ought never to imagine that we comprehend the attributes of this divine Being, or to suppose that his perfections have any analogy or likeness to the perfections of a human creature. Wisdom, Thought, Design, Knowledge; these we justly ascribe to him; because these words are honourable among men, and we have no other language or other conceptions by which we can express our adoration of him. But let us beware, lest we think, that our ideas anywise correspond to his perfections, or that his attributes have any resemblance to these qualities among men. He is infinitely superior to our limited view and comprehension; and is more the object of worship in the temple, than of disputation in the schools.

In reality, Cleanthes, continued he, there is no need of having recourse to that affected scepticism so displeasing to you, in order to come at this determination. Our ideas reach no further than our experience. We have no experience of divine attributes and operations. I need not conclude my syllogism.[31] You can draw the inference yourself. And it is a pleasure to me (and I hope to you too) that just reasoning and sound piety here concur in the same conclusion, and both of them establish the adorably mysterious and incomprehensible nature of the Supreme Being.

Not to lose any time in circumlocutions, said Cleanthes, addressing himself to Demea, much less in replying to the pious declamations of Philo; I shall briefly explain how I conceive this matter. Look around the world: contemplate the whole and every part of it: you will find it to be nothing but one great machine, subdivided into an infinite number of lesser machines, which again admit of subdivisions to a degree

---

[29] Nicolas Malebranche (1638–1715), whose *The Search After Truth* (first published 1674–5) went through six editions in his lifetime. [eds]

[30] 'And God said unto Moses, I AM THAT I AM.' (Exodus 2:14) [eds]

[31] i.e. deductive reasoning. [eds]

beyond what human senses and faculties can trace and explain. All these various machines, and even their most minute parts, are adjusted to each other with an accuracy which ravishes into admiration all men who have ever contemplated them. The curious adapting of means to ends, throughout all nature, resembles exactly, though it much exceeds, the productions of human contrivance; of human designs, thought, wisdom, and intelligence. Since, therefore, the effects resemble each other, we are led to infer, by all the rules of analogy, that the causes also resemble; and that the Author of Nature is somewhat similar to the mind of man, though possessed of much larger faculties, proportioned to the grandeur of the work which he has executed. By this argument *à posteriori*,[32] and by this argument alone, we do prove at once the existence of a Deity, and his similarity to human mind and intelligence.

I shall be so free, Cleanthes, said Demea, as to tell you, that from the beginning, I could not approve of your conclusion concerning the similarity of the Deity to men; still less can I approve of the mediums by which you endeavour to establish it. What! No demonstration of the Being of God! No abstract arguments! No proofs *à priori*![33] Are these which have hitherto been so much insisted on by philosophers, all fallacy, all sophism? Can we reach no further in this subject than experience and probability? I will not say that this is betraying the cause of a Deity: but surely, by this affected candour, you give advantage to Atheists, which they never could obtain by the mere dint of argument and reasoning.

What I chiefly scruple in this subject, said Philo, is not so much that all religious arguments are by Cleanthes reduced to experience, as that they appear not to be even the most certain and irrefragable of that inferior kind. That a stone will fall, that fire will burn, that the earth has solidity, we have observed a thousand and a thousand times; and when any new instance of this nature is presented, we draw without hesitation the accustomed inference. The exact similarity of the cases gives us a perfect assurance of a similar event; and a stronger evidence is never desired nor sought after. But wherever you depart, in the least, from the similarity of the cases, you diminish proportionably the evidence; and may at last bring it to a very weak *analogy*, which is confessedly liable to error and uncertainty. After having experienced the circulation of the blood in human creatures, we make no doubt that it takes place in Titius and Mævius. But from its circulation in frogs and fishes, it is only a presumption, though a strong one, from analogy, that it takes place in men and other animals. The analogical reasoning is much weaker, when we infer the circulation of the sap in vegetables from our experience that the blood circulates in animals; and those, who hastily followed that imperfect analogy, are found, by more accurate experiments, to have been mistaken.

If we see a house, Cleanthes, we conclude, with the greatest certainty, that it had an architect or builder; because this is precisely that species of effect which we have experienced to proceed from that species of cause. But surely you will not affirm, that the universe bears such a resemblance to a house, that we can with the same certainty infer a similar cause, or that the analogy is here entire and perfect. The dissimilitude is so striking, that the utmost you can here pretend to is a guess, a conjecture, a presumption concerning a similar cause; and how that pretension will be received in the world, I leave you to consider.

It would surely be very ill received, replied Cleanthes; and I should be deservedly blamed and detested, did I allow, that the proofs of a Deity amounted to no more than a guess or conjecture. But is the whole adjustment of means to ends in a house and in the universe so slight a resemblance? The economy of final causes?[34]

---

[32] *à posteriori* (Latin for 'from what comes after'). An *a posteriori* argument is one based on something that can only be known after one has experienced it, e.g. that the world is orderly. [eds]

[33] *à priori* (Latin for 'from what comes before'). An *à priori* argument or proof is one based on premises that can be known before one has experienced them; e.g. (so Demea believes) that every event has a cause.

[34] i.e. the efficient or thrifty organisation of final causes. A 'final cause' is usually thought of as the end, purpose, or aim, of something; for example, the final cause of the eye is sight, of the legs locomotion. [eds]

The order, proportion, and arrangement of every part? Steps of a stair are plainly contrived, that human legs may use them in mounting; and this inference is certain and infallible. Human legs are also contrived for walking and mounting; and this inference, I allow, is not altogether so certain, because of the dissimilarity which you remark; but does it, therefore, deserve the name only of presumption or conjecture?

Good God! cried Demea, interrupting him, where are we? Zealous defenders of religion allow, that the proofs of a Deity fall short of perfect evidence! And you, Philo, on whose assistance I depended in proving the adorable mysteriousness of the Divine Nature, do you assent to all these extravagant opinions of Cleanthes? For what other names can I give them? or, why spare my censure, when such principles are advanced, supported by such an authority, before so young a man as Pamphilus?

You seem not to apprehend, replied Philo, that I argue with Cleanthes in his own way; and, by showing him the dangerous consequences of his tenets, hope at last to reduce him to our opinion. But what sticks most with you, I observe, is the representation which Cleanthes has made of the argument *à posteriori*;[35] and finding that that argument is likely to escape your hold and vanish into air, you think it so disguised that you can scarcely believe it to be set in its true light. Now, however much I may dissent, in other respects, from the dangerous principles of Cleanthes, I must allow that he has fairly represented that argument; and I shall endeavour so to state the matter to you, that you will entertain no further scruples with regard to it.

Were a man to abstract from every thing which he knows or has seen, he would be altogether incapable, merely from his own ideas, to determine what kind of scene the universe must be, or to give the preference to one state or situation of things above another. For as nothing which he clearly conceives could be esteemed impossible or implying a contradiction, every chimera of his fancy would be upon an equal footing; nor could he assign any just reason, why he adheres to one idea or system, and rejects the others which are equally possible.

Again; after he opens his eyes, and contemplates the world as it really is, it would be

impossible for him at first to assign the cause of any one event, much less of the whole of things or of the universe. He might set his fancy a rambling; and she might bring him in an infinite variety of reports and representations. These would all be possible; but being all equally possible, he would never of himself give a satisfactory account for his preferring one of them to the rest. Experience alone can point out to him the true cause of any phenomenon.

Now, according to this method of reasoning, Demea, it follows, (and is, indeed, tacitly allowed by Cleanthes himself,) that order, arrangements, or the adjustment of final causes, is not of itself, any proof of design; but only so far as it has been experienced to proceed from that principle. For ought we can know *à priori*, matter may contain the source or spring of order originally within itself as well as mind does; and there is no more difficulty in conceiving, that the several elements, from an internal unknown cause, may fall into the most exquisite arrangement, than to conceive that their ideas, in the great universal mind, from a like internal, unknown cause, fall into that arrangement. The equal possibility of both these suppositions is allowed. But, by experience, we find, (according to Cleanthes,) that there is a difference between them. Throw several pieces of steel together, without shape or form; they will never arrange themselves so as to compose a watch. Stone, and mortar, and wood, without an architect, never erect a house. But the ideas in a human mind, we see, by an unknown, inexplicable economy, arrange themselves so as to form the plan of a watch or house. Experience, therefore, proves, that there is an original principle of order in mind, not in matter. From similar effects we infer similar causes. The adjustment of means to ends is alike in the universe, as in a machine of human contrivance. The causes, therefore, must be resembling.

I was from the beginning scandalized, I must own, with this resemblance, which is asserted, between the Deity and human creatures; and must conceive it to imply such a degradation of Supreme Being as no sound Theist could endure. With your assistance, therefore, Demea, I shall endeavour to defend what you justly call the adorable mysteriousness of the Divine

---

[35] i.e. of the argument that there is evidence of overall design in the universe. [eds]

Nature, and shall refute this reasoning of Cleanthes, provided he allows that I have made a fair representation of it.

When Cleanthes had assented, Philo, after a short pause, proceeded in the following manner.

That all inferences, Cleanthes, concerning fact, are founded on experience; and that all experimental reasonings are founded on the supposition that similar causes prove similar effects, and similar effects similar causes; I shall not at present much dispute with you. But observe, I entreat you, with what extreme caution all just reasoners proceed in the transferring of experiments to similar cases. Unless the cases be exactly similar, they repose no perfect confidence in applying their past observation to any particular phenomenon. Every alteration of circumstances occasions a doubt concerning the event;[36] and it requires new experiments to prove certainly, that the new circumstances are of no moment or importance. A change in bulk, situation, arrangement, age, disposition of the air, or surrounding bodies; any of these particulars may be attended with the most unexpected consequences: and unless the objects be quite familiar to us, it is the higher temerity to expect with assurance, after any of these changes, an event similar to that which before fell under our observation. The slow and deliberate steps of philosophers[37] here, if anywhere, are distinguished from the precipitate march of the vulgar, who, hurried on by the smallest similitude, are incapable of all discernment or consideration.

But can you think, Cleanthes, that your usual phlegm[38] and philosophy have been preserved in so wide a step as you have taken, when you compared to the universe houses, ships, furniture, machines, and, from their similarity in some circumstances, inferred a similarity in their causes? Thought, design, intelligence, such as we discover in men and other animals, is no more than one of the springs and principles of the universe, as well as heat or cold, attraction or repulsion, and a hundred others, which fall under daily observation. It is an active cause, by which some particular parts of nature, we find, produce alterations on other parts. But can a conclusion, with any propriety, be transferred from parts to the whole? Does not the great disproportion bar all comparison and inference? From observing the growth of a hair, can we learn any thing concerning the generation of a man? Would the manner of a leaf's blowing,[39] even though perfectly known, afford us any instruction concerning the vegetation of a tree?

But, allowing that we were to take the *operations* of one part of nature upon another, for the foundation of our judgement concerning the *origin* of the whole, (which never can be admitted,) yet why select so minute, so weak, so bounded a principle as the reason and design of animals is found to be upon this planet? What peculiar privilege has this little agitation of the brain which we call *thought*, that we must thus make it the model of the whole universe? Our partiality in our own favour does indeed present[40] it on all occasions; but sound philosophy ought carefully to guard against so natural an illusion.

So far from admitting, continued Philo, that the operations of a part can afford us any just conclusion concerning the origin of the whole, I will not allow any one part to form a rule for another part, if the latter be very remote from the former. Is there any reasonable ground to conclude, that the inhabitants of other planets possess thought, intelligence, reason, or any thing similar to these faculties in men? When nature has so extremely diversified her manner of operation in this small globe, can we imagine that she incessantly copies herself throughout so immense a universe? And if thought, as we may well suppose, be confined merely to this narrow corner, and has even there so limited a sphere of action, with what propriety

---

[36] i.e. outcome. [eds]

[37] i.e. scientists. [eds]

[38] i.e. coolness. [eds]

[39] i.e. growing, blossoming, opening out. [eds]

[40] i.e. recommend. [eds]

can we assign it for the original cause of all things? The narrow views of a peasant, who makes his domestic economy the rule for the government of kingdoms, is in comparison a pardonable sophism.[41]

But were we ever so much assured, that a thought and reason, resembling the human, were to be found throughout the whole universe, and were its activity elsewhere vastly greater and more commanding than it appears in this globe; yet I cannot see, why the operations of a world constituted, arranged, adjusted, can with any propriety be extended to a world which is in its embryo state, and is advancing towards that constitution and arrangement. By observation, we know somewhat of the economy,[42] action, and nourishment of a finished animal; but we must transfer with great caution that observation to the growth of a foetus in the womb, and still more to the formation of an animalcule[43] in the loins of its male parent. Nature, we find, even from our limited experience, possesses an infinite number of springs and principles, which incessantly discover[44] themselves on every change of her position and situation. And what new and unknown principles would actuate her in so new and unknown a situation as that of the formation of a universe, we cannot, without the utmost temerity, pretend to determine.

A very small part of this great system, during a very short time, is very imperfectly discovered to us; and do we thence pronounce decisively concerning the origin of the whole?

Admirable conclusion! Stone, wood, brick, iron, brass, have not, at this time, in this minute globe of earth, an order or arrangement without human art and contrivance; therefore the universe could not originally attain its order and arrangement, without something similar to human art. But is a part of nature a rule for another part very wide of the former? Is it a rule for the whole? Is a very small part a rule for the universe? Is nature in one situation, a certain rule for nature in another situation vastly different from the former?

And can you blame me, Cleanthes, if I here imitate the prudent reserve of Simonides, who, according to the noted story, being asked by Hiero, *What God was?* desired a day to think of it, and then two days more; and after that manner continually prolonged the term, without ever bringing in his definition or description?[45] Could you even blame me, if I had answered at first, *that I did not know,* and was sensible that this subject lay vastly beyond the reach of my faculties? You might cry out sceptic and railer, as much as you pleased: but having found, in so many other subjects much more familiar, the imperfections and even contradictions of human reason, I never should expect any success from its feeble conjectures, in a subject so sublime, and so remote from the sphere of our observation. When two *species* of objects have always been observed to be conjoined together, I can *infer*, by custom, the existence of one wherever I *see* the existence of the other; and this I call an argument from experience. But how this argument can have place, where the objects, as in the present case, are single, individual, without parallel, or specific resemblance, may be difficult to explain. And will any man tell me with a serious countenance, that an orderly universe must arise from some thought and art like the human, because we have experience of it? To ascertain this reasoning, it were requisite that we had experience of the origin of worlds; and it is not sufficient, surely, that we have seen ships and cities arise from human art and contrivance.

Philo was proceeding in this vehement manner, somewhat between jest and earnest, as it appeared to me, when he observed some signs of impatience in Cleanthes, and then immediately

---

[41] i.e. plausible but fallacious argument. [eds]

[42] i.e. organization. [eds]

[43] i.e. microscopic animal. [eds]

[44] i.e. reveal. [eds]

[45] Simonides (550–470 BC), a lyric poet. Hiero was tyrant of Syracuse in Sicily. The story is in Cicero's *The Nature of the Gods* (I:xxii). [eds]

stopped short. What I had to suggest, said Cleanthes, is only that you would not abuse terms, or make use of popular expressions to subvert philosophical reasonings. You know, that the vulgar often distinguish reason from experience, even where the question relates only to matter of fact and existence; though it is found, that where that *reason* is properly analysed, that it is nothing but a species of experience. To prove by experience the origin of the universe from mind, is not more contrary to common speech, than to prove the motion of the earth from the same principle. And a caviller might raise all the same objections to the Copernican system, which you have urged against my reasonings. Have you other earths, might he say, which you have seen to move? Have...

Yes! cried Philo, interrupting him, we have other earths. Is not the moon another earth, which we see to turn round its centre? Is not Venus another earth, where we observe the same phenomenon? Are not the revolutions of the sun also a confirmation, from analogy, of the same theory? All the planets, are they not earths, which revolve about the sun? Are not the satellites moons, which move round Jupiter and Saturn, and along with these primary planets round the sun? These analogies and resemblances, with others which I have not mentioned, are the sole proofs of the Copernican system; and to you it belongs to consider, whether you have any analogies of the same kind to support your theory.

In reality, Cleanthes, continued he, the modern system of astronomy is now so much received by all inquirers, and has become so essential a part even of our earliest education, that we are not commonly very scrupulous in examining the reasons upon which it is founded. It is now become a matter of mere curiosity to study the first writers on that subject, who had the full force of prejudice to encounter, and were obliged to turn their arguments on every side in order to render them popular and convincing. But if we pursue Galilæo's famous Dialogues concerning the system of the world, we shall find, that that great genius, one of the

sublimest that ever existed, first bent all his endeavours to prove, that there was no foundation for the distinction commonly made between elementary and celestial substances. The schools,[46] proceeding from the illusions of sense, had carried this distinction very far; and had established the latter substances to be ingenerable, incorruptible, unalterable, impassible; and had assigned all the opposite qualities to the former. But Galilæo, beginning with the moon, proved its similarity in every particular to the earth; its convex figure, its natural darkness when not illuminated, its density, its distinction into solid and liquid, the variations of its phases, the mutual illuminations of the earth and moon, their mutual eclipses, the inequalities of the lunar surface, &c. After many instances of this kind, with regard to all the planets, men plainly saw that these bodies became proper objects of experience; and that the similarity of their nature enabled us to extend the same arguments and phenomena from one to the other.

In this cautious proceeding of the astronomers, you may read your own condemnation, Cleanthes; or rather may see, that the subject in which you are engaged exceeds all human reason and inquiry. Can you pretend to show any such similarity between the fabric of a house, and the generation of a universe? Have you ever seen nature in any such situation as resembles the first arrangement of the elements? Have worlds ever been formed under your eye, and have you had leisure to observe the whole progress of the phenomenon, from the first appearance of order to its final consummation? If you have, then cite your experience, and deliver your theory.

Part III

HOW the most absurd argument, replied Cleanthes, in the hands of a man of ingenuity and invention, may acquire an air of probability! Are you not aware, Philo, that it became necessary for Copernicus and his first disciples to prove the similarity of the terrestrial and celestial matter; because several philosophers, blinded by old systems,[47] and supported by some sensible

---

[46] i.e. organized bodies of teachers and scholars, especially in a university. [eds]

[47] i.e. systems of belief, theories. [eds]

appearances,[48] had denied this similarity? but that it is by no means necessary, that Theists should prove the similarity of the works of nature to those of Art; because this similarity is self-evident and undeniable? The same matter, a like form; what more is requisite to show an analogy between their causes, and to ascertain the origin of all things from a divine purpose and intention? Your objections, I must freely tell you, are no better than the abstruse cavils of those philosophers, who denied motion; and ought to be refuted in the same manner, by illustrations, examples, and instances, rather than by serious argument and philosophy.

Suppose, therefore, that an articulate voice were heard in the clouds, much louder and more melodious than any which human art could ever reach: suppose, that this voice were extended in the same instant over all nations, and spoke to each nation in its own language and dialect: suppose, that the words delivered not only contain a just sense and meaning, but convey some instruction altogether worthy of a benevolent Being, superior to mankind: could you possibly hesitate a moment concerning the cause of this voice? and must you not instantly ascribe it to some design or purpose? Yet I cannot see but all the same objections (if they merit that appellation) which lie against the system of Theism, may also be produced against this inference.

Might you not say, that all conclusions concerning fact were founded on experience: that when we hear an articulate voice in the dark, and thence infer a man, it is only the resemblance of the effects, which leads us to conclude that there is a like resemblance in the cause: but that this extraordinary voice, by its loudness, extent, and flexibility to all languages, bears so little analogy to any human voice, that we have no reason to suppose any analogy in their causes: and consequently, that a rational, wise, coherent speech proceeded, you know not whence, from some accidental whistling of the winds, not from any divine reason or intelligence? You see clearly your own objections in these cavils, and I hope too, you see clearly, that they cannot possibly have more force in the one case than in the other.

But to bring the case still nearer the present one of the universe, I shall make two suppositions, which imply not any absurdity or impossibility. Suppose that there is a natural, universal, invariable language, common to every individual of human race; and that books are natural productions, which perpetuate themselves in the same manner with animals and vegetables, by descent and propagation. Several expressions of our passions contain a universal language: all brute animals have a natural speech, which, however limited, is very intelligible to their own species. And as there are infinitely fewer parts and less contrivance in the finest composition of eloquence, than in the coarsest organized body, the propagation of an *Iliad* or *Æneid*[49] is an easier supposition than that of any plant or animal.

Suppose, therefore, that you enter into your library, thus peopled by natural volumes, containing the most refined reason and most exquisite beauty; could you possibly open one of them, and doubt, that its original cause bore the strongest analogy to mind and intelligence? When it reasons and discourses; when it expostulates, argues, and enforces its views and topics; when it applies sometimes to the pure intellect, sometimes to the affections; when it collects, disposes, and adorns every consideration suited to the subject; could you persist in asserting, that all this, at the bottom, had really no meaning; and that the first formation of this volume in the loins of its original parent proceeded not from thought and design? Your obstinacy, I know, reaches not that degree of firmness: even your sceptical play and wantonness would be abashed at so glaring an absurdity.

But if there be any difference, Philo, between this supposed case and the real one of the universe, it is all to the advantage of the latter. The anatomy of an animal affords many stronger instances of design than the perusal of Livy or Tacitus;[50] and any objection which you

---

[48] i.e. perceptible to the senses. [eds]

[49] Famous epic poems in Greek and Latin repectively. [eds]

[50] Titus Livius (59 BC–AD 17) and Gaius Cornelius Tacitus (*c.*AD 55–117), Roman historians. [eds]

start in the former case, by carrying me back to so unusual and extraordinary a scene as the first formation of worlds, the same objection has place on the supposition of our vegetating library. Choose, then, your party, Philo, without ambiguity or evasion; assert either that a rational volume is no proof of a rational cause, or admit of a similar cause to all the works of nature.

Let me here observe too, continued Cleanthes, that this religious argument, instead of being weakened by that scepticism so much affected by you, rather acquires force from it, and becomes more firm and undisputed. To exclude all argument or reasoning of every kind, is either affectation or madness. The declared profession of every reasonable sceptic is only to reject abstruse, remote, and refined arguments; to adhere to common sense and the plain instincts of nature; and to assent, wherever any reasons strike him with so full a force that he cannot, without the greatest violence, prevent it. Now the arguments for Natural Religion are plainly of this kind; and nothing but the most perverse, obstinate metaphysics can reject them. Consider, anatomize the eye; survey its structure and contrivance; and tell me, from your own feeling, if the idea of a contriver does not immediately flow in upon you with a force like that of sensation. The most obvious conclusion, surely, is in favour of design; and it requires time, reflection and study, to summon up those frivolous, though abstruse objections, which can support Infidelity.[51] Who can behold the male and female of each species, the correspondence of their parts and instincts, their passions, and whole course of life before and after generation, but must be sensible, that the propagation of the species is intended by Nature? Millions and millions of such instances present themselves through every part of the universe; and no language can convey a more intelligible irresistible meaning, than the curious adjustment of final causes. To what degree, therefore, of blind dogmatism must one have attained, to reject such natural and such convincing arguments?

Some beauties in writing we may meet with, which seem contrary to rules, and which gain the affections, and animate the imagination, in opposition to all the precepts of criticism, and to the authority of the established masters of art. And if the argument for Theism be, as you pretend, contradictory to the principles of logic; its universal, its irresistible influence proves clearly, that there may be arguments of a like irregular nature. Whatever cavils may be urged, an orderly world, as well as a coherent, articulate speech, will still be received as an incontestable proof of design and intention.

It sometimes happens, I own, that the religious arguments have not their due influence on an ignorant savage and barbarian; not because they are obscure and difficult, but because he never asks himself any question with regard to them. Whence arises the curious structure of an animal? From the copulation of its parents. And these whence? From *their* parents? A few removes set the objects at such a distance, that to him they are lost in darkness and confusion; nor is he actuated by any curiosity to trace them further. But this is neither dogmatism nor scepticism, but stupidity: a state of mind very different from your sifting, inquisitive disposition, my ingenious friend. You can trace causes from effects: you can compare the most distant and remote objects: and your greatest errors proceed not from barrenness of thought and invention, but from too luxuriant a fertility, which suppresses your natural good sense, by a profusion of unnecessary scruples and objections.

Here I could observe, Hermippus, that Philo was a little embarrassed and confounded: but while he hesitated in delivering an answer, luckily for him, Demea broke in upon the discourse, and saved his countenance.

Your instance, Cleanthes, said he, drawn from books and language, being familiar, has, I confess, so much more force on that account: but is there not some danger too in this very circumstance; and may it not render us presumptuous, by making us imagine we comprehend the Deity, and have some adequate idea of his nature and attributes? When I read a volume, I enter into the mind and intention of the author: I become him, in a manner, for the instant; and have an immediate feeling and conception of those ideas which revolved in his imagination while employed in that composition. But so near

---

[51] i.e. religious disbelief. [eds]

an approach we never surely can make to the Deity. His ways are not our ways. His attributes are perfect, but incomprehensible. And this volume of nature contains a great and inexplicable riddle, more than any intelligible discourse or reasoning.

The ancient Platonists, you know, were the most religious and devout of all the Pagan philosophers; yet many of them, particularly Plotinus,[52] expressly declare, that intellect or understanding is not to be ascribed to the Deity; and that our most perfect worship of him consists, not in acts of veneration, reverence, gratitude, or love; but in a certain mysterious self-annihilation, or total extinction of all our faculties. These ideas are, perhaps, too far stretched; but still it must be acknowledged, that, by representing the Deity as so intelligible, and comprehensible, and so similar to a human mind, we are guilty of the grossest and most narrow partiality, and make ourselves the model of the whole universe.

All the *sentiments* of the human mind, gratitude, resentment, love, friendship, approbation, blame, pity, emulation, envy, have a plain reference to the state and situation of man, and are calculated for preserving the existence and promoting the activity of such a being in such circumstances. It seems, therefore, unreasonable to transfer such sentiments to a supreme existence, or to suppose him actuated by them; and the phenomena besides of the universe will not support us in such a theory. All our *ideas* derived from the senses are confusedly false and illusive; and cannot therefore be supposed to have place in a supreme intelligence: and as the ideas of internal sentiment, added to those of the external senses, compose the whole furniture of human understanding, we may conclude, that none of the *materials* of thought are in any respect similar in the human and in the divine intelligence. Now, as to the *manner* of thinking; how can we make any comparison between them, or suppose them anywise resembling? Our thought is fluctuating, uncertain, fleeting, successive, and compounded; and were we to remove these circumstances, we absolutely annihilate its essence, and it would in such a case be an abuse of terms to apply to it the name of thought or reason. At least if it appear more pious and respectful (as it really is) still to retain these terms, when we mention the Supreme Being, we ought to acknowledge, that their meaning, in that case, is totally incomprehensible; and that the infirmities of our nature do not permit us to reach any ideas which in the least correspond to the ineffable sublimity of the Divine attributes.

Part IV

IT seems strange to me, said Cleanthes, that you, Demea, who are so sincere in the cause of religion, should still maintain the mysterious, incomprehensible nature of the Deity, and should insist so strenuously that he has no manner of likeness or resemblance to human creatures. The Deity, I can readily allow, possesses many powers and attributes of which we can have no comprehension: but if our ideas, so far as they go, be not just, and adequate, and correspondent to his real nature, I know not what there is in this subject worth insisting on. Is the name, without any meaning, of such mighty importance? Or how do you mystics, who maintain the absolute incomprehensibility of the Deity, differ from Sceptics or Atheists, who assert, that the first cause of all is unknown and unintelligible? Their temerity must be very great, if, after rejecting the production by a mind, I mean a mind resembling the human, (for I know of no other,) they pretend to assign, with certainty, any other specific intelligible cause: and their conscience must be very scrupulous indeed, if they refuse to call the universal unknown cause a God or Deity; and to bestow on him as many sublime eulogies and unmeaning epithets as you shall please to require of them.

Who could imagine, replied Demea, that Cleanthes, the calm philosophical Cleanthes, would attempt to refute his antagonists, by affixing a nickname to them; and, like the common bigots and inquisitors of the age, have recourse to invective and declamation, instead of reasoning? Or does he not perceive, that these topics

---

[52] Plotinus (*c.*AD 203–262), an Egyptian who opened a school in Rome. He developed Plato's teaching along mystical lines and had an influence upon the evolution of Christianity. [eds]

are easily retorted, and that Anthropomorphite[53] is an appellation as invidious, and implies as dangerous consequences, as the epithet of Mystic, with which he has honoured us? In reality, Cleanthes, consider what it is you assert when you represent the Deity as similar to a human mind and understanding. What is the soul of man? A composition of various faculties, passions, sentiments, ideas; united, indeed, into one self or person, but still distinct from each other. When it reasons, the ideas, which are the parts of its discourse, arrange themselves in a certain form or order; which is not preserved entire for a moment, but immediately gives place to another arrangement. New opinions, new passions, new affections, new feelings arise, which continually diversify the mental scene, and produce in it the greatest variety and most rapid succession imaginable. How is this compatible with that perfect immutability and simplicity which all true Theists ascribe to the Deity? By the same act, say they, he sees past, present, and future: his love and his hatred, his mercy and justice, are one individual operation: he is entire in every point of space; and complete in every instant of duration. No succession, no change, no acquisition, no diminution. What he is implies not in it any shadow of distinction or diversity. And what he is this moment he ever has been, and ever will be, without any new judgement, sentiment, or operation. He stands fixed in one simple, perfect state: nor can you ever say, with any propriety, that this act of his is different from that other; or that this judgement or idea has been lately formed, and will give place, by succession, to any different judgement or idea.

I can readily allow, said Cleanthes, that those who maintain the perfect simplicity of the Supreme Being, to the extent in which you have explained it, are complete Mystics, and chargeable with all the consequences which I have drawn from their opinion. They are, in a word, Atheists, without knowing it. For though it be

allowed, that the Deity possesses attributes of which we have no comprehension, yet ought we never to ascribe to him any attributes which are absolutely incompatible with that intelligent nature essential to him. A mind, whose acts and sentiments and ideas are not distinct and successive; one, that is wholly simple, and totally immutable, is a mind which has no thought, no reason, no will, no sentiment, no love, no hatred; or, in a word, is no mind at all. It is an abuse of terms to give it that appellation; and we may as well speak of limited extension without figure, or of number without composition.[54]

Pray consider, said Philo, whom you are at present inveighing against. You are honouring with the appellation of *Atheist* all the sound, orthodox divines, almost, who have treated of this subject; and you will at last be, yourself, found, according to your reckoning, the only sound Theist in the world. But if idolaters be Atheists, as, I think, may justly be asserted, and Christian Theologians the same, what becomes of the argument, so much celebrated, derived from the universal consent of mankind?[55]

But because I know you are not much swayed by names and authorities, I shall endeavour to show you, a little more distinctly, the inconveniences of that Anthropomorphism, which you have embraced; and shall prove, that there is no ground to suppose a plan of the world to be formed in the Divine mind, consisting of distinct ideas, differently arranged, in the same manner as an architect forms in his head the plan of a house which he intends to execute.

It is not easy, I own, to see what is gained by this supposition, whether we judge of the matter by *Reason* or by *Experience*. We are still obliged to mount higher, in order to find the cause of this cause, which you had assigned as satisfactory and conclusive.

If *Reason* (I mean abstract reason, derived from enquiries *à priori*) be not alike mute with regard to all questions concerning cause and

---

[53] i.e. one who ascribes, as an article of religious belief, a human form and personality to God. A sect of this belief arose in Egypt in the fourth century AD. [eds]

[54] i.e. of a defined area without any shape, or of a quantity which is not composed of smaller quantities. [eds]

[55] Philo refers to Cicero's words attributed to an Epicurean: 'a belief which all men by nature share must necessarily be true; therefore it must be admitted that the gods exist' *The Nature of the Gods* translated by H. Rackham, Loeb, London, 1933, p.45). [eds]

effect, this sentence at least it will venture to pronounce, That a mental world, or universe of ideas, requires a cause as much, as does a material world, or universe of objects; and, if similar in its arrangement, must require a similar cause. For what is there in this subject, which should occasion a different conclusion or inference? In an abstract view, they are entirely alike; and no difficulty attends the one supposition, which is not common to both of them.

Again, when we will needs force *Experience* to pronounce some sentence, even on these subjects which lie beyond her sphere, neither can she perceive any material difference in this particular, between these two kinds of worlds; but finds them to be governed by similar principles, and to depend upon an equal variety of causes in their operations. We have specimens in miniature of both of them. Our own mind resembles the one; a vegetable or animal body the other. Let experience, therefore, judge from these samples. Nothing seems more delicate, with regard to its causes, than thought; and as these causes never operate in two persons after the same manner, so we never find two persons who think exactly alike. Nor indeed does the same person think exactly alike at any two different periods of time. A difference of age, of the disposition of his body, of weather, of food, of company, of books, of passions; any of these particulars, or others more minute, are sufficient to alter the curious machinery of thought, and communicate to it very different movements and operations. As far as we can judge, vegetables and animal bodies are not more delicate in their motions, nor depend upon a greater variety or more curious adjustments of springs and principles.

How, therefore, shall we satisfy ourselves concerning the cause of that Being whom you suppose the Author of Nature, or, according to your system of Anthropomorphism, the ideal world, into which you trace the material? Have we not the same reason to trace that ideal world into another ideal world, or new intelligent principle? But if we stop, and go no further; why go so far? why not stop at the material world? How

can we satisfy ourselves without going on *in infinitum*? And, after all, what satisfaction is there in that infinite progression? Let us remember the story of the Indian philosopher and his elephant.[56] It was never more applicable than to the present subject. If the material world rests upon a similar ideal world, this ideal world must rest upon some other; and so on, without end. It were better, therefore, never to look beyond the present material world. By supposing it to contain the principle of its order within itself, we really assert it to be God; and the sooner we arrive at that Divine Being, so much the better. When you go one step beyond the mundane system, you only excite an inquisitive humour which it is impossible ever to satisfy.

To say, that the different ideas which compose the reason of the Supreme Being, fall into order of themselves, and by their own nature, is really to talk without any precise meaning. If it has a meaning, I would fain know, why it is not as good sense to say, that the parts of the material world fall into order of themselves and by their own nature. Can the one opinion be intelligible, while the other is not so?

We have, indeed, experience of ideas, which fall into order of themselves, and without any *known* cause. But, I am sure, we have a much larger experience of matter which does the same; as, in all instances of generation and vegetation, where the accurate analysis of the cause exceeds all human comprehension. We have also experience of particular systems of thought and of matter which have no order; of the first in madness, of the second in corruption.[57] Why, then, should we think, that order is more essential to one than the other? And if it requires a cause in both, what do we gain by your system, in tracing the universe of objects into a similar universe of ideas? The first step which we make leads us on for ever. It were, therefore, wise in us to limit all our inquiries to the present world, without looking further. No satisfaction can ever be attained by these speculations, which so far exceed the narrow bounds of human understanding.

[56] The story is of an Indian philosopher who believed the world to be supported by an elephant, which in turn was supported by a tortoise. [eds]

[57] i.e. decay, decomposition. [eds]

It was usual with the Peripatetics, you know, Cleanthes, when the cause of any phenomenon was demanded, to have recourse to their *faculties* or *occult qualities*; and to say, for instance, that bread nourished by its nutritive faculty, and senna purged by its purgative. But it has been discovered, that this subterfuge was nothing but the disguise of ignorance; and that these philosophers, though less ingenuous, really said the same thing with the sceptics or the vulgar, who fairly confessed that they knew not the cause of these phenomena. In like manner, when it is asked, what cause produces order in the ideas of the Supreme Being; can any other reason be assigned by you, Anthropomorphites, than that it is a *rational* faculty, and that such is the nature of the Deity? But why a similar answer will not be equally satisfactory in accounting for the order of the world, without having recourse to any such intelligent creator as you insist on, may be difficult to determine. It is only to say, that *such* is the nature of material objects, and that they are all originally possessed of a *faculty* of order and proportion. These are only more learned and elaborate ways of confessing our ignorance; nor has the one hypothesis any real advantage above the other, except in its greater conformity to vulgar prejudices.

You have displayed this argument with great emphasis, replied Cleanthes: You seem not sensible, how easy it is to answer it. Even in common life, if I assign a cause for any event, is it any objection, Philo, that I cannot assign the cause of that cause, and answer every new question which may incessantly be started? And what philosophers could possibly submit to so rigid a rule? philosophers, who confess ultimate causes to be totally unknown; and are sensible, that the most refined principles into which they trace the phenomena, are still to them as inexplicable as these phenomena themselves are to the vulgar. The order and arrangement of nature, the curious adjustment of final causes, the plain use and intention of every part and organ; all these bespeak in the clearest language an intelligent cause or author. The heavens and the earth join

in the same testimony: the whole chorus of Nature raises one hymn to the praises of its Creator.[58] You alone, or almost alone, disturb this general harmony. You start abstruse doubts, cavils, and objections: you ask me, what is the cause of this cause? I know not; I care not; that concerns not me. I have found a Deity; and here I stop my inquiry. Let those go further, who are wiser or more enterprising.

I pretend to be neither, replied Philo: and for that very reason, I should never perhaps have attempted to go so far; especially when I am sensible, that I must at last be contented to sit down with the same answer, which, without further trouble, might have satisfied me from the beginning. If I am still to remain in utter ignorance of causes, and can absolutely give an explication of nothing, I shall never esteem it any advantage to shove off for a moment a difficulty, which, you acknowledge, must immediately, in its full force, recur[59] upon me. Naturalists indeed very justly explain particular effects by more general causes, though these general causes themselves should remain in the end totally inexplicable; but they never surely thought it satisfactory to explain a particular effect by a particular cause, which was no more to be accounted for than the effect itself. An ideal system, arranged of itself, without a precedent design, is not a whit more explicable than a material one, which attains its order in a like manner; nor is there any more difficulty in the latter supposition than in the former.

Part V

BUT to show you still more inconveniences, continued Philo, in your Anthropomorphism, please to take a new survey of your principles. *Like effects prove like causes.* This is the experimental argument; and this, you say too, is the sole theological argument. Now, it is certain, that the liker the effects are which are seen, and the liker the causes which are inferred, the stronger is the argument. Every departure on either side diminishes the probability, and renders the experiment

---

[58] In *The Nature of the Gods*, Cicero's Stoic says 'for when we gaze upward to the sky and contemplate the heavenly bodies, what can be so obvious and so manifest as that there must exist some power possessing transcendent intelligence by whom these things are ruled?' (*op.cit.*, p.125). [eds]

[59] i.e. bounce back. [eds]

less conclusive. You cannot doubt of this principle; neither ought you to reject its consequences.

All the new discoveries in astronomy, which prove the immense grandeur and magnificence of the works of Nature, are so many additional arguments for a Deity, according to the true system of Theism; but, according to your hypothesis of experimental Theism, they become so many objections, by removing the effect still further from all resemblance to the effects of human art and contrivance. For, if Lucretius,[60] even following the old system of the world, could exclaim,

> Quis regere immensi summam, quis hebere profundi[61]
> Indu manu validas potis est moderanter habenas?
> Quis pariter coelos omnes convertere? et omnes
> Ignibus ætheriis terras suffire feraces?
> Omnibus inque locis esse omni tempore præsto?

If Tully[62] esteemed this reasoning so natural, as to put it into the mouth of his Epicurean: 'Quibus enim oculis animi intueri potuit vester Plato fabricam illam tanti operis, qua construi a Deo atque ædificari mundum facit? quæ molito? quæ ferramenta? qui vectes? quæ machinæ? qui ministri tanti muneris fuerunt? quemadmodum autem obedire et parere voluntati architecti aer, ignis, aqua, terra potuerunt?'[63] If this argument, I say, had any force in former ages, how much greater must it have at present, when the bounds of Nature are so infinitely enlarged, and such a magnificent scene is opened to us? It is still more unreasonable to form our idea of so unlimited a cause from our experience of the narrow productions of human design and invention.

The discoveries by microscopes, as they open a new universe in miniature, are still objections, according to you, arguments, according to me. The further we push our researches of this kind, we are still led to infer the universal cause of all to be vastly different from mankind, or from any object of human experience and observation.

And what say you to the discoveries in anatomy, chemistry, botany?…These surely are no objections, replied Cleanthes; they only discover new instances of art and contrivance. It is still the image of mind reflected on us from innumerable objects. Add, a mind *like the human,* said Philo. I know of no other, replied Cleanthes. And the liker the better, insisted Philo. To be sure, said Cleanthes.

Now, Cleanthes, said Philo, with an air of alacrity and triumph, mark the consequences. *First,* By this method of reasoning, you renounce all claim to infinity in any of the attributes of the Deity. For, as the cause ought only to be proportioned to the effect, and the effect, so far as it falls under our cognizance, is not infinite; what pretensions have we, upon your suppositions, to ascribe that attribute to the Divine Being? You will still insist, that, by removing him so much from all similarity to human creatures, we give in to the most arbitrary hypothesis, and at the same time weaken all proofs of his existence.

Secondly, You have no reason, on your theory, for ascribing perfection to the Deity, even in

---

[60] Titus Lucretius Carus (*c.*99–55 BC), a Roman poet, wrote *On the Nature of Things*, a poem expounding Epicurean philosophy. [eds]

[61] Who is strong enough to rule the sum of the immeasurable, who to hold in his hand and control the mighty bridle of the unfathomable? Who to turn about all the heavens at one time and warm the fruitful worlds with ethereal fires, or to be present in all places and at all times? (*On the Nature of Things*, translated by W.D.H. Rouse, revised by M. Ferguson Smith, Loeb, London, 1975, p.181). [eds]

[62] i.e. Cicero. (See note 1 above, p.7). [eds]

[63] What power of mental vision enabled your master Plato to descry the vast and elaborate architectural process which, as he makes out, the deity adopted in building the structure of the universe? What method of engineering was employed? What tools and levers and derricks? What agents carried out so vast an undertaking? And how were air, fire, water and earth enabled to obey and execute the will of the architect? (*The Nature of the Gods, op.cit.*, p.23). [eds]

his finite capacity, or for supposing him free from every error, mistake, or incoherence, in his undertakings. There are many inexplicable difficulties in the works of Nature, which, if we allow a perfect author[64] to be proved *à priori,* are easily solved, and become only seeming difficulties, from the narrow capacity of man, who cannot trace infinite relations. But according to your method of reasoning, these difficulties become all real; and perhaps will be insisted on, as new instances of likeness to human art and contrivance. At least, you must acknowledge, that it is impossible for us to tell, from our limited views, whether this system contains any great faults, or deserves any considerable praise, if compared to other possible, and even real systems. Could a peasant, if the Æneid were read to him, pronounce that poem to be absolutely faultless, or even assign to it its proper rank among the productions of human wit, he, who had never seen any other production?

But were this world ever so perfect a production, it must still remain uncertain, whether all the excellences of the work can justly be ascribed to the workman. If we survey a ship, what an exalted idea must we form of the ingenuity of the carpenter who framed so complicated, useful, and beautiful a machine? And what surprise must we feel, when we find him a stupid mechanic, who imitated others, and copied an art, which, through a long succession of ages, after multiplied trials, mistakes, corrections, deliberations, and controversies, had been gradually improving? Many worlds might have been botched and bungled, throughout an eternity, ere this system was struck out; much labour lost; many fruitless trials made; and a slow, but continued improvement carried on during infinite ages in the art of world-making. In such subjects, who can determine, where the truth; nay, who can conjecture where the probability lies, amidst a great number of hypotheses which may be proposed, and a still greater which may be imagined?

And what shadow of an argument, continued Philo, can you produce, from your hypothesis, to prove the unity of the Deity? A great number of men join in building a house or ship, in rearing a city, in framing a commonwealth; why may not several deities combine in contriving and framing a world? This is only so much greater similarity to human affairs. By sharing the work among several, we may so much further limit the attributes of each, and get rid of that extensive power and knowledge, which must be supposed in one deity, and which, according to you, can only serve to weaken the proof of his existence. And if such foolish, such vicious creatures as man, can yet often unite in framing and executing one plan, how much more those deities or demons, whom we may suppose several degrees more perfect!

To multiply causes without necessity, is indeed contrary to true philosophy: but this principle applies not to the present case. Were one deity antecedently proved by your theory, who were possessed of every attribute requisite to the production of the universe; it would be needless, I own, (though not absurd,) to suppose any other deity existent. But while it is still a question, Whether all these attributes are united in one subject, or dispersed among several independent beings, by what phenomena in nature can we pretend to decide the controversy? Where we see a body raised in a scale, we are sure that there is in the opposite scale, however concealed from sight, some counterpoising weight equal to it; but it is still allowed to doubt, whether that weight be an aggregate of several distinct bodies, or one uniform united mass. And if the weight requisite very much exceeds any thing which we have ever seen conjoined in any single body, the former supposition becomes still more probable and natural. An intelligent being of such vast power and capacity as is necessary to produce the universe, or, to speak in the language of ancient philosophy, so prodigious an animal exceeds all analogy, and even comprehension.

But further, Cleanthes: men are mortal, and renew their species by generation; and this is common to all living creatures. The two great sexes of male and female, says Milton,[65] animate the world. Why must this circumstance, so universal, so essential, be excluded from those

---

[64] i.e. creator, originator. [eds]

[65] 'Communicating male and femal light,
   Which two great sexes animate the World'
   (John Milton, *Paradise Lost,* Book VIII, ll.150–1). [eds]

numerous and limited deities? Behold, then, the theogony[66] of ancient times brought back upon us.

And why not become a perfect Anthropomorphite? Why not assert the deity or deities to be corporeal, and to have eyes, a nose, mouth, ears, etc.? Epicurus maintained, that no man had ever seen reason but in a human figure; therefore the gods must have a human figure. And this argument, which is deservedly so much ridiculed by Cicero,[67] becomes, according to you, solid and philosophical.

In a word, Cleanthes, a man who follows your hypothesis is able perhaps to assert, or conjecture, that the universe, sometime, arose from something like design: but beyond that position he cannot ascertain one single circumstance; and is left afterwards to fix every point of his theology by the utmost license of fancy and hypothesis. This world, for aught he knows, is very faulty and imperfect, compared to a superior standard; and was only the first rude essay[68] of some infant deity, who afterwards abandoned it, ashamed of his lame performance: it is the work only of some dependent, inferior deity; and is the object of derision to his superiors: it is the production of old age and dotage in some superannuated deity; and ever since his death, has run on at adventures, from the first impulse and active force which it received from him. You justly give signs of horror, Demea, at these strange suppositions, but these, and a thousand more of the same kind, are Cleanthes's suppositions, not mine. From the moment the attributes of the Deity are supposed finite, all these have place. And I cannot, for my part, think that so wild and unsettled a system of theology is, in any respect, preferable to none at all.

These suppositions I absolutely disown, cried Cleanthes: they strike me, however, with no horror; especially, when proposed in that rambling way in which they drop from you. On the contrary, they give me pleasure, when I see, that, by the utmost indulgence of your imagination, you never get rid of the hypothesis of design in the universe, but are obliged at every turn to have recourse to it. To this concession I adhere steadily; and this I regard as a sufficient foundation for religion.

Part VI

IT must be a slight fabric, indeed, said Demea, which can be erected on so tottering a foundation. While we are uncertain whether there is one deity or many; whether the deity or deities, to whom we owe our existence, be perfect or imperfect, subordinate or supreme, dead or alive; what trust or confidence can we repose in them? What devotion or worship address them? What veneration or obedience pay them? To all the purposes of life the theory of religion becomes altogether useless: and even with regard to speculative consequences, its uncertainty, according to you, must render it totally precarious and unsatisfactory.

To render it still more unsatisfactory, said Philo, there occurs to me another hypothesis, which must acquire an air of probability from the method of reasoning so much insisted on by Cleanthes. That like effects arise from like causes: this principle he supposes the foundation of all religion. But there is another principle of the same kind, no less certain, and derived from the same source of experience; that where several known circumstances are observed to be similar, the unknown will also be found similar. Thus, if we see the limbs of a human body, we conclude that it is also attended with a human head, though hid from us. Thus, if we see, through a chink in a wall, a small part of the sun, we conclude, that, were the wall removed, we should see the whole body. In short, this method of reasoning is so obvious and familiar, that no scruple can ever be made with regard to its solidity.

---

[66] i.e. the generation or birth of the gods. [eds]

[67] Philo refers to Cicero's *The Nature of the Gods*: 'since it is agreed that the gods are supremely happy, and no one can be happy without virtue, and virtue cannot exist without reason, and reason is only found in human shape, it follows that the gods possess the form of man.' (*op. cit.*, p.49) [eds]

[68] i.e. rough attempt. [eds]

Now, if we survey the universe, so far as it falls under our knowledge, it bears a great resemblance to an animal or organized body, and seems actuated with a like principle of life and motion. A continual circulation of matter in it produces no disorder: a continual waste in every part is incessantly repaired: the closest sympathy is perceived throughout the entire system: and each part or member, in performing its proper offices, operates both to its own preservation and to that of the whole. The world, therefore, I infer, is an animal; and the Deity is the SOUL of the world, actuating it, and actuated by it.

You have too much learning, Cleanthes, to be at all surprised at this opinion, which, you know, was maintained by almost all the Theists of antiquity, and chiefly prevails in their discourses and reasonings. For though, sometimes, the ancient philosophers reason from final causes, as if they thought the world the workmanship of God; yet it appears rather their favourite notion to consider it as his body, whose organization renders it subservient to him. And it must be confessed, that, as the universe resembles more a human body than it does the works of human art and contrivance, if our limited analogy could ever, with any propriety, be extended to the whole of nature, the inference seems juster in favour of the ancient than the modern theory.

There are many other advantages, too, in the former theory, which recommended it to the ancient theologians. Nothing more repugnant to all their notions, because nothing more repugnant to common experience, than mind without body; a mere spiritual substance, which fell not under their senses nor comprehension, and of which they had not observed one single instance throughout all nature. Mind and body they knew, because they felt both: an order, arrangement, organization, or internal machinery, in both, they likewise knew, after the same manner: and it could not but seem reasonable to transfer this experience to the universe; and to suppose the divine mind and body to be also coeval,[69] and to have, both of them, order and arrangement naturally inherent in them, and inseparable from them.

Here therefore is a new species of *Anthropomorphism*, Cleanthes, on which you may deliberate; and a theory which seems not liable to any considerable difficulties. You are too much superior, surely, to *systematical prejudices*, to find any more difficulty in supposing an animal body to be, originally, of itself, or from unknown causes, possessed of order and organization, than in supposing a similar order to belong to mind. But the *vulgar prejudice* , that body and mind ought always to accompany each other, ought not, one should think, to be entirely neglected; since it is founded on *vulgar experience,* the only guide which you profess to follow in all these theological inquiries. And if you assert, that our limited experience is an unequal standard, by which to judge of the unlimited extent of nature; you entirely abandon your own hypothesis, and must thenceforward adopt our Mysticism, as you call it, and admit of the absolute incomprehensibility of the Divine Nature.

This theory, I own, replied Cleanthes, has never before occurred to me, though a pretty natural one; and I cannot readily, upon so short an examination and reflection, deliver any opinion with regard to it. You are very scrupulous, indeed, said Philo: were I to examine any system of yours, I should not have acted with half that caution and reserve, in starting objections and difficulties to it. However, if any thing occur to you, you will oblige us by proposing it.

Why then, replied Cleanthes, it seems to me, that, though the world does, in many circumstances, resemble an animal body; yet is the analogy also defective in many circumstances the most material: no organs of sense; no seat of thought or reason; no one precise origin of motion and action. In short, it seems to bear a stronger resemblance to a vegetable[70] than to an animal, and your inference would be so far inconclusive in favour of the soul of the world.

But, in the next place, your theory seems to imply the eternity of the world; and that is a principle, which, I think, can be refuted by the strongest reasons and probabilities. I shall suggest an argument to this purpose, which, I believe, has not been insisted on by any writer. Those, who

---

[69] i.e. of the same age. [eds]

[70] i.e. plant. [eds]

reason from the late origin of arts and sciences, though their inference wants not force, may perhaps be refuted by considerations derived from the nature of human society, which is in continual revolution, between ignorance and knowledge, liberty and slavery, riches and poverty; so that it is impossible for us, from our limited experience, to foretell with assurance what events may or may not be expected. Ancient learning and history seem to have been in great danger of entirely perishing after the inundation of the barbarous nations; and had these convulsions continued a little longer, or been a little more violent, we should not probably have now known what passed in the world a few centuries before us. Nay, were it not for the superstition of the Popes, who preserved a little jargon of Latin, in order to support the appearance of an ancient and universal church, that tongue must have been utterly lost; in which case, the Western world, being totally barbarous, would not have been in a fit disposition for receiving the Greek language and learning, which was conveyed to them after the sacking of Constantinople.[71] When learning and books had been extinguished, even the mechanical arts would have fallen considerably to decay; and it is easily imagined, that fable or tradition might ascribe to them a much later origin than the true one. This vulgar argument, therefore, against the eternity of the world, seems a little precarious.

But here appears to be the foundation of a better argument. Lucullus[72] was the first that brought cherry-trees from Asia to Europe; though that tree thrives so well in many European climates, that it grows in the woods without any culture. Is it possible, that throughout a whole eternity, no European had ever passed into Asia, and thought of transplanting so delicious a fruit into his own country? Or if the tree was once transplanted and propagated, how could it ever afterwards perish? Empires may rise and fall, liberty and slavery succeed alternately, ignorance and knowledge give place to each other; but the cherry-tree will still remain in the woods of Greece, Spain and Italy, and will never be affected by the revolutions of human society.

It is not two thousand years since vines were transplanted into France; though there is no climate in the world more favourable to them. It is not three centuries since horses, cows, sheep, swine, dogs, corn, were known in America. Is it possible, that during the revolutions of a whole eternity, there never arose a Columbus, who might open the communication between Europe and that continent? We may as well imagine, that all men would wear stockings for ten thousand years, and never have the sense to think of garters to tie them. All these seem convincing proofs of the youth, or rather infancy of the world; as being founded on the operation of principles more constant and steady than those by which human society is governed and directed. Nothing less than a total convulsion of the elements will ever destroy all the European animals and vegetables which are now to be found in the Western world.

And what argument have you against such convulsions? replied Philo. Strong and almost incontestable proofs may be traced over the whole earth, that every part of this globe has continued for many ages entirely covered with water. And though order were supposed inseparable from matter, and inherent in it; yet may matter be susceptible of many and great revolutions, through the endless periods of eternal duration. The incessant changes, to which every part of it is subject, seem to intimate some such general transformations; though, at the same time, it is observable, that all changes and corruptions of which we have ever had experience, are but passages from one state of order to another; nor can matter ever rest in total deformity and confusion. What we see in the parts, we may infer in the whole; at least, that is the method of reasoning on which you rest your whole theory. And were I obliged to defend any particular system of this nature, which I never willingly should do, I esteem none more plausible than that which ascribes an eternal inherent principle of order to the world, though attended with great and continual revolutions and alterations. This at once solves all difficulties; and if the solution, by being so general, is not entirely

---

[71] The Turks finally captured Constantinople (modern Istanbul) in 1453. [eds]

[72] L. Licinius Lucullus (*c.*110 BC–57 BC), Roman general who conquered a substantial part of what is modern Turkey. [eds]

complete and satisfactory, it is at least a theory that we must sooner or later have recourse to, whatever system we embrace. How could things have been as they are, were there not an original inherent principle of order somewhere, in thought or in matter? And it is very indifferent to which of these we give the preference. Chance has no place, on any hypothesis, sceptical or religious. Every thing is surely governed by steady, inviolable laws. And were the inmost essence of things laid open to us, we should then discover a scene, of which, at present, we can have no idea. Instead of admiring the order of natural beings, we should clearly see that it was absolutely impossible for them, in the smallest article, ever to admit of any other disposition.

Were any one inclined to revive the ancient Pagan Theology, which maintained, as we learn from Hesiod,[73] that this globe was governed by thirty thousand deities, who arose from the unknown powers of nature: you would naturally object, Cleanthes, that nothing is gained by this hypothesis; and that it is as easy to suppose all men and animals, beings more numerous, but less perfect, to have sprung immediately from a like origin. Push the same inference a step further, and you will find a numerous society of deities as explicable as one universal deity, who possesses within himself the powers and perfections of the whole society. All these systems, then, of Scepticism, Polytheism, and Theism, you must allow, on your principles, to be on a like footing, and that no one of them has any advantage over the others. You may thence learn the fallacy of your principles.

Part VII

BUT here, continued Philo, in examining the ancient system of the soul of the world, there strikes me, all on a sudden, a new idea, which, if just, must go near to subvert all your reasoning, and destroy even your first inferences, on which you repose such confidence. If the universe bears a greater likeness to animal bodies and to vegetables, than to the world of human art, it is more probable that its cause resembles the cause of the former than that of the latter, and its origin ought rather to be ascribed to generation

or vegetation, than to reason or design. Your conclusion, even according to your own principles, is therefore lame and defective.

Pray open up this argument a little further, said Demea, for I do not rightly apprehend it in that concise manner in which you have expressed it.

Our friend Cleanthes, replied Philo, as you have heard, asserts, that since no question of fact can be proved otherwise than by experience, the existence of a Deity admits not of proof from any other medium. The world, says he, resembles the works of human contrivance; therefore its cause must also resemble that of the other. Here we may remark, that the operation of one very small part of nature, to wit man, upon another very small part, to wit that inanimate matter lying within his reach, is the rule by which Cleanthes judges of the origin of the whole; and he measures objects, so widely disproportioned, by the same individual standard. But to waive all objections drawn from this topic, I affirm, that there are other parts of the universe (besides the machines of human invention) which bear still a greater resemblance to the fabric of the world, and which, therefore, afford a better conjecture concerning the universal origin of this system. These parts are animals and vegetables. The world plainly resembles more an animal or a vegetable, than it does a watch or a knitting-loom. Its cause, therefore, it is more probable, resembles the cause of the former. The cause of the former is generation or vegetation. The cause, therefore, of the world, we may infer to be something similar or analogous to generation or vegetation.

But how is it conceivable, said Demea, that the world can arise from any thing similar to vegetation or generation?

Very easily, replied Philo. In like manner as a tree sheds its seeds into the neighbouring fields, and produces other trees; so the great vegetable, the world, or this planetary system, produces within itself certain seeds, which, being scattered into the surrounding chaos, vegetate into new worlds. A comet, for instance, is the seed of a world; and after it has been fully ripened, by passing from sun to sun, and star to star, it is at last tossed into the unformed

---

[73] Hesiod (*c.*8th century BC), one of the earliest Greek poets, wrote the *Theogony*, a mythical account of the origin of the world and the genealogy of the gods. [eds]

elements, which everywhere surround this universe, and immediately sprouts up into a new system.

Or if, for the sake of variety (for I see no other advantage), we should suppose this world to be an animal; a comet is the egg of this animal: and in like manner as an ostrich lays its egg in the sand, which, without any further care, hatches the egg, and produces a new animal; so... I understand you, says Demea: but what wild, arbitrary suppositions are these! What *data* have you for such extraordinary conclusions? And is the slight, imaginary resemblance of the world to a vegetable or an animal sufficient to establish the same inference with regard to both? Objects, which are in general so widely different, ought they to be a standard for each other?

Right, cries Philo: this is the topic on which I have all along insisted. I have still asserted, that we have no *data* to establish any system of cosmogony.[74] Our experience, so imperfect in itself, and so limited both in extent and duration, can afford us no probable conjecture concerning the whole of things. But if we must needs fix on some hypothesis; by what rule, pray, ought we to determine our choice? Is there any other rule than the greater similarity of the objects compared? And does not a plant or an animal, which springs from vegetation or generation, bear a stronger resemblance to the world, than does any artificial machine, which arises from reason and design?

But what is this vegetation and generation of which you talk? said Demea. Can you explain their operations, and anatomize that fine internal structure on which they depend?

As much, at least, replied Philo, as Cleanthes can explain the operations of reason, or anatomize that internal structure on which *it* depends. But without any such elaborate disquisitions, when I see an animal, I infer, that it sprang from generation; and that with as great certainty as you conclude a house to have been reared by design. These words, *generation, reason,* mark only certain powers and energies in nature, whose effects are known, but whose essence is incomprehensible; and one of these principles, more than the other, has no privilege for being made a standard to the whole of nature.

In reality, Demea, it may reasonably be expected, that the larger the views are which we take of things, the better will they conduct us in our conclusions concerning such extraordinary and such magnificent subjects. In this little corner of the world alone, there are four principles, *reason, instinct, generation, vegetation,* which are similar to each other, and are the causes of similar effects. What a number of other principles may we naturally suppose in the immense extent and variety of the universe, could we travel from planet to planet, and from system to system, in order to examine each part of this mighty fabric? Any one of these four principles above mentioned, (and a hundred others which lie open to our conjecture,) may afford us a theory by which to judge of the origin of the world; and it is a palpable and egregious[75] partiality to confine our view entirely to that principle by which our own minds operate. Were this principle more intelligible on that account, such a partiality might be somewhat excusable: but reason, in its internal fabric and structure, is really as little known to us as instinct or vegetation; and, perhaps, even that vague, undeterminate word, *Nature,* to which the vulgar refer every thing, is not at the bottom more inexplicable. The effects of these principles are all known to us from experience; but the principles themselves, and their manner of operation, are totally unknown; nor is it less intelligible, or less conformable to experience, to say, that the world arose by vegetation, from a seed shed by another world, than to say that it arose from a divine reason or contrivance, according to the sense in which Cleanthes understands it.

But methinks, said Demea, if the world had a vegetative quality, and could sow the seeds of new worlds into the infinite chaos, this power would be still an additional argument for design in its author. For whence could arise so wonderful a faculty but from design? Or how can order spring from any thing which perceives not that order which it bestows?

---

[74] i.e. of the origin of the universe. [eds]

[75] i.e. flagrant. [eds]

You need only look around you, replied Philo, to satisfy yourself with regard to this question. A tree bestows order and organization on that tree which springs from it, without knowing the order; an animal in the same manner on its offspring; a bird on its nest; and instances of this kind are even more frequent in the world than those of order, which arise from reason and contrivance. To say, that all this order in animals and vegetables proceeds ultimately from design, is begging the question; nor can that great point be ascertained otherwise than by proving, *à priori*, both that order is, from its nature, inseparably attached to thought; and that it can never of itself, or from original unknown principles, belong to matter.

But further, Demea; this objection which you urge can never be made use of by Cleanthes, without renouncing a defence which he has already made against one of my objections. When I inquired concerning the cause of that supreme reason and intelligence into which he resolves every thing; he told me, that the impossibility of satisfying such inquiries could never be admitted as an objection in any species of philosophy. *We must stop somewhere*, says he; *nor is it ever within the reach of human capacity to explain ultimate causes, or show the last connections of any objects. It is sufficient, if any steps, so far as we go, are supported by experience and observation.* Now, that vegetation and generation, as well as reason, are experienced to be principles of order in nature, is undeniable. If I rest my system of cosmogony on the former, preferably to the latter, it is at my choice. The matter seems entirely arbitrary. And when Cleanthes asks me what is the cause of my great vegetative or generative faculty, I am equally entitled to ask him the cause of his great reasoning principle. These questions we have agreed to forbear on both sides; and it is chiefly his interest on the present occasion to stick to this agreement. Judging by our limited and imperfect experience, generation has some privileges above reason: for we see every day the latter arise from the former, never the former from the latter.

Compare, I beseech you, the consequences on both sides. The world, say I, resembles an animal; therefore it is an animal, therefore it arose from generation. The steps, I confess, are wide; yet there is some small appearance of analogy in each step. The world, says Cleanthes, resembles a machine, therefore it is a machine, therefore it arose from design. The steps are here equally wide, and the analogy less striking. And if he pretends to carry on *my* hypothesis a step further, and to infer design or reason from the great principle of generation, on which I insist; I may, with better authority, use the same freedom to push further *his* hypothesis, and infer a divine generation or theogony from his principle of reason. I have at least some faint shadow of experience, which is the utmost that can ever be attained in the present subject. Reason, in innumerable instances, is observed to arise from the principle of generation, and never to arise from any other principle.

Hesiod, and all the ancient mythologists, were so struck with this analogy, that they universally explained the origin of nature from an animal birth, and copulation. Plato too, so far as he is intelligible, seems to have adopted some such notion in his Timæus.[76]

The Brahmins[77] assert, that the world arose from an infinite spider, who spun this whole complicated mass from his bowels, and annihilates afterwards the whole or any part of it, by absorbing it again, and resolving it into his own essence. Here is a species of cosmogony, which appears to us ridiculous; because a spider is a little contemptible animal, whose operations we are never likely to take for a model of the whole universe. But still here is a new species of analogy, even in our globe. And were there a planet wholly inhabited by spiders, (which is very possible,) this inference would there appear as natural and irrefragable as that which in our planet ascribes the origin of all things to design and intelligence, as explained by Cleanthes. Why an orderly system may not be spun from the belly as well as from the brain, it will be difficult for him to give a satisfactory reason.

---

[76] Plato sets forth his cosmogony in the dialogue *Timæus*. Much in this dialogue is obscure and contentious, but it seems fairly clear from it that Plato regards the whole universe as a single 'animal', a living and moving thing with a body and an intelligent soul. [eds]

[77] The highest priestly caste amongst the Hindus. [eds]

I must confess, Philo, replied Cleanthes, that of all men living, the task which you have undertaken, of raising doubts and objections, suits you best, and seems, in a manner, natural and unavoidable to you. So great is your fertility of invention, that I am not ashamed to acknowledge myself unable, on a sudden, to solve regularly such out-of-the-way difficulties as you incessantly start upon me: though I clearly see, in general, their fallacy and error. And I question not, but you are yourself, at present, in the same case, and have not the solution so ready as the objection: while you must be sensible, that common sense and reason are entirely against you; and that such whimsies as you have delivered, may puzzle, but never can convince us.

Part VIII

WHAT you ascribe to the fertility of my invention, replied Philo, is entirely owing to the nature of the subject. In subjects adapted to the narrow compass of human reason, there is commonly but one determination, which carries probability or conviction with it; and to a man of sound judgement, all other suppositions, but that one, appear entirely absurd and chimerical.[78] But in such questions as the present, a hundred contradictory views may preserve a kind of imperfect analogy; and invention has here full scope to exert itself. Without any great effort of thought, I believe that I could, in an instant, propose other systems of cosmogony, which would have some faint appearance of truth, though it is a thousand, a million to one, if either yours or any one of mine be the true system.

For instance, what if I should revive the old Epicurean hypothesis?[79] This is commonly, and I believe justly esteemed the most absurd system that has yet been proposed; yet I know not whether, with a few alterations, it might not be brought to bear a faint appearance of probability. Instead of supposing matter infinite, as Epicurus did, let us suppose it finite. A finite number of particles is only susceptible of finite

transpositions: and it must happen, in an eternal duration, that every possible order or position must be tried an infinite number of times. This world, therefore, with all its events, even the most minute, has before been produced and destroyed, and will again be produced and destroyed, without any bounds and limitations. No one, who has a conception of the powers of infinite, in comparison of finite, will ever scruple this determination.

But this supposes, said Demea, that matter can acquire motion, without any voluntary agent or first mover.

And where is the difficulty, replied Philo, of that supposition? Every event, before experience, is equally difficult and incomprehensible; and every event, after experience, is equally easy and intelligible. Motion, in many instances, from gravity, from elasticity, from electricity, begins in matter, without any known voluntary agent: and to suppose always, in these cases, an unknown voluntary agent, is mere hypothesis; and hypothesis attended with no advantages. The beginning of motion in matter itself is as conceivable *à priori* as its communication from mind and intelligence.

Besides, why may not motion have been propagated by impulse through all eternity, and the same stock of it, or nearly the same, be still upheld in the universe? As much is lost by the composition of motion, as much is gained by its resolution. And whatever the causes are, the fact is certain, that matter is, and always has been, in continual agitation, as far as human experience or tradition reaches. There is not probably, at present, in the whole universe, one particle of matter at absolute rest.

And this very consideration too, continued Philo, which we have stumbled on in the course of the argument, suggests a new hypothesis of cosmogony, that is not absolutely absurd and improbable. Is there a system, an order, an economy of things, by which matter can preserve that perpetual agitation which seems essential to it, and yet maintain a constancy in the forms which

[78] i.e. wild and fanciful. [eds]

[79] In Lucretius' explanation: '[the atoms] being many and shifted in many ways, they are harried and set in motion with blows throughout the universe from infinity, thus by trying every motion and combination, at length they fall into such arrangements as this sum of things consists of' (*On the Nature of Things, op.cit.,* p.85). [eds]

it produces? There certainly is such an economy; for this is actually the case with the present world. The continual motion of matter, therefore, in less than infinite transpositions, must produce this economy or order; and by its very nature, that order, when once established, supports itself, for many ages, if not to eternity. But wherever matter is so poised, arranged, and adjusted, as to continue in perpetual motion, and yet preserve a constancy in the forms, its situation must, of necessity, have all the same appearance of art and contrivance which we observe at present. All the parts of each form must have a relation to each other, and to the whole; and the whole itself must have a relation to the other parts of the universe; to the element in which the form subsists; to the materials with which it repairs its waste and decay; and to every other form which is hostile or friendly. A defect in any of these particulars destroys the form; and the matter of which it is composed is again set loose, and is thrown into irregular motions and fermentations, till it unite itself to some other regular form. If no such form be prepared to receive it, and if there be a great quantity of this corrupted matter in the universe, the universe itself is entirely disordered; whether it be the feeble embryo of a world in its first beginnings that is thus destroyed, or the rotten carcase of one languishing in old age and infirmity. In either case, a chaos ensues; till finite, though innumerable revolutions produce at last some forms, whose parts and organs are so adjusted as to support the forms amidst a continued succession of matter.

Suppose (for we shall endeavour to vary the expression), that matter were thrown into any position, by a blind, unguided force; it is evident that this first position must, in all probability, be the most confused and most disorderly imaginable, without any resemblance to those works of human contrivance, which, along with a symmetry of parts, discover[80] an adjustment of means to ends, and a tendency to self-preservation. If the actuating force cease after this operation, matter must remain for ever in disorder, and continue an immense chaos, without any proportion or activity. But suppose that the actuating force, whatever it be, still continues in matter, this first position will immediately give place to a second, which will likewise in all probability be as disorderly as the first, and so on, through many successions of changes and revolutions. No particular order or position ever continues a moment unaltered. The original force, still remaining in activity, gives a perpetual restlessness to matter. Every possible situation is produced, and instantly destroyed. If a glimpse or dawn of order appears for a moment, it is instantly hurried away, and confounded, by that never-ceasing force which actuates every part of matter.

Thus the universe goes on for many ages in a continued succession of chaos and disorder. But is it not possible that it may settle at last, so as not to lose its motion and active force (for that we have supposed inherent in it), yet so as to preserve an uniformity of appearance, amidst the continual motion and fluctuation of its parts? This we find to be the case with the universe at present. Every individual is perpetually changing, and every part of every individual; and yet the whole remains, in appearance, the same. May we not hope for such a position, or rather be assured of it, from the eternal revolutions of unguided matter; and may not this account for all the appearing wisdom and contrivance which is in the universe? Let us contemplate the subject a little, and we shall find, that this adjustment, if attained by matter of a seeming stability in the forms, with a real and perpetual revolution or motion of parts, affords a plausible, if not a true solution of the difficulty.

It is in vain, therefore, to insist upon the uses of the parts in animals or vegetables, and their curious adjustment to each other. I would fain know, how an animal could subsist, unless its parts were so adjusted? Do we not find, that it immediately perishes whenever this adjustment ceases, and that its matter corrupting tries some new form? It happens indeed, that the parts of the world are so well adjusted, that some regular form immediately lays claim to this corrupted matter: and if it were not so, could the world subsist? Must it not dissolve as well as the animal, and pass through new positions and situations; till in a great, but finite succession, it falls at last into the present or some such order?

---

[80] i.e. reveal. [eds]

It is well, replied Cleanthes, you told us, that this hypothesis was suggested on a sudden, in the course of the argument. Had you had leisure to examine it, you would soon have perceived the insuperable objections to which it is exposed. No form, you say, can subsist, unless it possess those powers and organs requisite for its subsistence: some new order or economy must be tried, and so on, without intermission; till at last some order, which can support and maintain itself, is fallen upon. But according to this hypothesis, whence arise the many conveniences and advantages which men and all animals possess? Two eyes, two ears, are not absolutely necessary for the subsistence of the species. Human race might have been propagated and preserved, without horses, dogs, cows, sheep, and those innumerable fruits and products which serve to our satisfaction and enjoyment. If no camels had been created for the use of man in the sandy deserts of Africa and Arabia, would the world have been dissolved? If no loadstone[81] had been framed to give that wonderful and useful direction to the needle, would human society and the human kind have been immediately extinguished? Though the maxims of Nature be in general very frugal, yet instances of this kind are far from being rare; and any one of them is a sufficient proof of design, and of a benevolent design, which gave rise to the order and arrangement of the universe.

At least, you may safely infer, said Philo, that the foregoing hypothesis is so far incomplete and imperfect, which I shall not scruple to allow. But can we ever reasonably expect greater success in any attempts of this nature? Or can we ever hope to erect a system of cosmogony, that will be liable to no exceptions, and will contain no circumstance repugnant to our limited and imperfect experience of the analogy of Nature? Your theory itself cannot surely pretend to any such advantage, even though you have run into *Anthropomorphism*, the better to preserve a conformity to common experience. Let us once

more put it to trial. In all instances which we have ever seen, ideas are copied from real objects, and are ectypal,[82] not archetypal, to express myself in learned terms: you reverse this order, and give thought the precedence. In all instances which we have ever seen, thought has no influence upon matter, except where that matter is so conjoined with it as to have an equal reciprocal influence upon it. No animal can move immediately any thing but the members of its own body; and indeed, the equality of action and reaction seems to be an universal law of nature: but your theory implies a contradiction to this experience. These instances, with many more, which it were easy to collect, (particularly the supposition of a mind or system of thought that is eternal, or, in other words, an animal ingenerable and immortal); these instances, I say, may teach all of us sobriety[83] in condemning each other, and let us see, that as no system of this kind ought ever to be received from a slight analogy, so neither ought any to be rejected on account of a small incongruity. For that is an inconvenience from which we can justly pronounce no one to be exempted.

All religious systems, it is confessed, are subject to great and insuperable difficulties. Each disputant triumphs in his turn; while he carries on an offensive war, and exposes the absurdities, barbarities, and pernicious tenets of his antagonist. But all of them, on the whole, prepare a complete triumph for the *Sceptic*, who tells them, that no system ought ever to be embraced with regard to such subjects: for this plain reason, that no absurdity ought ever to be assented to with regard to any subject. A total suspense of judgement is here our only reasonable resource. And if every attack, as is commonly observed, and no defence, among Theologians, is successful; how complete must be *his* victory, who remains always, with all mankind, on the offensive, and has himself no fixed station or abiding city, which he is ever, on any occasion, obliged to defend?

---

[81] i.e. magnet. [eds]

[82] i.e. of the nature of a copy, not of an original. [eds]

[83] i.e. restraint. [eds]

Part IX

BUT if so many difficulties attend the argument *à posteriori*, said Demea; had we not better adhere to that simple and sublime argument *à priori*, which, by offering to us infallible demonstration, cuts off at once all doubt and difficulty? By this argument, too, we may prove the INFINITY of the Divine attributes, which, I am afraid, can never be ascertained with certainty from any other topic. For how can an effect, which either is finite, or, for aught we know, may be so; how can such an effect, I say, prove an infinite cause? The unity too of the Divine Nature, it is very difficult, if not absolutely impossible, to deduce merely from contemplating the works of nature; nor will the uniformity alone of the plan, even were it allowed, give us any assurance of that attribute. Whereas the argument *à priori*...

You seem to reason, Demea, interposed Cleanthes, as if those advantages and conveniences in the abstract argument[84] were full proofs of its solidity. But it is first proper, in my opinion, to determine what argument of this nature you choose to insist on; and we shall afterwards, from itself, better than from its *useful* consequences, endeavour to determine what value we ought to put upon it.

The argument, replied Demea, which I would insist on, is the common one. Whatever exists must have a cause or reason of its existence; it being absolutely impossible for any thing to produce itself, or be the cause of its own existence. In mounting up, therefore, from effects to causes, we must either go on in tracing an infinite succession, without any ultimate cause at all; or must at last have recourse to some ultimate cause, that is *necessarily* existent: now, that the first supposition is absurd, may be thus proved. In the infinite chain or succession of causes and effects, each single effect is determined to exist by the power and efficacy of that cause which immediately preceded; but the whole external chain or succession, taken together, is not determined or caused by any thing; and yet it is evident that it requires a cause or reason, as much as any particular object which begins to exist in time. The question is still reasonable, why this particular succession of causes existed from eternity, and not any other succession, or no succession at all. If there be no necessarily existent being, any supposition which can be formed is equally possible; nor is there any more absurdity in Nothing's having existed from eternity, than there is in that succession of causes which constitutes the universe. What was it, then, which determined Something to exist rather than Nothing, and bestowed being on a particular possibility, exclusive of the rest? *External causes*, there are supposed to be none. *Chance* is a word without a meaning. Was it *Nothing*? But that can never produce any thing. We must, therefore, have recourse to a necessarily existent Being, who carries the REASON of his existence in himself, and who cannot be supposed not to exist, without an express contradiction. There is, consequently such a Being; that is, there is a Deity.

I shall not leave it to Philo, said Cleanthes, though I know that the starting objections is his chief delight, to point out the weakness of this metaphysical reasoning. It seems to me so obviously ill-grounded, and at the same time of so little consequence to the cause of true piety and religion, that I shall myself venture to show the fallacy of it.

I shall begin with observing, that there is an evident absurdity in pretending to demonstrate a matter of fact, or to prove it by any arguments *à priori*. Nothing is demonstrable, unless the contrary implies a contradiction. Nothing, that is distinctly conceivable, implies a contradiction. Whatever we conceive as existent, we can also conceive as non-existent. There is no being, therefore, whose non-existence implies a contradiction. Consequently there is no being, whose existence is demonstrable. I propose this argument as entirely decisive, and am willing to rest the whole controversy upon it.

It is pretended that the Deity is a necessarily existent being; and this necessity of his existence is attempted to be explained by asserting, that if we knew his whole essence or nature, we should perceive it to be as impossible for him not to exist, as for twice two not to be four. But it is evident that this can never happen, while our faculties remain the same as at present. It will still be possible for us, at any time, to conceive the non-existence of what we formerly conceived

---

[84] i.e. the *à priori* argument. [eds]

to exist; nor can the mind ever lie under a necessity of supposing any object to remain always in being; in the same manner as we lie under a necessity of always conceiving twice two to be four. The words, therefore, *necessary existence,* have no meaning; or, which is the same thing, none that is consistent.

But further, why may not the material universe be the necessarily existent being, according to this pretended explication of necessity? We dare not affirm that we know all the qualities of matter; and for aught we can determine, it may contain some qualities, which, were they known, would make its non-existence appear as great a contradiction as that twice two is five. I find only one argument employed to prove, that the material world is not the necessarily existent Being: and this argument is derived from the contingency both of the matter and the form of the world. 'Any particle of matter,' it is said, 'may be *conceived* to be annihilated; and any form may be *conceived* to be altered. Such an annihilation or alteration, therefore, is not impossible.' But it seems a great partiality not to perceive, that the same argument extends equally to the Deity, so far as we have any conception of him; and that the mind can at least imagine him to be non-existent, or his attributes to be altered. It must be some unknown, inconceivable qualities, which can make his non-existence appear impossible, or his attributes unalterable: and no reason can be assigned, why these qualities may not belong to matter. As they are altogether unknown and inconceivable, they can never be proved incompatible with it.

Add to this, that in tracing an eternal succession of objects, it seems absurd to inquire for a general cause or first author. How can any thing, that exists from eternity, have a cause, since that relation implies a priority in time, and a beginning of existence?

In such a chain, too, or succession of objects, each part is caused by that which preceded it, and causes that which succeeds it. Where then is the difficulty? But the WHOLE, you say, wants a cause. I answer, that the uniting of these parts into a whole, like the uniting of several distinct countries into one kingdom, or several distinct members into one body, is performed merely by an arbitrary act of the mind, and has no influence on the nature of things. Did I show you the particular causes of each individual in a collection of twenty particles of matter, I should think it very unreasonable, should you afterwards ask me, what was the cause of the whole twenty. This is sufficiently explained in explaining the cause of the parts.

Though the reasonings which you have urged, Cleanthes, may well excuse me, said Philo, from starting any further difficulties, yet I cannot forbear insisting still upon another topic. It is observed by arithmeticians, that the products of 9, compose always either 9, or some lesser product of 9, if you add together all the characters of which any of the former products is composed. Thus, of 18, 27, 36, which are products of 9, you make 9 by adding 1 to 8, 2 to 7, 3 to 6. Thus, 369 is a product also of 9; and if you add 3, 6, and 9, you make 18, a lesser product of 9. To a superficial observer, so wonderful a regularity may be admired as the effect either of chance or design: but a skilful algebraist immediately concludes it to be the work of necessity, and demonstrates, that it must forever result from the nature of these numbers. Is it not probable, I ask, that the whole economy of the universe is conducted by a like necessity, though no human algebra can furnish a key which solves the difficulty? And instead of admiring the order of natural beings, may it not happen, that, could we penetrate into the intimate nature of bodies, we should clearly see why it was absolutely impossible they could ever admit of any other disposition? So dangerous is it to introduce this idea of necessity into the present question! and so naturally does it afford an inference directly opposite to the religious hypothesis!

But dropping all these abstractions, continued Philo, and confining ourselves to more familiar topics, I shall venture to add an observation, that the argument *à priori* has seldom been found very convincing, except to people of a metaphysical head, who have accustomed themselves to abstract reasoning, and who, finding from mathematics, that the understanding frequently leads to truth through obscurity, and contrary to first appearances, have transferred the same habit of thinking to subjects where it ought not to have place. Other people, even of good sense and the best inclined to religion, feel always some deficiency in such arguments, though they are not perhaps able to explain distinctly where it lies; a certain proof that men ever did, and ever will derive their religion from other sources than from this species of reasoning.

Part X

IT is my opinion, I own, replied Demea, that each man feels, in a manner, the truth of religion within his own breast, and, from a consciousness of his imbecility and misery, rather than from any reasoning, is led to seek protection from that Being, on whom he and all nature is dependent. So anxious or so tedious are even the best scenes of life, that futurity is still the object of all our hopes and fears. We incessantly look forward, and endeavour, by prayers, adoration, and sacrifice, to appease those unknown powers, whom we find, by experience, so able to afflict and oppress us. Wretched creatures that we are! what resource for us amidst the innumerable ills of life, did not religion suggest some methods of atonement,[85] and appease those terrors with which we are incessantly agitated and tormented?

I am indeed persuaded, said Philo, that the best, and indeed the only method of bringing every one to a due sense of religion, is by just representations of the misery and wickedness of men. And for that purpose a talent of eloquence and strong imagery is more requisite than that of reasoning and argument. For is it necessary to prove what every one feels within himself? It is only necessary to make us feel it, if possible, more intimately and sensibly.

The people, indeed, replied Demea, are sufficiently convinced of this great and melancholy truth. The miseries of life; the unhappiness of man; the general corruptions of our nature; the unsatisfactory enjoyment of pleasures, riches, honours; these phrases have become almost proverbial in all languages. And who can doubt of what all men declare from their own immediate feeling and experience?

In this point, said Philo, the learned are perfectly agreed with the vulgar; and in all letters, *sacred* and *profane*, the topic of human misery has been insisted on with the most pathetic eloquence that sorrow and melancholy could inspire. The poets, who speak from sentiment, without a system, and whose testimony has therefore the more authority, abound in images of this nature. From Homer down to Dr Young,[86] the whole inspired tribe have ever been sensible, that no other representation of things would suit the feeling and observation of each individual.

As to authorities, replied Demea, you need not seek them. Look round this library of Cleanthes. I shall venture to affirm, that, except authors of particular sciences, such as chemistry or botany, who have no occasion to treat of human life, there is scarce one of those innumerable writers, from whom the sense of human misery has not, in some passage or other, extorted a complaint and confession of it. At least, the chance is entirely on that side; and no one author has ever, so far as I can recollect, been so extravagant as to deny it.

There you must excuse me, said Philo: Leibnitz[87] has denied it; and is perhaps the first who ventured upon so bold and paradoxical an opinion; at least, the first who made it essential to his philosophical system.

And by being the first, replied Demea, might he not have been sensible of his error? For is this a subject in which philosophers can propose to make discoveries especially in so late an age? And can any man hope by a simple denial (for the subject scarcely admits of reasoning), to bear down the united testimony of mankind, founded on sense and consciousness?

And why should man, added he, pretend to an exemption from the lot of all other animals? The whole earth, believe me, Philo, is cursed and polluted. A perpetual war is kindled amongst all living creatures. Necessity, hunger, want, stimulate the strong and courageous: fear, anxiety, terror, agitate the weak and infirm. The first entrance into life gives anguish to the new-born

---

[85] Literally, at-one-ment, i.e. reconciliation after discord. [eds]

[86] Edward Young (1683–1765), author of *Night Thoughts*, a book that reflects on life's vicissitudes, death and immortality. [eds]

[87] Gottfried Wilhelm Leibnitz (1646–1716), German philosopher and mathematician born at Leipzig. Founder of the Society (later Academy) of Sciences at Berlin; independently discovered the infinitesimal calculus; argued a pre-established harmony between spirit and matter, and that, in creating the world, God created the best of all possible worlds. See the introduction to Voltaire's *Candide*. [eds]

infant and to its wretched parent: weakness, impotence, distress, attend each stage of that life: and it is at last finished in agony and horror.

Observe too, says Philo, the curious artifices of Nature, in order to embitter the life of every living being. The stronger prey upon the weaker, and keep them in perpetual terror and anxiety. The weaker too, in their turn, often prey upon the stronger, and vex and molest them without relaxation. Consider that innumerable race of insects, which either are bred on the body of each animal, or, flying about, infix their stings in him. These insects have others still less than themselves, which torment them. And thus on each hand, before and behind, above and below, every animal is surrounded with enemies, which incessantly seek his misery and destruction.

Man alone, said Demea, seems to be, in part, an exception to this rule. For by combination in society, he can easily master lions, tigers, and bears, whose greater strength and agility naturally enable them to prey upon him.

On the contrary, it is here chiefly, cried Philo, that the uniform and equal maxims of Nature are most apparent. Man, it is true, can, by combination, surmount all his *real* enemies, and become master of the whole animal creation: but does he not immediately raise up to himself *imaginary* enemies, the demons of his fancy, who haunt him with superstitious terrors, and blast every enjoyment of life? His pleasure, as he imagines, becomes, in their eyes, a crime: his food and repose give them umbrage[88] and offence: his very sleep and dreams furnish new materials to anxious fear: and even death, his refuge from every other ill, presents only the dread of endless and innumerable woes. Nor does the wolf molest more the timid flock, than superstition does the anxious breast of wretched mortals.

Besides, consider, Demea: this very society, by which we surmount those wild beasts, our natural enemies; what new enemies does it not raise to us? What woe and misery does it not occasion? Man is the greatest enemy of man. Oppression, injustice, contempt, contumely,[89] violence, sedition, war, calumny, treachery, fraud; by these they mutually torment each other; and they would soon dissolve that society which they had formed, were it not for the dread of still greater ills, which must attend their separation.

But though these external insults, said Demea, from animals, from men, from all the elements, which assault us, form a frightful catalogue of woes, they are nothing in comparison of those which arise within ourselves, from the distempered condition of our mind and body. How many lie under the lingering torment of diseases? Hear the pathetic[90] enumeration of the great poet.

> Intestine stone and ulcer, colic-pangs,
> Demoniac frenzy, moping melancholy,
> And moon-struck madness, pining atrophy,
> Marasmus, and wide-wasting pestilence.
> Dire was the tossing, deep the groans:
> DESPAIR
> Tended the sick, busiest from couch to couch.
> And over them triumphant DEATH his dart
> Shook: but delay'd to strike, though oft invok'd
> With vows, as their chief good and final hope.[91]

The disorders of the mind, continued Demea, though more secret, are not perhaps less dismal and vexatious. Remorse, shame, anguish, rage, disappointment, anxiety, fear, dejection, despair; who has ever passed through life without cruel inroads from these tormentors? How many have scarcely ever felt any better sensations? Labour and poverty, so abhorred by every one, are the certain lot of the far greater number; and those few privileged persons, who enjoy ease and opulence, never reach contentment or true felicity. All the goods of life united would not make a very happy man; but all the ills united would

---

[88] i.e. displeasure. [eds]

[89] i.e. insult, scorn. [eds]

[90] i.e. moving. [eds]

[91] John Milton, *Paradise Lost*, Book XI ll.484–93 (omitting l.488). [eds]

make a wretch indeed; and any one of them almost (and who can be free from every one?) nay often the absence of one good (and who can possess all?) is sufficient to render life ineligible.[92]

Were a stranger to drop on a sudden into this world, I would show him, as a specimen of its ills, an hospital full of diseases, a prison crowded with malefactors and debtors, a field of battle strewed with carcases, a fleet foundering in the ocean, a nation languishing under tyranny, famine, or pestilence. To turn the gay side of life to him and give him a notion of its pleasures; whither should I conduct him? to a ball, to an opera, to court? He might justly think, that I was only showing him a diversity of distress and sorrow.

There is no evading such striking instances, said Philo, but by apologies, which still further aggravate the charge. Why have all men, I ask, in all ages, complained incessantly of the miseries of life?... They have no just reason, says one: these complaints proceed only from their discontented, repining, anxious disposition... And can there possibly, I reply, be a more certain foundation of misery, than such a wretched temper?

But if they were really as unhappy as they pretend, says my antagonist, why do they remain in life?...

Not satisfied with life, afraid of death.

This is the secret chain, say I, that holds us. We are terrified, not bribed to the continuance of our existence.

It is only a false delicacy, he may insist, which a few refined spirits indulge, and which has spread these complaints among the whole race of mankind... And what is this delicacy, I ask, which you blame? Is it any thing but a greater sensibility to all the pleasures and pains of life? and if the man of a delicate, refined temper, by being so

much more alive than the rest of the world, is only so much more unhappy, what judgement must we form in general of human life?

Let men remain at rest, says our adversary, and they will be easy.[93] They are willing artificers of their own misery.... No! reply I: an anxious languor follows their repose; disappointment, vexation, trouble, their activity and ambition.

I can observe something like what you mention in some others, replied Cleanthes: but I confess I feel little or nothing of it in myself, and hope that it is not so common as you represent it.

If you feel not human misery yourself, cried Demea, I congratulate you on so happy a singularity. Others, seemingly the most prosperous, have not been ashamed to vent their complaints in the most melancholy strains. Let us attend to the great, the fortunate emperor, Charles V.,[94] when, tired with human grandeur, he resigned all his extensive dominions into the hands of his son. In the last harangue which he made on that memorable occasion, he publicly avowed, *that the greatest prosperities which he had ever enjoyed, had been mixed with so many adversities, that he might truly say he had never enjoyed any satisfaction or contentment.* But did the retired life, in which he sought for shelter, afford him any greater happiness? If we may credit his son's account, his repentance commenced the very day of his resignation.

Cicero's fortune, from small beginnings, rose to the greatest lustre and renown; yet what pathetic complaints of the ills of life do his familiar letters, as well as philosophical discourses, contain? And suitably to his own experience, he introduces Cato,[95] the great, the fortunate Cato, protesting in his old age, that had he a new life in his offer, he would reject the present.

Ask yourself, ask any of your acquaintance, whether they would live over again the last ten or twenty years of their lives. No! but the next twenty, they say, will be better:

---

[92] i.e. unfit to be chosen, undesirable. [eds]

[93] i.e. free from pain, care and apprehension. [eds]

[94] Charles V. (1500–58), ruler of Spain, the Netherlands, much of Italy and Spanish America and Holy Roman Emperor. Abdicated in favour of his son Philip II in 1555 and retired to Yuste in Extremadura, Spain. [eds]

[95] Cato the Censor (234 BC–149 BC), a Roman famous for his opposition to luxury and hostility to Carthage, for the destruction of which he constantly called. [eds]

And from the dregs of life, hope to receive
What the first sprightly running could not
give.[96]

Thus at last they find (such is the greatness of human misery, it reconciles even contradictions), that they complain at once of the shortness of life, and of its vanity and sorrow.

And is it possible, Cleanthes, said Philo, that after all these reflections, and infinitely more, which might be suggested, you can still persevere in your Anthropomorphism, and assert the moral attributes of the Deity, his justice, benevolence, mercy, and rectitude, to be of the same nature with these virtues in human creatures? His power we allow is infinite: whatever he wills is executed: but neither man nor any other animal is happy: therefore he does not will their happiness. His wisdom is infinite: he is never mistaken in choosing the means to any end: but the course of Nature tends not to human or animal felicity: therefore it is not established for that purpose. Through the whole compass of human knowledge, there are no inferences more certain and infallible than these. In what respect, then, do his benevolence and mercy resemble the benevolence and mercy of men?

Epicurus's old questions are yet unanswered. Is he willing to prevent evil, but not able? then is he impotent. Is he able, but not willing? then is he malevolent. Is he both able and willing? whence then is evil?

You ascribe, Cleanthes (and I believe justly), a purpose and intention to Nature. But what, I beseech you, is the object of that curious artifice and machinery, which she has displayed in all animals? The preservation alone of individuals, and propagation of the species. It seems enough for her purpose, if such a rank[97] be barely upheld in the universe, without any care or concern for the happiness of the members that compose it. No resource for this purpose: no machinery, in order merely to give pleasure or ease: no fund of pure joy and contentment: no indulgence, without some want or necessity accompanying it. At least, the few phenomena of this nature are overbalanced by opposite phenomena of still greater importance.

Our sense of music, harmony, and indeed beauty of all kinds, gives satisfaction, without being absolutely necessary to the preservation and propagation of the species. But what racking pains, on the other hand, arise from gouts, gravels, megrims,[98] tooth-aches, rheumatisms, where the injury to the animal machinery is either small or incurable? Mirth, laughter, play, frolic, seem gratuitous satisfactions, which have no further tendency: spleen,[99] melancholy, discontent, superstition, are pains of the same nature. How then does the Divine benevolence display itself, in the sense of you Anthropomorphites? None but we Mystics, as you were pleased to call us, can account for this strange mixture of phenomena, by deriving it from attributes, infinitely perfect, but incomprehensible.

And have you at last, said Cleanthes, smiling, betrayed your intentions, Philo? Your long agreement with Demea did indeed a little surprise me; but I find you were all the while erecting a concealed battery against me. And I must confess, that you have now fallen upon a subject worthy of your noble spirit of opposition and controversy. If you can make out the present point, and prove mankind to be unhappy or corrupted, there is an end at once of all religion. For to what purpose establish the natural attributes of the Deity, while the moral are still doubtful and uncertain?

You take umbrage very easily, replied Demea, at opinions the most innocent, and the most generally received, even amongst the religious and devout themselves: and nothing can be more surprising than to find a topic like this, concerning the wickedness and misery of man, charged with no less than Atheism and profaneness. Have not all pious divines and preachers, who have indulged their rhetoric on

---

[96] From John Dryden's play *Aureng-Zebe* IV:i, ll.41–2. Hume has substituted 'hope' for 'think'. [eds]

[97] i.e. creatures with feeling. [eds]

[98] Gravels: urinary crystals that obstruct the passage of urine; megrims: headaches, migraines. [eds]

[99] i.e. gloominess and irritability. [eds]

so fertile a subject; have they not easily, I say, given a solution of any difficulties which may attend it? This world is but a point in comparison of the universe; this life but a moment in comparison of eternity. The present evil phenomena, therefore, are rectified in other regions, and in some future period of existence. And the eyes of men, being then opened to larger views of things, see the whole connection of general laws; and trace, with adoration, the benevolence and rectitude of the Deity, through all the mazes and intricacies of his providence.

No! replied Cleanthes, No! These arbitrary suppositions can never be admitted, contrary to matter of fact, visible and uncontroverted. Whence can any cause be known but from its known effects? Whence can any hypothesis be proved but from the apparent phenomena? To establish one hypothesis upon another, is building entirely in the air; and the utmost we ever attain, by these conjectures and fictions, is to ascertain the bare possibility of our opinion; but never can we, upon such terms, establish its reality.

The only method of supporting Divine benevolence, and it is what I willingly embrace, is to deny absolutely the misery and wickedness of man. Your representations are exaggerated; your melancholy views mostly fictitious; your inferences contrary to fact and experience. Health is more common than sickness; pleasure than pain; happiness than misery. And for one vexation which we meet with, we attain, upon computation, a hundred enjoyments.

Admitting your position, replied Philo, which yet is extremely doubtful, you must at the same time allow, that if pain be less frequent than pleasure, it is infinitely more violent and durable. One hour of it is often able to outweigh a day, a week, a month of our common insipid enjoyments; and how many days, weeks, and months, are passed by several in the most acute torments? Pleasure, scarcely in one instance, is ever able to reach ecstasy and rapture; and in no one instance can it continue for any time at its highest pitch and altitude. The spirits evaporate, the nerves relax, the fabric is disordered, and the enjoyment quickly degenerates into fatigue and uneasiness. But pain often, good God, how

often! rises to torture and agony; and the longer it continues, it becomes still more genuine agony and torture. Patience is exhausted, courage languishes, melancholy seizes us, and nothing terminates our misery but the removal of its cause, or another event,[100] which is the sole cure of all evil, but which, from our natural folly, we regard with still greater horror and consternation.

But not to insist upon these topics, continued Philo, though most obvious, certain, and important; I must use the freedom to admonish you, Cleanthes, that you have put this controversy upon a most dangerous issue, and are unawares introducing a total scepticism into the most essential articles of natural and revealed theology. What! no method of fixing a just foundation for religion, unless we allow the happiness of human life, and maintain a continued existence even in this world, with all our present pains, infirmities, vexations, and follies, to be eligible and desirable! But this is contrary to every one's feeling and experience: it is contrary to an authority so established as nothing can subvert. No decisive proofs can ever be produced against this authority; nor is it possible for you to compute, estimate, and compare, all the pains and all the pleasures in the lives of all men and of all animals: and thus, by your resting the whole system of religion on a point, which, from its very nature, must for ever be uncertain, you tacitly confess, that that system is equally uncertain.

But allowing you what never will be believed, at least what you never possibly can prove, that animal, or at least human happiness, in this life, exceeds its misery, you have yet done nothing: for this is not, by any means, what we expect from infinite power, infinite wisdom, and infinite goodness. Why is there any misery at all in the world? Not by chance surely. From some cause then. Is it from the intention of the Deity? But he is perfectly benevolent. Is it contrary to his intention? But he is almighty. Nothing can shake the solidity of this reasoning, so short, so clear, so decisive; except we assert, that these subjects exceed all human capacity, and that our common measures of truth and falsehood are not applicable to them; a topic which I have all along insisted on, but which you have, from the beginning, rejected with scorn and indignation.

---

[100] i.e. death. [eds]

But I will be contented to retire still from this intrenchment,[101] for I deny that you can ever force me in it. I will allow, that pain or misery in man is *compatible* with infinite power and goodness in the Deity, even in your sense of these attributes: what are you advanced by all these concessions? A mere possible compatibility is not sufficient. You must *prove* these pure, unmixed, and uncontrollable attributes from the present mixed and confused phenomena, and from these alone. A hopeful undertaking! Were the phenomena ever so pure and unmixed, yet being finite, they would be insufficient for that purpose. How much more, where they are also so jarring and discordant!

Here, Cleanthes, I find myself at ease in my argument. Here I triumph. Formerly, when we argued concerning the natural attributes of intelligence and design, I needed all my sceptical and metaphysical subtilty to elude your grasp. In many views of the universe and of its parts, particularly the latter, the beauty and fitness of final causes strike us with such irresistible force, that all objections appear (what I believe they really are) mere cavils and sophisms;[102] nor can we then imagine how it was ever possible for us to repose any weight on them. But there is no view of human life, or of the condition of mankind, from which, without the greatest violence,[103] we can infer the moral attributes, or learn that infinite benevolence, conjoined with infinite power and infinite wisdom, which we must discover by the eyes of faith alone. It is your turn now to tug the labouring oar, and to support your philosophical subtilties against the dictates of plain reason and experience.

Part XI

I SCRUPLE not to allow, said Cleanthes, that I have been apt to suspect the frequent repetition of the word *infinite*, which we meet with in all theological writers, to savour more of panegyric[104] than of philosophy; and that any purposes of reasoning, and even of religion, would be better served, were we to rest contented with more accurate and more moderate expressions. The terms, *admirable, excellent, superlatively great, wise,* and *holy*; these sufficiently fill the imaginations of men; and any thing beyond, besides that it leads into absurdities, has no influence on the affections or sentiments. Thus, in the present subject, if we abandon all human analogy, as seems your intention, Demea, I am afraid we abandon all religion, and retain no conception of the great object of our adoration. If we preserve human analogy, we must for ever find it impossible to reconcile any mixture of evil in the universe with infinite attributes; much less can we ever prove the latter from the former. But supposing the Author of Nature to be finitely perfect, though far exceeding mankind, a satisfactory account may then be given of natural and moral evil, and every untoward phenomenon be explained and adjusted. A less evil may then be chosen, in order to avoid a greater; inconveniences be submitted to, in order to reach a desirable end; and in a word, benevolence, regulated by wisdom, and limited by necessity, may produce just such a world as the present. You, Philo, who are so prompt at starting views, and reflections, and analogies, I would gladly hear, at length, without interruption, your opinion of this new theory; and if it deserve our attention, we may afterwards, at more leisure, reduce it into form.

My sentiments, replied Philo, are not worth being made a mystery of; and therefore, without ceremony, I shall deliver what occurs to me with regard to the present subject. It must, I think, be allowed, that if a very limited intelligence, whom we shall suppose utterly unacquainted with the universe, were assured, that it were the production of a very good, wise, and powerful Being, however finite, he would, from his conjectures, form *beforehand* a different notion of it from what

---

[101] A logical impasse or fix. Hume originally wrote 'retrenchment' but his nephew who published the *Dialogues* made the alteration. [eds]

[102] i.e. plausible but fallacious argument. [eds]

[103] i.e. improper use of language and argument. [eds]

[104] i.e. formal praise. [eds]

we find it to be by experience; nor would he ever imagine, merely from these attributes of the cause, of which he is informed, that the effect could be so full of vice and misery and disorder, as it appears in this life. Supposing now, that this person were brought into the world, still assured that it was the workmanship of such a sublime and benevolent Being; he might, perhaps, be surprised at the disappointment; but would never retract his former belief, if founded on any very solid argument; since such a limited intelligence must be sensible of his own blindness and ignorance, and must allow, that there may be many solutions of those phenomena, which will for ever escape his comprehension. But supposing, which is the real case with regard to man, that this creature is not antecedently convinced of a supreme intelligence, benevolent and powerful, but is left to gather such a belief from the appearances of things; this entirely alters the case, nor will he ever find any reason for such a conclusion. He may be fully convinced of the narrow limits of his understanding; but this will not help him in forming an inference concerning the goodness of superior powers, since he must form that inference from what he knows, not from what he is ignorant of. The more you exaggerate his weakness and ignorance, the more diffident you render him, and give him the greater suspicion that such subjects are beyond the reach of his faculties. You are obliged, therefore, to reason with him merely from the known phenomena, and to drop every arbitrary supposition or conjecture.

Did I show you a house or palace, where there was not one apartment convenient or agreeable; where the windows, doors, fires, passages, stairs, and the whole economy[105] of the building, were the source of noise, confusion, fatigue, darkness, and the extremes of heat and cold; you would certainly blame the contrivance, without any further examination. The architect would in vain display his subtilty, and prove to you, that if this door or that window were altered, greater ills would ensue. What he says may be strictly true: the alteration of one particular, while the other parts of the building remain, may only augment the inconveniences.

But still you would assert in general, that, if the architect had had skill and good intentions, he might have formed such a plan of the whole, and might have adjusted the parts in such a manner, as would have remedied all or most of these inconveniences. His ignorance, or even your own ignorance of such a plan, will never convince you of the impossibility of it. If you find any inconveniences and deformities in the building, you will always, without entering into any detail, condemn the architect.

In short, I repeat the question: Is the world, considered in general, and as it appears to us in this life, different from what a man or such a limited being, would, *beforehand*, expect from a very powerful, wise, and benevolent Deity? It must be strange prejudice to assert the contrary. And from thence I conclude, that however consistent the world may be, allowing certain suppositions and conjectures, with the idea of such a Deity, it can never afford us an inference concerning his existence. The consistence is not absolutely denied, only the inference. Conjectures, especially where infinity is excluded from the Divine attributes, may perhaps be sufficient to prove a consistence, but can never be foundation for any inference.

There seem to be *four* circumstances, on which depend all, or the greatest part of the ills, that molest sensible creatures;[106] and it is not impossible but all these circumstances may be necessary and unavoidable. We know so little beyond common life, or even of common life, that, with regard to the economy of a universe, there is no conjecture, however wild, which may not be just; nor any one, however plausible, which may not be erroneous. All that belongs to human understanding, in this deep ignorance and obscurity, is to be sceptical, or at least cautious, and not to admit of any hypothesis whatever; much less of any which is supported by no appearance of probability. Now, this I assert to be the case with regard to all the causes of evil, and the circumstances on which it depends. None of them appear to human reason in the least degree necessary or unavoidable; nor can we suppose them such, without the utmost license of imagination.

---

[105] i.e. management, organization. [eds]

[106] i.e. creatures possessed of feeling. [eds]

The *first* circumstance which introduces evil, is that contrivance or economy of the animal creation, by which pains, as well as pleasures, are employed to excite all creatures to action, and make them vigilant in the great work of self-preservation. Now pleasure alone, in its various degrees, seems to human understanding sufficient for this purpose. All animals might be constantly in a state of enjoyment: but when urged by any of the necessities of nature, such as thirst, hunger, weariness; instead of pain, they might feel a diminution of pleasure, by which they might be prompted to seek that object which is necessary to their subsistence. Men pursue pleasure as eagerly as they avoid pain; at least they might have been so constituted. It seems, therefore, plainly possible to carry on the business of life without any pain. Why then is any animal ever rendered susceptible of such a sensation? If animals can be free from it an hour, they might enjoy a perpetual exemption from it; and it required as particular a contrivance of their organs to produce that feeling, as to endow them with sight, hearing, or any of the senses. Shall we conjecture, that such a contrivance was necessary, without any appearance of reason? and shall we build on that conjecture as on the most certain truth?

But a capacity of pain would not alone produce pain, were it not for the *second* circumstance, viz. the conducting of the world by general laws; and this seems nowise necessary to a very perfect Being. It is true, if every thing were conducted by particular volitions,[107] the course of nature would be perpetually broken, and no man could employ his reason in the conduct of life. But might not other particular volitions remedy this inconvenience? In short, might not the Deity exterminate all ill, wherever it were to be found; and produce all good, without any preparation or long progress of causes and effects?

Besides, we must consider, that, according to the present economy of the world, the course of nature, though supposed exactly regular, yet to us appears not so, and many events are uncertain, and many disappoint our expectations. Health and sickness, calm and tempest, with an infinite number of other accidents, whose causes are unknown and variable, have a great influence both on the fortunes of particular persons and on the prosperity of public societies;[108] and indeed all human life, in a manner, depends on such accidents. A being, therefore, who knows the secret springs of the universe, might easily, by particular volitions, turn all these accidents to the good of mankind, and render the whole world happy, without discovering[109] himself in any operation. A fleet, whose purposes were salutary to society, might always meet with a fair wind. Good princes enjoy sound health and long life. Persons born to power and authority, be framed with good tempers and virtuous dispositions. A few such events as these, regularly and wisely conducted, would change the face of the world; and yet no more seem to disturb the course of nature or confound human conduct, than the present economy of things, where the causes are secret, and variable, and compounded. Some small touches given to Caligula's[110] brain in his infancy, might have converted him into a Trajan.[111] One wave, a little higher than the rest, by burying Cæsar and his fortune in the bottom of the ocean, might have restored liberty to a considerable part of mankind. There may, for aught we know, be good reasons, why Providence interposes not in this manner; but they are unknown to us; and though the mere supposition, that such reasons exist, may be sufficient to *save* the conclusion concerning the Divine attributes, yet surely it can never be sufficient to *establish* that conclusion.

---

[107] i.e. not general but individual acts of will. [eds]

[108] i.e. states, countries. [eds]

[109] i.e. revealing. [eds]

[110] Gaius Caesar Caligula, Roman emperor AD 37–41, whose reign was marked by cruelty, vice and madness. He was eventually murdered. [eds]

[111] Marcus Ulpius Traianus, Roman emperor AD 98–117, a great soldier and a simple and unassuming man. [eds]

If every thing in the universe be conducted by general laws, and if animals be rendered susceptible of pain, it scarcely seems possible but some ill must arise in the various shocks of matter, and the various concurrence and opposition of general laws; but this ill would be very rare, were it not for the *third* circumstance, which I proposed to mention, viz. the great frugality with which all powers and faculties are distributed to every particular being. So well adjusted are the organs and capacities of all animals, and so well fitted to their preservation, that, as far as history or tradition reaches, there appears not to be any single species which has yet been extinguished in the universe. Every animal has the requisite endowments; but these endowments are bestowed with so scrupulous an economy, that any considerable diminution must entirely destroy the creature. Wherever one power is increased, there is a proportional abatement in the others. Animals which excel in swiftness are commonly defective in force. Those which possess both are either imperfect in some of their senses, or are oppressed with the most craving wants. The human species, whose chief excellency is reason and sagacity, is of all others the most necessitous, and the most deficient in bodily advantages; without clothes, without arms, without food, without lodging, without any convenience of life, except what they owe to their own skill and industry. In short, nature seems to have formed an exact calculation of the necessities of her creatures; and, like a *rigid master*, has afforded them little more powers or endowments than what are strictly sufficient to supply those necessities. An *indulgent parent* would have bestowed a large stock, in order to guard against accidents, and secure the happiness and welfare of the creature in the most unfortunate concurrence of circumstances. Every course of life would not have been so surrounded with precipices, that the least departure from the true path, by mistake or necessity, must involve us in misery and ruin. Some reserve, some fund, would have been provided to insure happiness; nor would the powers and the necessities have been adjusted with so rigid an economy. The Author of Nature is inconceivably powerful: his force is supposed great, if not altogether inexhaustible: nor is there any reason, as far as we can judge, to make him observe this strict frugality in his dealings with his creatures. It would have been better, were his power extremely limited, to have created fewer animals, and to have endowed these with more faculties for their happiness and preservation. A builder is never esteemed prudent, who undertakes a plan beyond what his stock will enable him to finish.

In order to cure most of the ills of human life, I require not that man should have the wings of the eagle, the swiftness of the stag, the force of the ox, the arms of the lion, the scales of the crocodile or rhinoceros; much less do I demand the sagacity of an angel or cherubim.[112] I am contented to take an increase in one single power or faculty of his soul. Let him be endowed with a greater propensity to industry and labour; a more vigorous spring and activity of mind; a more constant bent to business and application. Let the whole species possess naturally an equal diligence with that which many individuals are able to attain by habit and reflection; and the most beneficial consequences, without any alloy of ill, is the immediate and necessary result of this endowment. Almost all the moral, as well as natural evils of human life, arise from idleness; and were our species, by the original constitution of their frame, exempt from this vice or infirmity, the perfect cultivation of land, the improvement of arts and manufactures, the exact execution of every office and duty, immediately follow; and men at once may fully reach that state of society, which is so imperfectly attained by the best regulated government. But as industry is a power, and the most valuable of any, Nature seems determined, suitably to her usual maxims, to bestow it on men with a very sparing hand; and rather to punish him severely for his deficiency in it, than to reward him for his attainments. She has so contrived his frame, that nothing but the most violent necessity can oblige him to labour; and she employs all his other wants to overcome, at least in part, the want of diligence, and to endow him with some share of a faculty of which she has thought fit naturally to bereave him. Here our demands may be allowed very humble, and therefore the more reasonable. If we required the endowments of superior penetration and judgement, of a more delicate taste of beauty, of a nicer

---

[112] Strictly, the Hebrew plural for creatures like angels. [eds]

sensibility to benevolence and friendship; we might be told, that we impiously pretend to break the order of Nature; that we want to exalt ourselves into a higher rank of being; that the presents which we require, not being suitable to our state and condition, would only be pernicious to us. But it is hard; I dare to repeat it, it is hard, that being placed in a world so full of wants and necessities, where almost every being and element is either our foe or refuses us their assistance... we should also have our own temper[113] to struggle with, and should be deprived of that faculty which can alone fence against these multiplied evils.

The *fourth* circumstance, whence arises the misery and ill of the universe, is the inaccurate workmanship of all the springs and principles of the great machine of nature. It must be acknowledged, that there are few parts of the universe, which seem not to serve some purpose, and whose removal would not produce a visible defect and disorder in the whole. The parts hang all together; nor can one be touched without affecting the rest, in a greater or less degree. But at the same time, it must be observed, that none of these parts or principles, however useful, are so accurately adjusted, as to keep precisely within those bounds in which their utility consists; but they are, all of them, apt, on every occasion, to run into the one extreme or the other. One would imagine, that this grand production has not received the last hand of the maker; so little finished is every part, and so coarse are the strokes with which it is executed. Thus, the winds are requisite to convey the vapours along the surface of the globe, and to assist men in navigation: but how oft, rising up to tempests and hurricanes, do they become pernicious? Rains are necessary to nourish all the plants and animals of the earth: but how often are they defective? how often excessive? Heat is requisite to all life and vegetation; but is not always found in the due proportion. On the mixture and secretion of the humours and juices of the body depend the health and prosperity of the animal: but the parts perform not regularly their proper function. What more useful than all the passions of the mind, ambition, vanity, love, anger? But how oft do they break their bounds, and cause the greatest convulsions in society? There is nothing so advantageous in the universe, but what frequently becomes pernicious, by its excess or defect; nor has Nature guarded, with the requisite accuracy, against all disorder or confusion. The irregularity is never perhaps so great as to destroy any species; but is often sufficient to involve the individuals in ruin and misery.

On the concurrence, then, of these *four* circumstances, does all or the greatest part of natural evil depend. Were all living creatures incapable of pain, or were the world administered by particular volitions, evil never could have found access into the universe: and were animals endowed with a large stock of powers and faculties, beyond what strict necessity requires; or were the several springs and principles of the universe so accurately framed as to preserve always the just temperament and medium; there must have been very little ill in comparison of what we feel at present. What then shall we pronounce on this occasion? Shall we say, that these circumstances are not necessary, and that they might easily have been altered in the contrivance of the universe? This decision seems too presumptuous for creatures so blind and ignorant. Let us be more modest in our conclusions. Let us allow, that, if the goodness of the Deity (I mean a goodness like the human) could be established on any tolerable reasons *à priori*, these phenomena, however untoward, would not be sufficient to subvert that principle; but might easily, in some unknown manner, be reconcilable to it. But let us still assert, that as this goodness is not antecedently established, but must be inferred from the phenomena, there can be no grounds for such an inference, while there are so many ills in the universe, and while those ills might so easily have been remedied, as far as human understanding can be allowed to judge on such a subject. I am Sceptic enough to allow, that the bad appearances, notwithstanding all my reasonings, may be compatible with such attributes as you suppose; but surely they can never prove these attributes. Such a conclusion cannot result from Scepticism, but must arise from the phenomena, and from our confidence in the reasonings which we deduce from these phenomena.

---

[113] i.e. constitution, habitual disposition. [eds]

Look round this universe. What an immense profusion of beings, animated and organized, sensible and active! You admire this prodigious variety and fecundity. But inspect a little more narrowly these living existences, the only beings worth regarding. How hostile and destructive to each other! How insufficient all of them for their own happiness! How contemptible or odious to the spectator! The whole presents nothing but the idea of a blind Nature, impregnated by a great vivifying principle, and pouring forth from her lap, without discernment or parental care, her maimed and abortive children!

Here the Manichæan[114] system occurs as a proper hypothesis to solve the difficulty: and no doubt, in some respects, it is very specious,[115] and has more probability than the common hypothesis, by giving a plausible account of the strange mixture of good and ill which appears in life. But if we consider, on the other hand, the perfect uniformity and agreement of the parts of the universe, we shall not discover in it any marks of the combat of a malevolent with a benevolent being. There is indeed an opposition of pains and pleasures in the feelings of sensible creatures: but are not all the operations of Nature carried on by an opposition of principles, of hot and cold, moist and dry, light and heavy? The true conclusion is, that the original Source of all things is entirely indifferent to all these principles; and has no more regard to good above ill, than to heat above cold, or to drought above moisture, or to light above heavy.

There may *four* hypotheses be framed concerning the first causes of the universe: *that* they are endowed with perfect goodness; *that* they have perfect malice; *that* they are opposite, and have both goodness and malice; *that* they have neither goodness nor malice. Mixed phenomena can never prove the two former unmixed principles; and the uniformity and steadiness of general laws seem to oppose the third. The fourth, therefore, seems by far the most probable.

What I have said concerning natural evil will apply to moral, with little or no variation; and we have no more reason to infer, that the rectitude of the Supreme Being resembles human rectitude, than that his benevolence resembles the human. Nay, it will be thought, that we have still greater cause to exclude from him moral sentiments, such as we feel them; since moral evil, in the opinion of many, is much more predominant above moral good than natural evil above natural good.

But even though this should not be allowed, and though the virtue which is in mankind, should be acknowledged much superior to the vice, yet so long as there is any vice at all in the universe, it will very much puzzle you Anthropomorphites, how to account for it. You must assign a cause for it, without having recourse to the first cause. But as every effect must have a cause, and that cause another, you must either carry on the progression *in infinitum*, or rest on that original principle, who is the ultimate cause of all things...

Hold! Hold! cried Demea: whither does your imagination hurry you? I joined in alliance with you, in order to prove the incomprehensible nature of the Divine Being, and refute the principles of Cleanthes, who would measure every thing by human rule and standard. But I now find you running into all the topics of the greatest libertines and infidels, and betraying that holy cause which you seemingly espoused. Are you secretly, then, a more dangerous enemy than Cleanthes himself?

And are you so late in perceiving it? replied Cleanthes. Believe me, Demea, your friend Philo, from the beginning, has been amusing himself at both our expense; and it must be confessed, that the injudicious reasoning of our vulgar theology has given him but too just a handle of ridicule. The total infirmity of human reason, the absolute incomprehensibility of the Divine Nature, the great and universal misery, and still greater wickedness of men; these are strange topics, surely, to be so fondly cherished by orthodox divines and doctors. In ages of stupidity and ignorance, indeed, these principles may safely be espoused; and perhaps no views of

---

[114] The Manichæans taught that the universe is governed by two independent principles, one the source of good, the other the source of evil. [eds]

[115] i.e. plausible. [eds]

things are more proper to promote superstition, than such as encourage the blind amazement, the diffidence, and melancholy of mankind. But at present...

Blame not so much, interposed Philo, the ignorance of these reverend gentlemen. They know how to change their style with the times. Formerly it was a most popular theological topic to maintain, that human life was vanity and misery, and to exaggerate all the ills and pains which are incident to men. But of late years, divines, we find, begin to retract this position; and maintain, though still with some hesitation, that there are more goods than evils, more pleasures than pains, even in this life. When religion stood entirely upon temper and education, it was thought proper to encourage melancholy; as indeed mankind never have recourse to superior powers so readily as in that disposition. But as men have now learned to form principles, and to draw consequences, it is necessary to change the batteries, and to make use of such arguments as will endure at least some scrutiny and examination. This variation is the same (and from the same causes) with that which I formerly remarked with regard to Scepticism.

Thus Philo continued to the last his spirit of opposition, and his censure of established opinions. But I could observe that Demea did not at all relish the latter part of the discourse; and he took occasion soon after, on some pretence or other, to leave the company.

Part XII

AFTER Demea's departure, Cleanthes and Philo continued the conversation in the following manner. Our friend, I am afraid, said Cleanthes, will have little inclination to revive this topic of discourse, while you are in company; and to tell truth, Philo, I should rather wish to reason with either of you apart on a subject so sublime and interesting. Your spirit of controversy, joined to your abhorrence of vulgar superstition, carries you strange lengths, when engaged in an argument; and there is nothing so sacred and venerable, even in your own eyes, which you spare on that occasion.

I must confess, replied Philo, that I am less cautious on the subject of Natural Religion than on any other; both because I know that I can never, on that head, corrupt the principles of any man of common sense; and because no one, I am confident, in whose eyes I appear a man of common sense, will ever mistake my intentions. You, in particular, Cleanthes, with whom I live in unreserved intimacy; you are sensible, that notwithstanding the freedom of my conversation, and my love for singular arguments, no one has a deeper sense of religion impressed on his mind, or pays more profound adoration to the Divine Being, as he discovers[116] himself to reason, in the inexplicable contrivance and artifice of nature. A purpose, an intention, a design, strikes everywhere the most careless, the most stupid thinker; and no man can be so hardened in absurd systems, as at all times to reject it. *That Nature does nothing in vain*, is a maxim established in all the schools, merely from the contemplation of the works of Nature, without any religious purpose; and, from a firm conviction of its truth, an anatomist, who had observed a new organ or canal, would never be satisfied till he had also discovered its use and intention. One great foundation of the Copernican system is the maxim, *That Nature acts by the simplest methods, and chooses the most proper means to any end*; and the astronomers often, without thinking of it, lay this strong foundation of piety and religion. The same thing is observable in other parts of philosophy: and thus all the sciences almost lead us insensibly to acknowledge a first intelligent Author; and their authority is often so much the greater, as they do not directly profess that intention.

It is with pleasure I hear Galen[117] reason concerning the structure of the human body. The anatomy of a man, says he, discovers above six hundred different muscles; and whoever duly considers these, will find, that, in each of them, Nature must have adjusted at least ten different circumstances, in order to attain the end which she proposed; proper figure, just magnitude, right disposition of the several ends, upper and lower position of the whole, the due insertion of the several nerves, veins, and arteries: so that, in

---

[116] i.e. reveals. [eds]

[117] Claudius Galen (AD 131–200), Greek physician, wrote widely on anatomy and the theory of science and medicine. The work referred to is *The Formation of the Foetus*.

the muscles alone, above six thousand several views and intentions must have been formed and executed. The bones he calculates to be two hundred and eighty-four: the distinct purposes aimed at in the structure of each, above forty. What a prodigious display of artifice, even in these simple and homogeneous parts! But if we consider the skin, ligaments, vessels, glandules, humours,[118] the several limbs and members of the body; how must our astonishment rise upon us, in proportion to the number and intricacy of the parts so artificially adjusted! The further we advance in these researches, we discover new scenes of art and wisdom: but descry still, at a distance, further scenes beyond our reach; in the fine internal structure of the parts, in the economy of the brain, in the fabric of the seminal[119] vessels. All these artifices are repeated in every different species of animal, with wonderful variety, and with exact propriety, suited to the different intentions of Nature, in framing each species. And if the infidelity[120] of Galen, even when these natural sciences were still imperfect, could not withstand such striking appearances, to what pitch of pertinacious obstinacy must a philosopher in this age have attained, who can now doubt of a Supreme Intelligence!

Could I meet with one of this species (who, I thank God, are very rare), I would ask him: Supposing there were a God, who did not discover himself immediately to our senses, were it possible for him to give stronger proofs of his existence, than what appear on the whole face of Nature? What indeed could such a Divine Being do, but copy the present economy of things; render many of his artifices so plain, that no stupidity could mistake them; afford glimpses of still greater artifices, which demonstrate his prodigious superiority above our narrow apprehensions; and conceal altogether a great many from such imperfect creatures? Now, according to all rules of just reasoning, every fact must pass for undisputed, when it is supported by all the arguments which its nature

admits of; even though these arguments be not in themselves, very numerous or forcible: how much more, in the present case, where no human imagination can compute their number, and no understanding estimate their cogency![121]

I shall further add, said Cleanthes, to what you have so well urged, that one great advantage of the principle of Theism, is, that it is the only system of cosmogony which can be rendered intelligible and complete, and yet can throughout preserve a strong analogy to what we every day see and experience in the world. The comparison of the universe to a machine of human contrivance, is so obvious and natural, and is justified by so many instances of order and design in Nature, that it must immediately strike all unprejudiced apprehensions, and produce universal approbation. Whoever attempts to weaken this theory, cannot pretend to succeed by establishing in its place any other that is precise and determinate: it is sufficient for him if he start doubts and difficulties; and by remote and abstract views of things, reach that suspense of judgement, which is here the utmost boundary of his wishes. But, besides that this state of mind is in itself unsatisfactory, it can never be steadily maintained against such striking appearances as continually engage us into the religious hypothesis. A false, absurd system, human nature, from the force of prejudice, is capable of adhering to with obstinacy and perseverance: but no system at all, in opposition to a theory supported by strong and obvious reason, by natural propensity, and by early education, I think it absolutely impossible to maintain or defend.

So little, replied Philo, do I esteem this suspense of judgement in the present case to be possible, that I am apt to suspect there enters somewhat of a dispute of words into this controversy, more than is usually imagined. That the works of Nature bear a great analogy to the productions of art, is evident; and according to all the rules of good reasoning, we ought to infer, if

---

[118] Glandules, i.e. small glands; humours, i.e. fluids. [eds]

[119] i.e. reproductive. [eds]

[120] i.e. disbelief. [eds]

[121] i.e. power of compelling assent. [eds]

we argue at all concerning them, that their causes have a proportional analogy. But as there are also considerable differences, we have reason to suppose a proportional difference in the causes; and in particular, ought to attribute a much higher degree of power and energy to the supreme cause, than any we have ever observed in mankind. Here then the existence of a DEITY is plainly ascertained by reason: and if we make it a question, whether, on account of these analogies, we can properly call him a *mind* or *intelligence*, notwithstanding the vast difference which may reasonably be supposed between him and human minds; what is this but a mere verbal controversy? No man can deny the analogies between the effects: to restrain ourselves from inquiring concerning the causes is scarcely possible. From this inquiry, the legitimate conclusion is, that the causes have also an analogy: and if we are not contented with calling the first and supreme cause a GOD or DEITY, but desire to vary the expression; what can we call him but MIND or THOUGHT, to which he is justly supposed to bear a considerable resemblance?

All men of sound reason are disgusted with verbal disputes, which abound so much in philosophical and theological inquiries; and it is found, that the only remedy for this abuse, must arise from clear definitions, from the precision of those ideas which enter into any argument, and from the strict and uniform use of those terms which are employed. But there is a species of controversy, which, from the very nature of language and of human ideas, is involved in perpetual ambiguity, and can never, by any precaution or any definitions, be able to reach a reasonable certainty or precision. These are the controversies concerning the degrees of any quality or circumstance. Men may argue to all eternity, whether Hannibal be a great, or a very great, or a superlatively great man, what degree of beauty Cleopatra possessed, what epithet of praise Livy or Thucydides is entitled to, without bringing the controversy to any determination.[122] The disputants may here agree in their sense, and differ in the terms, or *vice versa*; yet never be

able to define their terms, so as to enter into each other's meaning: because the degrees of these qualities are not, like quantity or number, susceptible of any exact mensuration, which may be the standard in the controversy. That the dispute concerning Theism is of this nature, and consequently is merely verbal, or perhaps, if possible, still more incurably ambiguous, will appear upon the slightest inquiry. I ask the Theist, if he does not allow, that there is a great and immeasurable, because incomprehensible difference between the *human* and the *divine* mind: the more pious he is, the more readily will he assent to the affirmative, and the more will he be disposed to magnify the difference: he will even assert, that the difference is of a nature which cannot be too much magnified. I next turn to the Atheist, who, I assert, is only nominally so, and can never possibly be in earnest; and I ask him, whether, from the coherence and apparent sympathy in all the parts of this world, there be not a certain degree of analogy among all the operations of Nature, in every situation and in every age; whether the rotting of a turnip, the generation of an animal, and the structure of human thought, be not energies that probably bear some remote analogy to each other: it is impossible he can deny it: he will readily acknowledge it. Having obtained this concession, I push him still further in his retreat; and I ask him, if it be not probable, that the principle which first arranged, and still maintains order in this universe, bears not also some remote inconceivable analogy to the other operations of nature, and, among the rest, to the economy[123] of human mind and thought. However reluctant, he must give his assent. Where then, cry I to both these antagonists, is the subject of your dispute? The Theist allows, that the original intelligence is very different from human reason: the Atheist allows, that the original principle of order bears some remote analogy to it. Will you quarrel, gentlemen, about the degrees, and enter into a controversy, which admits not of any precise meaning, nor consequently of any determination? If you should be so obstinate, I should

---

[122] Hannibal (247 BC–182 BC), Cathaginian general, eventually defeated by Roman power. Titus Livius (59 BC–AD 17), Roman historian. Thucydides (*c*.460 BC–400 BC), great Athenian historian. Cleopatra (69 BC–30 BC), ruler of Egypt and successively mistress of Julius Caesar and Mark Antony. [eds]

[123] i.e. organization. [eds]

not be surprised to find you insensibly change sides; while the Theist, on the one hand, exaggerates the dissimilarity between the Supreme Being, and frail, imperfect, variable, fleeting, and mortal creatures; and the Atheist, on the other, magnifies the analogy among all the operations of Nature, in every period, every situation, and every position. Consider then, where the real point of controversy lies, and if you cannot lay aside your disputes, endeavour, at least, to cure yourselves of your animosity.

And here I must also acknowledge, Cleanthes, that as the works of Nature have a much greater analogy to the effects of *our* art and contrivance, than to those of *our* benevolence and justice, we have reason to infer, that the natural attributes of the Deity have a greater resemblance to those of men, than his moral have to human virtues. But what is the consequence? Nothing but this, that the moral qualities of man are more defective in their kind than his natural abilities. For, as the Supreme Being is allowed to be absolutely and entirely perfect, whatever differs most from him, departs the furthest from the supreme standard of rectitude and perfection.[124]

These, Cleanthes, are my unfeigned sentiments on this subject; and these sentiments, you know, I have ever cherished and maintained. But in proportion to my veneration for true religion, is my abhorrence of vulgar superstitions; and I indulge a peculiar pleasure, I confess, in pushing such principles, sometimes into absurdity, sometimes into impiety. And you are sensible, that all bigots, notwithstanding their great aversion to the latter above the former, are commonly equally guilty of both.

My inclination, replied Cleanthes, lies, I own, a contrary way. Religion, however corrupted, is still better than no religion at all. The doctrine of a future state[125] is so strong and necessary a security to morals, that we never ought to abandon or neglect it. For if finite and temporary rewards and punishments have so great an effect, as we daily find; how much greater must be expected from such as are infinite and eternal?

How happens it then, said Philo, if vulgar superstition be so salutary to society, that all history abounds so much with accounts of its pernicious consequences on public affairs? Factions, civil wars, persecutions, subversions of government, oppression, slavery; these are the dismal consequences which always attend its prevalency over the minds of men. If the religious spirit be ever mentioned in any historical narration, we are sure to meet afterwards with a detail of the miseries which attend it. And no period of time can be happier or more prosperous, than those in which it is never regarded or heard of.

The reason of this observation, replied Cleanthes, is obvious. The proper office of religion is to regulate the heart of men, humanize their conduct, infuse the spirit of temperance, order, and obedience; and as its operation is silent, and only enforces the motives of morality and justice, it is in danger of being overlooked, and confounded with these other motives. When it distinguishes itself, and acts as a separate principle over men, it has departed from its proper sphere, and has become only a cover to faction and ambition.

And so will all religion, said Philo, except the philosophical and rational kind. Your reasonings are more easily eluded than my facts.

---

[124] It seems evident, that the dispute between the Sceptics and Dogmatists is entirely verbal, or at least regards only the degrees of doubt and assurance which we ought to indulge with regard to all reasoning; and such disputes are commonly, at the bottom, verbal, and admit not of any precise determination. No philosophical Dogmatist denies that there are difficulties both with regard to the senses and to all science, and that these difficulties are in a regular, logical method, absolutely insolvable. No Sceptic denies that we lie under an absolute necessity, notwithstanding these difficulties, of thinking, and believing, and reasoning, with regard to all kinds of subjects, and even of frequently assenting with confidence and security. The only difference, then, between these sects, if they merit that name, is, that the Sceptic, from habit, caprice, or inclination, insists most on the difficulties; the Dogmatist, for like reasons, on the necessity. [Hume]

The above paragraph appeared as a note in Hume's manuscript but Hume deleted it later and rewrote it at the end of the manuscript. Some editors incorporate it into the main body of the text on the assumption that this was Hume's intention. [eds]

[125] i.e. an after-life. [eds]

The inference is not just, because finite and temporary rewards and punishments have so great influence, that therefore such as are infinite and eternal must have so much greater. Consider, I beseech you, the attachment which we have to present things, and the little concern which we discover[126] for objects so remote and uncertain. When divines are declaiming against the common behaviour and conduct of the world, they always represent this principle as the strongest imaginable (which indeed it is); and describe almost all human kind as lying under the influence of it, and sunk into the deepest lethargy and unconcern about their religious interests. Yet these same divines, when they refute their speculative antagonists, suppose the motives of religion to be so powerful, that, without them, it were impossible for civil society to subsist; nor are they ashamed of so palpable a contradiction. It is certain, from experience, that the smallest grain of natural honesty and benevolence has more effect on men's conduct, than the most pompous views suggested by theological theories and systems. A man's natural inclination works incessantly upon him; it is for ever present to the mind, and mingles itself with every view and consideration: whereas religious motives, where they act at all, operate only by starts and bounds; and it is scarcely possible for them to become altogether habitual to the mind. The force of the greatest gravity, say the philosophers, is infinitely small, in comparison of that of the least impulse; yet it is certain, that the smallest gravity will, in the end, prevail above a great impulse; because no strokes or blows can be repeated with such constancy as attraction and gravitation.

Another advantage of inclination: it engages on its side all the wit and ingenuity of the mind; and when set in opposition to religious principles, seeks every method and art of eluding them: in which it is almost always successful. Who can explain the heart of man, or account for those strange salvos and excuses, with which people satisfy themselves, when they follow their inclinations in opposition to their religious duty? This is well understood in the world; and none but fools ever repose less trust in a man, because they hear, that from study and philosophy, he has entertained some speculative doubts with regard to theological subjects. And when we have to do with a man, who makes a great profession of religion and devotion, has this any other effect upon several, who pass for prudent, than to put them on their guard, lest they be cheated and deceived by him?

We must farther consider, that philosophers, who cultivate reason and reflection, stand less in need of such motives to keep them under the restraint of morals; and that the vulgar, who alone may need them, are utterly incapable of so pure a religion as represents the Deity to be pleased with nothing but virtue in human behaviour. The recommendations to the Divinity are generally supposed to be either frivolous observances, or rapturous ecstasies, or a bigoted credulity. We need not run back into antiquity, or wander into remote regions, to find instances of this degeneracy. Amongst ourselves, some have been guilty of that atrociousness, unknown to the Egyptian and Grecian superstitions, of declaiming in express terms, against morality; and representing it as a sure forfeiture of the Divine favour, if the least trust or reliance be laid upon it.

But even though superstition or enthusiasm should not put itself in direct opposition to morality; the very diverting of the attention, the raising up a new and frivolous species of merit, the preposterous distribution which it makes of praise and blame, must have the most pernicious consequences, and weaken extremely men's attachment to the natural motives of justice and humanity.

Such a principle of action likewise, not being any of the familiar motives of human conduct, acts only by intervals on the temper; and must be roused by continual efforts, in order to render the pious zealot satisfied with his own conduct, and make him fulfil his devotional task. Many religious exercises are entered into with seeming fervour, where the heart, at the time, feels cold and languid: a habit of dissimulation is by degrees contracted; and fraud and falsehood become the predominant principle. Hence the reason of that vulgar observation, that the highest zeal in religion and the deepest hypocrisy, so far from being inconsistent, are often or commonly united in the same individual character.

---

[126] i.e. reveal. [eds]

The bad effects of such habits, even in common life, are easily imagined; but where the interests of religion are concerned, no morality can be forcible enough to bind the enthusiastic[127] zealot. The sacredness of the cause sanctifies every measure which can be made use of to promote it.

The steady attention alone to so important an interest as that of eternal salvation, is apt to extinguish the benevolent affections, and beget a narrow, contracted selfishness. And when such a temper is encouraged, it easily eludes all the general precepts of charity and benevolence.

Thus, the motives of vulgar superstition have no great influence on general conduct; nor is their operation very favourable to morality, in the instances where they predominate.

Is there any maxim in politics more certain and infallible, than that both the number and authority of priests should be confined within very narrow limits; and that the civil magistrate ought, for ever, to keep his *fasces*[128] and *axes* from such dangerous hands? But if the spirit of popular religion were so salutary to society, a contrary maxim ought to prevail. The greater number of priests, and their greater authority and riches, will always augment the religious spirit. And though the priests have the guidance of this spirit, why may we not expect a superior sanctity of life, and greater benevolence and moderation, from persons who are set apart for religion, who are continually inculcating it upon others, and who must themselves imbibe a greater share of it? Whence comes it then, that, in fact, the utmost a wise magistrate can propose with regard to popular religions, is, as far as possible, to make a saving game of it, and to prevent their pernicious consequences with regard to society? Every expedient which he tries for so humble a purpose is surrounded with inconveniences. If he admits only one religion among his subjects, he must sacrifice, to an uncertain prospect of tranquillity, every consideration of public liberty, science, reason, industry, and even his own independency. If he gives indulgence to several sects, which is the wiser maxim, he must preserve a very philosophical indifference to all of them, and carefully restrain the pretensions of the prevailing sect; otherwise he can expect nothing but endless disputes, quarrels, factions, persecutions, and civil commotions.

True religion, I allow, has no such pernicious consequences: but we must treat of religion, as it has commonly been found in the world; nor have I any thing to do with that speculative tenet of Theism, which, as it is a species of philosophy, must partake of the beneficial influence of that principle, and at the same time must lie under a like inconvenience, of being always confined to very few persons.

Oaths are requisite in all courts of judicature; but it is a question whether their authority arises from any popular religion. It is the solemnity and importance of the occasion, the regard to reputation, and the reflecting on the general interests of society, which are the chief restraints upon mankind. Custom-house oaths and political oaths are but little regarded even by some who pretend to principles of honesty and religion; and a Quaker's asseveration is with us justly put upon the same footing with the oath of any other person. I know, that Polybius[129] ascribes the infamy of Greek faith to the prevalency of the Epicurean philosophy: but I know also, that Punic[130] faith had as bad a reputation in ancient times as Irish evidence has in modern; though we cannot account for these vulgar observations by the same reason. Not to mention that Greek faith was infamous before the rise of the Epicurean philosophy; and Euripides,[131] in a passage which I shall point out to you, has

---

[127] The word here suggests self-deluding. [eds]

[128] Bundles of sticks with an axe projecting, carried before the chief Roman magistrates. Philo disapproves of the surrender of civil, temporal power to priests. [eds]

[129] Polybius (*c*.204 BC–122 BC), Greek historian who spent most of his life at Rome. [eds]

[130] i.e. Carthaginian. [eds]

[131] Euripides' *Iphigenia in Tauris* (*c*.414 BC) contains a scene in which Iphigenia deceives Thoas, using her sanctity as a priestess to cover her lies, remarking 'Greeks are never to be trusted'. [eds]

glanced a remarkable stroke of satire against his nation, with regard to this circumstance.

Take care, Philo, replied Cleanthes, take care: push not matters too far: allow not your zeal against false religion to undermine your veneration for the true. Forfeit not this principle, the chief, the only great comfort in life; and our principal support amidst all the attacks of adverse fortune. The most agreeable reflection, which it is possible for human imagination to suggest, is that of genuine Theism, which represents us as the workmanship of a Being perfectly good, wise, and powerful; who created us for happiness, and who, having implanted in us immeasurable desires of good, will prolong our existence to all eternity, and will transfer us into an infinite variety of scenes, in order to satisfy those desires, and render our felicity complete and durable. Next to such a Being himself (if the comparison be allowed), the happiest lot which we can imagine, is that of being under his guardianship and protection.

These appearances, said Philo, are most engaging and alluring; and with regard to the true philosopher, they are more than appearances. But it happens here, as in the former case, that, with regard to the greater part of mankind, the appearances are deceitful, and that the terrors of religion commonly prevail above its comforts.

It is allowed, that men never have recourse to devotion so readily as when dejected with grief or depressed with sickness. Is not this a proof, that the religious spirit is not so nearly allied to joy as to sorrow?

But men, when afflicted, find consolation in religion, replied Cleanthes. Sometimes, said Philo: but it is natural to imagine, that they will form a notion of those unknown beings, suitably to the present gloom and melancholy of their temper, when they betake themselves to the contemplation of them. Accordingly, we find the tremendous images to predominate in all religions; and we ourselves, after having employed the most exalted expression in our descriptions of the Deity, fall into the flattest contradictions in affirming that the damned are infinitely superior in number to the elect.

I shall venture to affirm, that there never was a popular religion, which represented the state of departed souls in such a light, as would render it eligible[132] for human kind that there should be such a state. These fine models of religion are the mere product of philosophy. For as death lies between the eye and the prospect of futurity, that event is so shocking to Nature, that it must throw a gloom on all the regions which lie beyond it; and suggest to the generality of mankind the idea of Cerberus and Furies;[133] devils, and torrents of fire and brimstone.

It is true, both fear and hope enter into religion; because both these passions, at different times, agitate the human mind, and each of them forms a species of divinity suitable to itself. But when a man is in a cheerful disposition, he is fit for business or company or entertainment of any kind; and he naturally applies himself to these, and thinks not of religion. When melancholy and dejected, he has nothing to do but brood upon the terrors of the invisible world, and to plunge himself still deeper in affliction. It may indeed happen, that after he has, in this manner, engraved the religious opinions deep into his thought and imagination, there may arrive a change of health and circumstances, which may restore his good humour, and raising cheerful prospects of futurity, make him run into the other extreme of joy and triumph. But still it must be acknowledged, that, as terror is the primary principle of religion, it is the passion which always predominates in it, and admits but of short intervals of pleasure.

Not to mention, that these fits of excessive, enthusiastic joy, by exhausting the spirits, always prepare the way for equal fits of superstitious terror and dejection; nor is there any state of mind so happy as the calm and equable. But this state it is impossible to support, where a man thinks that he lies in such profound darkness and uncertainty, between an eternity of happiness and an eternity of misery. No wonder that such an opinion disjoints the ordinary frame of the mind, and throws it into the utmost confusion. And though that opinion is seldom so steady in its operation as to influence all the actions; yet it

---

[132] i.e. desirable. [eds]

[133] Cerberus was a dog with fifty heads, in Roman mythology, reputedly stationed at the entrance to the underworld. The Furies were avenging deities in Greek mythology. [eds]

is apt to make a considerable breach in the temper,[134] and to produce that gloom and melancholy so remarkable in all devout people.

It is contrary to common sense to entertain apprehensions or terrors upon account of any opinion whatsoever, or to imagine that we run any risk hereafter, by the freest use of our reason. Such a sentiment implies both an *absurdity* and an *inconsistency*. It is an absurdity to believe that the Deity has human passions, and one of the lowest of human passions, a restless appetite for applause. It is an inconsistency to believe, that, since the Deity has this human passion, he has not others also; and, in particular, a disregard to the opinions of creatures so much inferior.

To know God, says Seneca,[135] *is to worship him.* All other worship is indeed absurd, superstitious, and even impious. It degrades him to the low condition of mankind, who are delighted with entreaty, solicitation, presents, and flattery. Yet is this impiety the smallest of which superstition is guilty. Commonly, it depresses the Deity far below the condition of mankind; and represents him as a capricious demon, who exercises his power without reason and without humanity! And were that Divine Being disposed to be offended at the vices and follies of silly mortals, who are his own workmanship, ill would it surely fare with the votaries of most popular superstitions. Nor would any of human race merit his *favour,* but a very few, the philosophical Theists, who entertain, or rather indeed endeavour to entertain, suitable notions of his Divine perfections: as the only persons entitled to his *compassion* and *indulgence* would be the philosophical Sceptics, a sect almost equally rare, who, from a natural diffidence of their own capacity, suspend, or endeavour to suspend, all judgement with regard to such sublime and such extraordinary subjects.

If the whole of Natural Theology, as some people seem to maintain, resolves itself into one simple, though somewhat ambiguous, at least undefined proposition, *That the cause or causes of order in the universe probably bear some remote analogy to human intelligence:* if this proposition be not capable of extension, variation, or more particular explication: if it affords no inference that affects human life, or can be the source of any action or forbearance: and if the analogy, imperfect as it is, can be carried no further than to the human intelligence, and cannot be transferred, with any appearance of probability, to the qualities of the mind; if this really be the case, what can the most inquisitive, contemplative, and religious man do more than give a plain, philosophical assent to the proposition, as often as it occurs, and believe that the arguments on which it is established exceed the objections which lie against it? Some astonishment, indeed, will naturally arise from the greatness of the object; some melancholy from its obscurity; some contempt of human reason, that it can give no solution more satisfactory with regard to so extraordinary and magnificent a question. But believe me, Cleanthes, the most natural sentiment, which a well-disposed mind will feel on this occasion, is a longing desire and expectation, that Heaven would be pleased to dissipate, at least alleviate, this profound ignorance, by affording some more particular revelation to mankind, and making discoveries[136] of the nature, attributes, and operations of the Divine object of our faith. A person, seasoned with a just sense of the imperfections of natural reason, will fly to revealed truth with the greatest avidity: while the haughty Dogmatist, persuaded that he can erect a complete system of Theology by the mere help of philosophy, disdains any further aid, and rejects this adventitious instructor. To be a philosophical Sceptic is, in a man of letters, the first and most essential step towards being a sound, believing Christian; a proposition which I would willingly recommend to the attention of Pamphilus: and I hope Cleanthes will forgive me for interposing so far in the education and instruction of his pupil.

---

[134] i.e. habitual disposition. [eds]

[135] Lucius Annaeus Seneca (d. AD 65), tutor to the young Nero, dramatist and philosopher. The reference is to his *Moral Letters* XCV 50: 'the first way to worship the gods is to believe in the gods'. [eds]

[136] i.e. revelations. [eds]

Cleanthes and Philo pursued not this conversation much further: and as nothing ever made greater impression on me, than all the reasonings of that day, so I confess, that, upon a serious review of the whole, I cannot but think, that Philo's principles are more probable than Demea's; but that those of Cleanthes approach still nearer to the truth.

Source: The Philosophical Works of David Hume, Volume II, Little, Brown and Company, Boston, 1854.

Wolfgang Amadeus Mozart
The Magic Flute

Libretto by Emanuel Schikaneder
Translated from the German by
Robert Philip

Contents

Wolfgang Amadeus Mozart
The Magic Flute

The German libretto printed here corresponds with the version used in the EMI recording conducted by Wolfgang Sawallisch, supplied on cassette (AC 1629 and AC 1630, Grey). The sung sections are all complete but Schikaneder's spoken dialogue, as in most modern performances, is abbreviated, and a few of the stage directions have had to be adapted to match the cuts in dialogue. The beginning of each sung section is indicated by an appropriate heading and number, the end is marked by the sign ¶

Although this is a new translation which aims to convey the sense of the German as closely as possible, it includes (inevitably) quotations from several distinguished earlier translations, notably those of Andrew Porter and Lionel Salter. Porter's version for the English National Opera (published by Faber, 1980) provides the most complete translation in English of the spoken dialogue of the original and the stage directions.

ERSTER AKT

ACT ONE

The setting is a rocky landscape, overgrown here and there with trees. There are practicable mountains on either side, and a round temple. Tamino comes down, right, from a rock, in a magnificent Japanese hunting costume, carrying a bow but no arrows. A serpent pursues him.

Nr. 1 Introduktion

No. 1 Introduction

TAMINO. Zu Hilfe! Zu Hilfe! sonst bin ich verloren!
der listigen Schlange zum Opfer erkoren!
Barmherzige Götter! Schon nahet sie sich!
Ach! rettet mich, ach! schützet mich!

TAMINO. Help me! Help me! Or I am lost.
Condemned to be a sacrifice to the cunning serpent.
Merciful gods! It's coming closer!
Ah, save me! Ah, defend me!

(He falls in a swoon; immediately the door of the temple opens; three veiled ladies come out, each with a silver javelin.)

DIE DAMEN. Stirb, Ungeheu'r! durch unsre Macht!
Triumph! Triumph! Sie ist vollbracht,
die Heldentat! Er ist befreit
durch unsres Armes Tapferkeit!

THE LADIES. Die, monster, by our power!
Victory! Victory! The heroic deed
is accomplished! He is set free
by the valour of our arm!

ERSTE DAME. Ein holder Jüngling, sanft und schön –

FIRST LADY (*gazing at him*). A pleasing youth, gentle and fair –

ZWEITE DAME. So schön als ich noch nie gesehn!

SECOND LADY. Fairer than any I ever saw.

DRITTE DAME. Ja, ja, gewiss, zum Malen schön!

THIRD LADY. Yes, indeed, fair enough to paint.

ALLE DREI. Würd' ich mein Herz der Liebe weihn,
so müsst' es dieser Jüngling sein.
Lasst uns zu unsrer Fürstin eilen,
ihr diese Nachricht zu erteilen.
Vielleicht, dass dieser schöne Mann
die vor'ge Ruh' ihr geben kann.

ALL THREE. If ever I gave my heart to love,
it would have to be to this youth.
Let us hurry to our Queen
and report this news to her.
Perhaps this handsome man
may restore her former peace.

ERSTE DAME. So geht und sagt es ihr,
Ich bleib' indessen hier.

ZWEITE DAME. Nein, nein, geht ihr nur hin,
Ich wache hier für ihn!

DRITTE DAME. Nein, nein, das kann nicht sein!
Ich schütze ihn allein.

ERSTE DAME. Ich bleib' indessen hier!

ZWEITE DAME. Ich wache hier für ihn!

DRITTE DAME. Ich schütze ihn allein!

ERSTE DAME. Ich bleibe!

ZWEITE DAME. Ich wache!

DRITTE DAME. Ich schütze!

ALLE DREI. Ich! Ich! Ich!

Ich sollte fort? Ei, ei! wie fein!
Sie wären gern bei ihm allein.
Nein, nein, das kann nicht sein!
Was wollte ich darum nicht geben,
könnt' ich mit diesem Jüngling leben!
Hätt' ich ihn doch so ganz allein!
Doch keine geht; es kann nicht sein!
Am besten ist es nun, ich geh'.
Du Jüngling, schön und liebevoll
du trauter Jüngling, lebe wohl,
bis ich dich wiederseh'.¶

TAMINO.
Wo bin ich?
Ist's Phantasie, dass ich noch
lebe? Wie? Die Schlange tot zu
meinen Füssen?

Was hör' ich?
Eine Gestalt nähert sich. Ich will sie von ferne beobachten!

FIRST LADY. Then go and tell her
while I stay here.

SECOND LADY. No, no, you go,
I'll keep watch here.

THIRD LADY. No, no, that cannot be,
I'll guard him by myself.

FIRST LADY. I'll stay here.

SECOND LADY. I'll keep watch.

THIRD LADY. I'll guard him by myself.

FIRST LADY. I'll stay!

SECOND LADY. I'll keep watch!

THIRD LADY. I'll guard him!

ALL THREE. I! I! I!

(*each to herself*)

Should I go? Indeed! The very idea!
They would like to be alone with him.
No, no, that cannot be!
I would give anything
to live with this youth!
If only I could be alone with him!
Still no-one leaves. It cannot be!
It would be better if I go.
O youth, so fair and lovable,
dear youth, farewell,
until I see you again.¶

(*All three go off through the door of the temple, which opens and closes by itself*).

TAMINO (*coming to and looking around fearfully*).
Where am I?
Am I dreaming that I am still alive?
What's this? The
serpent dead at my feet?

(*Panpipes are heard in the distance, accompanied quietly by the orchestra. Tamino speaks through the introduction.*)

What is that I hear?

Someone is approaching. I'll observe him from a safe distance.
(*He hides behind a tree.*)
Papageno comes down the footpath. On his back he is carrying a large birdcage which reaches high above his head, and in which there are various birds. He also holds panpipes in both hands. He pipes and sings.

Nr. 2 Lied

PAPAGENO. Der Vogelfänger bin ich ja,
stets lustig, heissa hopsasa!
Ich Vogelfänger bin bekannt
bei alt und jung im ganzen Land.
Weiss mit dem Locken umzugehn,
und mich aufs Pfeifen zu verstehn!
Drum kann ich froh und lustig sein,
denn alle Vögel sind ja mein.
Der Vogelfänger bin ich ja,
stets lustig, heissa hopsasa!
Ich Vogelfänger bin bekannt
bei alt und jung im ganzen Land.
Ein Netz für Mädchen möchte ich,
ich fing sie dutzendweis' für mich!
Dann sperrte ich sie bei mir ein,
und alle Mädchen wären mein.
Wenn alle Mädchen wären mein,
so tauschte ich brav Zucker ein,
die, welche mir am liebsten wär,
der gäb' ich gleich den Zucker her.
Und küsste sie mich zärtlich dann,
war' sie mein Weib und ich ihr Mann.
Sie schlief an meiner Seite ein,
ich wiegte wie ein Kind sie ein.¶

TAMINO. Heda!

PAPAGENO. Was da?!

TAMINO. Sag mir, du lustiger Freund,
wer bist du?

PAPAGENO. Wer ich bin? – Dumme Frage! –
Ein Mensch wie du. – Wenn ich dich nun fragte,
wer du bist.

TAMINO. Ich bin Prinz!

PAPAGENO. Prinz?

TAMINO. Sag, wovon lebst du?

PAPAGENO. Von Essen und Trinken, wie alle
Menschen.

TAMINO. Und wodurch erhältst du das?

PAPAGENO. Ich fange für die sternflammende
Königin verschiedene Vögel, und dafür erhalt' ich
täglich Speise und Trank.

TAMINO. Sag mir, guter Freund,
warst du schon so glücklich,
diese Göttin der Nacht zu sehen?

PAPAGENO. Seh…? Die sternflammende
Königin sehn? Sehn! Wa… warum blickst du
so verdächtig nach mir?

TAMINO. Weil ich zeifle, ob du ein Mensch bist.

No. 2 Song

PAPAGENO. Yes, I am the birdcatcher,
and always merry – hopsasa!
As birdcatcher I am known
by old and young throughout the land.
I know how to set decoys
and make myself understood on my pipes.
So I can be cheerful and happy,
for all the birds belong to me.
Yes, I am the birdcatcher,
and always merry – hopsasa!
As birdcatcher I am known
by old and young throughout the land.
If I had a net for girls,
I'd catch them by the dozen for myself!
I'd keep them by me, caged up,
and all the girls would be mine.
If all the girls were mine,
I'd trade some for the best sugar,
and then the one that I liked best –
I'd give her all the sugar,
And then she would kiss me tenderly,
she would be my wife and I her husband.
She would sleep at my side
and I would rock her like a child.¶

After the aria, he goes towards the temple door.

TAMINO. Hey, there!

PAPAGENO. What there?

TAMINO. Tell me, my merry friend,
who are you?

PAPAGENO. Who am I? – *(Aside)* Stupid
question! – *(Aloud)* A human being like yourself,
And what if I asked you who you are?

TAMINO. I am a prince.

PAPAGENO. A prince?

TAMINO. Tell me, how do you live?

PAPAGENO. By eating and drinking, like everyone.

TAMINO. And where do you get food and drink
from?

PAPAGENO. I catch all sorts of birds for the star-
blazing Queen,
and in return I get food and drink every day.

TAMINO. Tell me, good friend,
have you ever had the good fortune
to see this goddess of the night?

PAPAGENO. See… ? See the star-blazing Queen?
See her?! But why are you looking at me so
suspiciously?

TAMINO. Because I'm not sure whether
you are a human being.

PAPAGENO. Was?

TAMINO. Nach deinen Federn, die dich bedecken, da halt' ich dich…

PAPAGENO. Doch für keinen Vogel! Du – du – du… bleib zurück, sag' ich, und traue mir nicht, denn ich – ich habe Riesenkraft!

TAMINO. Riesenkraft?

Also warst du wohl gar mein Erretter, der diese giftige Schlange bekämpft hat?!

PAPAGENO. Schlange? – Ist sie tot oder lebendig?

TAMINO. Sie ist tot! Sag, wie hast du dieses Ungeheuer bekämpft?

PAPAGENO. Die – d… – erdrosselt! Ich bin in meinem Leben noch nicht so stark gewesen wie heut'.

DIE DAMEN. Papageno!

PAPAGENO. Ah! Das geht mich an!

TAMINO. Wer sind diese verschleierten Damen?

PAPAGENO. Na, das si… also wer sie eigentlich sind, weiss ich selbst nicht, ich weiss nur, dass sie mir täglich meine Vögel adnehmen und mir dafür süsse Feigen bringen.

TAMINO. Sie sind vermutlich sehr schön?

PAPAGENO. Das glaub' ich nicht! Eh, wenn sie so schön wären, würden sie ihre Gesichter nicht bedecken.

DIE DAMEN. Papageno!

PAPAGENO. O je! – Hier, meine Schönen, übergeb' ich meine Vögel.

ERSTE DAME. Dafür schickt dir unsere Fürstin heute zum ersten Mal statt Wein reines, helles Wasser!

ZWEITE DAME. Und mir befahl sie, dass ich statt Zuckerbrot diesen Stein dir überbringen soll.

PAPAGENO. W – w – was? Steine soll ich fressen?

DRITTE DAME. Und statt der süssen Feigen, habe ich die Ehre, dir dies goldene Schloss vor den Mund zu schlagen.

PAPAGENO. Mmmmmmm…

ERSTE DAME. Damit du künftig nie mehr Fremde belügst…

ZWEITE DAME. … und dass dich nie mehr der Heldentaten rühmst, die andre vollbrachten.

PAPAGENO. Hm, hm, hm.

PAPAGENO. What?

TAMINO. Judging by the feathers you are covered in, I'd take you for… *(He goes up to him.)*

PAPAGENO. Not a bird! You – you – Just you keep your distance and don't trust me. I have the strength of a giant!

TAMINO. The strength of a giant? *(He looks at the serpent.)* So you are my saviour, who conquered this poisonous serpent?

PAPAGENO. Serpent? *(He looks round, and retreats a few steps, trembling.)* Is it dead or alive?

TAMINO. It's dead. Tell me, how did you vanquish this monster?

PAPAGENO. I – er – strangled it. *(Aside)* I've never been so strong in all my life as I am today! *(The Three Ladies enter.)*

THE LADIES *(threatening)*. Papageno!

PAPAGENO. Ah, that's for me.

TAMINO. Who are these veiled ladies?

PAPAGENO. Well, they are… Well, I don't know who they are, actually; I only know that they come every day, take my birds, and give me sweet figs in return.

TAMINO. Presumably they are very beautiful?

PAPAGENO. I don't think so. After all, if they were beautiful they wouldn't cover up their faces.

THE LADIES. Papageno!

PAPAGENO. Oh dear! Here, fair ladies, here are my birds.

FIRST LADY. In exchange, for the first time, our Queen today sends you pure, clear water instead of wine. *(She gives him a beautiful flask of water.)*

SECOND LADY. And she commands me to give you this stone instead of sweetmeats.

PAPAGENO. What? Am I to eat stones?

THIRD LADY. And instead of sweet figs, I have the honour of fastening your mouth with this golden padlock. *(She fastens the padlock on him.)*

PAPAGENO. Mmmmmmm…

FIRST LADY. So that in future you will never again tell lies to strangers…

SECOND LADY. … and never again boast of heroic deeds accomplished by others.

PAPAGENO. Hm, hm, hm.

DRITTE DAME. Wir waren's, Jüngling, die dich befreiten. – Hier dieses Gemälde schickt dir die grosse Fürstin; es ist das Bildnis ihrer Tochter Pamina. Findest du, sagte sie, dass diese Züge dir nicht gleichgültig sind, dann ist Glück, Ehr' und Ruhm dein Los.
Auf Wiedersehn!

ERSTE DAME. Auf Wiedersehn!

ZWEITE DAME. Adieu, Papageno!

PAPAGENO. Mmmmmmm…

THIRD LADY. It was we, young man, who saved you. Here, our great Queen sends you this painting; it is a portrait of her daughter Pamina. She says, if you are not indifferent to these features, you will be rewarded with happiness, honour and fame. Farewell! *(Goes out.)*

FIRST LADY. Farewell! *(Goes out.)*

SECOND LADY. Adieu, Papageno! *(Goes out, laughing.)*

PAPAGENO. Mmmmmmm…
(Tamino has been gazing at the portrait ever since he received it; love has seized him, so that he seems deaf to all this talking.)

Nr. 3 Arie

TAMINO. Dies Bildnis ist bezaubernd schön, wie noch kein Auge je gesehn!
Ich fühl' es, wie dies Götterbild
mein Herz mit neuer Regung füllt.
Dies Etwas kann ich zwar nicht nennen,
doch fühl' ich's hier wie Feuer brennen.
Soll die Empfindung Liebe sein?
Ja, ja! Die Liebe ist's allein.
O wenn ich sie nur finden könnte!
O wenn sie doch hier vor mir stände!
Ich würde … würde warm und rein…
Was würde ich?
Ich würde sie voll Entzücken
an diesen heissen Busen drücken,
und ewig wäre sie dann mein!¶

ERSTE DAME. Rüste dich mit Mut unter Standhaftigkeit, schöner Jüngling!

ZWEITE DAME. Die Fürstin hat jedes deiner Worte gehört…

DRITTE DAME. Hat dieser Jüngling, sprach sie, auch soviel Mut und Tapferkeit, als er zärtlich ist, so ist meine Tochter gewiss gerettet.

TAMINO. Wo ist sie?

ERSTE DAME. Ein mächtiger Herrscher hat sie ihrer Mutter entrissen.

TAMINO. Kommt, Mädchen, führt mich! Pamina sei gerettet! Was ist das?

ERSTE DAME. Es verkündet die Ankunft unserer Königin!

DIE DREI DAMEN. Sie kommt! – Sie kommt! – Sie kommt!

No. 3 Aria

TAMINO. This portrait is enchantingly fair, such as no eyes have ever seen!
I feel that this divine picture
is filling my heart with a new emotion.
Something I cannot name;
but I feel it here burning like fire.
Can this sensation be love?
Yes, yes! It can only be love.
Oh, if only I might find her!
If only she stood before me!
I would … would warmly, chastely…
What would I do?
Enraptured, I would
press her to my burning heart,
and she would be mine forever!¶

(He turns to go. The Three Ladies return.)

FIRST LADY. Arm yourself with courage and steadfastness, fair youth!

SECOND LADY. The Queen has heard your every word.

THIRD LADY. She says, if this young man is as bold and brave as he is loving, my daughter is certainly saved.

TAMINO. Where is she?

FIRST LADY. A powerful ruler has abducted her from her mother.

TAMINO. Come, ladies, lead me to her! Let Pamina be rescued! *(Thunder.)* What is that?

FIRST LADY. It heralds the arrival of our Queen. *(Thunder.)*

THE THREE LADIES. She comes! She comes! She comes! *(Thunder.)*

Transformation

The mountains split asunder, and the scene is transformed into a magnificent chamber. The Queen is seated on a throne decorated with transparent stars.

Nr. 4 Rezitativ und Arie

KÖNIGIN. O zittre nicht, mein lieber Sohn!
du bist unschuldig, weise, fromm.
Ein Jüngling, so wie du, vermag am besten,
dies tiefbetrübte Mutterherz zu trösten.
Zum Leiden bin ich auserkoren;
denn meine Tochter fehlet mir.
Durch sie ging all mein Glück verloren,
ein Bösewicht entfloh mit ihr.
Noch seh' ich ihr Zittern
mit bangem Erschüttern,
ihr ängstliches Beben,
ihr schüchternes Streben!
Ich musste sie mir rauben sehen.
"Ach helft!" war alles, was sie sprach;
allein vergebens war ihr Flehen,
denn meine Hilfe war zu schwach.
Du wirst sie zu befreien gehen,
du wirst der Tochter Retter sein!
Und werd' ich dich als Sieger sehen,
so sei sie dann auf ewig dein!¶

TAMINO. Ist denn auch Wirklichkeit, was ich sah?
Ihr guten Götter, täuscht mich nicht!

Nr. 5 Quintett

PAPAGENO. Hm! hm! hm! hm!

TAMINO. Der Arme kann von Strafe sagen,
denn seine Sprache ist dahin!

PAPAGENO. Hm! hm! hm! hm!

TAMINO. Ich kann nichts tun, als dich beklagen,
weil ich zu schwach zu helfen bin.

PAPAGENO. Hm! hm! hm! hm!

ERSTE DAME. Die Königin begnadigt dich,
erlässt die Strafe dir durch mich.

PAPAGENO. Nun plaudert Papageno wieder.

ZWEITE DAME. Ja, plaudre, lüge nur nicht wieder.

PAPAGENO. Ich lüge nimmermehr, nein, nein!

DIE DAMEN. Dies Schloss soll deine Warnung
sein.

No. 4 Recitative and Aria

QUEEN. O tremble not, my beloved son!
You are innocent, wise and good.
A youth like you can best console
this sorely afflicted mother's heart.
I am condemned to sorrow,
for my daughter is taken from me.
With her is all my happiness lost,
a villain has stolen her away.
I still can see her trembling
with fearful agitation,
her anguished shaking,
her timid struggles.
I had to watch her being taken.
'Ah, help!' was all that she could say;
but all her tears were in vain,
I was too weak to help her.
You shall go to set her free,
you shall be my daughter's rescuer!
And when I see you victorious,
then shall she be yours forever!¶

She goes out with the Three Ladies. The stage is changed back as it was before.

TAMINO. Can it be true, what I saw?
O ye good gods, do not deceive me!
(He is about to leave. Papageno steps in his way.)

No. 5 Quintet

PAPAGENO. *(With the padlock on his mouth, sadly points at it.)* Hm! hm! hm! hm!

TAMINO. The poor fellow can still complain of his punishment, even though he is speechless!

PAPAGENO. Hm! hm! hm! hm!

TAMINO. I can do nothing but pity you,
for I am too weak to help.

PAPAGENO. Hm! hm! hm! hm!
(The Three Ladies return.)

FIRST LADY. The Queen pardons you,
and lifts her punishment through me.
(She takes the padlock from his mouth.)

PAPAGENO. Now Papageno can chatter again.

SECOND LADY. Yes, chatter, but do not lie again.

PAPAGENO. I'll never lie again, no, no!

THE LADIES. This lock shall be your warning.

PAPAGENO. Dies Schloss soll meine Warnung sein.

ALLE. Bekämen doch die Lügner alle
ein solches Schloss vor ihren Mund!
Statt Hass, Verleumdung, schwarzer Galle,
bestünde Lieb' und Bruderbund.

ERSTE DAME. O Prinz, nimm dies Geschenk von mir,
dies sendet unsre Fürstin dir.
Die Zauberflöte wird dich schützen,
im grössten Unglück unterstützen.

DIE DAMEN. Hiermit kannst du allmächtig handeln,
der Menschen Leidenschaft verwandeln,
der Traurige wird freudig sein,
den Hagestolz nimmt Liebe ein.

ALLE. O! so eine Flöte ist mehr
als Gold und Kronen wert,
denn durch sie wird Menschenglück
und Zufriedenheit vermehrt.

PAPAGENO. Nun, ihr schönen Frauenzimmer,
darf ich? So empfehl' ich mich.

DIE DAMEN. Dich empfehlen kannst du immer,
doch bestimmt die Fürstin dich,
mit dem Prinzen ohn' Verweilen,
nach Sarastros Burg zu eilen.

PAPAGENO. Nein! dafür bedank' ich mich!
Von euch selbsten hörte ich,
dass er wie ein Tigertier;
sicher liess ohn' alle Gnaden
mich Sarastro rupfen, braten,
setzte mich den Hunden für!

DIE DAMEN. Dich schützt der Prinz, trau ihm allein!
dafür sollst du sein Diener sein.

PAPAGENO. Dass doch der Prinz beim Teufel wäre!
Mein Leben ist mir lieb;
am Ende schleicht, bei meiner Ehre,
er von mir wie ein Dieb.

ERSTE DAME. Hier, nimm dies Kleinod, es ist dein.

PAPAGENO. Ei! ei! was mag darinnen sein?

DIE DAMEN. Darinnen hörst du Glöckchen tönen.

PAPAGENO. Werd' ich sie auch wohl spielen können?

DIE DAMEN. O ganz gewiss, ja! ja! gewiss.

ALLE. Silberglöckchen, Zauberflöten
sind zu eurem (unserm) Schutz vonnöten.
Lebet wohl! wir wollen gehn,
lebet wohl! auf Wiedersehn.

TAMINO. Doch, schöne Damen, saget an –

TAMINO UND PAPAGENO.
Wie man die Burg wohl finden kann?

PAPAGENO. This lock shall be my warning.

ALL. If only all liars received
such a padlock over their mouths,
Then hate, slander and black rancour
would change to love and brotherhood.

FIRST LADY (*gives Tamino a golden flute*). O Prince,
take this gift from me,
sent to you by our Queen.
This magic flute will protect you,
and sustain you in the greatest misfortune.

THE LADIES. With it you have limitless power
to transform the sorrows of humanity;
the mourner will become merry,
the old bachelor will turn to love.

ALL. Oh, such a flute is worth more
than gold or crowns,
for by its power human joy
and contentment will be increased.

PAPAGENO. Now, fair ladies,
may I? Thus I take my leave.

THE LADIES. You may take your leave,
but our lady has decided that you are
to accompany the prince without delay
to Sarastro's castle.

PAPAGENO. No, thank you very much!
I heard it from you yourselves,
that he is like a wild tiger;
surely Sarastro would without mercy
have me plucked and roasted,
and thrown to the dogs.

THE LADIES. The Prince will protect you, trust in him, and you will be his servant.

PAPAGENO (*aside*). The devil take this Prince!
My life is precious to me;
In the end, he's bound to give me the slip like a thief.

FIRST LADY. (*Gives him a small chest of bells.*) Here, take this chest, it is yours.

PAPAGENO. Aha! What can be inside?

THE LADIES. Inside you can hear bells ringing.

PAPAGENO. And shall I be able to play them?

THE LADIES. Oh, certainly, yes, certainly.

ALL. Silver bells, magic flute,
are needed for your (our) protection.
Farewell! We must go,
farewell! Till we meet again.
(*The Three Ladies turn to go.*)

TAMINO. But fair ladies, tell us –

TAMINO AND PAPAGENO.
How will we find the castle?

DIE DAMEN. Drei Knaben, jung, schön, hold
und weise,
umschweben euch auf eurer Reise,
sie werden eure Führer sein;
folgt ihrem Rate ganz allein.

TAMINO UND PAPAGENO.
Drei Knaben, jung, schön, hold und weise,
umschweben uns auf unsrer Reise.

DIE DAMEN. Sie werden eure Führer sein;
folgt ihrem Rate ganz allein.

ALLE. So lebet wohl! wir wollen gehn,
lebt wohl! auf Wiedersehen.

THE LADIES. Three boys, young, fair, gentle and
wise,
will hover round you on your journey.
They will be your guides:
follow their counsel and none other.

TAMINO AND PAPAGENO.
Three boys, young, fair, gentle and wise,
will hover round us on our journey.

THE LADIES. They will be your guides;
follow their counsel and none other.

ALL. So farewell! We must go;
farewell! Until we meet again. *(They all go out.)*

Transformation

The scene is tranformed into a magnificent Egyptian room, with beautiful cushions, a splendid Turkish table, and carpets. Enter Monostatos. Pamina is brought in by slaves.

Nr. 6 Terzett

MONOSTATOS. Du feines Täubchen, nur herein!

PAMINA. O welche Marter! welche Pein!

MONOSTATOS. Verloren ist dein Leben!

PAMINA. Der Tod macht mich nicht beben,
nur meine Mutter dauert mich,
sie stirbt vor Gram ganz sicherlich.

MONOSTATOS. He! Sklaven! legt ihr Fesseln an!
Mein Hass soll dich verderben!

PAMINA. O lass mich lieber sterben,
weil nichts, Barbar! dich rühren kann.

MONOSTATOS. Nun fort! nun fort! Lasst mich mit
ihr allein.

PAPAGENO. Wo bin ich wohl? wo mag ich sein?
Aha! da find' ich Leute. Gewagt! ich geh' hinein.
Schön Mädchen, jung und fein,
viel weisser noch als Kreide –

PAPAGENO UND MONOSTATOS.
Hu! das ist der Teufel sicherlich!
Hab Mitleid! verschone mich! Hu! Hu!¶

PAMINA. Mutter! Mutter! –

Wie, noch schlägt dieses Herz! –
Zu neuen Qualen erwacht. Oh, das ist hart,
mir bitterer als der Tod.

No. 6 Trio

MONOSTATOS. My fine little dove, inside with you!

PAMINA. Oh, what torment! What agony!

MONOSTATOS. Your life is lost!

PAMINA. Death does not make me tremble –
I sorrow only for my mother;
she will surely die of grief.

MONOSTATOS. Hey, slaves! Put her in chains!
My hatred will destroy you!
(Slaves attach fetters to her.)

PAMINA. O let me rather die,
barbarian! For nothing can touch your heart.
(She falls in a swoon on a sofa.)

MONOSTATOS. And now get out! Leave me alone
with her.
The slaves leave. Papageno appears outside at the window, without being seen at first.

PAPAGENO. Where am I now? Wherever can I be?
Aha! There's someone there. Risky, but I'll go in.
(He enters) Pretty maiden, young and fair,
even whiter than chalk –
Papageno and Monostatos come face to face and each is terrified by the other.

PAPAGENO AND MONOSTATOS.
Oo! That is surely the Devil!
Have pity! Spare me! Oo! Oo!¶

(They both run off.)

PAMINA. *(speaking as if in a dream)* Mother, mother!
(recovering and looking around)
What? My heart is still beating!
Awoken to new torments. Oh, that is cruel;
more bitter than death itself.

PAPAGENO. Bin ich nicht ein
Narr, dass ich mich schrecken liess? –
Es gibt doch schwarze Vögel in der Welt,
warum nicht auch schwarze Menschen. –
Ah, da ist das schöne Fräuleinbild noch. –
Du, Tochter der nächtlichen Königin…

PAMINA. Nächtliche Königin? –
Wer bist du?

PAPAGENO. Ein Abgesandter der
sternflammenden Königin.

PAMINA. Meiner Mutter?

PAPAGENO. Ja.

PAMINA. Dein Name?

PAPAGENO. Papageno.

PAMINA. Papageno?! Oh, ich erinnere mich, den
Namen oft gehört zu haben, dich selbst
aber sah ich noch nie.

PAPAGENO. Ich dich ebensowenig.

PAMINA. Du kennst also meine gute,
zärtliche Mutter?

PAPAGENO. Wenn du die Tochter der
nächtlichen Königin bist – ja.

PAMINA. Oh, ich bin es.

PAPAGENO. Das werde ich gleich nach diesem
Bild erkennen:

die Augen braun, – richtig,
braun, – Lippen rot, – richtig, rot, –
blonde Haare – blonde Haare, alles trifft ein,
bis auf Hände und Füsse, nach diesem Gemälde
solltest du weder Hände noch Füsse haben.

PAMINA. Erlaube mir?! Ja, ich bin's!

PAPAGENO. Ha!

PAMINA. Doch wie kam es in deine Hände?

PAPAGENO. Ich kam heute früh wie gewöhnlich
zu deiner Mutter Palast, eben als ich im
Begriffe war, meine Vögel abzugeben, da, sah ich
einen Menschen vor mir, der sich Prinz
nennen lässt.

PAMINA. Ein Prinz?

PAPAGENO. Ja! Dieser Prinz hat deine Mutter
so für sich eingenommen, dass sie ihm dein
Bildnis schenkte und ihm befahl, dich zu befreien.

PAMINA. Mich zu befreien?!

PAPAGENO. Pscht! Sein Entschluss war so
schnell wie seine Liebe zu dir.

PAMINA. Er liebt mich also?

PAPAGENO. Mm. Komm, du wirst Augen
machen, wenn du den schönen Jüngling
erblickst.

PAPAGENO. *(returns)* Am I not a fool to be so
frightened? After all, there are black
birds in this world, why not black people, too?
Ah, that lovely girl is still there.
Daughter of the Queen of the Night!

PAMINA. Queen of the Night?
Who are you?

PAPAGENO. An ambassador from the star-blazing
Queen.

PAMINA. My mother?

PAPAGENO. Yes.

PAMINA. What is your name?

PAPAGENO. Papageno.

PAMINA. Papageno? I remember hearing the
name often, but I have never seen you
before.

PAPAGENO. I have never seen you before either.

PAMINA. So you know my dear, sweet
mother?

PAPAGENO. If you are the daughter of the
Queen of the Night, yes.

PAMINA. Oh, I am.

PAPAGENO. I shall soon see from this picture.
*(He looks at the portrait which was given earlier to the
Prince, and which Papageno now carries on a ribbon round
his neck.)* Eyes brown: yes, brown.
Lips red: yes, red. Blond hair: yes, blond hair.
Everything fits, except the hands and feet.
According to this painting, you shouldn't
have any hands or feet.

PAMINA. May I? Yes, it's me.

PAPAGENO. Ha!

PAMINA. But how did it come into your hands?

PAPAGENO. I went to your mother's palace
this morning as usual, and just as I was about
to deliver my birds, I saw before me
someone who called himself a prince.

PAMINA. A prince?

PAPAGENO. Yes. This prince so captivated
your mother that she gave him your portrait
and commanded him to rescue you.

PAMINA. To rescue me?

PAPAGENO. Oh yes, he made up his mind as quickly
as falling in love with you.

PAMINA. *(joyfully)* He loves me?

PAPAGENO. Aha. Come, you will be all eyes
when you see the handsome young man.

PAMINA. Wohlan denn, es sei gewagt!
Aber wenn dies ein Fallstrick ware? Wenn dieser
ein böser Geist aus Sarastros Gefolge wäre?

PAPAGENO. Ich? ein böser Geist?

PAMINA. Hm!

PAPAGENO. Wo denkst du hin? Bei mir ist von
Geist keine Spur!

PAMINA. Vergib, Freund, wenn ich dich
beleidigte! Du hast ein gefühlvolles Herz.

PAPAGENO. Freilich hab' ich ein gefühlvolles
Herz, was nützt mir das alles. Ich möchte mir
oft alle meine Federn ausrupfen, wenn ich
bedenke, dass Papageno noch keine Papagena
hat.

PAMINA. Armer Mann, du hast also noch
kein Weib?

PAPAGENO. Noch nicht einmal ein Mädchen,
viel weniger ein Weib, und unsereiner hat
auch bisweilen so seine lustigen Stunden,
wo man gerne… gesellschaftliche Unterhaltung
pflegen möchte.

PAMINA. Geduld, Freund, der Himmel wird auch für
dich sorgen. Er wird dir eine Freundin schicken,
ehe du dir's vermutest.

PAPAGENO. Wenn er sie nur bald schickte!

Nr. 7 Duett

PAMINA. Bei Männern, welche Liebe fühlen,
fehlt auch ein gutes Herze nicht.

PAPAGENO. Die süssen Triebe mitzufühlen,
ist dann der Weiber erste Pflicht.

BEIDE. Wir wollen uns der Liebe freun,
wir leben durch die Lieb' allein.

PAMINA. Die Lieb' versüsset jede Plage,
ihr opfert jede Kreatur.

PAPAGENO. Sie würzet unsre Lebenstage,
sie wirkt im Kreise der Natur.

BEIDE. Ihr hoher Zweck zeigt deutlich an,
nichts Edlers sei als Weib und Mann.
Mann und Weib, und Weib und Mann
reichen an die Gottheit an.

PAMINA. Let's go, then, and take the risk.
But what if this should be a trap?
What if this man were an evil spirit
from Sarastro's retinue.

PAPAGENO. Me, an evil spirit?

PAMINA. Mm.

PAPAGENO. What are you thinking of?
I haven't a trace of spirit in me!

PAMINA. Forgive me, my friend, if I offended you.
You have a tender heart.

PAPAGENO. Indeed I have a tender heart.
But what good does it do me? I could often
pluck out all my feathers when I think
that Papageno still hasn't a Papagena.

PAMINA. Poor man, you still don't have a wife?

PAPAGENO. Not even a sweetheart, let alone a
wife. And after all, people like us have cheerful
moments from time to time,
when we'd enjoy some agreeable company.

PAMINA. Patience, my friend, heaven will
provide for you, too. It will send you a girlfriend
sooner than you expect.

PAPAGENO. If only it would send her soon!

No. 7 Duet

PAMINA. Men who know the feeling of love
cannot lack a good heart.

PAPAGENO. To return these sweet desires
is woman's first duty.

BOTH. We gladly rejoice in Love,
and live by love alone.

PAMINA. Love sweetens every trouble;
all creatures pay homage to it.

PAPAGENO. It seasons the days of our lives,
and turns the wheel of Nature.

BOTH. Its higher purpose is clear;
nothing is nobler than man and wife.
Man and wife, and wife and man,
attain to divinity. *(They both go out.)*

Start of Cassette Side 2

Transformation

The scene changes to a grove. At the back of the stage is a beautiful temple, with the inscription 'Temple of Wisdom'. This temple is joined by colonnades to two other temples: the one on the right has the inscription 'Temple of Reason'; the one on the left, 'Temple of Nature'.
(Three Boys lead in Tamino; each holds a silver palm-branch in his hand.)

Nr. 8 Finale

DIE DREI KNABEN. Zum Ziele führt dich diese Bahn,
doch musst du, Jüngling, männlich siegen.
Drum höre unsre Lehre an;
Sei standhaft, duldsam und verschwiegen!

TAMINO. Ihr holden Kleinen, sagt mir an,
ob ich Paminen retten kann?

KNABEN. Dies kundzutun steht uns nicht an:
Sei standhaft, duldsam und verschwiegen!
Bedenke dies; kurz, sei ein Mann!
Dann, Jüngling, wirst du männlich siegen.

TAMINO. Die Weisheitslehre dieser Knaben
sei ewig mir ins Herz gegraben!
Wo bin ich nun? was wird mit mir?
ist dies der Sitz der Götter hier?
Doch zeigen die Pforten, es zeigen die Säulen,
dass Klugheit und Arbeit und Künste hier weilen;
wo Tätigkeit thronet und Müssiggang weicht,
erhält seine Herrschaft das Laster nicht leicht.
Ich wage mich mutig zur Pforte hinein;
die Absicht ist edel und lauter und rein.
Erzittre, feiger Bösewicht!
Paminen retten ist mir Pflicht!

EINE STIMME. Zurück!

TAMINO. Zurück? So wag' ich hier mein Glück.

EINE STIMME. Zurück!

TAMINO. Auch hier ruft man 'zurück'?
Da seh' ich noch eine Tür!
vielleicht find' ich den Eingang hier.

SPRECHER. Wo willst du, kühner Fremdling, hin?
Was suchst du hier im Heiligtum?

TAMINO. Der Lieb und Tugend Eigentum.

SPRECHER. Die Worte sind von hohem Sinn,
allein, wie willst du diese finden?
Dich leitet Lieb' und Tugend nicht,
weil Tod und Rache dich entzünden.

No. 8 Finale

THE THREE BOYS. This path leads you to your goal.
But, youth, you must conquer like a man.
So listen to our teaching:
Be steadfast, patient and discreet!

TAMINO. Gracious boys; tell me first:
Can I save Pamina?

BOYS. It is not for us to make that known:
Be steadfast, patient and discreet!
Remember this; in short, be a man!
Then, youth, you will conquer manfully.
(They go out.)

TAMINO. May the wise teaching of these boys
be ever engraved on my heart!
Where am I now? What will happen to me?
Is this the seat of the gods?
These gates, these columns prove
that wisdom, industry, and art reside here;
where action rules and idleness retreats,
vice cannot easily gain control.
I will boldly pass through the door,
my purpose is noble, honourable and pure.
Tremble, cowardly villain!
My duty is to save Pamina!
(He approaches the door on the right.)

A VOICE. Go back!

TAMINO. Go back? Then I will try my luck here.
(He approaches the door on the left.)

A VOICE. Go back!

TAMINO. Here too they call 'go back'?
I see one more door.
Perhaps I will find an entrance here.
(He knocks, and an old priest appears.)

SPEAKER (OLD PRIEST). Where do you wish to go, bold stranger?
What do you seek in this sanctuary?

TAMINO. The realm of Love and Virtue.

SPEAKER. Your words are lofty,
but how do you expect to find it?
Love and virtue do not guide you,
for death and vengeance inflame you.

TAMINO. Nur Rache für den Bösewicht!

SPRECHER. Den wirst du wohl bei uns nicht finden.

TAMINO. Sarastro herrscht in diesen Gründen?

SPRECHER. Ja! ja! Sarastro herrschet hier.

TAMINO. Doch in dem Weisheitstempel nicht?

SPRECHER. Er herrscht im Weisheitstempel hier.

TAMINO. So ist denn alles Heuchelei!

SPRECHER. Willst du schon wieder gehn?

TAMINO. Ja, ich will gehn, froh und frei,
nie euren Tempel sehn.

SPRECHER. Erklär dich näher mir,
dich täuschet ein Betrug.

TAMINO. Sarastro wohnet hier?
Das ist mir schon genug.

SPRECHER. Wenn du dein Leben liebst, so rede,
bleibe da!
Sarastro hassest du?

TAMINO. Ich hass' ihn ewig, ja!

SPRECHER. So gib mir deine Gründe an.

TAMINO. Er ist ein Unmensch, ein Tyrann!

SPRECHER. Ist das, was du gesagt, erwiesen?

TAMINO. Durch ein unglücklich Weib bewiesen,
das Gram und Jammer niederdrückt.

SPRECHER. Ein Weib hat also dich berückt?
Ein Weib tut wenig, plaudert viel;
du, Jüngling, glaubst dem Zungenspiel?
O, legte doch Sarastro dir
die Absicht seiner Handlung für!

TAMINO. Die Absicht ist nur allzu klar!
Riss nicht der Räuber ohn Erbarmen
Paminen aus der Mutter Armen?

SPRECHER. Ja, Jüngling, was du sagst, ist wahr.

TAMINO. Wo ist sie, die er uns geraubt?
Man opferte vielleicht sie schon?

SPRECHER. Dir dies zu sagen, teurer Sohn!
ist jetzt und mir noch nicht erlaubt.

TAMINO. Erklär dies Rätsel, täusch mich nicht!

SPRECHER. Die Zunge bindet Eid und Pflicht.

TAMINO. Wann also wird das Dunkel schwinden?

SPRECHER. Sobald dich führt der Freundschaft
Hand ins Heiligtum zum ew'gen Band.

TAMINO. O ew'ge Nacht, wann wirst du schwinden?
Wann wird das Licht mein Auge finden?

CHOR. Bald, Jüngling, oder nie!

TAMINO. Bald, sagt ihr, oder nie?
Ihr Unsichtbaren, saget mir,
lebt denn Pamina noch?

TAMINO. Only vengeance against the villain!

SPEAKER. You will not find one among us.

TAMINO. Does Sarastro rule in these precincts?

SPEAKER. Yes, Sarastro rules here.

TAMINO. But not in the Temple of Wisdom?

SPEAKER. He rules here in the Temple of Wisdom.

TAMINO. Then all is hypocrisy!

SPEAKER. Do you wish to go on your way?

TAMINO. Yes, I shall go, happy and free,
and never see your Temple.

SPEAKER. Explain yourself further;
some deceit has misled you.

TAMINO. Sarastro dwells here?
That is quite enough for me.

SPEAKER. If you value your life, stay and speak.
Do you hate Sarastro?

TAMINO. I shall hate him forever, yes!

SPEAKER. Give me your reasons.

TAMINO. He is a monster, a tyrant!

SPEAKER. Is there proof of what you say?

TAMINO. The proof is an unhappy woman,
oppressed by sorrow and grief.

SPEAKER. Has a woman so deceived you?
A woman does little, gossips much;
you, young man, believe wagging tongues?
If only Sarastro could reveal to you
the purpose of his actions!

TAMINO. His purpose is all too clear!
Did not the robber snatch without pity
Pamina from her mother's arms?

SPEAKER. Yes, young man, what you say is true.

TAMINO. Where is she whom he stole from us?
Has she perhaps already been sacrificed?

SPEAKER. I am not yet permitted
to tell you this, dear son.

TAMINO. Explain this riddle, do not deceive me!

SPEAKER. Oath and duty bind my tongue.

TAMINO. When will this darkness fade away?

SPEAKER. As soon as friendship's hand leads you
to the sanctuary's eternal bond. (He goes out.)

TAMINO (alone). O endless night, when will you vanish?
When will my eyes see the light?

CHORUS (from within). Soon, youth, or never!

TAMINO. Soon, you say, or never?
Then tell me, invisible ones,
is Pamina still alive?

CHOR. Pamina lebet noch.

TAMINO. Sie lebt? sie lebt?
Ich danke euch dafür!
O! wenn ich doch im Stande wäre,
Allmächtige! zu eurer Ehre,
mit jedem Tone meinen Dank
zu schildern, wie er hier entsprang!

TAMINO. Wie stark ist nicht dein Zauberton!
weil, holde Flöte, durch dein Spielen
selbst wilde Tiere Freude fühlen.
Doch, nur Pamina bleibt davon,
Pamina, Pamina, höre mich!
Umsonst! Wo? ach! wo, wo find' ich dich?

TAMINO. Ha! das ist Papagenos Ton!

Vielleicht sah er Pamina schon,
vielleicht eilt sie mit ihm zu mir,
vielleicht führt mich der Ton zu ihr!

PAMINA UND PAPAGENO.
Schnelle Füsse, rascher Mut
schützt vor Feindes List und Wut;
fänden wir Tamino doch,
sonst erwischen sie uns noch!

PAMINA. Holder Jüngling!

PAPAGENO. Stille, stille, ich kann's besser!

PAMINA UND PAPAGENO.
Welche Freude ist wohl grösser!
Freund Tamino hört uns schon;
hierher kam der Flötenton!
Welch ein Glück, wenn ich ihn finde!
nur geschwinde, nur geschwinde!

MONOSTATOS. Nur geschwinde, nur geschwinde!
Ha! Hab' ich euch noch erwischt!
Nur herbei mit Stahl und Eisen!
Wart, man wird euch Mores weisen!
Den Monostatos berücken!
Nun herbei mit Band und Stricken!
He! ihr Sklaven, kommt herbei!

PAMINA UND PAPAGENO.
Ach, nun ist's mit uns vorbei!

CHORUS. Pamina is still alive.

TAMINO (*joyfully*). Alive? She is alive?
I thank you for that! (*He takes his flute.*)
Oh, if only I were able,
almighty gods, in your honour,
to express with every note
my gratitude, as it springs up here (*indicating his heart*).
He plays; wild animals of all kinds come out to listen to him. He stops, and they run away. Birds sing to his playing.

TAMINO. How powerful is your magic tone,
sweet flute, for when you play
even wild beasts feel joy.
Yet Pamina stays far away.
Pamina, Pamina, hear me!
In vain! Where, ah where shall I find you?
(*Papageno answers from within on his pipes.*)

TAMINO. Ha! that is Papageno's call!
(*He plays. Papageno answers.*)
Perhaps he has already seen Pamina,
perhaps she is hurrying to me with him,
perhaps the sound will lead me to her!
(*He hurries out. Enter Papageno and Pamina without fetters.*)

PAMINA AND PAPAGENO.
Swift feet, and bold courage
protect us from our enemy's cunning and rage;
if only we could find Tamino –
otherwise we may yet be captured.

PAMINA (*calling*). Gentle youth!

PAPAGENO. Hush, hush, I can do better!
(*He pipes, and Tamino replies on his flute.*)

PAMINA AND PAPAGENO.
What joy is greater than this?
Friend Tamino has already heard us;
the sound of his flute reached us.
What happiness if I find him!
Quickly, quickly!
(*As they are about to hurry off, Monostatos enters.*)

MONOSTATOS (*mocking them*). Quickly, quickly!
Ha! now I've captured you!
Bring here fetters and chains!
Just wait, I'll teach you manners!
You would deceive Monostatos!
Bring here shackles and ropes!
Hey, you slaves, come here!
(*The slaves come with fetters.*)

PAMINA AND PAPAGENO.
Ah, now we're done for!

PAPAGENO. Wer viel wagt, gewinnt oft viel!
Komm, du schönes Glockenspiel,
lass die Glöckchen klingen, klingen,
dass die Ohren ihnen singen.

MONOSTATOS UND DIE SKLAVEN.
Das klinget so herrlich, das klinget so schön!
La-ra-la, la la la-ra-la!
Nie hab' ich so etwas gehört und gesehn!
La-ra-la, la la la-ra-la!

PAMINA UND PAPAGENO.
Könnte jeder brave Mann
solche Glöckchen finden,
seine Feinde würden dann
ohne Mühe schwinden;
und er lebte ohne sie
in der besten Harmonie.
Nur der Freundschaft Harmonie
mildert die Beschwerden,
ohne diese Sympathie
ist kein Glück auf Erden.

CHOR. Es lebe Sarastro. Sarastro lebe!

PAPAGENO. Was soll das bedeuten? Ich zittre, ich bebe!

PAMINA. O! Freund, nun ist's um uns getan;
dies kündigt den Sarastro an!

PAPAGENO. O wär ich eine Maus,
wie wollt' ich mich verstecken!
Wär' ich so klein wie Schnecken,
so kröch' ich in mein Haus!
Mein Kind, was werden wir nun sprechen?

PAMINA. Die Wahrheit! wär' sie auch Verbrechen!

CHOR. Es lebe Sarastro. Sarastro soll leben!
Er ist es, dem wir uns mit Freuden ergeben!
Stets mög' er des Lebens als Weiser sich freun!
Er ist unser Abgott, dem alle sich weihn!

PAMINA. Herr! Ich bin zwar Verbrecherin!
ich wollte deiner Macht entfliehn.
Allein, die Schuld liegt nicht an mir:
Der böse Mohr verlangte Liebe,
darum, o Herr! entfloh ich dir.

SARASTRO. Steh auf, erheitre dich, o Liebe!
denn ohne erst in dich zu dringen,
weiss ich von deinem Herzen mehr;
du liebest einen andern sehr.
Zur Liebe will ich dich nicht zwingen,
doch geb' ich dir die Freiheit nicht.

PAPAGENO. Nothing venture, nothing gain!
Come, my pretty chime of bells,
let your bells ring and ring
and make their ears sing!
(He plays on his instrument.)

MONOSTATOS AND THE SLAVES.
That sounds so pretty, that sounds so lovely,
La-ra-la, la la la-ra-la!
Never did I hear and see anything like that!
La-ra-la, la la la-ra-la!
(They go out as if marching.)

PAMINO AND PAPAGENO.
If every honest man
could find such bells,
his enemies would then
vanish without effort;
he would live without them
in perfect harmony.
Only the harmony of friendship
eases all hardships,
and without this sympathy
there is no joy on earth.
(A loud march with trumpets and drums strikes up.)

CHORUS *(from within)*. Long live Sarastro!

PAPAGENO. What can that mean? I tremble and shake!

PAMINA. Oh, my friend, now we're finished;
this announces Sarastro's approach.

PAPAGENO. If only I were a mouse –
how I'd hide myself!
If I were as tiny as a snail
I'd creep into my house!
My child, what will we say now?

PAMINA. The truth – even if it were a crime.
A procession of attendants; at the end Sarastro rides out in a triumphal chariot drawn by six lions.

CHORUS. Long live Sarastro – long may he live!
To him we dedicate ourselves with joy!
May he ever, in his wisdom, live happily!
He is the idol to whom we devote ourselves!
(This chorus is sung until Sarastro alights from the chariot.)

PAMINA *(kneeling)*. My lord, I have transgressed.
I wished to escape your power.
Yet the guilt is not mine:
the wicked Moor demanded love –
and that is why, my lord, I ran away.

SARASTRO. Arise, take heart, my dear!
for without questioning you I know
more from your own heart;
you love another deeply.
I will not force you to love,
yet I will not give you your freedom.

PAMINA. Mich rufet ja die Kindespflicht,
denn meine Mutter –

SARASTRO. Steht in meiner Macht;
du würdest um dein Glück gebracht,
wenn ich dich ihren Händen liesse.

PAMINA. Mir klingt der Muttername süsse!
Sie ist es, sie ist es –

SARASTRO. Und ein stolzes Weib!
Ein Mann muss eure Herzen leiten,
denn ohne ihn pflegt jedes Weib
aus ihrem Wirkungskreis zu schreiten.

MONOSTATOS. Du stolzer Jüngling, nur hierher!
Hier ist Sarastro, unser Herr.

PAMINA. Er ist's!

TAMINO. Sie ist's!

PAMINA. Ich glaub' es kaum!

TAMINO. Es ist kein Traum!

PAMINA UND TAMINO.
Es schling' mein Arm sich um ihn (sie) her,
und wenn es auch mein Ende wär'!

CHOR. Was soll das heissen?

MONOSTATOS. Welch eine Dreistigkeit!
Gleich auseinander, das geht zu weit!

Dein Sklave liegt zu deinen Füssen,
lass den verwegnen Frevler büssen!
Bedenk, wie frech der Knabe ist!
Durch dieses seltnen Vogels List
wollt er Pamina dir entführen,
allein ich wusst' ihn aufzuspüren.
Du kennst mich, meine Wachsamkeit –

SARASTRO. Verdient, dass man ihr Lorbeer streut!

He! gebt dem Ehrenmann sogleich –

MONOSTATOS. Schon deine Gnade macht mich
reich!

SARASTRO. – Nur sieben und siebenzig Sohlen-
streich'!

MONOSTATOS. Ach, Herr! den Lohn verhofft' ich
nicht!

SARASTRO. Nicht Dank! es ist ja meine Pflicht!

CHOR. Es lebe Sarastro, der göttliche Weise!
er lohnet und strafet in ähnlichem Kreise.

PAMINA. The duty of a child summons me,
for my mother –

SARASTRO. Lies in my power;
your happiness would be destroyed
if I delivered you into her hands.

PAMINA. To me my mother's name sounds sweet!
She is, she is –

SARASTRO. She is an arrogant woman!
A man must guide your heart,
for without that, every woman tends
to step out of her rightful place.
(Monostatos leads Tamino in.)

MONOSTATOS. Now, proud youth, come here!
Here is Sarastro, our master.

PAMINA. It is he!

TAMINO. It is she!

PAMINA. I can hardly believe it!

TAMINO. This is no dream!

PAMINA AND TAMINO.
My arms will embrace him (her)
even if that should mean my death!
(They embrace.)

CHORUS. Whatever can this mean?

MONOSTATOS. What impudence!
Get away from each other, you go too far!
(He separates them and kneels before Sarastro.)

Your slave lies at your feet:
let the reckless sinner be punished!
Consider the boy's cheek!
Through the cunning of this rare bird
he meant to steal Pamina from you,
and I alone knew how to track him down.
You know me, my vigilance –

SARASTRO. Deserves a path strewn with laurel
leaves!
You there! Give this worthy man at once –

MONOSTATOS. Your generosity makes me rich!

SARASTRO. – Seventy-seven lashes on the soles of his
feet.

MONOSTATOS *(kneels)*. Ah, sir, I hardly hoped for
such payment!

SARASTRO. Do not thank me, it is my duty!
(Monostatos is led away.)

CHORUS. Long live Sarastro, the godly wise man!
He rewards and punishes in equal degree.

SARASTRO. Führt diese beiden Fremdlinge
in unsern Prüfungstempel ein;
bedecket ihre Häupter dann,
sie müssen erst gereinigt sein.

SARASTRO. Take these two strangers
into our temple of trial;
then cover their heads,
for they must first be purified.
*Two men each bring a kind of sack, and cover the heads of
the two strangers.*

CHOR. Wenn Tugend und Gerechtigkeit
den Grossen Pfad mit Ruhm bestreut,
dann ist die Erd' ein Himmelreich,
und Sterbliche den Göttern gleich.

CHORUS. If virtue and righteousness
spread glory on the path of the great,
then the earth will be a heavenly kingdom
and mortals will be like the gods.

ZWEITER AKT

ACT TWO

*The scene is a palm grove; all the trees are silver, with gold leaves. There are eighteen seats made of palm leaves. By each
seat stands a pyramid and a large black horn bound with gold. In the centre is the largest pyramid, and also the largest
trees. Sarastro and the other priests enter in solemn procession, each with a palm-branch in his hand. A march with wind
instruments accompanies the procession.*

Nr. 9 Marsch der Priester

No. 9 March of the Priests

SARASTRO. Ihr in den Weisheitstempel
eingeweihten Diener der grossen Göttin Osiris und
Isis, ich erkläre euch, dass unsere heutige
Versammlung von grosser Bedeutung ist. –
Tamino, ein Königssohn, wandelt an der
nördlichen Pforte unsers Tempels. Er will den
nächtlichen Schleier von sich reissen und ins
Heiligtum des grössten Lichtes blicken, ihm
freundschaftlich die Hand zu bieten, sei heute
eine unserer wichtigsten Pflichten.

SARASTRO. Servants of the great gods
Osiris and Isis, initiated in the Temple of
Wisdom, I declare unto you that our assembly
today is of the greatest importance. Tamino,
a king's son, is waiting at the north door of
our Temple. He wishes to tear from himself
the veil of night and look into the sanctuary
of supreme light. Let it be one of our most solemn
duties today to offer him the hand of friendship.

ERSTER PRIESTER. Er besitzt Tugend?

FIRST PRIEST *(rises)*. Does he possess virtue?

SARASTRO. Tugend.

SARASTRO. Virtue.

SPRECHER. Auch Verschwiegenheit?

SPEAKER. And discretion?

SARASTRO. Verschwiegenheit.

SARASTRO. Discretion.

ERSTER PRIESTER. Ist wohltätig?

FIRST PRIEST. And goodwill?

SARASTRO. Wohltätig. Haltet ihr ihn für würdig,
so folgt meinem Beispiel.

SARASTRO. Goodwill. If you deem him worthy,
then follow my example.
(They blow their horns three times.)

Pamina, das tugendhafte Mädchen, haben die
Götter dem Jüngling bestimmt; dies ist der Grund,
warum ich sie der stolzen Mutter entriss, –
das Weib dünkt sich gross zu sein und versucht,
unsern festen Tempelbau zu zerstören.
Das soll sie nicht. Tamino selbst soll ihn mit uns
befestigen.

Pamina, that virtuous maiden, has been chosen by
the gods for this youth; that is the reason
why I removed her from her arrogant mother.
That woman thinks herself important and
is trying to destroy the strong foundation of our Temple. But she shall not! Tamino himself shall join us in
strengthening it.
(The threefold chord on the horns is repeated by everyone.)

SPRECHER. Grosser Sarastro, wird Tamino auch
die schweren Prüfungen bestehen? – Er ist Prinz!

SPEAKER *(rises)*. Great Sarastro, will Tamino also
withstand the severe trials that await him?
Remember, he is a prince!

SARASTRO. Mehr noch – er ist Mensch!

SPRECHER. Wenn er aber im harten Kampfe unterliegt?

SARASTRO. Dann wird er der Götter Freuden früher fühlen als wir.

Man führe Tamino mit seinem Reisegefährten in den Vorhof des Tempels! Und ihr, Freunde, vollziehet euer heiliges Amt und lehret die beiden die Weisheit und Macht der Götter erkennen!

SARASTRO. Even more; he is a human being!

SPEAKER. But what if he is defeated in the struggle?

SARASTRO. Then he will experience the joys of the gods sooner than we.
(The threefold chord is repeated.)

Let Tamino and his travelling companion be led into the forecourt of the Temple! And you, my friends, fulfil your sacred office and teach them both to acknowledge the wisdom and power of the gods.
The Speaker and one priest go out; all the priests stand together with their palm branches.

Nr. 10 Arie und Chor

No. 10 Aria and Chorus

SARASTRO. O Isis und Osiris, schenket
der Weisheit Geist dem neuen Paar!
Die ihr der Wandrer Schritte lenket,
stärkt mit Geduld sie in Gefahr!

CHOR. Stärkt mit Geduld sie in Gefahr!

SARASTRO. Lasst sie der Prüfung Früchte sehen;
doch sollten sie zu Grabe gehen,
so lohnt der Tugend kühnen Lauf,
nehmt sie in euren Wohnsitz auf!

CHOR. Nehmt sie in euren Wohnsitz auf!¶

SARASTRO. O Isis and Osiris, grant
the spirit of wisdom to the new pair!
Ye that guide the steps of wanderers,
strengthen them with perseverance in danger.

CHORUS. Strengthen them with perseverance in danger.

SARASTRO. Let them see the fruits of their trial,
but if they should go to the grave,
reward the bold course of their virtue
and receive them into your dwelling place.

CHORUS. Receive them into your dwelling place.¶

Sarastro goes out, and all the others follow.

Transformation

Night. Thunder rolls in the distance. The scene is transformed into a small forecourt of the temple, in which the ruins of fallen columns and pyramids can be seen, together with some thornbushes. On both sides stand practicable, tall, ancient Egyptian portals, with other side buildings beyond.
Tamino and Papageno are led in by two priests, who remove the sacks from them and then leave.

TAMINO. Eine schreckliche Nacht. –
Papageno, bist du noch bei mir?

PAPAGENO. Ja, leider.

O weh! O weh!

TAMINO. Du hast Furcht?

PAPAGENO. F... Furcht. Furcht eben nicht,
nur, es läuft mir so eiskalt über den Rücken.

O weh! O...

TAMINO. Papageno, sei ein Mann!

PAPAGENO. Ich wollt', ich wär' ein Mädchen!

Oh! D... das ist mein letzter Augenblick!

TAMINO. What a dreadful night!
Papageno, are you still with me?

PAPAGENO. Yes, unfortunately.
(Clap of thunder.)
Oh dear, oh dear!

TAMINO. Are you afraid?

PAPAGENO. Af-f-fraid? Not exactly afraid,
it's just that ice-cold shivers are running down
my spine.
(Loud clap of thunder.)
Oh dear! Oh …

TAMINO. Papageno, be a man!

PAPAGENO. I wish I were a girl
(Very loud clap of thunder.)
Oh! m-my last moment has come!
(Two priests enter carrying torches.)

ZWEITER PRIESTER. Ihr Fremdlinge, was sucht ihr? Was treibt euch an, in unsre Mauern zu dringen?

TAMINO. Freundschaft und Liebe!

ZWEITER PRIESTER. Bist du bereit, sie mit deinem Leben zu erkämpfen?

TAMINO. Ja! Weisheitslehre sei mein Sieg: Pamina mein Lohn!

ZWEITER PRIESTER. Reiche mir deine Hand! – Du wirst Pamina sehen, sie aber nicht sprechen dürfen; das ist der Anfang deiner Prüfung.

ERSTER PRIESTER. Papageno!

PAPAGENO. Hm.

ERSTER PRIESTER. Willst auch du die Weisheitslehre erkämpfen?

PAPAGENO. Na… kämpfen ist meine Sache nicht, i… ich bin so ein Naturmensch, der sich mit Schlaf, Speise und Trank begnügt; und wenn es mal sein könnte, dass ich mir ein schönes Weibchen fange…

ERSTER PRIESTER. Das wirst du nie erhalten, wenn du dich nicht unseren Prüfungen unterziehst und selbst den Tod nicht scheust!

PAPAGENO. Ich bleibe ledig!

ERSTER PRIESTER. Wenn nun aber Sarastro für dich ein Mädchen hätte, das an Farbe und Kleidung dir ganz gleich wäre …

PAPAGENO. Mir ganz gleicht? Hört! Mir ganz gleicht?! Ist sie jung?

ERSTER PRIESTER. Sehr jung!

PAPAGENO. Hmm…

ERSTER PRIESTER. Und heisst Papagena.

PAPAGENO. Pa… wie? wie? Papage…

ERSTER PRIESTER. …na!

PAPAGENO. Na? Ah, Papagena. Die möchte ich aus blosser Neugierde sehen!

ERSTER PRIESTER. Sehen kannst du sie, aber kein Wort mit ihr sprechen! Wird dein Geist soviel Standhaftigkeit besitzen?

PAPAGENO. O ja!

SECOND PRIEST. Strangers, what do you seek? What has driven you to penetrate within our walls (masonry)?

TAMINO. Friendship and love.

SECOND PRIEST. Are you prepared to fight for them with your life?

TAMINO. Yes! May the knowledge of wisdom be my victory, and Pamina my reward!

SECOND PRIEST. Give me your hand. You will see Pamina, but you will not be allowed to speak to her. That is the beginning of your trial.

FIRST PRIEST. Papageno?

PAPAGENO. Hm?

FIRST PRIEST. Are you, too, willing to fight for the knowledge of wisdom?

PAPAGENO. Well… fighting isn't really my line; I'm a child of Nature, satisfied with sleep, food and drink; and if I could only catch a beautiful little wife …

FIRST PRIEST. You will never achieve that unless you undergo our trials, not shrinking even in the face of death.

PAPAGENO. I'll stay single!

FIRST PRIEST. But what if Sarastro had a girl for you, just like you in colours and clothing?

PAPAGENO. Just like me? You hear that? Just like me! Is she young?

FIRST PRIEST. Very young.

PAPAGENO. Mmm…

FIRST PRIEST. And her name is Papagena.

PAPAGENO. Pa… what? What? Papage…

FIRST PRIEST. …na!

PAPAGENO. Na? Oh, I see, Papagena. I'd like to see her, just out of curiosity!

FIRST PRIEST. You may see her, but not speak a single word to her. Will your spirit be able to summon up so much steadfastness?

PAPAGENO. Oh, yes!

Nr. 11 Duett

ZWEI PRIESTER. Bewahret euch vor Weibertücken:
dies ist des Bundes erste Pflicht!
Manch weiser Mann liess sich berücken,
er fehlte und versah sich's nicht;
verlassen sah er sich am Ende,
vergolten seine Treu' mit Hohn!
Vergebens rang er seine Hände,
Tod und Verzweiflung war sein Lohn.¶

PAPAGENO. He. Lichter her! Das ist doch
wunderlich, sooft einen die Herren verlassen,
sieht man mit offenen Augen nichts.

TAMINO. Ertrag es mit Geduld und denk,
es ist der Götter Wille.

Nr. 12 Quintett

DIE DAMEN. Wie? wie? wie? ihr an diesem
Schreckensort?
Nie, nie, nie, kommt ihr glücklich wieder fort!
Tamino, dir ist Tod geschworen;
du Papageno, bist verloren!

PAPAGENO. Nein, nein, nein, das wär zu viel!

TAMINO. Papageno, schweige still!
Willst du dein Gelübde brechen,
nichts mit Weibern hier zu sprechen?

PAPAGENO. Du hörst ja, wir sind beide hin.

TAMINO. Stille, sag' ich, schweige still!

PAPAGENO. Immer still und immer still!

DIE DAMEN. Ganz nah ist euch die Königin,
sie drang im Tempel heimlich ein.

PAPAGENO. Wie, was? sie soll im Tempel sein?

TAMINO. Stille, sag' ich! schweige still!
Wirst du immer so vermessen
deiner Eidespflicht vergessen?

DIE DAMEN. Tamino, hör, du bist verloren!
Gedenke an die Königin!
Man zischelt viel sich in die Ohren
von dieser Priester falschem Sinn.

TAMINO. Ein Weiser prüft und achtet
nicht
was der gemeine Pöbel spricht.

DIE DAMEN. Man sagt, we ihrem Bunde schwört,
der fährt zur Höll' mit Haupt und Haar.

PAPAGENO. Das wär' beim Teufel unerhört!
Sag an, Tamino, ist das wahr?

No. 11 Duet

TWO PRIESTS. Guard yourself from women's treachery: this is the first duty of our order.
Many a wise man has let himself be bewitched,
has failed without realising it;
at last he has found himself abandoned,
his faith repaid with scorn!
In vain he has wrung his hands,
for death and despair were his reward.¶

(The two priests go out.)

PAPAGENO. Hey, lights! It's astonishing,
whenever these gentlemen leave you you can
see nothing even with your eyes wide open.

TAMINO. Bear it with patience and remember that it
is the will of the gods.
(The three Ladies appear through the trapdoor.)

No. 12 Quintet

THE LADIES. What? What? What? You in this
dreadful place.
Never, never, never will you have the luck to escape!
Tamino, death is sworn for you;
you, Papageno, are lost!

PAPAGENO. No, no, no, that would be too much!

TAMINO. Papageno, be silent!
Will you break your vow
not to speak to women here?

PAPAGENO. But you heard them, we are both done for.

TAMINO. Silence, I say, be silent!

PAPAGENO. Always silent, always silent!

THE LADIES. The Queen is very near to you.
She has secretly entered the temple.

PAPAGENO. What? She is in the temple?

TAMINO. Silence, I say, be silent!
Do you always dare
to forget your sworn duty?

THE LADIES. Tamino, listen, you are lost!
Think of the Queen!
There are many rumours about
the false ways of these priests.

TAMINO *(to himself)*. A wise man seeks proof,
and pays no attention to
what the common rabble says.

THE LADIES. It is said that whoever takes their oath
goes straight to Hell, body and soul.

PAPAGENO. That's enough to frighten the Devil!
Tell me, Tamino, is that true?

TAMINO. Geschwätz von Weibern nachgesagt,
von Heuchlern aber ausgedacht.

PAPAGENO. Doch sagt es auch die Königin.

TAMINO. Sie ist ein Weib, hat Weibersinn.
Sei still, mein Wort sei dir genug:
denk deiner Pflicht und handle klug!

DIE DAMEN.
Warum bist du mit uns so spröde?

Auch Papageno schweigt? so rede!

PAPAGENO. Ich möchte gerne … woll …

TAMINO. Still!

PAPAGENO. Ihr seht, dass ich nicht soll!

TAMINO. Still!

PAPAGENO. Dass ich nicht kann das Plaudern lassen, ist wahrlich eine Schand' für mich.

TAMINO. Dass du nicht kannst das Plaudern lassen,
ist wahrlich eine Schand' für dich.

DIE DAMEN. Wir müssen sie mit Scham verlassen,
es plaudert keiner sicherlich.

TAMINO UND PAPAGENO.
Sie müssen uns mit Scham verlassen,
es plaudert keiner sicherlich.

ALLE. Von festem Geiste ist ein Mann,
er denket, was er sprechen kann.

CHOR.
Entweiht ist die heilige Schwelle.
hinab mit den Weibern zur Hölle!

DIE DAMEN. O weh! o weh!

PAPAGENO. O weh! o weh!¶

ZWEITER PRIESTER. Tamino! Dein standhaft männliches Betragen hat gesiegt. Wir wollen nun unsere Wanderschaft fortsetzen.

ERSTER PRIESTER. Was seh' ich, Freund,
steh auf! Wie ist dir?

PAPAGENO. Sch! Ich lieg' in einer Ohnmacht!

ERSTER PRIESTER. Auf, sammle dich!

PAPAGENO. Aber sagt mir nur,
meine Herren, wenn mir die Götter eine Papagena bestimmt haben, warum sie unter soviel Mühen und Qualen erringen?

TAMINO. Gossip repeated by women,
but thought up by hypocrites.

PAPAGENO. But the Queen says so too.

TAMINO. She is a woman, with a woman's mind.
Be quiet, let my word be enough for you;
think of your duty and keep your wits about you.

THE LADIES (*to Tamino*).
Why are you so reserved with us?
(*Tamino indicates discreetly that he may not speak.*)
Papageno too is silent? Speak!

PAPAGENO. I would gladly … I would …

TAMINO. Silence!

PAPAGENO (*to the ladies secretly*). You see that I may not!

TAMINO. Silence!

PAPAGENO. That I cannot give up chattering
is truly a disgrace for me.

TAMINO. That you cannot give up chattering,
is truly a disgrace for you.

THE LADIES. In shame we must leave you.
Clearly, neither of you will talk.

TAMINO AND PAPAGENO.
In shame you must leave us.
Clearly, neither of us will talk.

ALL. A man is strong in spirit;
he thinks before he speaks.
(*The three Ladies are about to go, when the initiates cry from within:*)

CHORUS.
The sacred threshold is defiled.
Cast these women down to hell!
A dreadful chord on full orchestra, thunder, lightning and a crash, followed immediately by two loud thunderclaps.

THE LADIES. Oh, woe! Oh, woe!
(*They fall through the trapdoor.*)

PAPAGENO (*falls to the ground*). Oh, woe! Oh woe!¶

The threefold chord is sounded. The two priests enter, carrying torches.

SECOND PRIEST. Tamino! Your steadfast, manly behaviour has triumphed. We shall now continue our journey.
(*He hands Tamino the sack, and they go out.*)

FIRST PRIEST. What do I see, friend?
Stand up! How are you feeling?

PAPAGENO. Sssh! I've fainted.

FIRST PRIEST. Get up, pull yourself together!

PAPAGENO (*gets up*). But tell me one thing, gentlemen; if the gods have provided Papagena for me, why do I have to go through all this pain and torment to get her?

ERSTER PRIESTER. Diese Neugierige Frage mag dir deine Vernunft beantworten.

FIRST PRIEST. Let your reason answer that impertinent question.

PAPAGENO. O je!

PAPAGENO. Oh dear!

ERSTER PRIESTER. Komm jetzt!

FIRST PRIEST. Come along now! *(He hands the sack to Papageno.)*

PAPAGENO. Bei so einer ewigen Wanderschaft möcht' einem die Liebe auf immer vergehn.

PAPAGENO. With this endless wandering, love might pass a man by for ever. *(They go out.)*

Transformation

The scene is transformed into a peaceful garden. Trees are placed in the form of a horseshoe; in the centre, an arbour of flowers and roses, in which Pamina is asleep. The moonlight shines on her face. In front there is a grass seat. Monostatos enters, hesitates, and then sits down.

MONOSTATOS. Ha! Da find' ich ja die spröde Schöne! Welcher Mensch würde bei so einem Anblick kalt und unempfindlich bleiben? Wenn ich wüsste, dass ich so ganz allein und unbelauscht wäre – ein Küsschen, dächte ich, liesse sich entschuldigen.

MONOSTATOS. Ah, now I've found the prim little beauty! What creature of flesh and blood could remain cold and unmoved at such a sight? If I could be sure I was quite alone and unobserved, a little kiss, I think, might be forgiven.

Nr. 13 Arie

MONOSTATOS. Alles fühlt der Liebe Freuden,
schnäbelt, tändelt, herzet, küsst,
und ich soll die Liebe meiden,
weil ein Schwarzer hässlich ist!
Ist mir denn kein Herz gegeben?
Bin ich nicht von Fleisch und Blut?
Immer ohne Weibchen leben
wäre wahrlich Höllenglut!
Drum so will ich, weil ich lebe,
schnäbeln, küssen, zärtlich sein!
Lieber guter Mond, vergebe:
eine Weisse nahm mich ein.
Weiss ist schön, ich muss sie küssen:
Mond, verstecke dich dazu!
Sollt' es dich zu sehr verdriessen,
o so mach die Augen zu!¶

No. 13 Aria

MONOSTATOS. Every creature feels the joys of love,
bills and coos, flirts, hugs, kisses,
but I must shun love
because a black man is ugly!
Was I not given a heart?
Am I not of flesh and blood?
To live forever without a wife
would be to burn in hell!
And so I will, while I live,
bill and coo, kiss, be amorous!
Dear, beloved moon, forgive me:
A white woman has captured me.
White is beautiful, I must kiss her:
Moon, hide yourself from me!
If it vexes you too much,
then close your eyes!¶

(He steals slowly and quietly towards Pamina. The Queen appears, to the sound of thunder, from the centre trapdoor, so that she stands directly in front of Pamina.)

KÖNIGIN. Zurück!

QUEEN. Get back!

MONOSTATOS. O weh! Die Königin der Nacht!

MONOSTATOS. Woe is me, the Queen of the Night!

PAMINA. Mutter! Meine Mutter!

PAMINA *(wakening)*. Mother, my mother! *(She falls into her arms.)*

MONOSTATOS. Mutter? Das muss man von weitem belauschen!

MONOSTATOS. Mother?
This must be overheard from a distance.
(He slinks out.)

KÖNIGIN. Wo ist der Jüngling, den ich zu dir sandte?

QUEEN. Where is the young man I sent to you?

PAMINA. Er hat sich den Eingeweihten gewidmet!

PAMINA. He has dedicated himself to the initiates.

KÖNIGIN. Den Eingeweihten? Unglückliche Tochter! Nun bist du mir auf ewig entrissen. – Nimm hier diesen Dolch! Er ist für Sarastro geschliffen. Du wirst ihn töten und den mächtigen Sonnenkreis mir überliefern!

PAMINA. Aber liebste Mutter!

KÖNIGIN. Kein Wort!

Nr. 14 Arie

KÖNIGIN. Der Hölle Rache kocht in meinem Herzen;
Tod und Verzweiflung flammet um mich her!
Fühlt nicht durch dich Sarastro Todes-schmerzen,
so bist du meine Tochter nimmermehr!
Verstossen sei auf ewig, verlassen sei auf ewig,
zertrümmert sei auf ewig alle Bande der Natur –
wenn nicht durch dich Sarastro wird erblassen!
Hört! Rachegötter! Hört der Mutter Schwur!¶

Start of Cassette Side 3

PAMINA.
Morden soll ich? – Das kann ich nicht!
Das kann ich nicht! O Götter, was soll ich tun?

MONOSTATOS.
Dich mir anvertrauen!

PAMINA. Ha!

MONOSTATOS. Warum zitterst du?
Vor meiner schwarzen Farbe, oder vor dem geplanten Mord?!

PAMINA. Du weisst also?

MONOSTATOS. Alles! Du hast nur einen Weg, dich und deine Mutter zu retten.

PAMINA. Und der wäre?

MONOSTATOS. Mich zu lieben.

PAMINA. Nein!

MONOSTATOS. So stirb!

SARASTRO. Zurück!

MONOSTATOS. Herr, ich bin unschuldig.

SARASTRO. Geh!

MONOSTATOS. Jetzt such' ich die Mutter auf.

PAMINA. Herr, strafe meine Mutter nicht!
Der Schmerz über meine Abwesenheit …

SARASTRO. Ich weiss alles, allein, du sollst sehen, wie ich mich an deiner Mutter räche.

QUEEN. The initiates? Unhappy daughter! Now you are taken from me for ever. Take this dagger! It has been sharpened for Sarastro. You will kill him and bring me the mighty circle of the sun.

PAMINA. But dearest mother!

QUEEN. Not a word!

No. 14 Aria

QUEEN. The vengeance of hell boils in my heart;
death and despair flame around me!
If Sarastro does not suffer the pains of death through you,
you will be my daughter no more!
Be cast out forever, abandoned forever,
Let all ties of nature be shattered for ever –
if Sarastro does not die through you!
Hear me, gods of vengeance! Hear a mother's vow!¶
(She sinks down.)

PAMINA. *(with the dagger in her hand).*
Shall I murder? I cannot, I cannot! O gods, what shall I do?

MONOSTATOS *(entering quickly, stealthily, and gleefully).* Entrust yourself to me! *(He takes the dagger from her.)*

PAMINA *(screams with fright).* Ah!

MONOSTATOS. What are you trembling at? My black skin, or the murder plan?

PAMINA. So you know?

MONOSTATOS. Everything! You have only one way to save yourself and your mother.

PAMINA. And that is?

MONOSTATOS. To love me!

PAMINA. No!

MONOSTATOS. Then die!

SARASTRO *(enters and quickly restrains him).* Get back!

MONOSTATOS. Sir, I am innocent.

SARASTRO. Away with you!

MONOSTATOS *(as he leaves).* Now I'll go and find her mother.
(Goes out.)

PAMINA. Sir, do not punish my mother! Her grief at my absence …

SARASTRO. I know everything. But you shall see how I take revenge on your mother.

Nr. 15 Arie

SARASTRO. In diesen heil'gen Hallen
kennt man die Rache nicht,
und ist ein Mensch gefallen,
führt Liebe ihn zur Pflicht.
Dann wandelt er an Freundes Hand,
vergnügt und froh ins bessre Land.
In diesen heil'gen Mauern,
wo Mensch den Menschen liebt,
kann kein Verräter lauern,
weil man dem Feind vergibt.
Wen solche Lehren nicht erfreun,
verdienet nicht, ein Mensch zu sein.¶

No. 15 Aria

SARASTRO. Within these sacred halls
vengeance is unknown,
and a human being who falls,
is guided back to duty by love,
walking with the hand of friendship,
content and happy, to a better land.
Within these sacred walls,
where humankind loves humankind,
no traitor can lurk,
for we forgive our enemies.
Anyone who does not rejoice at such teaching
is not worthy to be a human being.¶

(They go out.)

Transformation

The scene is transformed into a hall, in which the flying-machine can be used. The flying-machine is covered with roses and flowers, in which a door opens. In front are two grass seats. Tamino and Papageno are led in, without sacks, by the two priests.

ZWEITER PRIESTER. Hier seid ihr beide euch allein überlassen; Prinz, – noch einmal, vergesst nicht: schweigen!

SECOND PRIEST. Here you two will be left alone. Prince, once again, do not forget: be silent! *(He goes out.)*

ERSTER PRIESTER. Papageno!

FIRST PRIEST. Papageno!

PAPAGENO. Hm.

PAPAGENO. Mm?

ERSTER PRIESTER. Wer an diesem Ort sein Stillschweigen bricht, den strafen die Götter durch Donner und Blitz. Leb wohl!

FIRST PRIEST. Anyone who breaks his vow of silence in this place will be punished by the gods with thunder and lightning. Farewell! *(He goes out.)*

PAPAGENO. Leb wohl! Auf Wiedersehen! Lustig! Das ist ein lustiges Leben. – Wär' ich doch lieber in meiner Strohhütte im Wald geblieben, da hört' ich doch wenigstens manchmal einen Vogel pfeifen.

PAPAGENO. Farewell! Goodbye! This is a jolly life! If only I had stayed in my straw hut in the forest, then at least I would hear a bird singing occasionally.

TAMINO. Ssst!

TAMINO. Ssh!

PAPAGENO. Mit mir werd' ich noch sprechen dürfen, wir zwei können auch miteinander reden, weil: wir sind ja Männer!

PAPAGENO. I'm allowed to talk to myself, And we can talk to each other, too; we are men.

TAMINO. Ssst!

TAMINO. Ssh!

PAPAGENO. Lalalala …

PAPAGENO. Lalalala …

TAMINO. Sst!

TAMINO. Ssh!

PAPAGENO. Lalala …

PAPAGENO. Lalala …

TAMINO. Sst!

TAMINO. Ssh!

PAPAGENO. Lalala! – Nicht einmal einen Tropfen Wasser bekommt man bei diesen Leuten.

PAPAGENO. Lalala … You don't even get a drop of water from these people.
(An ugly old woman comes out of the trap-door holding, on a tray, a large cup of water.)

WEIB. Hier, mein Engel!

WOMAN. Here you are, my angel!

PAPAGENO. Ist der Becher für mich?

PAPAGENO. Is that cup for me?

WEIB. Freilich, mein Engel, freilich!

WOMAN. Of course, my angel, of course!

PAPAGENO. Ha! Brr!
Wasser! – Komm, Alte, setz dich her zu mir,
sag einmal, wie alt bist du denn?

WEIB. Achtzehn Jahr' und zwei Minuten.

PAPAGENO. Achtzig Jahr' und zwei Minuten.

WEIB. Achtzehn Jahr' und zwei Minuten.

PAPAGENO. Hahaha! Achtzehn! Haha! Ei, du
junger Engel! Du, du, hast du auch einen
Geliebten?

WEIB. Freilich, er ist zehn Jahre älter.

PAPAGENO. Um zehn Jahre älter –, das muss
eine feurige Liebe sein! Wie nennt er sich denn,
dein Geliebter?

WEIB. Papageno!

PAPAGENO. Ah! Papageno?! W … ? Ah …
Papageno? Ich wäre dein Geliebter?

WEIB. Ja, mein Engel.

PAPAGENO. Wie heisst denn du?

WEIB. Ich heisse …

PAPAGENO. Oi! oje …

PAPAGENO. O weh! Nun sprech' ich kein
Wort mehr.

PAPAGENO (drinks). Ugh! Brr! Water!
Here, old girl, come and sit by me. Tell me,
how old are you?

WOMAN. Eighteen years and two minutes.

PAPAGENO. Eighty years and two minutes.

WOMAN. Eighteen years and two minutes.

PAPAGENO. Hahaha! Eighteen! Hahaha!
You young angel! And do you have a sweetheart?

WOMAN. Of course; he is ten years older.

PAPAGENO. Ten years older! That must be a
passionate love affair! What's his name, then, your
sweetheart?

WOMAN. Papageno.

PAPAGENO. Ah! Papageno? Wh…? Eh?
Papageno? I'm to be your sweetheart?

WOMAN. Yes, my angel.

PAPAGENO (quickly takes the water and dashes it in her
face). What's your name, then?

WOMAN. My name is … (Clap of thunder.)

PAPAGENO. Oi! Ooo …
(The old woman hobbles hurriedly away.)

PAPAGENO. Oh woe! Now I shan't speak another
word.
*The three boys appear in a flying-machine decked with roses.
In the centre of it is a lavishly spread table. One boy has the
flute, and another the box of bells.*

Nr. 16 Terzett

DIE KNABEN. Seid uns zum zweiten Mal
willkommen,
ihr Männer, in Sarastros Reich.
Er schickt, was man euch abgenommen,
die Flöte und die Glöckchen euch.
Wollt ihr die Speisen nicht verschmähen,
so esset, trinket froh davon.
Wenn wir zum dritten Mal uns sehen,
ist Freude eures Mutes Lohn.
Tamino, Mut! nah ist das Ziel!
Du, Papageno, schweige still!¶

PAPAGENO. Tamino, wollen wir nicht speisen?

PAPAGENO. Er bläst! Blas nur fort auf deiner
Flöte –, ich will hier meines Brocken blasen!
Hm, der Sarastro führt eine gute Küche!
Nun muss ich versuchen, ob auch der Keller so
gut bestellt ist. Hm! das ist Götterwein!

No. 16 Trio

THE BOYS. A second time we bid you welcome,

gentlemen, in Sarastro's realm.
He sends what was taken from you –
your flute and your bells.
If you will not scorn this food,
then eat and drink of it with pleasure.
When we meet for the third time
your courage will be rewarded with joy.
Tamino, courage! The goal is near!
You, Papageno, keep silent!¶

*During the trio they place the table in the centre of the stage
and fly away.*

PAPAGENO. Tamino, can we not eat?
(Tamino plays his flute.)

PAPAGENO. He's playing! All right then, play your
flute. I'll play with these scraps.
Mm, Sarastro has a good cook.
Now I must see if his cellar is as good.
Mm, wine of the gods!

PAMINA. Du hier? Gütige Götter, Dank euch, dass ihr mich diesen Weg geführt habt. Ich hörte deine Flöte – und so lief ich schnell dem Tone nach. Aber du bist traurig? Sprichst nicht eine Silbe mit deiner Pamina? Liebst du mich nicht mehr? O Papageno, sag du mir, was ist mit meinem Freund?

PAPAGENO.
Wir …

PAMINA. Wie, auch du? Liebster, einziger Tamino … Oh, das ist mehr als Kränkung, mehr als Tod!

Nr. 17 Arie

PAMINA. Ach, ich fühl's, es ist entschwunden, ewig hin der Liebe Glück! Nimmer kommt ihr, Wonnestunden, meinem Herzen mehr zurück! Sieh, Tamino, diese Tränen fliessen, Trauter, dir allein; fühlst du nicht der Liebe Sehnen, so wird Ruh' im Tode sein.¶

PAPAGENO. Siehst du, Tamino ich kann auch schweigen, wenn's sein muss.

Ah, das geht uns an!

Wir kommen schon!

Tamino, na, eile nicht so, wir kommen schon noch zeitig genug, um uns braten zu lassen.

PAMINA. *(enters joyfully)* You here? Dear gods, thank you for leading me this way. I heard your flute and ran towards the sound as fast as I could. But you are sad? You say nothing to your Pamina? Don't you love me any more? Papageno, tell me, what is the matter with my friend?

PAPAGENO *(with his mouth full of food, indicates to her to go away)*. We …

PAMINA. What, you as well? Dearest, my only Tamino, … Oh, this is more than wounding, worse than death!

No. 17 Aria

PAMINA. Ah, I feel it has all vanished, the happiness of love gone for ever. Never will you return, hours of delight, back again to my heart. See, Tamino, these tears flow, beloved, for you alone; if you do not feel love's yearning, my peace will be in death.¶

(She goes out.)

PAPAGENO *(eats quickly)*. You see, Tamino, I can keep silent if I have to. *(The threefold trombone-chord.)* Ah, that's for us! *(The threefold trombone-chord.)* All right, we're coming! *(Tamino drags him off by force.)* Tamino, not so fast, we shall still arrive in time to get roasted. *(They go off.)*

Transformation

The scene is transformed into the vault of the pyramids. Sarastro, the Speaker, and several priests. Two priests carry an illuminated pyramid on their shoulders; each priest has a transparent pyramid the size of a lantern in his hand.

Nr. 18 Chor

CHOR. O Isis und Osiris! welche Wonne! Die düstre Nacht verscheucht der Glanz der Sonne. Bald fühlt der edle Jüngling neues Leben, bald ist er unserm Dienste ganz ergeben. Sein Geist ist kühn, sein Herz ist rein, bald wird er unser würdig sein.¶

No. 18 Chorus

CHORUS. O Isis and Osiris, what rapture! The rays of the sun banish the dark night. Soon the noble youth will feel new life. Soon he will be wholly dedicated to our order. His spirit is bold, his heart is pure. Soon he will be worthy of us.¶

(Tamino is led in.)

SARASTRO. Tamino, dein Betragen war bisher männlich und gelassen; nun hast du noch zwei gefährliche Wege zu wandern. Mögen die Götter dich ferner geleiten! Man bringe Pamina!

SARASTRO. Tamino, your conduct so far has been manly and composed. You now have two further dangerous paths to take. May the gods accompany you further! Bring in Pamina!
(A silence reigns over all the priests; Pamina is led in, covered with the same kind of sack which the initiates were wearing. Sarastro unties the sack.)

PAMINA. Wo bin ich? Saget mir, wo ist mein Tamino?

PAMINA. Where am I? Tell me, where is my Tamino?

SARASTRO. Er wartet auf dich, um dir das letzte Lebewohl zu sagen.

SARASTRO. He is waiting for you, to bid you a last farewell.

PAMINA. Das letzte Lebewohl!? Tamino!

PAMINA. A last farewell? Tamino!

Nr. 19 Terzett

No. 19 Trio

PAMINA. Soll ich dich, Teurer, nicht mehr sehn?

PAMINA. Shall I, dear one, never see you again?

SARASTRO. Ihr werdet froh euch wiedersehn!

SARASTRO. You will meet again in joy!

PAMINA. Dein warten tödliche Gefahren!

PAMINA. Deadly perils await you!

TAMINO UND SARASTRO. Die Götter mögen mich (ihn) bewahren!

TAMINO AND SARASTRO. The gods will protect me (him)!

PAMINA. Du wirst dem Tode nicht entgehen, mir flüstert dieses Ahnung ein.

PAMINA. You will not escape from death, foreboding whispers to me.

TAMINO UND SARASTRO.
Der Götter Wille mag geschehen, ihr Wink soll mir (ihm) Gesetze sein!

TAMINO AND SARASTRO.
The will of the gods must be done, their sign shall be my (his) law!

PAMINA. O liebtest du, wie ich dich liebe, du würdest nicht so ruhig sein.

PAMINA. Oh, if you loved as I love you, you would not be so calm.

TAMINO UND SARASTRO.
Glaub mir, ich fühle (er fühlet) gleiche Triebe, werd' (wird) ewig dein Getreuer sein.

TAMINO AND SARASTRO.
Believe me, I feel (he feels) the same desire, I will be (he will be) forever true to you.

SARASTRO. Die Stunde schlägt, nun müsst ihr scheiden!

SARASTRO. The hour strikes, now you must part.

TAMINO AND PAMINA. Wie bitter sind der Trennung Leiden!

TAMINO AND PAMINA. How bitter are the sorrows of parting!

SARASTRO. Tamino muss nun wieder fort!

SARASTRO. Tamino must leave again.

TAMINO. Pamina, ich muss wirklich fort!

TAMINO. Pamina, now I must be on my way.

PAMINA. Tamino muss nun wirklich fort!

PAMINA. Tamino now must be on his way.

SARASTRO. Nun muss er fort!

SARASTRO. Now he must go.

TAMINO. Nun muss ich fort!

TAMINO. Now I must go.

PAMINA. So musst du fort!

PAMINA. Now you must go.

TAMINO. Pamina, lebe wohl!

TAMINO. Pamina, farewell.

PAMINA. Tamino, lebe wohl!

PAMINA. Tamino, farewell.

SARASTRO. Nun eile fort!
Dich ruft dein Wort!
Die Stunde schlägt!
Wir sehn uns wieder!

SARASTRO. Hurry away!
Your vow calls you.
The hour strikes.
We will meet again.

TAMINO UND PAMINA. Ach, goldne Ruhe, kehre wieder!¶

TAMINO AND PAMINA. Ah, golden peace, come back again.¶

(They leave.)

PAPAGENO.
Tamino! Tamino! Willst du mich denn gänzlich
verlassen?

STIMME. Zurück!

PAPAGENO. Barmherzige Götter! Wenn ich jetzt
nur wüsste, wo ich hereinkam!

STIMME. Zurück!

PAPAGENO. Jetzt kann ich weder vorwärts noch
rückwärts, muss vielleicht am Ende gar hier
verhungern. – Schon recht! Warum bin ich auch
mitgereist?!

ERSTER PRIESTER. Mensch!

PAPAGENO. Hier!

ERSTER PRIESTER. Du hättest verdient, auf
immer in finsteren Klüften der Erde zu wandern.
Nie wirst du das himmlische Vergnügen der
Eingeweihten fühlen!

PAPAGENO. Je nun, es gibt noch mehr Leute
meinesgleichen! Mir wäre jetzt ein gutes Glas
Wein das himmlischste Vergnügen!

ERSTER PRIESTER. Man wird dich damit
bedienen.

PAPAGENO. Juchhe! Da ist es schon!
Herrlich! Himmlisch! Göttlich. Ich bin jetzt so
vergnügt, dass ich bis zur Sonne fliegen wollte,
wenn ich Flügel hätte – mir, mir wird ganz
wunderlich ums Herz! Ich möchte … ich
wünschte … ja, was denn?

Nr. 20 Arie

PAPAGENO. Ein Mädchen oder Weibchen
wünscht Papageno sich!
O, so ein sanftes Täubchen
wär' Seligkeit für mich!
Dann schmeckte mir Trinken und Essen,
dann könnt' ich mit Fürsten mich messen,
des Lebens als Weiser mich freun,
und wie im Elysium sein!
Ein Mädchen, *etc.*
Ach, kann ich denn keiner von allen
den reizenden Mädchen gefallen?
Helf' eine mir nur aus der Not,
sonst gräm' ich mich wahrlich zu Tod!
Ein Mädchen, *etc.*
Wird keine mir Liebe gewähren,
so muss mich die Flamme verzehren,
doch küsst' mich ein weiblicher Mund,
so bin ich schon wieder gesund.¶

PAPAGENO (*entering*).
Tamino, Tamino! Will you abandon
me altogether? (*He goes to the door through which
Tamino was led off.*)

A VOICE. Get back! (*Clap of thunder; fire bursts from the
door.*)

PAPAGENO. Merciful gods!
If only I knew where I came in! (*He goes to the door
from which he came in.*)

A VOICE. Get back! (*Thunder and fire, as before.*)

PAPAGENO. Now I can't go on, and I can't go back.
Perhaps I have to starve to death here. Well, it serves
me right. Why did I ever come with him? (*The First
Priest enters with his pyramid.*)

FIRST PRIEST. Mortal!

PAPAGENO. Here!

FIRST PRIEST. You really deserve to wander for
ever in the dark caverns of the earth.
You will never feel the heavenly joy of the
initiates.

PAPAGENO. Ah well, there are lots of other people
like me! At the moment the most
heavenly joy would be a good glass of wine.

FIRST PRIEST. Your wish will be granted.
(*He goes off. Immediately a large glass of red wine rises out
of the floor.*)

PAPAGENO. Hooray, there it is!
(*Drinks.*) Glorious, heavenly, divine! I'm now so full of
joy that I would fly to the sun if I
had wings. Oh, I have such a strange feeling in my
heart. I'd like … I want … Well what, then?

No. 20 Aria

PAPAGENO. A little maiden or a little wife,
that is what Papageno wants.
Oh, such a gentle sweetheart
would be bliss to me!
Then drinking and eating would be a pleasure,
then I could be as happy as a prince,
I would enjoy life as much as a wise man,
as if I were in heaven.
A little maiden, *etc.*
Ah, can I not please a single one
of all the charming girls?
If one does not help me in my need,
I'll surely grieve to death!
A little maiden, *etc.*
If no-one will give me love,
the flames will consume me;
but if a woman's lips will kiss me,
I will be cured straight away.¶

WEIB. Da bin ich schon, mein Engel!

PAPAGENO. Die Alte hat sich meiner erbarmt!

WEIB. Ja, mein Engel.

PAPAGENO. An dem Glockenspiel muss was
hin sein!

WEIB. Mein Engel, wenn du mir versprichst,
mir ewig treu zu bleiben, dann sollst du sehen,
wie zärtlich dein Weibchen dich lieben wird.

PAPAGENO. Ei, ei, du zärtliches Närrchen!

WEIB. Reich mir zum Pfand unseres Bundes
deine Hand.

PAPAGENO. Nur nicht so hastig, mein lieber
Engel! So ein Bündnis braucht seine reifliche
Überlegung!

WEIB. Papageno, ich rate dir, zaudere nicht,
deine Hand, oder du bist auf immer hier
eingekerkert.

PAPAGENO. Eingekerkert?

WEIB. Wasser und Brot wird deine tägliche Kost
sein, ohne Freund, ohne Freundin musst du
leben und der Welt auf immer entsagen.

PAPAGENO. Wasser trinken? Bah! Der Welt
entsagen? Na, da will ich doch lieber eine Alte
nehmen, als gar keine! Hier hast du meine Hand
mit der Versicherung, dass ich dir immer getreu
bleibe, solang ich keine Schönere finde.

WEIB. Das schwörst du?

PAPAGENO. Das schwör' ich!

Papagena!

ERSTER PRIESTER. Fort mit dir, junges Weib!
Er ist deiner noch nicht würdig!

PAPAGENO. Herr mischen sie sich nicht in
meine Familienangelegenheiten!

(The old woman comes in, dancing and supporting herself on her stick.)

WOMAN. Here I am, my angel!

PAPAGENO. The old girl has taken pity on me!

WOMAN. Yes, my angel.

PAPAGENO. There must be something wrong
with the bells!

WOMAN. My angel, if you promise to be true
to me for ever, you will see how tenderly
your little wife will love you.

PAPAGENO. Oh, you tender little creature!

WOMAN. Give me your hand as a pledge of our
union.

PAPAGENO. Not so fast, my dear angel!
Such a union needs careful consideration.

WOMAN. Papageno, I warn you not to hesitate.
Give me your hand, or you'll be imprisoned here
for ever.

PAPAGENO. Imprisoned?

WOMAN. Bread and water will be your daily diet,
and you'll have to live without a friend, man or woman, and renounce the world forever.

PAPAGENO. Drink water? Ugh! Renounce the
world? Then I'd rather take an old woman
than none at all. Here is my hand, with the promise
that I'll always be faithful to you
(aside) until I find someone prettier.

WOMAN. You swear it?

PAPAGENO. I swear it.
(The woman is transformed into a young girl, who is dressed exactly the same as Papageno.)
Papagena!
(He is about to embrace her. The First Priest enters and takes her quickly by the hand.)

FIRST PRIEST. Away with you, young woman!
He is not yet worthy of you. *(He drags Papagena away.)*

PAPAGENO. You sir, don't interfere
in my family affairs!

Start of Cassette Side 4

Transformation

The scene is transformed into a small garden. The three boys descend.

<table>
<tr><td>

Nr. 21 Finale

DIE KNABEN. Bald prangt, den Morgen zu verkünden,
die Sonn' auf goldner Bahn,
bald soll der Aberglaube schwinden,
bald siegt der weise Mann.
O holde Ruhe, steig hernieder,
kehr in der Menschen Herzen wieder,
dann ist die Erd' ein Himmelreich,
und Sterbliche den Göttern gleich.

ERSTER KNABE. Doch seht, Verzweiflung quält Paminen!

ZWEITER UND DRITTER KNABE.
Wo ist sie denn?

ERSTER KNABE. Sie ist von Sinnen –

DIE KNABEN. Sie quält verschmähter Liebe Leiden,
lasst uns der Armen Trost bereiten;
fürwahr, ihr Schicksal geht uns nah!
O wäre nur ihr Jüngling da!
Sie kommt, lasst uns bei Seite gehn,
damit wir, was sie mache, sehn.

PAMINA. Du also bist mein Bräutigam?
Durch dich vollend' ich meinen Gram!

DIE KNABEN.
Welch dunkle Worte sprach sie da?
Die Arme ist dem Wahnsinn nah.

PAMINA. Geduld, mein Trauter, ich bin dein,
bald werden wir vermählet sein!

DIE KNABEN. Wahnsinn tobt ihr im Gehirne.
Selbstmord steht auf ihrer Stirne.
Holdes Mädchen, sieh uns an!

PAMINA. Sterben will ich, weil der Mann,
den ich nimmermehr kann hassen,
seine Traute kann verlassen!
Dies gab meine Mutter mir!

DIE KNABEN. Selbstmord strafet Gott an dir!

PAMINA. Lieber durch dies Eisen sterben,
als durch Liebesgram verderben;
Mutter! durch dich leide ich,
und dein Fluch verfolget mich.

DIE KNABEN. Mädchen, willst du mit uns gehn?

</td><td>

No. 21 Finale   [No.21a]

THE BOYS. Soon, to announce
morning, the sun will shine
on its golden course;
soon superstition will vanish,
soon the wise man will triumph.
O noble peace, descend to us,
return to the hearts of men once more;
then earth will be a heavenly kingdom
and mortals will be like the gods.

FIRST BOY. But look, despair torments Pamina!

SECOND AND THIRD BOYS.
Where is she?

FIRST BOY. She is beside herself –

THE BOYS. The sorrows of rejected love torment her.
Let us comfort the poor girl;
truly, her fate is dear to us!
Oh, if only her young man were here!
She is coming, let us step aside
and see what she does.
(Pamina enters, half mad, holding a dagger.)

PAMINA. So you shall be my bridegroom?
Through you shall I end my grief!

THE BOYS *(to themselves)*.
What dark words did she speak?
The poor girl is near madness.

PAMINA. Patience, beloved, I am yours,
soon we shall be married!

THE BOYS. Madness rages in her mind,
on her brow is suicide.
(To Pamina) Fair maiden, look at us!

PAMINA. I will die, for the man
whom I can never hate
is able to leave his true love.
(Indicates the dagger.) My mother gave me this.

THE BOYS. God will punish your suicide!

PAMINA. Better to die by this dagger
than to waste away from love's grief;
Mother! Because of you I suffer,
and your curse pursues me.

THE BOYS. Maiden, will you go with us?

</td></tr>
</table>

PAMINA. Ha! des Jammers Mass ist voll!
falscher Jüngling, lebe wohl!
Sieh, Pamina stirbt durch dich!
Dieses Eisen töte mich!

DIE KNABEN. Ha! Unglückliche, halt ein!
Sollte dies dein Jüngling sehen,
würde er vor Gram vergehen;
denn er liebet dich allein.

PAMINA. Was? er fühlte Gegenliebe,
und verbarg mir seine Triebe,
wandte sein Gesicht von mir!
Warum sprach er nicht mit mir?

DIE KNABEN. Dieses müssen wir verschweigen,
doch wir wollen dir ihn zeigen,
und du wirst mit Staunen sehn,
dass er dir sein Herz geweiht,
und den Tod für dich nicht scheut.
Komm, wir wollen zu ihm gehn!

PAMINA. Führt mich hin, ich möcht' ihn sehn!

ALLE. Zwei Herzen, die von Liebe brennen,
kann Menschenohnmacht niemals trennen;
verloren ist der Feinde Müh',
die Götter selbst beschützen sie.

PAMINA. Ah! The measure of sorrow is full.
False young man, farewell!
See, Pamina dies because of you.
May this dagger kill me!
(She is about to stab herself.)

THE BOYS *(holding her arm)*. Ha! Unhappy girl, stop!
If your young man should see this,
he would die of grief;
for he loves you alone.

PAMINA. What? He returned my love,
but hid his feelings from me,
and turned his face away?
Why did he not speak to me?

THE BOYS. About this we must be silent,
but we will show him to you,
and you will be amazed to see
that his heart is dedicated to you
and that for you he would not shrink from death.
Come, we shall go to him!

PAMINA. Lead me on, I want to see him!

ALL. Two hearts that burn with love
can never be parted by human weakness;
in vain is the effort of their enemies,
the gods themselves protect them. *(They leave.)*

Transformation

The scene is transformed into two large mountains; in one is a waterfall, and its rush and roar can be heard; the other spits fire. Each mountain has a grating through which fire and water can be seen. Where the fire burns, the horizon must be bright red, and where the water is, a black mist lies. To each side are rocks, each closed by an iron gate.
Tamino is lightly clothed, without sandals. Two men in black armour lead Tamino in. In their helmets fire burns. They read to him the transparent inscription which is written on a pyramid. This pyramid stands high in the centre, near the grating.

[No.21b]

DIE ZWEI GEHARNISCHTEN.
Der, welcher wandert diese Strasse voll
Beschwerden,
wird rein durch Feuer, Wasser, Luft und Erden.
Wenn er des Todes Schrecken überwinden kann,
schwingt er sich aus der Erde himmelan;
erleuchtet wird er dann im Stande sein,
sich den Mysterien der Isis ganz zu weihn.

TAMINO. Mich schreckt kein Tod, als Mann zu
handeln,
den Weg der Tugend fortzuwandeln:
schliesst mir die Schreckenspforten auf!
ich wage froh den kühnen Lauf.

PAMINA. Tamino, halt! ich muss
dich sehn!

TAMINO. Was hör ich? Paminens Stimme?

DIE ZWEI GEHARNISCHTEN.
Ja, ja, das ist Paminens Stimme.

THE TWO MEN IN ARMOUR.
He who treads this path beset
with hardships,
will be made pure by fire, water, air and earth.
If he can overcome the fears of death
he will soar from earth toward Heaven;
then, enlightened, he will be able
to dedicate himself wholly to the mysteries of Isis.

TAMINO. No fear of death will prevent me acting as
a man,
and following the way of virtue:
unlock the gates of fear for me!
I gladly venture on the courageous path. *(He is about to go.)*

PAMINA *(from within)*. Tamino, stop! I must
see you!

TAMINO. What do I hear? Pamina's voice?

THE TWO MEN IN ARMOUR.
Yes, yes, that is Pamina's voice.

TAMINO, DIE ZWEI GEHARNISCHTEN. Wohl mir (dir), nun kann sie mit mir (dir) gehn, nun trennet uns (euch) kein Schicksal mehr, wenn auch der Tod beschieden wär'.

TAMINO. Ist mir erlaubt, mit ihr zu sprechen?

DIE ZWEI GEHARNISCHTEN.
Dir ist erlaubt, mit ihr zu sprechen.

TAMINO, DIE ZWEI GEHARNISCHTEN. Welch Glück, wenn wir uns (euch) wiedersehn, froh Hand in Hand in Tempel gehn! Ein Weib, das Nacht und Tod nicht scheut, ist würdig und wird eingeweiht.

PAMINA. Tamina mein! O welch ein Glück!

TAMINO. Pamina mein! O welch ein Glück! Hier sind die Schreckenspforten, die Not und Tod mir dräun.

PAMINA. Ich werde aller Orten an deiner Seite sein. Ich selbsten führe dich, die Liebe leitet mich! Sie mag den Weg mit Rosen streun, weil Rosen stets bei Dornen sein. Spiel du die Zauberflöte an; sie schützt uns auf unsrer Bahn. Es schnitt in einer Zauberstunde mein Vater sie aus tiefstem Grunde der tausendjähr' gen Eiche aus, bei Blitz und Donner, Sturm und Braus. Nun komm und spiel die Flöte an; sie leite uns auf grauser Bahn.

PAMINA, TAMINO, DIE ZWEI GEHARNISCHTEN. Wir (Ihr) wandeln durch des Tones Macht froh durch des Todes düstre Nacht.

PAMINA UND TAMINO.
Wir wandelten durch Feuergluten bekämpften mutig die Gefahr. Dein Ton sei Schutz in Wasserfluten, so wie er es im Feuer war!

PAMINA UND TAMINO.
Ihr Götter, welch ein Augenblick! Gewähret ist uns Isis' Glück!

TAMINO, THE TWO MEN IN ARMOUR. Happy am I (are you), now can she go with me (you); now no fate can separate us (you) again, even if death should be our (your) lot.

TAMINO. Am I allowed to speak to her?

THE TWO MEN IN ARMOUR.
You are allowed to speak to her.
(The two Priests go out.)

TAMINO, THE TWO MEN IN ARMOUR. What joy to meet again, and happily, hand in hand, to enter the temple! A woman who does not fear night and death is worthy and will be initiated.
(The gates are opened; Tamino and Pamina embrace.)

PAMINA. My Tamino! Oh, what joy!

TAMINO. My Pamina! Oh, what joy! Here are the gates of fear which threaten me with danger and death.

PAMINA. Everywhere I will be at your side. I myself will lead you, and Love will be my guide. *(She takes him by the hand.)* It will strew the way with roses, for roses are found with thorns. Play your magic flute; it will protect us on our way. In a magic hour my father cut it from the deepest heart of a thousand-year-old oak tree, amid thunder and lightning, storm and tempest. Now, come and play the flute; it will lead us on our dreadful path.

PAMINA, TAMINO, AND THE TWO MEN IN ARMOUR. We (you) walk by the power of music, cheerful through death's dark night.
The gates are slowly closed behind them. Tamino and Pamina can be seen walking. The crackling of fire and the howling of wind are heard, sometimes also the sound of muffled thunder and the roar of water. Tamino plays his flute, sometimes accompanied by muted kettledrums. As soon as they have come out of the fire, they embrace and remain in the centre.

PAMINA AND TAMINO.
We passed through glowing fire and bravely faced the danger. May your music protect us in the flood as it did in the fire!
Tamino plays; they are seen climbing down, and after a while coming up again. Immediately a door opens, to reveal the entrance to a temple which is brightly lit. A solemn silence. This sight should present the utmost splendour.

PAMINA AND TAMINO.
O gods, what a glorious moment! Guaranteed to us is the joy of Isis!

CHOR.
Triumph! Triumph! du edles Paar!
besieget hast du die Gefahr!
Der Isis Weihe ist nun dein!
Kommt, kommt, tretet in den Tempel ein!

CHORUS *(from within)*.
Triumph, triumph, noble pair!
you have overcome the danger!
The mysteries of Isis are now yours!
Come, come, enter the temple!

Transformation

The scene is changed back to the earlier garden.

[No.21c]

PAPAGENO. Papagena! Papagena! Papagena!
Weibchen, Täubchen, meine Schöne!
Vergebens! Ach, sie ist verloren;
ich bin zum Unglück schon geboren.
Ich plauderte, und das war schlecht,
und drum geschieht es mir schon recht!
Seit ich gekostet diesen Wein,
seit ich das schöne Weibchen sah,
so brennt's im Herzenskämmerlein,
so zwickt es hier, so zwickt es da.
Papagena, Herzensweibchen!
Papagena, liebes Täubchen!
's ist umsonst, es ist vergebens!
Müde bin ich meines Lebens.
Sterben macht der Lieb' ein End,
wenn's im Herzen noch so brennt.

Diesen Baum da will ich zieren,
mir an ihm den Hals zuschnüren,
weil das Leben mir missfällt,
Gute Nacht, du falsche Welt!
Weil du böse an mir handelst,
mir kein schönes Kind zubandelst,
so ist's aus, so sterbe ich;
schöne Mädchen, denkt an mich!
Will sich eine um mich Armen,
eh' ich hänge, noch erbarmen,
wohl, so lass ich's diesmal sein.
Rufet nur; ja, oder nein!
Keine hört mich; alles stille!
Also ist es euer Wille?
Papageno, frisch hinauf,
ende deinen Lebenslauf!
Nun, ich warte noch, es sei;
bis man zählet: eins, zwei drei!
Eins! … Zwei! … Drei! …
Nun wohlan, es bleibt dabei;
weil mich nichts zurücke hält,
gute Nacht, du falsche Welt!

PAPAGENO. Papagena! Papagena! Papagena!
Little wife, my dove, my beauty!
In vain! Ah, she is lost;
I was surely born to bad luck.
I chattered, and that was wrong,
so I got what I deserved.
Ever since I tasted that wine,
ever since I saw that pretty girl,
my heart has been on fire,
pinched all over (by the pangs of love).
Papagena! Wife of my heart!
Papagena, dearest dove!
It is in vain, it is useless.
I am weary of my life.
Death puts an end to love,
when your heart burns so.
(He takes a rope from his waist.)

I shall decorate this tree by tying
myself to it by the neck,
since life so displeases me.
Good night, false world!
Because you treated me badly,
and never gave me a sweetheart,
all is over, and so I die;
pretty maiden, think of me!
If just one girl will
take pity on me before I hang,
I will let it go this time.
Speak up: yes, or no! *(He looks around.)*
No one hears me; all is still.
So that is your decision?
Papageno, get on with it,
and end your weary life! *(He looks around.)*
I'll just wait a moment
until I've counted: one, two, three. *(He pipes.)*
One! … Two! … Three! …
Well, then, that's final;
since nothing holds me back,
good night, false world!
(He is about to hang himself.)

DIE KNABEN. Halt ein! O Papageno, und sei klug;
man lebt nur einmal, dies sei dir genug!

THE BOYS *(descending)*. Stop, Papageno, and be sensible;
you live only once, let that be enough!

PAPAGENO. Ihr habt gut reden, habt gut scherzen;
doch brennt es euch wie mich im Herzen,
ihr würdet auch nach Mädchen gehn.

DIE KNABEN. So lasse deine Glöckchen klingen,
dies wird dein Weibchen zu dir bringen!

PAPAGENO. Ich narr vergass das Zauberdinge!

Erklinge, Glockenspiel, erklinge!
Ich muss mein liebes Mädchen sehn!

Klinget, Glöckchen, klinget!
Schafft mein Mädchen her!
Bringt mein Weibchen her,
bringt sie her, mein Weibchen her!

DIE KNABEN. Nun, Papageno, sieh dich um!

PAPAGENO. Pa-pa-gena!

PAPAGENA. Pa-pa-geno!

PAPAGENO. Bist du mir nun ganz gegeben?

PAPAGENA. Nun bin ich dir ganz gegeben!

PAPAGENO. Nun, so sei mein liebes Weibchen!

PAPAGENA. Nun, so sei mein Herzenstäubchen!

BEIDE. Welche Freude wird das sein,
wenn die Götter uns bedenken,
unsrer Liebe Kinder schenken,
so liebe, kleine Kinderlein!

PAPAGENO. Erst einen kleinen Papageno …

PAPAGENA. Dann eine kleine Papagena …

PAPAGENO. Dann wieder einen Papageno …

PAPAGENA. Dann wieder eine Papagena …

BEIDE. Es ist das höchste der Gefühle,
wenn viele, viele Papageno
der Eltern Segen werden sein!

ALLE. Nur stille, stille, stille, stille,
bald dringen wir im Tempel ein.

MONOSTATOS. Doch Fürstin, halte Wort, erfülle,
dein Kind muss meine Gattin sein.

KÖNIGIN. Ich halte Wort, es ist mein Wille!
Mein Kind soll deine Gattin sein.

DIE DAMEN. Ihr Kind soll deine Gattin sein.

MONOSTATOS. Doch still, ich höre schrecklich rauschen
wie Donnerton und Wasserfall!

DIE KÖNIGIN UND DIE DAMEN.
Ja, fürchterlich ist dieses Rauschen,
wie fernen Donners Widerhall!

PAPAGENO. It's all very well for you to talk and joke,
but if your hearts were burning like mine,
you too would yearn for a sweetheart.

THE BOYS. Then let your bells ring;
they will bring your little wife to you!

PAPAGENO. What a fool! I forgot the magic! (*He takes out his instrument.*)
Ring out, bells, ring out!
I must see my dear sweetheart!
(*Playing*) Ring, little bells, ring!
Send my sweetheart here!
Bring my little wife here,
bring her here, my little wife here!
(*While Papageno is playing, the Three Boys run to their flying-machine and bring Papagena out.*)

THE BOYS. Now, Papageno, look round!

PAPAGENO. Pa-pa-gena!

PAPAGENA. Pa-pa-geno!

PAPAGENO. Are you really mine now?

PAPAGENA. I'm really yours now!

PAPAGENO. Then be my little wife!

PAPAGENA. Then be my heart's little dove!

BOTH. What a joy it will be
if the gods smile on us
and bless our love with children,
such dear little children!

PAPAGENO. First a little Papageno …

PAPAGENA. Then a little Papagena …

PAPAGENO. Then another Papageno …

PAPAGENA. Then another Papagena …

BOTH. It will be the highest joy of all,
if many, many Papagenos
bless their parents! (*They go out.*)
The Moor, the Queen and her Three Ladies appear from both trapdoors; they carry black torches in their hands.

ALL. Now softly, softly, softly, softly,
soon we will enter the temple.

MONOSTATOS. But Your Majesty, keep your promise: your child must be my wife.

QUEEN. I shall keep my word, it is my will!
My child shall be your wife.

THE LADIES. Her child shall be your wife.
Muffled thunder and the roar of water are heard.

MONOSTATOS. But listen, I hear a terrible roar,
like the noise of thunder and waterfall.

THE QUEEN AND THE LADIES.
Yes, fearful is that roar,
like the distant echo of thunder.

MONOSTATOS. Nun sind sie in des Tempels Hallen.

ALLE. Dort wollen wir sie überfallen, die Frömmler tilgen von der Erd' mit Feuersglut und mächt'gem Schwert!

MONOSTATOS UND DIE DAMEN. Dir, grosse Königin der Nacht, sei unsrer Rache Opfer gebracht!

ALLE. Zerschmettert ist unsere Macht, wir alle gestürzet in ewige Nacht!

MONOSTATOS. Now they are in the hall of the temple.

ALL. There we will attack them, wipe these hypocrites from the face of the earth with glowing fire and mighty sword!

MONOSTATOS AND THE LADIES. To you, great Queen of the Night, Let us bring the offering of our revenge! *A very loud chord, thunder, lightning and tempest.*

ALL. Our power is shattered, we are all cast into eternal night! *(They sink down.)*

Transformation

At once the whole scene changes to a sun. Sarastro stands on high; Tamino and Pamina, both in priestly robes. Egyptian priests flank them on each side. The Three Boys are holding flowers.

SARASTRO. Die Strahlen der Sonne vertreiben die Nacht, zernichten der Heuchler erschlichene Macht.

CHOR. Heil sei euch Geweihten! Ihr dranget durch Nacht. Dank sei dir, Osiris, Dank dir, Isis, gebracht! Es siegte die Stärke, und krönet zum Lohn die Schönheit und Weisheit mit ewiger Kron'!

SARASTRO. The rays of the sun drive out the night, and destroy the hypocrite's false power.

CHORUS. Hail to you, initiates! You have penetrated the night. Thanks be to thee, Osiris, thanks, Isis, be thine! Strength has triumphed, and rewards Beauty and Wisdom with an eternal crown!

Part E
Nature, Feeling and Society

Contents

Eighteenth-Century Poetry: A Selection

Prepared for the Course Team by
Michael Rossington

Contents

Eighteenth-Century Poetry: A Selection

Most of the following poems are selected from two anthologies, chosen and edited by Roger Lonsdale. The texts of the poems by Pope, Duck, Gray, Goldsmith and Crabbe are taken from The New Oxford Book of Eighteenth Century Verse *(Oxford University Press, 1984; repr. 1987); those by Montagu, 'Miss W–', Collier and Leapor, are taken from* Eighteenth-Century Women Poets: An Oxford Anthology *(Oxford University Press, 1989; repr. 1990). Full details of the textual sources of all these poems can be found in the endnotes to both books. (It must be stressed that these are extremely small samples from two rich and extensive anthologies which should be consulted in full, if at all possible.)*

We have largely adopted Lonsdale's editorial principles, most of which are common to both the above anthologies (for full details see Lonsdale, 1987, pp.xl–xli and Lonsdale, 1990, pp.xlvi–xlvii). The arrangement of the poems is 'basically chronological, in that poets are introduced successively by the date of their earliest [or only] poem [in this selection]' (Lonsdale, 1987, p.xl). The texts have been modernized in terms of their 'accidental' features: 'spelling and punctuation have been normalized, pervasive initial capitals and italics removed, and contractions expanded except when of metrical significance' (Lonsdale, 1987, p.xl). However, it should be noted that 'accidental features of texts were as often the responsibility of printers as of the writers themselves in the period; and that a general modernization of printing practices, especially affecting the initial capitalization of nouns, occurred in the mid-eighteenth century itself' (Lonsdale, 1990, p.xlvii). We have also reprinted, at the beginning of each poem, the dates provided by Lonsdale: 'The date of the poem is that of first publication. If the date of composition is verifiable and significantly different, this is also indicated' (Lonsdale, 1987, p.xli).

In addition to glosses provided either by Lonsdale (indicated thus: [Lonsdale]) on either the relevant page of the text itself or in the endnotes to his anthologies, or by the original author or editor, or in some cases by other modern editors (see below), we have also supplied some annotations of our own with the aim of explaining obscure words or unfamiliar usages. Our notes are indicated thus: [eds]. It has only been possible to annotate the texts of this selection of poems in a minimal way so that where notes from Lonsdale, the original author, or other modern editors have been used, they have been adopted selectively. Where relevant, cross-references are made to other poems or texts in A206 but largely not to other earlier or contemporary literary works or to the Bible. Moreover, we have been unable to reprint the invaluably detailed biographical headnotes which Lonsdale prefaces to the poems by women in his second anthology. The passages excerpted from his headnotes which are provided here are in no way representative of what are effectively introductory essays.

The text of Swift's 'The Lady's Dressing Room' is from Jonathan Swift, The Complete Poems, *edited by Pat Rogers (Yale University Press, 1983); the text of the extract from Thomson's* The Seasons *is taken from James Thomson,* The Seasons and the Castle of Indolence, *edited by James Sambrook (Oxford University Press, 1972); and the text of Macpherson's* Fragments of Ancient Poetry *is taken from James Macpherson,* Fragments of Ancient Poetry *(1760), introduced by John J. Dunn [for The Augustan Reprint Society] (William Andrews Clark Memorial Library, 1966). The texts of the poems by Burns, along with marginal glosses, notes and a glossary of common dialect words, are taken from Robert Burns,* The Kilmarnock Poems *(Poems, Chiefly in the Scottish Dialect, 1786), edited, with an introduction and notes by Donald A. Low (Dent, 1985). The editorial principles outlined above have been applied to the texts of poems by Burns, Thomson and Swift with the proviso that Low's texts are not modernized in the way that the rest of the poems in this selection have been. Glosses provided by Low, Sambrook and Rogers are indicated by their names in square brackets. Helpful glosses provided by other editors are indicated similarly: [Butt] refers to* The Poems of Alexander Pope: A one-volume edition of the Twickenham text with selected annotations, *edited by John Butt (Methuen, 1963); [DCP] to* George Crabbe, The Complete Poetical Works, *edited by Norma Dalrymple-Champneys and Arthur Pollard, 3 vols. (Clarendon Press, 1988); [Edwards] to* George Crabbe, Selected Poems, *edited with an introduction and notes by Gavin Edwards (Penguin, 1991); [Johnston] to* Selected Poems of Thomas Gray and William Collins, *edited by Arthur Johnston (Edward Arnold, 1967); [Lonsdale 1969] to* The Poems of Thomas Gray, William Collins, Oliver Goldsmith, *edited by Roger Lonsdale (Longman, 1969); [Lonsdale 1977] to* Thomas Gray and William Collins: Poetical Works, *edited by Roger Lonsdale (Oxford University Press, 1977); [Calder & Donnelly] to* Robert Burns: Selected Poetry, *edited by Angus Calder and William Donnelly (Penguin, 1991).*

Alexander Pope (1688–1744)

From *An Epistle to Richard Boyle, Earl of Burlington*

(1731)

    AT Timon's Villa let us pass a day,
Where all cry out, 'What sums are thrown away!'
So proud, so grand, of that stupendous air,
Soft and agreeable come never there.
Greatness, with Timon, dwells in such a draught
As brings all Brobdignag before your thought.
To compass this, his building is a town,
His pond an ocean, his parterre a down:
Who but must laugh, the master when he sees,
A puny insect, shiv'ring at a breeze!   10
Lo, what huge heaps of littleness around!
The whole, a laboured quarry above ground.
Two Cupids squirt before: a lake behind
Improves the keenness of the northern wind.
His gardens next your admiration call,
On ev'ry side you look, behold the wall!
No pleasing intricacies intervene,
No artful wildness to perplex the scene;
Grove nods at grove, each alley has a brother,
And half the platform just reflects the other.   20
The suff'ring eye inverted nature sees,
Trees cut to statues, statues thick as trees,
With here a fountain, never to be played,
And there a summer-house, that knows no shade;
Here Amphitrite sails through myrtle bow'rs;
There gladiators fight, or die, in flow'rs;
Unwatered see the drooping sea-horse mourn,
And swallows roost in Nilus' dusty urn.
    My Lord advances with majestic mien,
Smit with the mighty pleasure to be seen: 30
But soft – by regular approach – not yet –
First through the length of yon hot terrace sweat,
And when up ten steep slopes you've dragged your thighs,
Just at his study-door he'll bless your eyes.

---

l.1 At Timon's Villa: This description is intended to comprize the principles of a false Taste of Magnificence, and to exemplify what was said
before, that nothing but Good Sense can attain it [Pope]. Timon is
almost certainly nobody in particular, a personification of aristocratic
pride; but many of the details of the grounds and house derive from
actual offences against taste committed by Pope's contemporaries. [Butt]

His study! with what authors is it stored?
In books, not authors, curious is my Lord;
To all their dated backs he turns you round;
These Aldus printed, those Du Sueïl has bound.
Lo, some are vellum, and the rest as good
For all his Lordship knows, but they are wood.   40
For Locke or Milton 'tis in vain to look,
These shelves admit not any modern book.
    And now the chapel's silver bell you hear,
That summons you to all the pride of pray'r:
Light quirks of music, broken and uneven,
Make the soul dance upon a jig to heaven.
On painted ceilings you devoutly stare,
Where sprawl the saints of Verrio or Laguerre,
On gilded clouds in fair expansion lie,
And bring all paradise before your eye.   50
To rest, the cushion and soft dean invite,
Who never mentions hell to ears polite.
    But hark! the chiming clocks to dinner call;
A hundred footsteps scrape the marble hall:
The rich buffet well-coloured serpents grace,
And gaping Tritons spew to wash your face.
Is this a dinner? this a genial room?
No, 'tis a temple, and a hecatomb.
A solemn sacrifice, performed in state,
You drink by measure, and to minutes eat.   60
So quick retires each flying course, you'd swear
Sancho's dread doctor and his wand were there.
Between each act the trembling salvers ring,

---

l.35 The false Taste in Books: a satyr on the vanity in collecting them, more frequent in men of Fortune than the study to understand them. Many delight chiefly in the elegance of the print, or of the binding; some have carried it so far, as to cause the upper shelves to be filled with painted books of wood; others pique themselves so much upon books in a language they do not understand as to exclude the most useful in one they do. [Pope]

l.38 Aldus: Aldo Manutio, the Renaissance Venetian printer; Du Sueïl: Abbé Du Sueïl, a famous Paris binder of the eighteenth century. [Butt]

l.48 Verrio or Laguerre: Verrio (Antonio) [1639–1707] painted many ceilings, etc., at Windsor, Hampton-court, etc., and Laguerre [1663–1721] at Blenheim-castle, and other places. [Pope]

l.52 This is a fact: a reverend Dean preaching at Court, threatened the sinner with punishment in 'a place which he thought it not decent to name in so polite an assembly'. [Pope] Knightly Chetwood (1650–1720), Dean of Gloucester. [Butt]

l.57 genial: of or pertaining to a feast (*OED*). [Butt]

l.62 See [Cervantes] *Don Quixote*, ch.47. [Pope]

From soup to sweet-wine, and God bless the King.
In plenty starving, tantalised in state,
And complaisantly helped to all I hate,
Treated, caressed, and tired, I take my leave,
Sick of his civil pride from morn to eve;
I curse such lavish cost, and little skill,
And swear no day was ever passed so ill.   70
   Yet hence the poor are clothed, the hungry fed;
Health to himself, and to his infants bread,
The lab'rer bears: what his hard heart denies,
His charitable vanity supplies.
   Another age shall see the golden ear
Imbrown the slope, and nod on the parterre,
Deep harvests bury all his pride has planned,
And laughing Ceres reassume the land.

Lady Mary Wortley Montagu (née Pierrepont) (1689–1762)

Verses Written in the Chiosk* of the British Palace, at Pera, Overlooking the City of Constantinople, Dec. 26, 1717**

(Wr. 1717; pub. 1720)

'GIVE me, great God!' said I, 'a little farm,
In summer shady, and in winter warm;
Where a clear spring gives birth to a cool brook,
By nature sliding down a mossy rock.
Not artfully in leaden pipes conveyed,
Nor greatly falling in a forced cascade,
Pure and unsullied winding through the shade.'
All-bounteous Heaven has added to my prayer
A softer climate and a purer air.

---

l.71 The *Moral* of the whole, where PROVIDENCE is justified in giving wealth to those who squander it in this manner. A bad Taste employs more hands and diffuses Expence more than a good one. [Pope]

l.76 slope: A technical term for the artificial banks used by landscape gardeners. [Butt]

l.78 laughing Ceres: The smiling scene that a cornfield exhibits. [Butt]

*Chiosk: summer-house. [Lonsdale]

**In 1716 her husband was appointed Ambassador to Turkey and in August she accompanied him on the long journey via Hanover, Vienna, and Belgrade, reaching Constantinople in May 1717. Her letters make clear her curiosity about all aspects of Turkish life, and she also studied the Turkish language and literature ... before her death, no doubt aware that her family would seek to prevent it, she arranged the posthumous publication of her 'Embassy Letters' in 1763, which were later frequently reprinted. [Lonsdale]

Our frozen isle now chilling winter binds,   10
Deformed with rains, and rough with blasting winds;
The withered woods grow white with hoary frost,
By driving storms their verdant beauty's lost;
The trembling birds their leafless covert shun,
And seek in distant climes a warmer sun:
The water-nymphs their silenced urns deplore,
Even Thames benumbed, a river now no more:
The barren meadows give no more delight,
By glistening snow made painful to the sight.
   Here summer reigns with one eternal smile,   20
And double harvests bless the happy soil;
Fair fertile fields, to whom indulgent Heaven
Has every charm of every season given.
No killing cold deforms the beauteous year,
The springing flowers no coming winter fear.
But as the parent rose decays and dies,
The infant buds with brighter colours rise,
And with fresh sweets the mother's scent supplies.
Near them the violet glows with odours blessed,
And blooms in more than Tyrian purple dressed;   30
The rich jonquils their golden beams display,
And shine in glory emulating day;
These cheerful groves their living leaves retain,
The streams still murmur undefiled by rain,
And rising green adorns the fruitful plain.
The warbling kind uninterrupted sing,
Warmed with enjoyments of perpetual spring.
   Here, from my window, I at once survey
The crowded city and resounding sea;
In distant views see Asian mountains rise,   40
And lose their snowy summits in the skies;
Above those mountains high Olympus towers,
The parliamental seat of heavenly powers!
New to the sight, my ravished eyes admire
Each gilded crescent and each antique spire,
The marble mosques, beneath whose ample domes
Fierce warlike sultans sleep in peaceful tombs;
Those lofty structures, once the Christian boast,
Their names, their glories, and their beauties lost;
Those altars bright with gold, with sculpture graced,   50
By barbarous zeal of savage foes defaced;
Sophia alone her ancient sound retains,
Though unbelieving vows her shrine profanes;
Where holy saints have died in sacred cells,
Where monarchs prayed, the frantic dervish dwells.
How art thou fallen, imperial city, low!
Where are thy hopes of Roman glory now?
Where are thy palaces by prelates raised?

---

l.30 Tyrian purple: (of) the crimson colour got from molluscs of genera
Theis, Purpura and *Murex* (*OED*). [eds]

Where priestly pomp in purple lustre blazed,
Where Grecian artists all their skill displayed,   60
Before the happy sciences decayed;
So vast, that youthful kings might there reside,
So splendid, to content a patriarch's pride;
Convents where emperors professed of old,
The laboured pillars that their triumphs told,
Vain monuments of men that once were great,
Sunk undistinguished in one common fate.
    One little spot the small Fanar contains,
Of Greek nobility the poor remains;
Where other Helens show like powerful charms   70
As once engaged the warring world in arms;
Those names which royal ancestry can boast,
In mean mechanic arts obscurely lost;
Those eyes a second Homer might inspire,
Fixed at the loom, destroy their useless fire.
    Grieved at a view, which struck upon my mind
The short-lived vanity of humankind,
In gaudy objects I indulge my sight,
And turn where eastern pomp gives gay delight;
See the vast train in various habits dressed,   80
By the bright scimitar and sable vest
The vizier proud distinguished o'er the rest;
Six slaves in gay attire his bridle hold,
His bridle rich with gems, his stirrups gold;
His snowy steed adorned with lavish pride,
Whole troops of soldiers mounted by his side;
These toss the plumy crest, Arabian coursers guide,
With awful duty all decline their eyes,
No bellowing shouts of noisy crowds arise;
Silence, in solemn state, the march attends,   90
Till at the dread divan the slow procession ends.
    Yet not these prospects, all profusely gay –
The gilded navy that adorns the sea,
The rising city in confusion fair,
Magnificently formed, irregular,
Where woods and palaces at once surprise,
Gardens on gardens, domes on domes arise,
And endless beauties tire the wandering eyes –
So soothes my wishes, or so charms my mind,
As this retreat, secure from humankind.   100
No knave's successful craft does spleen excite,
No coxcomb's tawdry splendour shocks my sight,
No mob-alarm awakes my female fears,

---

l.68 The Fanar or Phanar was the Greek quarter of Constaninople.
[Lonsdale]

l.82 vizier: a high state official in the Turkish Empire (*OED*). [eds]

l.91 divan: Oriental court of justice (*OED*). [eds]

No unrewarded merit asks my tears,
Nor praise my mind, no envy hurts my ear,
Even fame itself can hardly reach me here;
Impertinence, with all her tattling train,
Fair-sounding flattery's delicious bane;
Censorious folly, noisy party rage,
The thousand tongues with which she must engage,
Who dare have virtue in a vicious age.   110

The Lover: A Ballad

(Wr. *c.* 1721–5; pub. 1747)

AT length, by so much importunity pressed,
Take, Molly, at once, the inside of my breast;
This stupid indifference so often you blame
Is not owing to nature, to fear, or to shame:
I am not as cold as a virgin in lead,
Nor is Sunday's sermon so strong in my head:
I know but too well how time flies along,
That we live but few years, and yet fewer are young.

But I hate to be cheated, and never will buy
Long years of repentance for moments of joy.   10
Oh! was there a man (but where shall I find
Good sense and good nature so equally joined?)
Would value his pleasure, contribute to mine;
Not meanly would boast, nor lewdly design;
Not over severe, yet not stupidly vain,
For I would have the power, though not give the pain.

No pedant, yet learnèd; not rake-helly gay,
Or laughing, because he has nothing to say;
To all my whole sex obliging and free,
Yet never be fond of any but me;   20
In public, preserve the decorums are just,
And show in his eyes he is true to his trust;
Then rarely approach, and respectfully bow,
Yet not fulsomely pert, nor yet foppishly low.

But when the long hours of public are past,
And we meet with champagne and a chicken at last,
May every fond pleasure that hour endear;
Be banished afar both discretion and fear.
Forgetting or scorning the airs of the crowd,
He may cease to be formal, and I to be proud,   30
Till lost in the joy, we confess that we live,
And he may be rude, and yet I may forgive.

And that my delight may be solidly fixed,
Let the friend and the lover be handsomely mixed;
In whose tender bosom my soul might confide,
Whose kindness can soothe me, whose counsel could guide.

---

l.17 rake-helly: a thorough scoundrel or rascal (*OED*). [eds]

From such a dear lover, as here I describe,
No danger should fright me, no millions should bribe;
But till this astonishing creature I know,
As I long have lived chaste, I will keep myself so.   40

I never will share with the wanton coquette,
Or be caught by a vain affectation of wit.
The toasters and songsters may try all their art,
But never shall enter the pass of my heart.
I loathe the lewd rake, the dressed fopling despise:
Before such pursuers the nice virgin flies:
And as Ovid has sweetly in parables told,
We harden like trees, and like rivers are cold.

From *Verses Addressed to the Imitator of the First Satire of the Second Book of Horace**

[A Reply to Alexander Pope]

(1733)

   WHEN God created thee, one would believe
He said the same as to the snake of Eve:
'To human race antipathy declare,
'Twixt them and thee be everlasting war.'
But oh! the sequel of the sentence dread,
And whilst you bruise their heel, beware your head.
   Nor think thy weakness shall be thy defence,
The female scold's protection in offence.
Sure 'tis as fair to beat who cannot fight,
As 'tis to libel those who cannot write.   10
And if thou draw'st thy pen to aid the law,
Others a cudgel, or a rod, may draw.
   If none with vengeance yet thy crimes pursue,
Or give thy manifold affronts their due;
If limbs unbroken, skin without a stain,
Unwhipped, unblanketed, unkicked, unslain,
That wretched little carcase you retain,
The reason is, not that the world wants eyes,
But thou'rt so mean, they see, and they despise:
When fretful porcupine, with rancorous will,   20

---

ll.47–8 The reference is to the transformations of Baucis and Philemon (into trees) and Arethusa (into a fountain) in Ovid, *Metamorphoses*, Books 8 and 5. [eds]

*She [first] met and corresponded with Pope [in 1714]. ...By 1729, when he referred contemptuously to her in the *Dunciad*, her relations with Pope had seriously deteriorated, possibly because she had mockingly rejected a passionate declaration of love on his part some years earlier. [Lonsdale]

ll.3–4 allude to Genesis 3:15 and ll.58–9 to Genesis 4:15. Some lines from Pope himself are adapted: in lines 26–7, *Epistle to Burlington*, 107–8, and in 31–3, the *First Satire of the Second Book*, 118, 69, 79–80. [Lonsdale]

From mounted back shoots forth a harmless quill,
Cool the spectators stand; and all the while
Upon the angry little monster smile.
Thus 'tis with thee: – whilst impotently safe,
You strike unwounding, we unhurt can laugh.
'Who but must laugh, this bully when he sees,
A puny insect shivering at a breeze?'
One over-matched by every blast of wind,
Insulting and provoking all mankind.
  Is this the thing to keep mankind in awe,   30
'To make those tremble who escape the law?'
Is this the ridicule to live so long,
'The deathless satire and immortal song?'
No: like thy self-blown praise, thy scandal flies;
And, as we're told of wasps, it stings and dies.
  If none do yet return th' intended blow,
You all your safety to your dullness owe:
But whilst that armour thy poor corpse defends,
'Twill make thy readers few, as are thy friends:
Those, who thy nature loathed, yet loved thy art,   40
Who liked thy head, and yet abhorred thy heart:
Chose thee to read, but never to converse,
And scorned in prose him whom they prized in verse:
Even they shall now their partial error see,
Shall shun thy writings like thy company;
And to thy books shall ope their eyes no more
Than to thy person they would do their door.
  Nor thou the justice of the world disown,
That leaves thee thus an outcast and alone;
For though in law to murder be to kill,   50
In equity the murder's in the will:
Then whilst with coward-hand you stab a name,
And try at least t'assassinate our fame,
Like the first bold assassin's be thy lot,
Ne'er be thy guilt forgiven, or forgot;
But, as thou hat'st, be hated by mankind,
And with the emblem of thy crooked mind
Marked on thy back, like Cain, by God's own hand,
Wander, like him, accursèd through the land.

Stephen Duck (1705–56)

From *The Thresher's Labour*

(1730)

  Soon as the harvest hath laid bare the plains,
And barns well filled reward the farmer's pains,
What corn each sheaf will yield intent to hear,
And guess from thence the profits of the year,
Or else impending ruin to prevent
By paying, timely, threat'ning landlord's rent,
He calls his threshers forth: around we stand,

With deep attention waiting his command.
To each our tasks he readily divides,
And, pointing, to our different stations guides.   10
As he directs, to different barns we go;
Here two for wheat, and there for barley two.
But first, to show what he expects to find,
These words, or words like these, disclose his mind:
'So dry the corn was carried from the field,
So easily 'twill thresh, so well 'twill yield.
Sure large day's work I well may hope for now;
Come, strip, and try, let's see what you can do.'
Divested of our clothes, with flail in hand,
At a just distance, front to front we stand;   20
And first the threshall's gently swung, to prove
Whether with just exactness it will move:
That once secure, more quick we whirl them round,
From the strong planks our crabtree staves rebound,
And echoing barns return the rattling sound.
Now in the air our knotty weapons fly,
And now with equal force descend from high:
Down one, one up, so well they keep the time,
The Cyclops' hammers could not truer chime;
Nor with more heavy strokes could Etna groan,   30
When Vulcan forged the arms for Thetis' son.
In briny streams our sweat descends apace,
Drops from our locks, or trickles down our face.
No intermission in our works we know;
The noisy threshall must for ever go.
Their master absent, others safely play;
The sleeping threshall doth itself betray.
Nor yet the tedious labour to beguile,
And make the passing minutes sweetly smile,
Can we, like shepherds, tell a merry tale: 40
The voice is lost, drowned by the noisy flail.
But we may think. – Alas! what pleasing thing
Here to the mind can the dull fancy bring?
The eye beholds no pleasant object here:
No cheerful sound diverts the list'ning ear.
The shepherd well may tune his voice to sing,
Inspired by all the beauties of the spring:
No fountains murmur here, no lambkins play,
No linnets warble, and no fields look gay;
'Tis all a dull and melancholy scene,   50
Fit only to provoke the Muse's spleen.
When sooty pease we thresh, you scarce can know
Our native colour, as from work we go:
The sweat, and dust, and suffocating smoke
Make us so much like Ethiopians look,

---

l.21 threshall: flail. [Lonsdale]

l.31 Thetis' son: The Greek warrior Achilles. [eds]

Bathetic

We scare our wives, when evening brings us home,
And frighted infants think the bugbear come.
Week after week we this dull task pursue,
Unless when winnowing days produce a new,
A new indeed, but frequently a worse: 60
The threshall yields but to the master's curse.
He counts the bushels, counts how much a day,
Then swears we've idled half our time away.
'Why look ye, rogues! D'ye think that this will do?
Your neighbours thresh as much again as you.'
Now in our hands we wish our noisy tools,
To drown the hated names of rogues and fools;
But wanting those, we just like schoolboys look   *Simile*
When th' angry master views the blotted book.
They cry their ink was faulty, and their pen;   70
We, 'The corn threshes bad, 'twas cut too green.'

Jonathan Swift (1667–1745)

The Lady's Dressing Room

(Wr. 1730; pub. 1732)

Five hours, (and who can do it less in?)
By haughty Celia spent in dressing;
The goddess from her chamber issues,
Arrayed in lace, brocade and tissues:
Strephon, who found the room was void,
And Betty otherwise employed,
Stole in, and took a strict survey,
Of all the litter as it lay:
Whereof, to make the matter clear,
An *inventory* follows here.   10

    And first, a dirty smock appeared,
Beneath the arm-pits well besmeared;
Strephon, the rogue, displayed it wide,
And turned it round on every side.
In such a case few words are best,
And Strephon bids us guess the rest;
But swears how damnably the men lie,
In calling Celia sweet and cleanly.

    Now listen while he next produces,
The various combs for various uses,   20
Filled up with dirt so closely fixed,
No brush could force a way betwixt;
A paste of composition rare,
Sweat, dandruff, powder, lead and hair,
A forehead cloth with oil upon't
To smooth the wrinkles on her front;
Here alum flower to stop the steams,

1.27 alum flower: powdered form of the mineral. [Rogers]

Exhaled from sour unsavoury streams;
There night-gloves made of Tripsy's hide,
Bequeathed by Tripsy when she died;   30
With puppy water, beauty's help,
Distilled from Tripsy's darling whelp.
Here gallipots and vials placed,
Some filled with washes, some with paste;
Some with pomatum, paints and slops,
And ointments good for scabby chops.
Hard by a filthy basin stands,
Fouled with the scouring of her hands;
The basin takes whatever comes,
The scrapings of her teeth and gums,   40
A nasty compound of all hues,
For here she spits, and here she spews.

    But oh! it turned poor Strephon's bowels,
When he beheld and smelt the towels;
Begummed, bemattered, and beslimed;
With dirt, and sweat, and ear-wax grimed.
No object Strephon's eye escapes,
Here, petticoats in frowzy heaps;
Nor be the handkerchiefs forgot,
All varnished o'er with snuff and snot.   50
The stockings who should I expose,
Stained with the moisture of her toes;
Or greasy coifs and pinners reeking,
Which Celia slept at least a week in?
A pair of tweezers next he found
To pluck her brows in arches round,
Or hairs that sink the forehead low,
Or on her chin like bristles grow.

    The virtues we must not let pass,
Of Celia's magnifying glass;   60
When frighted Strephon cast his eye on't,
It showed the visage of a giant:
A glass that can to sight disclose
The smallest worm in Celia's nose,
And faithfully direct her nail
To squeeze it out from head to tail;
For catch it nicely by the head,
It must come out alive or dead.

    Why, Strephon, will you tell the rest?
And must you needs describe the chest?   70
That careless wench! no creature warn her
To move it out from yonder corner,
But leave it standing full in sight,
For you to exercise your spite!

---

l.33 gallipots: small pots used for ointments and medicines. [Rogers]

l.48 frowzy: unkempt, slatternly. [Rogers]

In vain the workman showed his wit
With rings and hinges counterfeit
To make it seem in this disguise,
A cabinet to vulgar eyes;
Which Strephon ventured to look in,
Resolved to go through *thick* and *thin*;   80
He lifts the lid: there need no more,
He smelt it all the time before.

    As, from within Pandora's box,
When Epimethus oped the locks,
A sudden universal crew
Of human evils upward flew;
He still was comforted to find
That hope at last remained behind.

    So, Strephon, lifting up the lid,
To view what in the chest was hid,   90
The vapours flew from out the vent,
But Strephon cautious never meant
The bottom of the pan to grope,
And foul his hands in search of hope.

    O! ne'er may such a vile machine
Be once in Celia's chamber seen!
O! may she better learn to keep
'Those secrets of the hoary deep.'

    As mutton cutlets, prime of meat,
Which though with art you salt and beat,   100
As laws of cookery require,
And roast them at the clearest fire;
If from adown the hopeful chops
The fat upon a cinder drops,
To stinking smoke it turns the flame
Poisoning the flesh from whence it came;
And up exhales a greasy stench,
For which you curse the careless wench:
So things which must not be expressed,
When *plumped* into the reeking chest,   110
Send up an excremental smell
To taint the parts from which they fell:
The petticoats and gown perfume,
And waft a stink round every room.

    Thus finished his grand survey,
The swain disgusted slunk away,
Repeating in his amorous fits,
'Oh! Celia, Celia, Celia shits!'

---

ll.83–8 Epimethus, the brother of Promethus, married Pandora and, against advice, opened the box given to her by Jove; all the evils that beset the world promptly flew out, hope alone remaining in the box. [Rogers]

But Vengeance, goddess never sleeping,
Soon punished Strephon for his peeping.   120
His foul imagination links
Each dame he sees with all her stinks:
And, if unsavoury odours fly,
Conceives a lady standing by:
All women his description fits,
And both ideas jump like wits,
By vicious fancy coupled fast,
And still appearing in contrast.

    I pity wretched Strephon, blind
To all the charms of womankind;   130
Should I the queen of love refuse,
Because she rose from stinking ooze?
To him that looks behind the scene,
Statira's but some pocky quean.

    When Celia in her glory shows,
If Strephon would but stop his nose,
Who now so impiously blasphemes
Her ointments, daubs, and paints and creams;
Her washes, slops, and every clout,
With which she makes so foul a rout;   140
He soon would learn to think like me,
And bless his ravished eyes to see
Such order from confusion sprung,
Such gaudy *tulips* raised from *dung*.

---

l.126 jump: match; alluding to a proverbial phrase 'good wits jump', meaning something like 'great minds think alike'. [Rogers]

l.128 contrast: almost entirely a term of artistic description at this date, used of one element set in relief against another. [Rogers]

l.131 the queen of love: Venus, who arose from the sea. [Rogers]

l.134 Statira: the heroine of Lee's *Rival Queens* (1677) jointly with Roxana. [Rogers]

l.139 washes: as in l.34, a liquid to improve the complexion. [Rogers]

'Miss W–'

The Gentleman's Study, In Answer to [Swift's]*
The Lady's Dressing-Room

(1732)

SOME write of angels, some of goddess,
But I of dirty human bodies,
And lowly I employ my pen,
To write of naught but odious men;
And man I think, without a jest,
More nasty than the nastiest beast.

   In house of office, when they're bare,
And have not paper then to spare,
Their hands they'll take, half clean their bottom
And daub the wall, O – rot 'em;   10
And in a minute, with a t–d,
They'll draw them out a beast or bird,
And write there without ink or pen:
When finger's dry, there's a–se again.
But now high time to tell my story;
But 'tis not much to all men's glory.

   A milliner, one Mrs. South,
I had the words from her own mouth,
That had a bill, which was long owing
By Strephon, for cloth, lace and sewing;   20
And on a day to's lodging goes,
In hopes of payment for the clothes,
And meeting there, and 'twas by chance,
His valet Tom, her old acquaintance,
Who, with an odd but friendly grin,
Told her his master's not within,
But bid her if she pleased to stay,
He'd treat her with a pot of tea;
So brought her to the study, while
He'd go and make the kettle boil.   30

   She sat her down upon the chair,
For that was all that then was there,
And turned her eyes on every side,
Where strange confusion she espied.

---

*In view of the many speculations about Swift's mental state when he wrote his scatological verse, it is of interest that an unidentified woman promptly replied to his *The Lady's Dressing Room* (1732), with a poem which is, if anything, even more disgusted and disgusting, however modest its literary merits. (Although its content is unexpected, there is no evidence, internal or external, that it is not by a woman.) *The Gentleman's Study* was published anonymously in 1732 ... The attribution to Miss W——— is found on the title-page of Samuel Shepherd's *Chloe Surpriz'd; Or, The Second Part of the Lady's Dressing-Room* (Dublin, 1732). [Lonsdale]

There on a block a wig was set,
Whose inside did so stink with sweat;
The outside oiled with jessamine,
T' disguise the stench that was within.

And next a shirt, with gussets red,
Which Strephon slept in, when in bed;   40
But modesty forbids the rest,
It shan't be spoke, but may be guessed;
A napkin worn [up]on a head,
Enough, infection to have bred.

For there some stocks lay on the ground,
One side was yellow, t'other brown;
And velvet breeches (on her word),
The inside all bedaubed with t–d,
And just before, I'll not desist
To let you know they were be-pissed: 50
Four different stinks lay there together,
Which were sweat, turd, and piss, and leather.

There in a heap lay nasty socks,
Here tangled stockings with silver clocks,
And towels stiff with soap and hair,
Of stinking shoes there lay a pair;
A nightgown, with gold rich-brocaded,
About the neck was sadly faded.

A close-stool helped to make the fume;
Tobacco-spits about the room,   60
With phlegm and vomit on the walls;
Here powder, dirt, combs and wash-balls;
Oil-bottles, paper, pens, and wax,
Dice, pamphlets, and of cards some packs;
Pig-tail and snuff, and dirty gloves,
Some plain, some fringed, which most he loves;
A curling-iron stands upright,
False locks and oil lay down close by't;
A drabbled cloak hung on a pin,
And basin furred with piss within;   70
Of pipes a heap, some whole, some broke,
Some cut-and-dry for him to smoke;
And papers that his a–se has cleaned,
And handkerchiefs with snuff all stained:
The sight and smells did make her sick,
She did not come to herself for a week.

A coat that lay upon the table,
To reach so far she scarce was able,
But drew it to her, resolved to try
What's in the pockets, by and by.   80

1.69 drabbled: muddied. [Lonsdale]

1.72 cut-and-dry: tobacco. [Lonsdale]

The first things that present her view
Were dunning-letters, not a few;
And then the next did make her wonder,
To see of tavern-bills such a number;
And a fine snuff-box there lay hid,
With bawdy picture in the lid,
And as she touched it, by the mass,
It turned, and showed a looking-glass.

The rest she found, since I'm a-telling,
Advertisements of land he's selling,   90
A syringe, and some dirty papers,
A bawdy-house screw, with box of wafers.

Then all the shelves she searched around,
Where not one book was to be found;
But gallipots all in a row,
And glistening vials, a fine show!

What one pot held she thinks was this:
Diaclom magnum cum gummis,
And spread there was with art, *secundum*
Unguentum neopolitanum;   100
Pots of pomatum, panacea,
Injections for a gonorrhea;
Of empty ones there were a score,
Of newly filled as many more.
In plenty too stood box of pills,
Nor did there lack for chirurgeon's bills,
Nor nasty rags all stiff with matter,
Nor bottle of mercurial water,
The use of which he does determine
To cure his itch, and kill his vermin: 110
'Oh heaven!' says she, 'what creature's man?
All stink without, and worse within!'

With that she rose and went away,
For there she could no longer stay;
And scarce she got in the bedchamber,
And thought herself there out of danger,
But quick she heard with both her ears
Strephon come swearing up the stairs;
She swiftly crept behind the screen,
In order not for to be seen.   120

---

l.82 dunning-letters: demands for payment of debts. [Lonsdale]

l.92 screw: bill(?). [Lonsdale]

l.92 wafers: seals. [Lonsdale]

l.95 gallipots: earthen pots used by apothecaries. [Lonsdale]

ll.97–110 These lines refer to remedies for venereal disease. [Lonsdale]

Then in came Strephon, lovely sight!
Who had not slept a wink all night;
He staggers in, he swears, he blows,
With eyes like fire, and snotty nose;
A mixture glazed his cheeks and chin
Of claret, snuff, and odious phlegm;
And servant with him, to undress him,
And loving Strephon so caressed him:
'Come hither, Tom, and kiss your master;
Oons, to my groin come put a plaster.'   130

Tom dexterously his part he played,
To touch his bubo's not afraid;
Nor need he then to hesitate,
But strewed on the precipitate;
Then, in a moment, all the room
Did with the smell of ulcer fume,
And would have lasted very long,
Had not sour belches smelled as strong,
Which from her nose did soon depart,
When overcome with stink of fart,   140
And after, then came thick upon it
The odious, nauseous one of vomit,
That pourèd out from mouth and nose
Both on his bed, and floor, and clothes;
Nor was it lessened e'er a bit,
Nor overcome, by stink of s–t,
Which, in the pot and round about
The brim and sides, he squirted out;
But when poor Tom pulled off his shoes,
There was a greater stink of toes,   150
And sure, a nasty, loathsome smell
Must come from feet as black as hell.

Then tossed in bed Tom left his Honour,
And went to call up Peggy Connor
To empty th' pot, and mop the room,
To bring up ashes and a broom,
And, after that, mostly pleasantly,
To keep his master company.
The prisoner now being suffocated,
And saw the door was wide dilated,   160
She thought high time to post away,
For it was ten o'clock i' th' day;
And, ere that she got out of doors,
He turns, farts, hiccups, groans and snores.

Ladies, you'll think 'tis admirable
That this to all men's applicable;
And though they dress in silk and gold,
Could you their insides but behold,
There you fraud, lies, deceit would see,

---

l.132 bubo: inflammation of the groin. [Lonsdale]

And pride, and base impiety.   170
So let them dress the best they can,
They still are fulsome, wretched Man.

Mary Collier (1690? – c. 1762)

From **The Woman's Labour. An Epistle to Mr Stephen Duck***

[The Washerwoman]

(1739)

WHEN bright Orion glitters in the skies
In winter nights, then early we must rise;
The weather ne'er so bad, wind, rain or snow,
Our work appointed, we must rise and go,
While you on easy beds may lie and sleep,
Till light does through your chamber-windows peep
When to the house we come where we should go,
How to get in, alas! we do not know:
The maid quite tired with work the day before,
O'ercome with sleep; we standing at the door,   10
Oppressed with cold, and often call in vain,
Ere to our work we can admittance gain.
But when from wind and weather we get in,
Briskly with courage we our work begin;
Heaps of fine linen we before us view,
Whereon to lay our strength and patience too;
Cambrics and muslins, which our ladies wear,
Laces and edgings, costly, fine and rare,
Which must be washed with utmost skill and care;
With holland shirts, ruffles and fringes too,   20
Fashions which our forefathers never knew,
For several hours here we work and slave,
Before we can one glimpse of daylight have;
We labour hard before the morning's past,
Because we fear the time runs on too fast.

At length bright Sol illuminates the skies,
And summons drowsy mortals to arise;
Then comes our mistress to us without fail,
And in her hand, perhaps, a mug of ale

---

*After her father's death in the 1720s, she moved to Petersfield in
Hampshire, 'where my chief Employment was, Washing, Brewing and
such labour, still devoting what leisure time I had to Books', when she
could buy or borrow them. After the appearance of Stephen Duck's
Poems on Several Occasions (1730), she composed a reply to his criticism of
the idleness of rural women in *The Thresher's Labour*, 'to vindicate the
injured Sex', and perhaps also with some hope of attracting aristocratic
patronage of the kind enjoyed by Duck … In 1762 she claimed that she
had made little profit from *The Woman's Labour*: it had been published
'at my own charge, I lost nothing, neither did I gain much, others ran
away with the profit'. [Lonsdale]

To cheer our hearts, and also to inform   30
Herself what work is done that very morn;
Lays her commands upon us, that we mind
Her linen well, nor leave the dirt behind.
Not this alone, but also to take care
We don't her cambrics nor her ruffles tear;
And these most strictly does of us require,
To save her soap and sparing be of fire;
Tells us her charge is great, nay furthermore,
Her clothes are fewer than the time before.
Now we drive on, resolved our strength to try,   40
And what we can we do most willingly;
Until with heat and work, 'tis often known,
Not only sweat but blood runs trickling down
Our wrists and fingers: still our work demands
The constant action of our labouring hands.

   Now night comes on, from whence you have relief,
But that, alas! does but increase our grief.
With heavy hearts we often view the sun,
Fearing he'll set before our work is done;
For, either in the morning or at night,   50
We piece the summer's day with candlelight.
Though we all day with care our work attend,
Such is our fate, we know not when 'twill end.
When evening's come, you homeward take your way;
We, till our work is done, are forced to stay,
And, after all our toil and labour past,
Sixpence or eightpence pays us off at last;
For all our pains no prospect can we see
Attend us, but old age and poverty.

James Thomson (1700–48)

From *The Seasons*

['Summer', ll.1401–66; first pub. 1730; revised edn 1746)[*]

Which way, Amanda, shall we bend our course?
The choice perplexes. Wherefore should we choose?
All is the same with thee. Say, shall we wind
Along the streams? or walk the smiling mead?
Or court the forest glades? or wander wild
Among the waving harvests? or ascend,
While radiant Summer opens all its pride,

---

[*]*Summer* was first published in a separate edition in 1727; the first collected edition of *The Seasons* was published in 1730. The text before you is that of the final revised edition of *The Seasons* published in 1746.

l.1 Amanda: Elizabeth Young who had refused T.'s proposal of marriage in 1743. [Sambrook]

Thy hill, delightful Shene? Here let us sweep
The boundless landscape; now the raptured eye,
Exulting swift, to huge Augusta send,   10
Now to the sister hills that skirt her plain,
To lofty Harrow now, and now to where
Majestic Windsor lifts his princely brow.
In lovely contrast to this glorious view,
Calmly magnificent, then will we turn
To where the silver Thames first rural grows.
There let the feasted eye unwearied stray;
Luxurious, there, rove through the pendent woods
That nodding hang o'er Harrington's retreat;
And, stooping thence to Ham's embowering walks,   20
Beneath whose shades, in spotless peace retired,
With her the pleasing partner of his heart,
The worthy Queensberry yet laments his Gay,
And polished Cornbury woos the willing muse,
Slow let us trace the matchless vale of Thames;
Fair-winding up to where the muses haunt
In Twit'nam's bowers, and for their Pope implore
The healing god; to royal Hampton's pile,

---

l.8 Shene: The old name of Richmond, signifying in Saxon shining or splendour. [Thomson] Richmond Hill commanded one of the eighteenth century's most praised views; after 1736 it was T.'s home. [Sambrook]

l.10 Augusta: Augusta Trinobantum, a Roman name for London. [Sambrook]

l.11 the sister hills: Highgate and Hampstead. [Thomson]

l.14 contrast: juxtaposition of forms, colours, etc., as in painting. [Sambrook]

ll.18–24 'Harrington's retreat' (l.19) was Petersham Lodge built in the 1720s for William Stanhope, Earl of Harrington. The 'pendent woods' (l.18) belonged to one of the earliest English landscape gardens, laid out before 1713 by an earlier possessor of the estate – Henry Hyde, Earl of Rochester. Hyde's second daughter, Kitty, was the famous beauty and eccentric who married Charles Douglas (1698–1778), third Duke of Queensberry (referred to at l.23). John Gay the poet lived with the Queensberrys at Ham House (cf. l.20), near Twickenham for the last four years of his life. The Duchess also befriended Congreve, Swift, Prior, Pope, and T. Hyde's eldest son was Henry, Viscount Cornbury (1710–53 – referred to at l.24), a High Church Tory MP, author and friend of Bolingbroke, Pope, Swift, and T. The brilliant Ham House circle was a centre of opposition to Walpole and George II. [Sambrook]

l.27 Twit'nam's: Alexander Pope had laid out a famous garden at his house at Twickenham. He fell fatally ill early in 1744, shortly before T. wrote these lines, and died 30 May. [Sambrook]

To Clermont's terraced height, and Esher's groves,
Where in the sweetest solitude, embraced   30
By the soft windings of the silent Mole,
From courts and senates Pelham finds repose.
Enchanting vale! Beyond whate'er the muse
Has of Achaia or Hesperia sung!
O vale of bliss! O softly-swelling hills!
On which the Power of Cultivation lies,
And joys to see the wonders of his toil.
   Heavens! what a goodly prospect spreads around,
Of hills, and dales, and woods, and lawns, and spires,
And glittering towns, and gilded streams, till all   40
The stretching landscape into smoke decays!
Happy Britannia! where the Queen of Arts,
Inspiring vigour, Liberty, abroad
Walks unconfined even to thy farthest cots,
And scatters plenty with unsparing hand.
   Rich is thy soil, and merciful thy clime;
Thy streams unfailing in the Summer's drought;
Unmatched thy guardian-oaks; thy valleys float
With golden waves; and on thy mountains flocks
Bleat numberless; while, roving round their sides,   50
Bellow the blackening herds in lusty droves.
Beneath, thy meadows glow, and rise unquelled
Against the mower's scythe. On every hand
Thy villas shine. Thy country teems with wealth;
And Property assures it to the swain,
Pleased and unwearied in his guarded toil.
   Full are thy cities with the sons of art;
And trade and joy, in every busy street,
Mingling are heard: even Drudgery himself,

---

ll.29–32 Henry Pelham (1696–1754), the Whig politician, was Secretary at War, Paymaster-General, and, from 1743 to his death, Prime Minister. His estate, Claremont (cf. l.29) at Esher on the River Mole in Surrey had one of the most famous landscape gardens of the eighteenth century – laid out by Charles Bridgeman and Vanbrugh before 1726 and later remodelled by William Kent (illustrator of the 1730 edition of *The Seasons*). [Sambrook]

l.34 Achaia: the Roman province of southern Greece. [Sambrook]

l.34 Hesperia: 'western land'; the Greek name for Italy and the Roman name for Spain. T. means Italy. [Sambrook]

l.41 smoke: blue haze (as in a Claude Lorrain landscape painting). [Sambrook]

l.42 Here begins a patriotic panegyric highly characteristic of the eighteenth-century English georgic; the model is Virgil's praise of fruitful, prosperous Italy – the nurse of great men – cf. Georgics II.138–76. British Liberty the Queen of Arts scattering plenty – with the assistance of Property (l.55) and gay Drudgery (l.59) – is the political counterpart to nature, whose liberality is referred to [earlier in the poem]. [Sambrook]

As at the car he sweats, or, dusty, hews   60
The palace stone, looks gay. Thy crowded ports,
Where rising masts an endless prospect yield,
With labour burn, and echo to the shouts
Of hurried sailor, as he hearty waves
His last adieu, and, loosening every sheet,
Resigns the spreading vessel to the wind.

Mary Leapor * (1722–46)

Man the Monarch

(Wr. by 1746; pub. 1751)

AMAZED we read of Nature's early throes,
How the fair heavens and ponderous earth arose;
How blooming trees unplanted first began;
And beasts submissive to their tyrant, man:
To man, invested with despotic sway,
While his mute brethren tremble and obey;
Till heaven beheld him insolently vain,
And checked the limits of his haughty reign.
Then from their lord the rude deserters fly,
And, grinning back, his fruitless rage defy;   10
Pards, tigers, wolves to gloomy shades retire,
And mountain-goats in purer gales respire.
To humble valleys, where soft flowers blow,
And fattening streams in chrystal mazes flow,
Full of new life, the untamed coursers run,
And roll and wanton in the cheerful sun;
Round their gay hearts in dancing spirits rise,
And rouse the lightnings in their rolling eyes:
To craggy rocks destructive serpents glide,
Whose mossy crannies hide their speckled pride;   20
And monstrous whales on foamy billows ride.
Then joyful birds ascend their native sky:
But where! ah, where shall helpless woman fly?

---

l.65 sheet: sail. [Sambrook]

*She learned to read at an early age, and to write by the time she was 10
or 11, but her mother discouraged her early attempts at poetry. After
Anne Leapor's death in about 1742, she kept house for her father, but
spent her leisure in writing or reading, her neighbours fearing that she
would 'overstudy herself, and be mopish' … Her verse circulated locally
and eventually attracted the attention of Bridget Fremantle ('Artemisia'), the daughter of a former Rector of Hinton, who was impressed
by Leapor's writing and character … Miss Fremantle, assisted by a local
gentleman, began to organize a subscription for her, and her play and
samples of her verse were sent to London for advice … Although her
play was not accepted in London, the plan of publishing her poems
would presumably have gone ahead, had she not died of measles …
[Lonsdale]

l.11 Pards: leopards. [eds]

Here smiling Nature brought her choicest stores,
And roseate beauty on her favourite pours:
Pleased with her labour, the officious dame
Withheld no grace would deck the rising frame.
Then viewed her work, and viewed and smiled again,
And kindly whispered, 'Daughter, live and reign.'
But now the matron mourns her latest care,   30
And sees the sorrows of her darling fair;
Beholds a wretch, whom she designed a queen,
And weeps that e'er she formed the weak machine.
In vain she boasts her lip of scarlet dyes,
Cheeks like the morning, and far-beaming eyes;
Her neck refulgent, fair and feeble arms –
A set of useless and neglected charms.
She suffers hardship with afflictive moans:
Small tasks of labour suit her slender bones.
Beneath a load her weary shoulders yield,   40
Nor can her fingers grasp the sounding shield;
She sees and trembles at approaching harms,
And fear and grief destroy her fading charms.
Then her pale lips no pearly teeth disclose,
And time's rude sickle cuts the yielding rose.
Thus wretched woman's shortlived merit dies:
In vain to Wisdom's sacred help she flies,
Or sparkling Wit but lends a feeble aid:
'Tis all delirium from a wrinkled maid.

A tattling dame, no matter where or who –   50
Me it concerns not, and it need not you –
Once told this story to the listening Muse,
Which we, as now it serves our turn, shall use.

When our grandsire named the feathered kind,
Pondering their natures in his careful mind,
'Twas then, if on our author we rely,
He viewed his consort with an envious eye;
Greedy of power, he hugged the tottering throne,
Pleased with the homage, and would reign alone;
And, better to secure his doubtful rule,   60
Rolled his wise eyeballs, and pronounced her *fool*.
The regal blood to distant ages runs:
Sires, brothers, husbands, and commanding sons,
The sceptre claim; and every cottage brings
A long succession of domestic kings.

---

l.36 refulgent: shining. [eds]

l.54 grandsire: [i.e. Adam (cf. Genesis 2:19 – eds]. Mrs Leapor frequently
writes the Words *Sire, Fire, Spire, Hour,* &c. each as if two Syllables.
[original edition]

From *An Epistle to Artemisia*

['The Patrons of my early Song'] *

(Wr. by 1746; pub. 1751)

ONCE Delpho read – sage Delpho, learned and wise,
O'er the scrawled paper cast his judging eyes,
Whose lifted brows confessed a critic's pride,
While his broad thumb moved nimbly down the side.
His form was like some oracle profound:
The listening audience formed a circle round.
But Mira, fixing her presuming eyes
On the stern image, thus impatient cries:
'Sir, will they prosper? – Speak your judgement, pray.'
Replies the statue – 'Why, perhaps they may.'   10
For further answers we in vain implore:
The charm was over, and it spoke no more.

Cressida comes, the next unbidden guest:
Small was her top-knot, and her judgement less;
A decent virgin, blessed with idle time,
Now jingles bobbins, and now ponders rhyme:
Not ponders – reads; not reads – but looks 'em o'er
To little purpose, like a thousand more.

'Your servant, Molly.'
                        'I am yours the same.'
'I pay this visit, Molly, to your fame: 20
'Twas that that brought me here, or let me die.'
'My fame's obliged: and truly so am I.'
'Then fetch me something, for I must not stay
Above four hours.'
                        'But you'll drink some tea?'
We sip and read; we laugh and chat between.
'The air is pleasant, and the fields are green.
Well, Molly, sure, there never was thy fellow.
But don't my ruffles look exceeding yellow?
My apron's dirty – Mira, well, I vow
That thought of yours was very pretty now.   30
I've read the like, though I forget the place:
But, Mrs. Mira, how d'ye like my lace?'

Afflicted Mira, with a languid eye,
Now views the clock, and now the western sky:
'The sun grows lower: will you please to walk?'
'No; read some more.'
                        'But I had rather talk.'

---

*The subtitle, quoted from an earlier passage of the poem, suggests a consciously ironic contrast on her part with Pope's tribute to his literary mentors in *Epistle to Dr Arbuthnot*, lines 135–46. [Lonsdale]

l.14 top-knot: A knot or bow of ribbon worn on the top of the head (*OED*). [eds]

'Perhaps you're tired.'
                  'Truly, that may be.'
'Or think me weak.'
                  'Why, Cressy, thoughts are free.'
At last we part, with congees at the door:
'I'd thank you, Mira; but my thanks are poor.   40
I wish, alas! but wishes are in vain.
I like your garden; and I'll come again.
Dear, how I wish! – I do, or let me die,
That we lived near.'
             Thinks Mira, 'So don't I.'

This nymph, perhaps, as some had done before,
Found the cold welcome, and returned no more.

Then Vido next to Mira's cot appears,
And with some praise salutes her listening ears;
Whose maxim was, with truth not to offend,
And, right or wrong, his business to commend.   50
'Look here,' cries Mira, 'pray peruse this song:
Even I, its parent, see there's something wrong.'
'But you mistake: 'tis excellent indeed.'
'Then I'll correct it.'
            'No, there is no need.'
'Pray, Vido, look on these. Methinks they smell
Too much of Grub Street: that myself can tell.'
'Not so, indeed; they're easy and polite.'
'And can you bear 'em?'
              'I could read till night.'
But Mira, though too partial to the bays,
And, like her brethen, not averse to praise,   60
Had learned this lesson: praise, if planted wrong,
Is more destructive than a spiteful tongue.

Comes Codrus next, with talents to offend,
A simple tutor, and a saucy friend,
Who poured thick sonnets like a troubled spring,
And such as Butler's wide-mouthed mortals sing:
In shocking rhymes a nymph's perfections tells,
Like the harsh ting-tong of some village-bells.
Then a rude quarrel sings through either ear,
And Mira's levee once again is clear.   70

1.39 congees: farewells. [Lonsdale]

1.59 bays: leaves or sprigs of bay-tree woven into a wreath or garland to reward a poet; hence *fig.* the fame and repute attained by these. (*OED*). [eds]

1.66 This line alludes to Samuel Butler['s satire], *Hudibras*, II. iii. 383–4; 'His *Sonnets* charm'd th' attentive Crowd, By wide-mouth'd Mortal trol'd aloud.' [Lonsdale]

1.70 levee: reception of visitors on rising from bed. (*OED*). [eds]

Now the dull Muses took their usual rest;
The babes slept soundly in their tiny chest.
Not so their parent: fortune still would send
Some proud director, or ill-meaning friend:
At least we thought their sour meanings ill,
Whose lectures strove to cross a stubborn will.

Parthenia cries, 'Why, Mira, you are dull,
And ever musing, till you crack your skull;
Still poking o'er your what-d'ye-call – your Muse:
But prithee, Mira, when dost clean thy shoes?'   80

Then comes Sophronia, like a barbarous Turk:
'You thoughtless baggage, when d'ye mind your work?
Still o'er a table leans your bending neck:
Your head will grow preposterous, like a peck.
Go, ply your needle: you might earn your bread:
Or who must feed you when your father's dead?'
She sobbing answers, 'Sure, I need not come
To you for lectures: I have store at home.
What can I do?'
                    – 'Not scribble.'
                                        – 'But I will.'
'Then get thee packing – and be awkward still.'   90

Thus wrapped in sorrow, wretched Mira lay,
Till Artemisia swept the gloom away:
The laughing Muse, by her example led,
Shakes her glad wings, and quits the drowsy bed.

An Essay on Woman

(Wr. by 1746; pub. 1751)

WOMAN, a pleasing but a short-lived flower,
Too soft for business and too weak for power:
A wife in bondage, or neglected maid;
Despised, if ugly; if she's fair, betrayed.
'Tis wealth alone inspires every grace,
And calls the raptures to her plenteous face.
What numbers for those charming features pine,
If blooming acres round her temples twine!
Her lip the strawberry, and her eyes more bright
Than sparkling Venus in a frosty night;   10
Pale lilies fade and, when the fair appears,
Snow turns a negro and dissolves in tears,
And, where the charmer treads her magic toe,
On English ground Arabian odours grow;
Till mighty Hymen lifts his sceptred rod,
And sinks her glories with a fatal nod,
Dissolves her triumphs, sweeps her charms away,
And turns the goddess to her native clay.

---

l.72 The babes: her poems [original edition]

l.84 peck: a scythe (dialect) or peck measure. [Lonsdale]

But, Artemisia, let your servant sing
What small advantage wealth and beauties bring.   20
Who would be wise, that knew Pamphilia's fate?
Or who be fair, and joined to Sylvia's mate?
Sylvia, whose cheeks are fresh as early day,
As evening mild, and sweet as spicy May:
And yet that face her partial husband tires,
And those bright eyes, that all the world admires.
Pamphilia's wit who does not strive to shun,
Like death's infection or a dog-day's sun?
The damsels view her with malignant eyes,
The men are vexed to find a nymph so wise: 30
And wisdom only serves to make her know
The keen sensation of superior woe.
The secret whisper and the listening ear,
The scornful eyebrow and the hated sneer,
The giddy censures of her babbling kind,
With thousands ills that grate a gentle mind,
By her are tasted in the first degree,
Though overlooked by Simplicus and me.
Does thirst of gold a virgin's heart inspire,
Instilled by nature or a careful sire?   40
Then let her quit extravagance and play,
The brisk companion and expensive tea,
To feast with Cordia in her filthy sty
On stewed potatoes or on mouldy pie;
Whose eager eyes stare ghastly at the poor,
And fright the beggars from her hated door;
In greasy clouts she wraps her smoky chin,
And holds that pride's a never-pardoned sin.

If this be wealth, no matter where it falls;
But save, ye Muses, save your Mira's walls: 50
Still give me pleasing indolence and ease,
A fire to warm me and a friend to please.

Since, whether sunk in avarice or pride,
A wanton virgin or a starving bride,
Or wondering crowds attend her charming tongue,
Or, deemed an idiot, ever speaks the wrong;
Though nature armed us for the growing ill
With fraudful cunning and a headstrong will;
Yet, with ten thousand follies to her charge,
Unhappy woman's but a slave at large.   60

1.47 clouts: pieces of cloth (*OED*). [eds]

Thomas Gray (1716–71)

Elegy Written in a Country Churchyard

(Wr. 1746?–50; pub. 1751)

THE curfew tolls the knell of parting day,
The lowing herd wind slowly o'er the lea,
The ploughman homeward plods his weary way,
And leaves the world to darkness and to me.

Now fades the glimmering landscape on the sight,
And all the air a solemn stillness holds,
Save where the beetle wheels his droning flight,
And drowsy tinklings lull the distant folds;

Save that from yonder ivy-mantled tow'r
The moping owl does to the moon complain   10
Of such as, wand'ring near the secret bow'r,
Molest her ancient solitary reign.

Beneath those rugged elms, that yew-tree's shade,
Where heaves the turf in many a mould'ring heap,
Each in his narrow cell for ever laid,
The rude forefathers of the hamlet sleep.

The breezy call of incense-breathing morn,
The swallow twitt'ring from the straw-built shed,
The cock's shrill clarion or the echoing horn,
No more shall rouse them from their lowly bed.   20

For them no more the blazing hearth shall burn,
Or busy housewife ply her evening care:
No children run to lisp their sire's return,
Or climb his knees the envied kiss to share.

Oft did the harvest to their sickle yield,
Their furrow oft the stubborn glebe has broke;
How jocund did they drive their team afield!
How bowed the woods beneath their sturdy stroke!

Let not Ambition mock their useful toil,
Their homely joys and destiny obscure;   30
Nor Grandeur hear, with a disdainful smile,
The short and simple annals of the poor.

The boast of heraldry, the pomp of pow'r,
And all that beauty, all that wealth e'er gave,
Awaits alike the inevitable hour.
The paths of glory lead but to the grave.

Nor you, ye Proud, impute to these the fault,
If Mem'ry o'er their tomb no trophies raise,
Where through the long-drawn aisle and fretted vault
The pealing anthem swells the note of praise.   40

Can storied urn or animated bust
Back to its mansion call the fleeting breath?
Can Honour's voice provoke the silent dust,
Or Flatt'ry soothe the dull cold ear of Death?

Perhaps in this neglected spot is laid
Some heart once pregnant with celestial fire;
Hands that the rod of empire might have swayed,
Or waked to ecstasy the living lyre.

But Knowledge to their eyes her ample page
Rich with the spoils of time did ne'er unroll;   50
Chill Penury repressed their noble rage,
And froze the genial current of the soul.

Full many a gem of purest ray serene
The dark unfathomed caves of ocean bear:
Full many a flower is born to blush unseen
And waste its sweetness on the desert air.

Some village-Hampden that with dauntless breast
The little tyrant of his fields withstood;
Some mute inglorious Milton here may rest,
Some Cromwell guiltless of his country's blood.   60

Th' applause of list'ning senates to command,
The threats of pain and ruin to despise,
To scatter plenty o'er a smiling land,
And read their hist'ry in a nation's eyes,

Their lot forbade: nor circumscribed alone
Their growing virtues, but their crimes confined;
Forbade to wade through slaughter to a throne,
And shut the gates of mercy on mankind,

---

l.43 provoke: The sense is 'to arouse to action, call forth'. [Lonsdale 1969]

l.57 Hampden: John Hampden (1594–1643), a Buckinghamshire squire who in 1637 refused to pay 'ship-money', i.e. the levy on property imposed by Charles I in order to raise money for the building and support of the fleet. Hampden's trial publicised the illegality of Charles' attempt to impose a tax without Parliamentary approval. [Johnston]

The struggling pangs of conscious truth to hide,
To quench the blushes of ingenuous shame,   70
Or heap the shrine of Luxury and Pride
With incense kindled at the Muse's flame.

Far from the madding crowd's ignoble strife
Their sober wishes never learned to stray;
Along the cool sequestered vale of life
They kept the noiseless tenor of their way.

Yet ev'n these bones from insult to protect
Some frail memorial still erected nigh,
With uncouth rhymes and shapeless sculpture decked,
Implores the passing tribute of a sigh.   80

Their name, their years, spelt by th' unlettered muse,
The place of fame and elegy supply:
And many a holy text around she strews,
That teach the rustic moralist to die.

For who to dumb Forgetfulness a prey,
This pleasing anxious being e'er resigned,
Left the warm precincts of the cheerful day,
Nor cast one longing ling'ring look behind?

---

l.72 In the MS [The Eton Manuscript, entitled 'Stanza's Wrote in a Country Church-Yard'], preserved at Eton College, [which] clearly contains the earliest surviving version of the *Elegy*, [the following four] stanzas represent the original ending of the poem, and the evidence suggests that there was an interval of indefinite length before Gray returned to the poem, either omitting these stanzas or reworking them in his continuation.

> The thoughtless World to Majesty may bow
> Exalt the brave, idolize Success
> But more to Innocence their Safety owe
> Than Power and Genius e'er conspired to bless
>
> And thou, who mindful of the unhonour'd Dead
> Dost in these Notes their artless Tale relate
> By Night and lonely Contemplation led
> To linger in the gloomy Walks of Fate
>
> Hark how the sacred Calm, that broods around
> Bids ev'ry fierce tumultuous Passion cease
> In still small Accents whisp'ring from the Ground
> A grateful Earnest of eternal Peace
>
> No more with Reason thyself at Strife
> Give anxious Cares and endless Wishes room
> But thro' the cool sequester'd Vale of Life
> Pursue the silent Tenour of thy Doom.

[Lonsdale 1977]

l.85 For: 'For who, about to become a prey to dumb Forgetfulness (= oblivion).' [Lonsdale 1969].

l.86 This pleasing anxious being: life, which is a mixture of pleasure and distress. [Johnston]

On some fond breast the parting soul relies,
Some pious drops the closing eye requires;   90
Ev'n from the tomb the voice of Nature cries,
Ev'n in our ashes live their wonted fires.

For thee who, mindful of th' unhonoured dead,
Dost in these lines their artless tale relate;
If chance, by lonely Contemplation led,
Some kindred spirit shall inquire thy fate,

Haply some hoary-headed swain may say,
'Oft have we seen him at the peep of dawn
Brushing with hasty steps the dews away
To meet the sun upon the upland lawn.   100

'There at the foot of yonder nodding beech
That wreathes its old fantastic roots so high,
His listless length at noontide would he stretch,
And pore upon the brook that babbles by.

'Hard by yon wood, now smiling as in scorn,
Muttering his wayward fancies he would rove,
Now drooping, woeful wan, like one forlorn,
Or crazed with care, or crossed in hopeless love.

'One morn I missed him on the customed hill,
Along the heath and near his fav'rite tree;   110
Another came; nor yet beside the rill,
Nor up the lawn, nor at the wood was he;

'The next with dirges due in sad array
Slow through the church-way path we saw him borne.
Approach and read (for thou canst read) the lay,
Graved on the stone beneath yon aged thorn.'

THE EPITAPH

Here rests his head upon the lap of earth
A youth to fortune and to fame unknown.
Fair Science frowned not on his humble birth,
And Melancholy marked him for her own.   120

---

l.95 If chance: if by chance or if it should chance that. [Lonsdale 1969]

l.119 Science: Knowledge or learning in general. [Lonsdale 1969]

l.120 Melancholy: The meaning of this word is crucial to the 'Epitaph'. G. does not mean simply that the poet has been made melancholy (= gloomy) because his education made him aware of abilities which he has been unable to fulfil; if that had been the case the 'And' of this line would have logically been a 'But'. The favourite sense of 'melancholy', implying a valuable kind of sensibility, though not found in Johnson's *Dictionary*, was becoming fashionable at this time. The heightened sensibility of the melancholy man ideally expresses itself in benevolence and other social virtues, rather than merely in solitary wandering, although that usually precedes it ... Thus the melancholy which marks the young man explains not merely his solitary wanderings and sad wisdom about life, but the social virtues described in the next stanza. [Lonsdale 1969]

Large was his bounty and his soul sincere,
Heaven did a recompense as largely send:
He gave to Mis'ry all he had, a tear,
He gained from heav'n ('twas all he wished) a friend.

No farther seek his merits to disclose,
Or draw his frailties from their dread abode
(There they alike in trembling hope repose),
The bosom of his Father and his God.

James Macpherson (1736–96)

From *Fragments of Ancient Poetry*[*] (1760)

AUTUMN is dark on the mountains; grey mist rests on the hills.
The whirlwind is heard on the heath. Dark rolls the river
through the narrow plain. A tree stands alone on the hill, and
marks the grave of Connal. The leaves whirl round with the
wind, and strew the grave of the dead. At times are seen here the
ghosts of the deceased, when the musing hunter alone stalks
slowly over the heath.

WHO can reach the source of thy race, O Connal? and who
recount thy fathers? Thy family grew like an oak on the mountain, which meeteth the wind with its lofty head. But now it is
torn from the earth. Who shall supply the place of Connal?

HERE was the din of arms; and here the groans of the dying.
Mournful are the wars of Fingal! O Connal! it was here thou
didst fall. Thine arm was like a storm; thy sword, a beam of the
sky; thy height, a rock on the plain; thine eyes, a furnace of fire.
Louder than a storm was thy voice, when thou confoundedst the
field. Warriors fell by thy sword, as the thistle by the staff of a
boy.

DARGO the mighty came on, like a cloud of thunder. His brows
were contracted and dark. His eyes like two caves in a rock.
Bright rose their swords on each side; dire was the clang of their
steel.

THE daughter of Rinval was near; Crimora, bright in the
armour of man; her hair loose behind, her bow in her hand. She
followed the youth to the war, Connal her much-beloved. She
drew the string on Dargo; but erring pierced her Connal. He
falls like an oak on the plain; like a rock from the shaggy hill.
What shall she do, hapless maid! – He bleeds; her Connal dies.
All the night long she cries, and all the day, O Connal, my love,
and my friend! With grief the sad mourner died.

---

[*]This is the fifth of sixteen *Fragments of Ancient Poetry Collected in the Highlands of Scotland And Translated From the Galic or Erse Language*, published
by Macpherson in 1760, before he unveiled *Fingal* (1761), the epic which
he attributed to the ancient Gaelic warrior-bard Ossian. Though set out
as prose, it was accepted by a contemporary audience as 'poetry'. [eds]

EARTH here incloseth the loveliest pair on the hill. The grass grows between the stones of their tomb; I sit in the mournful shade. The wind sighs through the grass; and their memory rushes on my mind. Undisturbed you now sleep together; in the tomb of the mountain you rest alone.

Oliver Goldsmith (1730?–74)

The Deserted Village

(1770)

SWEET Auburn, loveliest village of the plain,
Where health and plenty cheered the labouring swain,
Where smiling spring its earliest visit paid,
And parting summer's lingering blooms delayed:
Dear lovely bowers of innocence and ease,
Seats of my youth, when every sport could please,
How often have I loitered o'er thy green,
Where humble happiness endeared each scene;
How often have I paused on every charm,
The sheltered cot, the cultivated farm,   10
The never-failing brook, the busy mill,
The decent church that topped the neighbouring hill,
The hawthorn bush, with seats beneath the shade,
For talking age and whispering lovers made.
How often have I blessed the coming day,
When toil remitting lent its turn to play,
And all the village train, from labour free,
Led up their sports beneath the spreading tree,
While many a pastime circled in the shade,
The young contending as the old surveyed;   20
And many a gambol frolicked o'er the ground,
And sleights of art and feats of strength went round.
And still as each repeated pleasure tired,
Succeeding sports the mirthful band inspired;
The dancing pair that simply sought renown,
By holding out to tire each other down;
The swain mistrustless of his smutted face,
While secret laughter tittered round the place;
The bashful virgin's sidelong looks of love,
The matron's glance that would those looks reprove.   30
These were thy charms, sweet village; sports like these,
With sweet succession, taught even toil to please;
These round thy bowers their cheerful influence shed,
These were thy charms – but all these charms are fled.

---

l.18 Led up: Led off, began. [Lonsdale, 1969]

l.25 simply: naïvely (rather than *merely*). [Lonsdale 1969]

Sweet smiling village, loveliest of the lawn,
Thy sports are fled and all thy charms withdrawn;
Amidst thy bowers the tyrant's hand is seen,
And desolation saddens all thy green:
One only master grasps the whole domain,
And half a tillage stints thy smiling plain: 40
No more thy glassy brook reflects the day,
But, choked with sedges, works its weedy way.
Along thy glades, a solitary guest,
The hollow-sounding bittern guards its nest;
Amidst thy desert walks the lapwing flies,
And tires their echoes with unvaried cries.
Sunk are thy bowers in shapeless ruin all,
And the long grass o'ertops the mouldering wall;
And trembling, shrinking from the spoiler's hand,
Far, far away, thy children leave the land.   50
    Ill fares the land, to hastening ills a prey,
Where wealth accumulates and men decay:
Princes and lords may flourish or may fade;
A breath can make them, as a breath has made;
But a bold peasantry, their country's pride,
When once destroyed, can never be supplied.
    A time there was, ere England's griefs began,
When every rood of ground maintained its man;
For him light labour spread her wholesome store,
Just gave what life required, but gave no more: 60
His best companions, innocence and health;
And his best riches, ignorance of wealth.
    But times are altered; trade's unfeeling train
Usurp the land and dispossess the swain;
Along the lawn, where scattered hamlets rose,
Unwieldy wealth and cumbrous pomp repose;
And every want to opulence allied,
And every pang that folly pays to pride.
These gentle hours that plenty bade to bloom,
Those calm desires that asked but little room,   70
Those healthful sports that graced the peaceful scene,
Lived in each look and brightened all the green;
These, far departing, seek a kinder shore,
And rural mirth and manners are no more.
    Sweet Auburn! parent of the blissful hour,
Thy glades forlorn confess the tyrant's power.
Here as I take my solitary rounds,
Amidst thy tangling walks and ruined grounds,
And, many a year elapsed, return to view
Where once the cottage stood, the hawthorn grew,   80

---

l.40 tillage: tilled or ploughed land, as distinct from pasturage. [Lonsdale 1969]

l.74 manners: customs. [Lonsdale 1969]

Remembrance wakes with all her busy train,
Swells at my breast and turns the past to pain.
    In all my wanderings round this world of care,
In all my griefs – and God has given my share –
I still had hopes my latest hours to crown,
Amidst these humble bowers to lay me down;
To husband out life's taper at the close
And keep the flame from wasting by repose.
I still had hopes, for pride attends us still,
Amidst the swains to show my book-learned skill,   90
Around my fire an evening group to draw,
And tell of all I felt and all I saw;
And, as a hare, whom hounds and horns pursue,
Pants to the place from whence at first she flew,
I still had hopes, my long vexations past,
Here to return – and die at home at last.
    O blest retirement, friend to life's decline,
Retreats from care that never must be mine,
How happy he who crowns in shades like these
A youth of labour with an age of ease;   100
Who quits a world where strong temptations try,
And, since 'tis hard to combat, learns to fly.
For him no wretches, born to work and weep,
Explore the mine or tempt the dangerous deep;
No surly porter stands in guilty state
To spurn imploring famine from the gate;
But on he moves to meet his latter end,
Angels around befriending virtue's friend;
Bends to the grave with unperceived decay,
While resignation gently slopes the way;   110
And, all his prospects brightening to the last,
His heaven commences ere the world be past!
    Sweet was the sound, when oft at evening's close
Up yonder hill the village murmur rose;
There, as I passed with careless steps and slow,
The mingling notes came softened from below;
The swain responsive as the milkmaid sung,
The sober herd that lowed to meet their young;
The noisy geese that gabbled o'er the pool,
The playful children just let loose from school;   120
The watchdog's voice that bayed the whispering wind,
And the loud laugh that spoke the vacant mind;
These all in sweet confusion sought the shade,
And filled each pause the nightingale had made.
But now the sounds of population fail,
No cheerful murmurs fluctuate in the gale,
No busy steps the grassgrown foot-way tread,
For all the bloomy flush of life is fled.

---

l.104 tempt: common poetical diction for 'venture on'. [Lonsdale 1969]

l.122 vacant: untroubled by thought, carefree. [Lonsdale 1969]

All but yon widowed, solitary thing
That feebly bends beside the plashy spring;   130
She, wretched matron, forced, in age, for bread,
To strip the brook with mantling cresses spread,
To pick her wintry faggot from the thorn,
To seek her nightly shed and weep till morn;
She only left of all the harmless train,
The sad historian of the pensive plain.
   Near yonder copse, where once the garden smiled,
And still where many a garden flower grows wild;
There, where a few torn shrubs the place disclose,
The village preacher's modest mansion rose.   140
A man he was to all the country dear,
And passing rich with forty pounds a year;
Remote from towns he ran his godly race,
Nor e'er had changed, nor wished to change, his place;
Unpractised he to fawn, or seek for power,
By doctrines fashioned to the varying hour;
Far other aims his heart had learned to prize,
More skilled to raise the wretched than to rise.
His house was known to all the vagrant train,
He chid their wanderings, but relieved their pain;   150
The long-remembered beggar was his guest,
Whose beard descending swept his aged breast;
The ruined spendthrift, now no longer proud,
Claimed kindred there and had his claims allowed;
The broken soldier, kindly bade to stay,
Sat by his fire and talked the night away;
Wept o'er his wounds or tales of sorrow done,
Shouldered his crutch and showed how fields were won.
Pleased with his guests, the good man learned to glow,
And quite forgot their vices in their woe;   160
Careless their merits or their faults to scan,
His pity gave ere charity began.
   Thus to relieve the wretched was his pride,
And even his failings leaned to virtue's side;
But in his duty prompt at every call,
He watched and wept, he prayed and felt, for all.
And, as a bird each fond endearment tries
To tempt its new-fledged offspring to the skies,
He tried each art, reproved each dull delay,
Allured to brighter worlds, and led the way.   170
   Beside the bed where parting life was laid,
And sorrow, guilt, and pain by turns dismayed,
The reverend champion stood. At his control,
Despair and anguish fled the struggling soul;

---

l.130 plashy: abounding in pools, marshy. [Lonsdale 1969]

l.142 passing: exceedingly. [Lonsdale 1969]

l.144 place: appointment, or (in this case) living. [Lonsdale 1969]

Comfort came down the trembling wretch to raise,
And his last faltering accents whispered praise.
   At church, with meek and unaffected grace,
His looks adorned the venerable place;
Truth from his lips prevailed with double sway,
And fools, who came to scoff, remained to pray.   180
The service past, around the pious man,
With steady zeal each honest rustic ran;
Even children followed with endearing wile,
And plucked his gown, to share the good man's smile.
His ready smile a parent's warmth expressed,
Their welfare pleased him and their cares distressed;
To them his heart, his love, his griefs were given,
But all his serious thoughts had rest in heaven.
As some tall cliff, that lifts its awful form,
Swells from the vale and midway leaves the storm,   190
Though round its breast the rolling clouds are spread,
Eternal sunshine settles on its head.
   Beside yon straggling fence that skirts the way,
With blossomed furze unprofitably gay,
There, in his noisy mansion, skilled to rule,
The village master taught his little school;
A man severe he was and stern to view;
I knew him well, and every truant knew;
Well had the boding tremblers learned to trace
The day's disasters in his morning face;   200
Full well they laughed, with counterfeited glee,
At all his jokes, for many a joke had he;
Full well the busy whisper, circling round,
Conveyed the dismal tidings when he frowned;
Yet he was kind, or, if severe in aught,
The love he bore to learning was in fault;
The village all declared how much he knew;
'Twas certain he could write and cipher too;
Lands he could measure, terms and tides presage,
And even the story ran that he could gauge.   210
In arguing too, the parson owned his skill,
For even though vanquished, he could argue still;
While words of learned length and thundering sound
Amazed the gazing rustics ranged around,
And still they gazed, and still the wonder grew,
That one small head could carry all he knew.

---

l.208 cipher: practise arithmetic. [Lonsdale]

l.209 terms: term of quarter days, when rents, wages, and other dues
were paid and tenures began and ended. [Lonsdale 1969]

l.209 tides: moveable feasts of the year. [Lonsdale 1969]

l.210 gauge: calculate capacity of vessels. [Lonsdale]

But past is all his fame. The very spot,
Where many a time he triumphed, is forgot.
Near yonder thorn, that lifts its head on high,
Where once the signpost caught the passing eye,   220
Low lies that house where nutbrown draughts inspired,
Where greybeard mirth and smiling toil retired,
Where village statesmen talked with looks profound,
And news much older than their ale went round.
Imagination fondly stoops to trace
The parlour splendours of that festive place;
The white-washed wall, the nicely sanded floor,
The varnished clock that clicked behind the door;
The chest contrived a double debt to pay,
A bed by night, a chest of drawers by day;   230
The pictures placed for ornament and use,
The twelve good rules, the royal game of goose;
The hearth, except when winter chilled the day,
With aspen boughs and flowers and fennel gay;
While broken teacups, wisely kept for show,
Ranged o'er the chimney, glistened in a row.
    Vain, transitory splendours! Could not all
Reprieve the tottering mansion from its fall!
Obscure it sinks, nor shall it more impart
An hour's importance to the poor man's heart;   240
Thither no more the peasant shall repair
To sweet oblivion of his daily care;
No more the farmer's news, the barber's tale,
No more the woodman's ballad shall prevail;
No more the smith his dusky brow shall clear,
Relax his ponderous strength and lean to hear;
The host himself no longer shall be found
Careful to see the mantling bliss go round;
Nor the coy maid, half willing to be pressed,
Shall kiss the cup to pass it to the rest.   250
    Yes! let the rich deride, the proud disdain,
These simple blessings of the lowly train;
To me more dear, congenial to my heart,
One native charm than all the gloss of art;
Spontaneous joys, where nature has its play,
The soul adopts and owns their firstborn sway;
Lightly they frolic o'er the vacant mind,
Unenvied, unmolested, unconfined:
But the long pomp, the midnight masquerade,
With all the freaks of wanton wealth arrayed,   260
In these, ere triflers half their wish obtain,
The toiling pleasure sickens into pain;
And, even while fashion's brightest arts decoy,
The heart distrusting asks, if this be joy.

---

l.248 mantling: frothing. [Lonsdale 1969]

Ye friends to truth, ye statesmen, who survey
The rich man's joys increase, the poor's decay,
'Tis yours to judge how wide the limits stand
Between a splendid and an happy land.
Proud swells the tide with loads of freighted ore,
And shouting Folly hails them from her shore;   270
Hoards, even beyond the miser's wish, abound,
And rich men flock from all the world around.
Yet count our gains. This wealth is but a name
That leaves our useful products still the same.
Not so the loss. The man of wealth and pride
Takes up a space that many poor supplied;
Space for his lake, his park's extended bounds,
Space for his horses, equipage and hounds;
The robe that wraps his limbs in silken sloth
Has robbed the neighbouring fields of half their growth;   280
His seat, where solitary sports are seen,
Indignant spurns the cottage from the green;
Around the world each needful product flies,
For all the luxuries the world supplies:
While thus the land, adorned for pleasure all,
In barren splendour feebly waits the fall.
  As some fair female unadorned and plain,
Secure to please while youth confirms her reign,
Slights every borrowed charm that dress supplies,
Nor shares with art the triumph of her eyes;   290
But when those charms are passed, for charms are frail,
When time advances and when lovers fail,
She then shines forth, solicitous to bless,
In all the glaring impotence of dress:
Thus fares the land, by luxury betrayed,
In nature's simplest charms at first arrayed;
But verging to decline, its splendours rise,
Its vistas strike, its palaces surprise;
While scourged by famine from the smiling land,
The mournful peasant leads his humble band;   300
And while he sinks, without one arm to save,
The country blooms – a garden and a grave.
  Where then, ah where, shall poverty reside,
To 'scape the pressure of contiguous pride?
If to some common's fenceless limits strayed,
He drives his flock to pick the scanty blade,
Those fenceless fields the sons of wealth divide,
And even the bare-worn common is denied.
  If to the city sped – what waits him there?
To see profusion that he must not share;   310

---

ll.305–8: G. seems here definitely to refer to the effect of the enclosure of common land (ll.39–50 might be similarly interpreted). [Lonsdale 1969]

To see ten thousand baneful arts combined
To pamper luxury and thin mankind;
To see those joys the sons of pleasure know
Extorted from his fellow-creature's woe.
Here, while the courtier glitters in brocade,
There the pale artist plies the sickly trade;
Here, while the proud their long-drawn pomps display,
There the black gibbet glooms beside the way.
The dome where Pleasure holds her midnight reign
Here, richly decked, admits the gorgeous train;   320
Tumultuous grandeur crowds the blazing square,
The rattling chariots clash, the torches glare.
Sure scenes like these no troubles e'er annoy!
Sure these denote one universal joy!
Are these thy serious thoughts? – Ah, turn thine eyes
Where the poor, houseless, shivering female lies.
She once, perhaps, in village plenty blessed,
Has wept at tales of innocence distressed;
Her modest looks the cottage might adorn,
Sweet as the primrose peeps beneath the thorn;   330
Now lost to all; her friends, her virtue fled,
Near her betrayer's door she lays her head,
And, pinched with cold and shrinking from the shower,
With heavy heart deplores that luckless hour,
When idly first, ambitious of the town,
She left her wheel and robes of country brown.
   Do thine, sweet Auburn, thine, the loveliest train,
Do thy fair tribes participate her pain?
Even now, perhaps, by cold and hunger led,
At proud men's doors they ask a little bread!   340
   Ah, no. To distant climes, a dreary scene,
Where half the convex world intrudes between,
Through torrid tracts with fainting steps they go,
Where wild Altama murmurs to their woe.
Far different there from all that charmed before
The various terrors of that horrid shore:
Those blazing suns that dart a downward ray,
And fiercely shed intolerable day;
Those matted woods where birds forget to sing,
But silent bats in drowsy clusters cling;   350
Those poisonous fields with rank luxuriance crowned,
Where the dark scorpion gathers death around;
Where at each step the stranger fears to wake
The rattling terrors of the vengeful snake;
Where crouching tigers wait their hapless prey,
And savage men more murderous still than they;

---

l.316 artist: workman. [Lonsdale]

l.318 glooms: frowns, lowers. [Lonsdale 1969]

l.319 dome: simply a building. [Lonsdale 1969]

l.344 Altama: a river in Georgia. [Lonsdale]

While oft in whirls the mad tornado flies,
Mingling the ravaged landscape with the skies.
Far different these from every former scene,
The cooling brook, the grassy-vested green,   360
The breezy covert of the warbling grove,
That only sheltered thefts of harmless love.
   Good heaven! what sorrows gloomed that parting day,
That called them from their native walks away;
When the poor exiles, every pleasure past,
Hung round their bowers and fondly looked their last,
And took a long farewell, and wished in vain
For seats like these beyond the western main;
And shuddering still to face the distant deep,
Returned and wept, and still returned to weep.   370
The good old sire the first prepared to go
To new-found worlds, and wept for others' woe;
But for himself, in conscious virtue brave,
He only wished for worlds beyond the grave.
His lovely daughter, lovelier in her tears,
The fond companion of his helpless years,
Silent went next, neglectful of her charms,
And left a lover's for a father's arms.
With louder plaints the mother spoke her woes,
And blessed the cot where every pleasure rose;   380
And kissed her thoughtless babes with many a tear,
And clasped them close, in sorrow doubly dear;
Whilst her fond husband strove to lend relief
In all the silent manliness of grief.
   O luxury! thou cursed by heaven's decree,
How ill exchanged are things like these for thee!
How do thy potions with insidious joy
Diffuse their pleasures only to destroy!
Kingdoms, by thee to sickly greatness grown,
Boast of a florid vigour not their own.   390
At every draught more large and large they grow,
A bloated mass of rank unwieldy woe;
Till sapped their strength and every part unsound,
Down, down they sink and spread a ruin round.
   Even now the devastation is begun,
And half the business of destruction done;
Even now, methinks, as pondering here I stand,
I see the rural virtues leave the land.
Down where yon anchoring vessel spreads the sail,
That idly waiting flaps with every gale,   400
Downward they move, a melancholy band,
Pass from the shore and darken all the strand.
Contented toil and hospitable care,
And kind connubial tenderness are there;

1.363 gloomed: made gloomy or melancholy.[Lonsdale 1969]

ll.403–6 These are the 'rural virtues' England is losing. [Lonsdale 1969]

And piety, with wishes placed above,
And steady loyalty and faithful love.
And thou, sweet Poetry, thou loveliest maid,
Still first to fly where sensual joys invade;
Unfit, in these degenerate times of shame,
To catch the heart or strike for honest fame;   410
Dear charming nymph, neglected and decried,
My shame in crowds, my solitary pride;
Thou source of all my bliss and all my woe,
That found'st me poor at first and keep'st me so;
Thou guide by which the nobler arts excel,
Thou nurse of every virtue, fare thee well!
Farewell, and oh, where'er thy voice be tried,
On Torno's cliffs or Pambamarca's side,
Whether where equinoctial fervours glow,
Or winter wraps the polar world in snow,   420
Still let thy voice, prevailing over time,
Redress the rigours of the inclement clime;
Aid slighted truth; with thy persuasive strain
Teach erring man to spurn the rage of gain;
Teach him that states of native strength possessed,
Though very poor, may still be very blest;
That trade's proud empire hastes to swift decay,
As ocean sweeps the laboured mole away;
While self-dependent power can time defy,
As rocks resist the billows and the sky.   430

George Crabbe (1754–1832)

The Village, Book I

(1783)

THE village life, and every care that reigns
O'er youthful peasants and declining swains;
What labour yields, and what, that labour past,
Age, in its hour of languor, finds at last;
What forms the real picture of the poor,
Demands a song – the Muse can give no more.
Fled are those times, if e'er such times were seen,
When rustic poets praised their native green;
No shepherds now, in smooth alternate verse,
Their country's beauty or their nymphs' rehearse;   10

---

l.418 Torno: a river in Sweden. [Lonsdale]

l.418 Pambamarca: a mountain in Ecuador, then in Peru. [Lonsdale]

l.419 equinoctial fervours: The intense heat at the Equator. [Lonsdale 1969]

ll.427–30 written by Johnson. [Lonsdale 1969]

Yet still for these we frame the tender strain,
Still in our lays fond Corydons complain,
And shepherds' boys their amorous pains reveal,
The only pains, alas! they never feel.
  On Mincio's banks, in Caesar's bounteous reign,
If Tityrus found the Golden Age again,
Must sleepy bards the flattering dream prolong,
Mechanic echoes of the Mantuan song?
From truth and nature shall we widely stray,
Where Virgil, not where Fancy leads the way?   20
  Yes, thus the Muses sing of happy swains,
Because the Muses never knew their pains.
They boast their peasants' pipes, but peasants now
Resign their pipes and plod behind the plough;
And few amid the rural tribe have time
To number syllables and play with rhyme;
Save honest Duck, what son of verse could share
The poet's rapture and the peasant's care?
Or the great labours of the field degrade
With the new peril of a poorer trade?   30
  From one chief cause these idle praises spring,
That themes so easy few forbear to sing;
They ask no thought, require no deep design,
But swell the song and liquefy the line;
The gentle lover takes the rural strain,
A nymph his mistress and himself a swain;
With no sad scenes he clouds his tuneful prayer,
But all, to look like her, is painted fair.
I grant indeed that fields and flocks have charms
For him that gazes or for him that farms;   40
But when amid such pleasing scenes I trace
The poor laborious natives of the place,
And see the mid-day sun, with fervid ray,

---

ll.12–20 References to a shepherd in Virgil's *Eclogues* ('Corydons', l.12),
to a tributary of the Po, near where Virgil lived ('Mincio's banks', l.15)
and to a character who stands for Virgil in the first eclogue ('Tityrus',
l.16) are specific; but it is not clear how far Virgil's poetry (and classical
culture) must be rejected along with its modern imitators, whether there
was once a golden age, or how far Crabbe wishes to generalize about
rural reality from his own experience of it. Lines 15–20 are Johnson's
unsuccessful attempt to clarify these issues, confused in Crabbe's original
which ran: [Edwards]

> In fairer scenes, where peaceful pleasures spring,
> Tityrus, the pride of Mantuan swains might sing:
> But charmed by him, or smitten with his views,
> Shall modern poets court the Mantuan muse?
> From Truth and Nature shall we widely stray,
> Where Fancy leads, or Virgil led the way? [Edwards]

l.18 Virgil was born at Andes, near Mantua. [DCP]

l.27 Duck: i.e. Stephen Duck, see p.111. [eds]

On their bare heads and dewy temples play;
While some, with feebler hands and fainter hearts,
Deplore their fortune, yet sustain their parts:
Then shall I dare these real ills to hide
In tinsel trappings of poetic pride?
   No, cast by Fortune on a frowning coast,
Which can no groves nor happy valleys boast; 50
Where other cares than those the Muse relates,
And other shepherds dwell with other mates;
By such examples taught, I paint the cot,
As truth will paint it, and as bards will not:
Nor you, ye poor, of lettered scorn complain,
To you the smoothest song is smooth in vain;
O'ercome by labour and bowed down by time,
Feel you the barren flattery of a rhyme?
Can poets soothe you, when you pine for bread,
By winding myrtles round your ruined shed? 60
Can their light tales your weighty griefs o'erpower,
Or glad with airy mirth the toilsome hour?
   Lo! where the heath, with withering brake grown o'er,
Lends the light turf that warms the neighbouring poor;
From thence a length of burning sand appears,
Where the thin harvest waves its withered ears;
Rank weeds, that every art and care defy,
Reign o'er the land and rob the blighted rye:
There thistles stretch their prickly arms afar,
And to the ragged infant threaten war; 70
There poppies, nodding, mock the hope of toil,
There the blue bugloss paints the sterile soil;
Hardy and high, above the slender sheaf,
The slimy mallow waves her silky leaf;
O'er the young shoot the charlock throws a shade,
And the wild tare clings round the sickly blade;
With mingled tints the rocky coasts abound,
And a sad splendour vainly shines around.
   So looks the nymph whom wretched arts adorn,
Betrayed by man, then left for man to scorn; 80
Whose cheek in vain assumes the mimic rose,
While her sad eyes the troubled breast disclose;
Whose outward splendour is but folly's dress,
Exposing most, when most it gilds distress.
   Here joyless roam a wild amphibious race,
With sullen woe displayed in every face;
Who far from civil arts and social fly,
And scowl at strangers with suspicious eye.
   Here too the lawless merchant of the main
Draws from his plough th' intoxicated swain; 90

---

l.79 This curious parallel is evidently derived from Goldsmith's *Deserted Village*, ll.285–94. [DCP]

Want only claimed the labour of the day,
But vice now steals his nightly rest away.
   Where are the swains, who, daily labour done,
With rural games played down the setting sun;
Who struck with matchless force the bounding ball,
Or made the pond'rous quoit obliquely fall;
While some huge Ajax, terrible and strong,
Engaged some artful stripling of the throng,
And, foiled, beneath the young Ulysses fell,
When peals of praise the merry mischief tell?   100
Where now are these? – Beneath yon cliff they stand,
To show the freighted pinnace where to land;
To load the ready steed with guilty haste;
To fly in terror o'er the pathless waste,
Or, when detected in their straggling course,
To foil their foes by cunning or by force;
Or, yielding part (which equal knaves contest),
To gain a lawless passport for the rest.
   Here, wand'ring long amid these frowning fields,
I sought the simple life that Nature yields;   110
Rapine and Wrong and Fear usurped her place,
And a bold, artful, surly, savage race;
Who, only skilled to take the finny tribe,
The yearly dinner, or septennial bribe,
Wait on the shore, and as the waves run high,
On the tossed vessel bend their eager eye,
Which to their coast directs its vent'rous way,
Theirs, or the ocean's, miserable prey.
   As on their neighbouring beach yon swallows stand,
And wait for favouring winds to leave the land,   120
While still for flight the ready wing is spread:
So waited I the favouring hour, and fled;
Fled from these shores where guilt and famine reign,
And cried, Ah! hapless they who still remain;
Who still remain to hear the ocean roar,
Whose greedy waves devour the lessening shore;
Till some fierce tide, with more imperious sway,
Sweeps the low hut and all it holds away;
When the sad tenant weeps from door to door,
And begs a poor protection from the poor!   130
   But these are scenes where Nature's niggard hand
Gave a spare portion to the famished land;
Hers is the fault, if here mankind complain
Of fruitless toil and labour spent in vain;

---

l.114 The yearly dinner: given after the election of the parish officers. [DCP]

l.114 septennial bribe: By the Parliament act of 1716, a general election had to be held every seven years. [DCP]

But yet in other scenes, more fair in view,
Where Plenty smiles – alas! she smiles for few,
And those who taste not, yet behold her store,
Are as the slaves that dig the golden ore,
The wealth around them makes them doubly poor.
Or will you deem them amply paid in health,   140
Labour's fair child, that languishes with wealth?
Go, then! and see them rising with the sun,
Through a long course of daily toil to run;
Like him to make the plenteous harvest grow,
And yet not share the plenty they bestow;
See them beneath the dog-star's raging heat,
When the knees tremble and the temples beat;
Behold them, leaning on their scythes, look o'er
The labour past, and toils to come explore;
See them alternate suns and showers engage,   150
And hoard up aches and anguish for their age;
Through fens and marshy moors their steps pursue,
When their warm pores imbibe the evening dew;
Then own that labour may as fatal be
To these thy slaves, as luxury to thee.
   Amid this tribe too oft a manly pride
Strives in strong toil the fainting heart to hide;
There may you see the youth of slender frame
Contend with weakness, weariness, and shame;
Yet urged along, and proudly loth to yield,   160
He strives to join his fellows of the field;
Till long-contending nature droops at last,
Declining health rejects his poor repast,
His cheerless spouse the coming danger sees,
And mutual murmurs urge the slow disease.
Yet grant them health, 'tis not for us to tell,
Though the head droops not, that the heart is well;
Or will you urge their homely, plenteous fare,
Healthy and plain and still the poor man's share?
Oh! trifle not with wants you cannot feel,   170
Nor mock the misery of a stinted meal;
Homely not wholesome, plain not plenteous, such
As you who envy would disdain to touch.
   Ye gentle souls, who dream of rural ease,
Whom the smooth stream and smoother sonnet please;
Go! if the peaceful cot your praises share,
Go, look within, and ask if peace be there:
If peace be his – that drooping weary sire,
Or theirs, that offspring round their feeble fire,
Or hers, that matron pale, whose trembling hand: 180

---

ll.144–5 These lines may have been dropped in 1807 because of their
political implications. [DCP]

l.172 Homely: Homely, as contrasted with wholesome, is here used in a
disparaging sense, meaning 'coarse' or 'rude'. [DCP]

Turns on the wretched hearth th' expiring brand.
Nor yet can time itself obtain for these
Life's latest comforts, due respect and ease;
For yonder see that hoary swain, whose age
Can with no cares except its own engage;
Who, propped on that rude staff, looks up to see
The bare arms broken from the withering tree,
On which, a boy, he climbed the loftiest bough,
Then his first joy, but his sad emblem now.
He once was chief in all the rustic trade,   190
His steady hand the straightest furrow made;
Full many a prize he won, and still is proud
To find the triumphs of his youth allowed.
A transient pleasure sparkles in his eyes,
He hears and smiles, then thinks again and sighs:
For now he journeys to his grave in pain;
The rich disdain him, nay, the poor disdain;
Alternate masters now their slave command,
And urge the efforts of his feeble hand;
Who, when his age attempts its task in vain,   200
With ruthless taunts of lazy poor complain.
Oft may you see him, when he tends the sheep,
His winter-charge, beneath the hillock weep;
Oft hear him murmur to the winds that blow
O'er his white locks and bury them in snow;
When, roused by rage and muttering in the morn,
He mends the broken hedge with icy thorn:
'Why do I live, when I desire to be
At once from life and life's long labour free?
Like leaves in spring, the young are blown away,   210
Without the sorrows of a slow decay;
I, like yon withered leaf, remain behind,
Nipped by the frost and shivering in the wind;
There it abides till younger buds come on,
As I, now all my fellow-swains are gone;
Then, from the rising generation thrust,
It falls, like me, unnoticed to the dust.
'These fruitful fields, these numerous flocks I see,
Are others' gain, but killing cares to me;
To me the children of my youth are lords,   220
Slow in their gifts but hasty in their words:

---

l.198 'A pauper who, being nearly past his labour, is employed by different masters, for a length of time proportioned to their occupations.'
[note by C in *Poems* (1807)] Unemployed men or 'roundsmen' were
sent by the Overseers of the Poor from house to house in order to get
work. The employer was obliged to give them food, and usually about
sixpence a day, which the parish supplemented according to their needs.
In some parishes a large proportion of the labouring population, including children of the age of ten and over, went on the 'rounds' especially
in winter. [DCP]

Wants of their own demand their care, and who
Feels his own want and succours others too?
A lonely, wretched man, in pain I go,
None need my help and none relieve my woe;
Then let my bones beneath the turf be laid,
And men forget the wretch they would not aid.'
    Thus groan the old, till, by disease oppressed,
They taste a final woe, and then they rest.
Theirs is yon house that holds the parish poor,   230
Whose walls of mud scarce bear the broken door;
There, where the putrid vapours, flagging, play,
And the dull wheel hums doleful through the day;
There children dwell, who know no parents' care,
Parents, who know no children's love, dwell there;
Heart-broken matrons on their joyless bed,
Forsaken wives, and mothers never wed;
Dejected widows with unheeded tears,
And crippled age with more than childhood-fears;
The lame, the blind, and, far the happiest they!   240
The moping idiot and the madman gay.
    Here too the sick their final doom receive,
Here brought amid the scenes of grief, to grieve,
Where the loud groans from some sad chamber flow,
Mixed with the clamours of the crowd below;
Here, sorrowing, they each kindred sorrow scan,
And the cold charities of man to man:
Whose laws indeed for ruined age provide,
And strong compulsion plucks the scrap from pride;
But still that scrap is bought with many a sigh,   250
And pride embitters what it can't deny.
    Say ye, oppressed by some fantastic woes,
Some jarring nerve that baffles your repose;
Who press the downy couch, while slaves advance
With timid eye to read the distant glance;
Who with sad prayers the weary doctor tease
To name the nameless ever-new disease;
Who with mock patience dire complaints endure,
Which real pain, and that alone, can cure;
How would ye bear in real pain to lie,   260
Despised, neglected, left alone to die?
How would ye bear to draw your latest breath,
Where all that's wretched paves the way for death?
    Such is that room which one rude beam divides,
And naked rafters form the sloping sides;
Where the vile bands that bind the thatch are seen,
And lath and mud is all that lie between,

---

l.230 C. was writing from experience, since he had been employed to
look after the pauper sick when practising medicine at Aldborough. The
parish poorhouse which he describes was probably kept in a squalid condition by the Overseers in order to discourage the poor from applying
for relief and so keep down the poor-rate. [DCP]

Save one dull pane, that, coarsely patched, gives way
To the rude tempest, yet excludes the day.
Here, on a matted flock, with dust o'erspread,   270
The drooping wretch reclines his languid head;
For him no hand the cordial cup applies,
Nor wipes the tear that stagnates in his eyes;
No friends with soft discourse his pain beguile,
Nor promise hope till sickness wears a smile.

But soon a loud and hasty summons calls,
Shakes the thin roof, and echoes round the walls.
Anon, a figure enters, quaintly neat,
All pride and business, bustle and conceit;
With looks unaltered by these scenes of woe,   280
With speed that, entering, speaks his haste to go,
He bids the gazing throng around him fly,
And carries fate and physic in his eye;
A potent quack, long versed in human ills,
Who first insults the victim whom he kills;
Whose murd'rous hand a drowsy bench protect,
And whose most tender mercy is neglect.

Paid by the parish for attendance here,
He wears contempt upon his sapient sneer;
In haste he seeks the bed where misery lies,   290
Impatience marked in his averted eyes;
And, some habitual queries hurried o'er,
Without reply, he rushes on the door;
His drooping patient, long inured to pain,
And long unheeded, knows remonstrance vain;
He ceases now the feeble help to crave
Of man, and mutely hastens to the grave.

But ere his death some pious doubts arise,
Some simple fears which 'bold bad' men despise;
Fain would he ask the parish priest to prove   300
His title certain to the joys above;
For this he sends the murmuring nurse, who calls
The holy stranger to these dismal walls;
And doth not he, the pious man, appear,
He, 'passing rich with forty pounds a year'?
Ah! no, a shepherd of a different stock,
And far unlike him, feeds this little flock;
A jovial youth, who thinks his Sunday's task
As much as God or man can fairly ask;
The rest he gives to loves and labours light,   310
To fields the morning and to feasts the night;
None better skilled the noisy pack to guide,
To urge their chase, to cheer them or to chide;
Sure in his shot, his game he seldom missed,
And seldom failed to win his game at whist;

---

l.305. 'A man he was to all the country dear,/And passing rich with forty
pounds a year'. (Goldsmith, *Deserted Village*, ll.141–2). [DCP]

Then, while such honours bloom around his head,
Shall he sit sadly by the sick man's bed
To raise the hope he feels not, or with zeal
To combat fears that ev'n the pious feel?
    Now once again the gloomy scene explore,   320
Less gloomy now; the bitter hour is o'er,
The man of many sorrows sighs no more.
    Up yonder hill, behold how sadly slow
The bier moves winding from the vale below;
There lie the happy dead, from trouble free,
And the glad parish pays the frugal fee.
No more, oh Death! thy victim starts to hear
Churchwarden stern, or kingly overseer;
No more the farmer gets his humble bow,
Thou art his lord, the best of tyrants thou!   330
    Now to the church behold the mourners come,
Sedately torpid and devoutly dumb;
The village children now their games suspend,
To see the bier that bears their ancient friend:
For he was one in all their idle sport,
And like a monarch ruled their little court;
The pliant bow he formed, the flying ball,
The bat, the wicket, were his labours all;
Him now they follow to his grave, and stand
Silent and sad, and gazing, hand in hand;   340
While bending low, their eager eyes explore
The mingled relics of the parish poor.
The bell tolls late, the moping owl flies round,
Fear marks the flight and magnifies the sound;
The busy priest, detained by weightier care,
Defers his duty till the day of prayer;
And, waiting long, the crowd retire distressed,
To think a poor man's bones should lie unblessed.

---

l.342 Paupers were sometimes buried in a common grave. [DCP]

ll.345–8 For republication in *Poems* (1807) Crabbe ... added a note to the end of Book I apologizing 'For the insertion of a circumstance by no means common' (the failure of a parson to turn up for a poor man's funeral): the *Anti-Jacobin Review* congratulated him on his apology. [Edwards]

l.346 When only a part of the service would need to be read. [DCP]

Robert Burns (1759–96)

Address to the Deil

O Prince, O chief of many throned pow'rs,
That led th' embattled Seraphim to war –

                                   Milton

O THOU, whatever title suit thee!
Auld Hornie, Satan, Nick, or Clootie,   *Cloven-hoof*
Wha in yon cavern grim an' sootie
     Clos'd under hatches,
Spairges about the brunstane cootie,   *bespatters, brimstone tub*
     To scaud poor wretches!   *scald*

Hear me, *auld Hangie*, for a wee,   *Hangman*
An' let poor, *damned bodies* bee;
I'm sure sma' pleasure it can gie,
     Ev'n to a *deil*,   10   *devil*
To skelp an' scaud poor dogs like me,   *smack*
     An' hear us squeel!

Great is thy pow'r, an' great thy fame;
Far kend an' noted is thy name;
An' though yon *lowan heugh's* thy hame,   *blazing pit*
     Thou travels far;
An' faith! thou's neither lag nor lame,   *backward*
     Nor blate nor scaur.   *bashful, afraid*

Whyles, ranging like a roaran lion,
For prey, a' holes an' corners tryin;   20
Whyles, on the strong-wing'd Tempest flyin,
     Tirlan the *kirks*;   *uncovering, churches*
Whyles, in the human bosom pryin,
     Unseen thou lurks.

I've heard my rev'rend *Graunie* say,   *grandmother*
In lanely glens ye like to stray;   *lonely*
Or where auld, ruin'd castles, gray,
     Nod to the moon,
Ye fright the nightly wand'rer's way,
     Wi' eldritch croon.   30   *unearthly moan*

When twilight did my *Graunie* summon
To say her pray'rs, douse, honest woman!   *sober*
Aft 'yont the dyke she's heard you bumman,   *behind, wall, humming*
     Wi' eerie drone;
Or, rustling, through the boortries coman   *elder trees*
     Wi' heavy groan.

---

l.2 Auld Hornie: Traditional Scotish nickname for the horned Devil.
[Low]

l.21 strong-wing'd Tempest: Tradition had it that the Devil raised strong
winds. [Low]

l.35 boortries: Elder trees were supposed to give protection against
witchcraft. [Low]

Ae dreary, windy, winter night,
The stars shot down wi' sklentan light,   *slanting*
Wi' you, *mysel,* I gat a fright,
    Ayont the lough;   40   *beyond, loch*
Ye, like a *rash-buss,* stood in sight,   *clump of rushes*
    Wi' waving sugh.   *sound of wind*

The cudgel in my neive did shake,   *fist*
Each bristl'd hair stood like a stake,
When wi' an eldritch, stoor *quaick, quaick,*   *harsh*
    Amang the springs,
Awa ye squatter'd like a *drake,*   *'flutter in water'* (B)
    On whistling wings.

Let *Warlocks* grim, an' wither'd *Hags,*
Tell how wi' you on ragweed nags,   50   *ragwort*
They skim the muirs an' dizzy crags,   *moors*
    Wi' wicked speed;
And in kirk-yards renew their leagues,
    Owre howcket dead.   *exhumed*

Thence, countra wives, wi' toil an' pain,
May plunge an' plunge the *kirn* in vain;   *churn*
For Oh! the yellow treasure's taen,
    By witching skill;
An' dawtet, twal-pint *Hawkie's* gane   *spoiled, twelve-, cow*
    As yell's the Bill.   60   *milkless as, bull*

Thence, mystic knots mak great abuse,
On *Young-Guidmen,* fond, keen an' croose;   *-husbands, confident*
When the best *wark-lume* i' the house,   *work-loom*
    By cantraip wit,   *magic*
Is instant made no worth a louse,
    Just at the bit.   *critical moment*

When thowes dissolve the snawy hoord,   *thaws, snowy drift*
An' float the jinglan icy boord,   *(on), cracking, surface*
Then, *Water-kelpies* haunt the foord,   *waterhorse demons, ford*
    By your direction,   70
An' nighted Trav'llers are allur'd
    To their destruction.

---

l.50 ragweed: Witches were said to ride on many kinds of steed — animals, enchanted humans, ragwort, ash branches, or straws. [Low]

l.61 mystic knots: knots devised in malice by witches. [Low]

l.63 wark-lume: According to a seventeenth-century tract, *Satan's Invisible World Discovered,* witches sometimes meddled with the weaver's craft. Burns uses the word with a sexual meaning. [Low]

l.69 Water-kelpies: Water-demons in the shape of horses, bent on drowing travellers (traditional in the Scottish Highlands). [Low]

An' aft your moss-traversing *Spunkies*   *wills o'the wisp*
Decoy the wight that late an' drunk is:
The bleezan, curst, mischievous monkies   *blazing*
          Delude his eyes,
Till in some miry slough he sunk is,
          Ne'er mair to rise.

When MASONS' mystic *word* an' *grip*
In storms an' tempests raise you up,   80
Some cock or cat, your rage maun stop',
          Or, strange to tell!
The *youngest Brother* ye wad whip
          Aff straught to H-ll.   *straight*

Lang syne in EDEN's bonie yard,   *long ago, garden*
When youthfu' lovers first were pair'd,
An' all the Soul of Love they shar'd,
          The raptur'd hour,
Sweet on the fragrant, flow'ry swaird,   *sward*
          In shady bow'r.   90

Then you, ye auld, snick-drawing dog!   *latch-*
Ye cam to paradise incog,   *unknown*
An' play'd on man a cursed brogue,   *trick*
          (Black be your fa'!)
An' gied the infant warld a shog,   *world, shock*
          'Maist ruin'd a'.

D'ye mind that day, when in a bizz,   *remember, stir*
Wi' reeket duds, an' reestet gizz,   *smoky clothes, 'cured' wig*
Ye did present your smoutie phiz   *ugly face*
          'Mang better folk,   100
An' sklented on the *man of Uzz*   *directed aslant*
          Your spitefu' joke?

An' how ye gat him i' your thrall,
An' brak him out o'house an' hal',
While scabs an' botches did him gall,   *'angry tumours' (B)*
          Wi' bitter claw,   *scratching*
An' lows'd his ill-tongu'd, wicked *Scawl*   *loosed, abusive woman*
          Was warst ava?   *worst of all*

But a' your doings to rehearse,
Your wily snares an' fechtin fierce,   110   *fighting*
Sin' that day MICHAEL did you pierce,

1.79 When MASONS' mystic word an' grip: Burns refers to the Masonic
password and handshake as having force to stir up the Devil in a storm;
then by contrast to the tradition that a cock, cat, or other unchristened
creature was needed in order to appease the Devil. A joke at the expense
of Masons, including the poet himself. [Low]

1.91 snick-drawing: An auld sneck-drawer, one who, from long experience, has acquired a great degree of facility in accomplishing any artful
purpose' (*Jamieson's Scots Dictionary*). [Low]

1.101 the *man of Uzz*: Job in the Old Testament. [Calder & Donnelly]

1.111 Vide Milton, [*Paradise Lost*] Book 6th. [Burns]

Down to this time,
Wad ding a' *Lallan* tongue, or *Erse*,   *weary, Lowland, Gaelic*
   In Prose or Rhyme.

An' now, auld *Cloots*, I ken ye're thinkan,
A certain *Bardie's* rantin, drinkin,   *poet*
Some luckless hour will send him linkan,   *going briskly*
   To your black pit;
But faith! he'll turn a corner jinkan,   *side-stepping*
   An' cheat you yet.   120

But fare-you-weel, auld *Nickie-ben*!
O wad ye tak a thought an' men'!   *and mend*
Ye aiblins might – I dinna ken–   *perhaps*
   Still hae a *stake* –   *chance*
I'm wae to think upo' yon den,   *unhappy*
   Ev'n for your sake.

Poor Mailie's Elegy

LAMENT in rhyme, lament in prose,
Wi' saut tears trickling down your nose;   *salt*
Our *Bardie's* fate is at a close,   *poet's*
   Past a' remead!   *cure*
The last, sad cape-stane of his woes;   *coping-stone*
   Poor *Mailie's* dead!

It's no the loss o' warl's gear,   *worldly property*
That could sae bitter draw the tear,
Or make our *Bardie*, dowie, wear   *sad*
   The mourning weed: 10
He's lost a friend and neebor dear,   *neighbour*
   In *Mailie* dead.

Thro' a' the town she trotted by him;   *village/farm*
A lang half-mile she could descry him;
Wi' kindly bleat, when she did spy him,
   She ran wi' speed:
A friend mair faithfu' ne'er came nigh him,
   Than *Mailie* dead.

I wat she was a *sheep* o'sense,   *know*
An' could behave hersel wi' mense: 20 *discretion*
I'll say't, she never brak a fence,   *broke*
   Thro' thievish greed.
Our *Bardie*, lanely, keeps the spence,   *lonely, inner room*
   Sin' *Mailie's* dead.

Or, if he wanders up the howe,   *valley*
Her living image in *her yowe*,   *ewe*
Comes bleating till him, owre the knowe,   *to*
   For bits o' bread;
An' down the briny pearls rowe   *roll*
   For *Mailie* dead.   30

She was nae get o' moorlan tips,   *offspring, tups*
Wi' tauted ket, an' hairy hips;   *matted fleece*
For her forbears were brought in ships,
   Frae 'yont the TWEED: *beyond*
A bonier *fleesh* ne'er cross'd the clips   *fleece, shears*
   Than *Mailie's* dead.

Wae worth that man wha first did shape,		*woe to*
That vile, wanchancie thing – *a raep*!		*unlucky, rope*
It maks guid fellows girn an' gape,		*'twist the features in rage' (B)*
Wi' chokin dread;	40	
An' *Robins's* bonnet wave wi'crape		
For *Mailie* dead.		

O, a' ye *Bards* on bonie DOON!	
An' wha on AIRE your chanters tune!	
Come, join the melancholious croon	*moan*
O' *Robin's* reed!	
His heart will never get aboon!	*above*
His *Mailie's* dead!	

The Cotter's Saturday Night

Inscribed to R. A****, Esq

Let not Ambition mock their useful toil,
    Their homely joys, and destiny obscure;
Nor Grandeur hear, with a disdainful smile,
    The short and simple annals of the Poor.

                    Gray

I

MY lov'd, my honor'd, much respected friend,	
No mercenary Bard his homage pays;	
With honest pride, I scorn each selfish end,	
My dearest meed, a friend's esteem and praise:	*reward*
To you I sing, in simple Scottish lays,	
The *lowly train* in life's sequester'd scene;	
The native feelings strong, the guileless ways,	
What A**** in a *Cottage* would have been;	
Ah! tho' his worth unknown, far happier there I ween!	*believe*

II

November chill blaws loud wi' angry sugh;	10	*blows, rushing sound*
The short'ning winter-day is near a close;		
The miry beasts retreating frae the pleugh;		*plough*
The black'ning trains o'craws to their repose:		*crows*
The toil-worn COTTER frae his labor goes,		*farm tenant/cottager*
This night his weekly moil is at an end,		*drudgery*
Collects his *spades*, his *mattocks* and his *hoes*		
Hoping the *morn* in ease and rest to spend,		
And weary, o'er the moor, his course does		
homeward bend.		

---

l.10 November chill: [B] ... has in mind Gray's *Elegy*, li. 2–3. [Low]

III

At length his lonely *Cot* appears in view   *cottage*
   Beneath the shelter of an aged tree;   20
The expectant *wee-things*, toddlan, stacher   *stagger*
     through
   To meet their *Dad*, wi' flichterin noise   *fluttering*
     and glee.
His wee-bit ingle, blinkan bonilie,   *little bit of fire*
   His clean hearth-stane, his thrifty *Wifie's*   *stone*
     smile,
The *lisping infant*, prattling on his knee,
   Does a' his weary *kiaugh* and care beguile,   *'carking anxiety'(B)*
And makes him quite forget his labor and his toil.

IV

Belyve, the *elder bairns* come drapping in,   *soon, dropping*
   At *Service* out, amang the Farmers roun';
Some ca' the pleugh, some herd, some tentie rin   *drive, careful, run*
   A cannie errand to a neebor town: 30   *quiet, neighbouring*
Their eldest hope, their *Jenny*, woman-grown,
   In youthfu' bloom, Love sparkling in her e'e,   *eye*
Comes hame, pehaps, to shew a braw new gown,   *good-looking*
   Or deposite her sair-won penny-fee,   *hard-won*
To help her *Parents* dear, if they in hardship be.

V

With joy unfeign'd, *brothers* and *sisters* meet,
   And each for other's weelfare kindly spiers: *asks*
The social hours, swift-wing'd, unnotic'd fleet;
   Each tells the uncos that he sees or hears.   *news/uncommon things*
The Parents partial eye their hopeful years;   40
   Anticipation forward points the view;
The *Mother*, wi' her needle and her sheers,
   Gars auld claes look amaist as weel's the new;   *makes, clothes*
The *Father* mixes a' wi' admonition due.

VI

Their Master's and their Mistress's command,
   The *youngkers* a' are warned to obey;
And mind their labor wi' an eydent hand,   *diligent*
   And ne'er, tho' out of sight, to jauk or play: *'daily, trifle' (B)*
'And O! be sure to fear the LORD alway!
   And mind your *duty*, duly, morn and night!   50
Lest in temptation's path ye gang astray,
   Implore his *counsel* and assisting *might*:
They never sought in vain that sought the
     LORD aright.'

---

l.22 flichterin: Glossed by Burns in 1787 as 'to flutter as young nestlings
when their dam approaches'. [Low]

VII

But hark! a rap comes gently to the door;
   Jenny, wha kens the meaning o' the same,
Tells how a neebor lad came o'er the moor,
   To do some errands, and convoy her hame.   *escort*
The wily Mother sees the *conscious flame*
   Sparkle in *Jenny's e'e,* and flush her cheek,   60
With heart-struck, anxious care enquires his name,
   While *Jenny* hafflins is afraid to speak;   *half*
Weel-pleas'd the Mother hears, it's nae wild, worthless *Rake.*

VIII

With kindly welcome, *Jenny* brings him ben;
   A *strappan youth*; he takes the Mother's eye;
Blythe *Jenny* sees the *visit's* no ill taen;
   The Father cracks of horses, pleughs and kye.   *talks, cattle*
The *Youngster's* artless heart o'erflows wi'joy,
   But blate and laithfu', scarce can weel behave;   *shy, bashful*
The Mother, wi' a woman's wiles, can spy   70
   What makes the *youth* sae bashfu' and sae grave;
Weel-pleas'd to think her *bairn's* respected like the lave.   *rest*

IX

O happy love! where love like this is found!
   O heart-felt raptures! bliss beyond compare!
I've paced much this weary, *mortal round,*
   And sage EXPERIENCE bids me this declare –
'If Heaven a draught of heavenly pleasure spare,
   One *cordial* in this melancholy *Vale,*
'Tis when a youthful, loving, *modest* Pair,
   In other's arms, breathe out the tender tale,   80
Beneath the milk-white thorn that scents the ev'ning gale.'

X

Is there, in human form, that bears a heart–
   A Wretch! a Villain! lost to love and truth!
That can, with studied, sly, ensnaring art,
   Betray sweet Jenny's unsuspecting youth?
Curse on his perjur'd arts! dissembling smooth!
   Are *Honor, Virtue, Conscience,* all exil'd?
Is there no Pity, no relenting Ruth,
   Points to the Parents fondling o'er their Child?
Then paints the *ruin'd Maid,* and *their* distraction wild!   90

XI

But now the Supper crown their simple board,
   The healsome *Porritch,* chief of SCOTIA's food: *wholesome, porridge*
The soupe their only *Hawkie* does afford,   *drink, cow*
   That 'yont the hallan snugly chows her cood: *beyond, partition, chews,*
                                                                   cud

---

l.93 Hawkie: Cow with the white face, pet name. [Low]

The *Dame* brings forth, in complimental mood,
   To grace the lad, her weel-hain'd kebbuck, fell,   *-kept, cheese, pungent*
And aft he's prest, and aft he ca's it guid;
   The frugal *Wifie*, garrulous, will tell,
How 'twas a towmond auld, sin' Lint was i' the bell.   *twelvemonth, flax, flower*

XII

The chearfu' Supper done, wi' serious face,   100
   They, round the ingle, form a circle wide;
The Sire turns o'er, with patriarchal grace,
   The big *ha'-Bible*, ance his *Father's* pride: *hall-*
His bonnet rev'rently is laid aside,
   His *lyart haffets* wearing thin and bare;   *grey, temples*
Those strains that once did sweet in ZION glide,
   He wales a portion with judicious care;   *chooses*
'And let us worship god!' he says with solemn air.

XIII

They chant their artless notes in simple guise;
   They tune their *hearts*, by far the noblest aim: 110
Perhaps *Dundee's* wild warbling measures rise,
   Or plaintive *Martyrs*, worthy of the name;
Or noble *Elgin* beets the heaven-ward flame,   *'adds fuel to' (B)*
   The sweetest far of SCOTIA'S holy lays:
Compar'd with these, *Italian trills* are tame;
   The tickl'd ears no heart-felt raptures raise;
Nae unison hae they, with our CREATOR'S praise.

XIV

The priest-like Father reads the sacred page,
   How *Abram* was the Friend of GOD on high;
Or, *Moses* bade eternal warfare wage,   120
   With *Amalek's* ungracious progeny;
Or how the *royal Bard* did groaning lye,
   Beneath the stroke of Heaven's avenging ire;
Or *Job's* pathetic plaint, and wailing cry;
   Or rapt *Isaiah's* wild, seraphic fire;
Or other *Holy Seers* that tune the *sacred lyre*.

XV

Perhaps the *Christian Volume* is the theme,
   How *guiltless blood for guilty man* was shed;
How HE, who bore in heaven the second name,
Had not on Earth whereon to lay His head: 130
How His first *followers* and *servants* sped;

---

l.96 weel-hain'd kebbuck: 'If cheese was to be kept for some time ... all
the whey had to be squeezed out, and pressing was a necessity ... Ayrshire Dunlop cheese became the country's national cheese' (A. Fenton,
Scottish Country Life, 1976, pp.152, 154). [Low]

l.117 Nae unison had they: The Scottish tradition in psalmody was for
everyone to keep the same pitch and sing together, in unison. [Low]

The *Precepts sage* they wrote to many a land:
How, *he*, who lone in *Patmos* banished,
   Saw in the sun a mighty angel stand;
And heard great *Bab'lon's* doom pronounc'd
      by Heaven's command.

XVI

Then kneeling down to HEAVEN'S ETERNAL KING
   The *Saint*, the *Father*, and the *Husband* prays:
Hope 'springs exulting on triumphant wing,'
   That *thus* they all shall meet in future days:
There, ever bask in *uncreated rays*,   140
   No more to sigh, or shed the bitter tear,
Together hymning their CREATOR'S praise,
   In *such society*, yet still more dear;
While circling Time moves round in an eternal sphere.

XVII

Compar'd with *this*, how poor Religion's pride,
   In all the pomp of *method,* and of *art,*
When men display to congregations wide,
   Devotion's ev'ry grace, except the *heart!*
The POWER, incens'd, the Pageant will desert,   150
   The pompous strain, the sacerdotal stole;
But haply, in some *Cottage* far apart,
   May hear, well pleas'd, the language of the *Soul;*
And in His *Book of Life* the Inmates poor enroll.

XVIII

Then homeward all take off their sev'ral way;
   The youngling *Cottagers* retire to rest:
The Parent-pair their *secret homage* pay,
   And proffer up to Heaven the warm request,
That HE who stills the *raven's* clam'rous nest,
   And decks the *lily* fair in flow'ry pride,
Would, in the way *His Wisdom* sees the best,   160
   For *them* and for their *little ones* provide;
But chiefly, in their hearts with *Grace divine* preside.

XIX

From scenes like these, old SCOTIA'S grandeur springs,
   That makes her lov'd at home, rever'd abroad:
Princes and lords are but the breath of kings,
   'An honest man's the noblest work of GOD:'
And *certes*, in fair Virtue's heavenly road,
   The *Cottage* leaves the *Palace* far behind:
What is a lordling's pomp? a cumbrous load,
   Disguising oft the *wretch* of human kind,   170
Studied in arts of Hell, in wickedness refin'd!

---

l.138 Pope's Windsor Forest. [Burns]

l.165 Princes and Lords: cf. Goldsmith, *The Deserted Village*, ll.53–5. [Low]

XX

O SCOTIA! my dear, my native soil!
　　For whom my warmest wish to heaven is sent!
Long may thy hardy sons of *rustic toil,*
　　Be blest with health, and peace, and sweet
　　　　content!
And O may Heaven their simple lives prevent
　　From *Luxury's* contagion, weak and vile!
Then howe'er *crowns* and *coronets* be rent,
　　A *virtuous Populace* may rise the while,
And stand a wall of fire around their　　　　　　　　180
　　much-lov'd ISLE.

XXI

O THOU! who pour'd the *patriotic tide,*
　　That stream'd thro' great, unhappy
　　　　WALLACE' heart;
Who dar'd to, nobly, stem tyrannic pride,
　　Or *nobly die,* the second glorious part:
(The Patriot's GOD, peculiarly thou art,
　　His *friend, inspirer, guardian* and *reward!*)
O never, never SCOTIA'S realm desert,
　　But still the *Patriot,* and the *Patriot-Bard,*
In bright succession raise, her *Ornament*
　　and *Guard!*

To A Mouse,

On turning her up in her Nest,
with the Plough, November, 1785

WEE , sleeket, cowran, tim'rous *beastie,*	*sleek, fearful, little creature*
O, what a panic's in thy breastie!	*little breast*
Thou need no start awa sae hasty,	
Wi'bickering brattle!	*sound of scamper*
I wad be laith to rin an' chase thee,	*loath, run*
Wi' murd'ring *pattle!*	*plough-staff*

I'm truly sorry Man's dominion
Has broken Nature's social union,
An' justifies that ill opinion,
　　　　Which makes thee startle,　　　　　　　　10
At me, thy poor, earth-born companion,
　　　　An' *fellow-mortal!*

---

l.181 the patriotic tide: William Wallace, victor of Stirling Bridge, was
executed by Edward I of England in 1305. [Low] 'The story of Wallace
poured a Scottish prejudice in my veins which will boil along there till
the flood-gates of life shut in eternal rest' (*Letters,* I, 136). [Burns]

l.6 pattle: a small long-handled spade carried on a plough to clear it of
mud, a plough-staff. [Low]

I doubt na, whyles, but thou may *thieve*,
What then? poor beastie, thou maun live!
A *daimen-icker* in a *thrave*   *occasional ear, 24 sheaves*
    'S a sma' request:
I'll get a blessin wi' the lave,   *what's left/the rest*
    An' never miss't!

Thy wee-bit *housie*, too, in ruin!
Its silly wa's the win's are strewin!   20   *frail, winds*
An' naething, now, to big a new ane,   *build*
    O'foggage green!   *rank grass*
An' bleak *December's winds* ensuin,
    Baith snell an' keen!   *bitter*

Thou saw the fields laid bare an' wast,   *waste*
An' weary *Winter* comin fast,
An' cozie here, beneath the blast,
    Thou thought to dwell,
Till crash! the cruel *coulter* past   *iron cutter of plough*
    Out thro' thy cell.   30

That wee-bit heap o' leaves an' stibble,   *stubble*
Has cost thee monie a weary nibble!
Now thou's turn'd out, for a' thy trouble,
    But house or hald,   *without refuge*
To thole the Winter's *sleety dribble*,   *endure*
    An' *cranreuch* cauld!   *hoar-frost*

But Mousie, thou art no thy-lane,   *not alone*
In proving *foresight* may be vain:
The best laid schemes *o' Mice* an' *Men*
    Gang aft agley,   40   *awry*
An' lea'e us nought but grief an' pain,
    For promis'd joy!

Still, thou art blest, compar'd wi' *me*!
The present only toucheth thee:
But Och! I *backward* cast my e'e,   *eye*
    On prospects drear!
An' *forward*, tho' I canna *see*,
    I *guess* an' *fear*!

---

l.15 daimen-icker: Ayrshire Scots, denoting an occasional ear of corn.
[Low]

l.15 thrave: two stooks of corn, or 24 sheaves, a measure of straw or fodder. [Low]

ll.43–8 Still, thou art blest, compar'd wi' me!: cf. Johnson, *Rasselas*, chapter 2, 'As he passed through the fields, and saw the animals around him, "Ye," said he, "are happy, and need not envy me that walk thus among you, burdened with myself; nor do I, ye gentle beings, envy your felicity, for it is not the felicity of man. I have many distresses from which ye are free; I fear pain when I do not feel it; I sometimes shrink at evils recollected and sometimes start at evils anticipated: surely the equity of Providence has balanced peculiar sufferings with peculiar enjoyments".' [Low] See Greene (1984), p.338. [eds]

Epistle to J.L ***** K,

*An Old Scotch Bard**

April 1st, 1785

WHILE briers an' woodbines budding green,
An' Paitricks scraichan loud at e'en,   *partridges, screaming, eve-*
And morning Poossie whiddan seen,   *ning*
     Inspire my Muse,   *hare, scudding*
This freedom, in an *unknown* frien',
     I pray excuse.

On Fasteneen we had a rockin,   *Shrove Tuesday, spinning*
To ca' the crack and weave our stockin;   *party*
And there was muckle fun and jokin,   *have a chat*
     Ye need na doubt;   10
At length we had a hearty yokin,   *set to*
     At *sang about.*   *singing in turn*

There was ae *sang,* amang the rest,
Aboon them a'it pleas'd me best,   *above*
That some kind husband had addrest,
     To some sweet wife:
It thirl'd the heart-strings thro' the breast,   *thrilled*
     A' to the life.

I've scarce heard ought describ'd sae weel,
What gen'rous, manly bosoms feel;   20
Thought I, 'Can this be *Pope,* or *Steele,*
     Or *Beattie's* wark;'   *work*
They tald me 'twas an odd kind chiel   *told, fellow*
     About *Muirkirk.*

---

*John Lapraik (1727–1807) was a tenant-farmer who had fallen on hard times: in 1785 he was imprisoned for debt in Ayr. While in prison, he wrote poetry for diversion. Following Burns's example, he published *Poems on Several Occasions* at Kilmarnock in 1788. His last years were spent as postmaster and Innkeeper in Muirkirk. [Low]

l.7 a rockin: The Revd. John Sheppard of Muirkirk described a rocking as taking place 'when neighbours visit one another in pairs, or three or more in company, during the moonlight of winter or spring … The custom seems to have arisen when spinning on the *rock* or *distaff* was in use, which therefore was carried along with the visitant to a neighbour's house [and] still prevails, though the rock is laid aside.' (*Memoirs of Ayrshire about 1780,* ed. W. Kirk Dickson, Scottish Historical Society, Miscellany vi, 1939, p.288). [Low]

l.13 ae sang: A reference to Lapraik's poem 'When I upon thy bosom lean,' said to have been written when Lapraik's wife had been fretting over their misfortunes. [Low]

ll.21–2 Pope … Steele … Beattie: Here as examples of writers skilled in expressing moral sentiments. Burns was familiar with the poetry of Pope, and with Steele's periodical essays. James Beattie (1735–1803), professor of moral philosophy at Aberdeen, was best known for his blank verse poem, *The Minstrel,* although he also wrote Scots verse. [Low]

It pat me fidgean-fain to hear't   *put, tingling with pleasure*
An' sae about him there I spier't;   *asked*
Then a' that kent him round declar'd,
     He had *ingine*,   *wit*
That nane excell'd it, few cam near't,
      It was sae fine.   30

That set him to a pint of ale,
An' either douse or merry tale,   *sober*
Or rhymes an' sangs he'd made himsel,
     Or witty catches,
'Tween Inverness and Teviotdale,
     He had few matches.

Then up I gat, an swoor an aith,   *swore, oath*
Tho' I should pawn my pleugh an' graith,   *plough, harness*
Or die a cadger pownie's death,   *hawker pony's*
     At some dyke-back,   40   *behind a wall*
A *pint* an' *gill* I'd gie them *baith*,
     To hear your crack.   *talk*

But first an' foremost, I should tell,
Amaist as soon as I could spell,
I to the *crambo-jingle* fell,   *rhyming*
     Tho' rude an' rough,
Yet crooning to a body's sel,   *humming, to oneself*
     Does well eneugh.   *enough*

I am nae *Poet*, in a sense,
But just a *Rhymer* like by chance,   50
An' hae to Learning nae pretence,
     Yet, what the matter?
Whene'er my Muse does on me glance,
     I jingle at her.

Your Critic-folk may cock their nose,
And say, 'How can you e'er propose,
You wha ken hardly *verse* frae *prose*,
     To mak a *sang*?'
But by your leaves, my learned foes,
     Ye're maybe wrang.   60   *wrong*

What's a' your jargon o' your Schools,
Your Latin names for horns an' stools;
If honest Nature made you *fools*,
     What sairs your Grammars?   *serves*
Ye'd better taen up *spades* and *shools*,   *shovels*
     Or *knappin-hammers*.   *stone-breaking*

A set o'dull, conceited Hashes,   *dunderheads*
Confuse their brains in *Colledge-classes*!
They *gang in* Stirks, and *come out* Asses,   *steers/young bullocks*
     Plain truth to speak;   70
An' syne they think to climb Parnassus   *then*
     By dint o' Greek!

Gie me ae spark o' Nature's fire,
That's a' the learning I desire;
Then tho' I drudge thro' dub an' mire   *puddle*
     At pleugh or cart,
My Muse, tho' hamely in attire,
     May touch the heart.

O for a spunk o' ALLAN'S glee,   *spark*
Or FERGUSSON'S, the bauld an' slee,   80   *bold, clever*
Or bright L*****K'S, my friend to be,
     If I can hit it!
That would be *lear* eneugh for me,   *learning*
     If I could get it.

Now, Sir, if ye hae friends enow,   *enough*
Tho' *real friends* I b'lieve are few,
Yet, if your catalogue be fow,   *full*
     I'se no insist;   *I'll*
But gif ye want ae friend that's true,   *if*
     I'm on your list.   90

I winna blaw about *mysel*,   *will not brag*
As ill I like my fauts to tell;   *faults*
But friends an' folk that wish me well,
     They sometimes roose me;   *praise*
Tho' I maun own, as monie still,
     As far abuse me.

There's ae *wee faut* they whiles lay to me,
I like the lasses – Gude forgie me!   *God forgive*
For monie a Plack they wheedle frae me,   *coin*
     At dance or fair: 100
Maybe some *ither thing* they gie me
     They weel can spare.

But MAUCHLINE Race or MAUCHLINE Fair,
I should be proud to meet you there;
We'se gie ae night's discharge to *care*,   *we'll*
     If we forgather,
An' hae a swap o' *rhymin-ware*,
     Wi' ane anither.

The *four-gill chap*, we'se gar him clatter,   *cup, we'll make*
An' kirs'n him wi' reekin water;   110   *christen, steaming*
Syne we'll sit down an' tak our whitter,   *draught*
     To chear our heart,
An' faith, we'se be *acquainted* better
     Before we part.

Awa ye selfish, warly race,   *worldly*
Wha think that havins, sense an' grace,   *manners*
Ev'n love an' friendship should give place
     To *catch-the-plack*!   *coining money*
I dinna like to see your face,   *do not*
     Nor hear your crack.   120

---

l.79 ALLAN: Allan Ramsay (1686–1785), Scottish poet. [eds]

l.80 FERGUSSON: Robert Fergusson (1750–74), Scottish poet. [eds]

But ye whom social pleasure charms,
Whose hearts the *tide of kindness* warms,
Who hold your *being* on the terms,
        'Each aids the others,'
Come to my bowl, come to my arms,
        My friends, my brothers!

But to conclude my lang epistle,
As my auld pen's worn to the grissle;
Twa lines frae you wad gar me fissle,   *make, tingle*
        Who am, most fervent,   130
While I can either sing, or whissle,
        Your friend and servant.

Glossary

a' *all*
ae *one*
aff *off*
aft(en) *often*
amaist *almost*
amang *among*
ance *once*
ane *one*
auld *old*
awa *away*
ay(e) *always*
baith *both*
ben *indoors/within*
bluid *blood*
bon(n)ie *attractive*
braw *fine/splendid*
ca' *call/name*
cauld *cold*
countra *country*
fa' *fall*
frae *from*
gae, gaen, gaun, *go, gone*
gang *etc go*
gat *got*
gie *etc give*
guid *good*
hae *have*
hame *home*
ither, *other, each other*
ilk(a) *each/every*
ken *know*

lang(er) *long(er)*
mair *more*
maist *most, almost*
maun *must*
meikle/mickle/muckle *much*
monie/mony *many*
na, nae, nane, naething *not,   no,
    none, nothing*
onie/ony *any*
owre *over, too*
sae *so*
sang *song*
sic/sich *such*
sma' *small*
tae *to*
taen *taken*
thegither *together*
tither *the other*
twa *two*
unco *very, odd*
wa' *wall*
wad *would, would have*
wee *small*
weel *well*
wha/whase *who, whose*
whare *where*
why(i)les *now, at times/
    sometimes*
yon *that*

(Low, 1985)

Jean-Jacques Rousseau
Émile

Prepared for the Course Team by
Linda Walsh

Contents

Jean-Jacques Rousseau
Émile

Émile *was published in 1762, in the same year as Rousseau's major political work,* The Social Contract, *and shortly after publication of his hugely successful novel,* La Nouvelle Héloïse *(published in London in 1760 and in Paris in 1761). Conceived primarily as a concise guide on the education of children and written in response to a request by Mme de Chenonceaux, a lady highly respected by Rousseau, the work grew in scope, eventually forming an educational treatise incorporating the elements of a philosophical treatise on the goodness of man, and the characters and narrative of a novel with an autobiographical bias. Rousseau offers advice on how to educate Émile, an imaginary pupil, from birth to manhood and goes on to offer guidance on the education of Sophie, Émile's future marriage partner, and on that of women in general. The guiding principle throughout is that any educational programme should respect the natural inclinations and abilities of the child concerned rather than bow uncritically to social conventions. The most controversial part of the book was the section dealing with Émile's religious education. This included the 'Profession of Faith of a Savoyard Priest', a semi-autobiographical, composite account of the advice offered to the young and spiritually adrift Rousseau by two priests he met in Turin and Savoy. The 'Profession of Faith' presented strong arguments in support of deism or natural religion and was seen as a threat to the orthodox Church in France. The Paris Parlement ordered that the book should be publicly burned and Rousseau was forced into exile. From then on he* devoted his literary energies to autobiographical, introspective works of self-justification which emphasised his alienation from contemporary society. The extracts which follow deal principally with the upbringing and education of babies and young children; the 'Profession of Faith' which is relevant to Émile's religious education; and the education of girls.

The text you are given is from a 1779 edition of an eighteenth-century translation (first published in London in 1762) of Rousseau's Émile *entitled* Emilius and Sophia: or, a New System of Education, *4 vols. (992 pp.), printed for J. Potts and D. Chamberlaine, Dublin, 1779. The translation is by William Kenrick but has been altered in places in order to take account of more recent or accurate interpretations of Rousseau's work, and of the French text of* Émile *established in the Pléiade edition (Oeuvres complètes de Jean-Jacques Rousseau, Éditions Gallimard, 1969, vol.IV). Some effort has been made to retain the spelling, capitalization and punctuation of Kenrick's translation. Modern equivalents of eighteenth-century terms are offered in footnotes where appropriate. Page references to Kenrick's translation are offered under the relevant headings.*

The passages from the 'Profession of Faith' contain only a very small proportion of Book IV (See Studies, *II). Occasional paragraphs or parts of paragraphs are omitted from the other selected passages of* Émile *due to limitations of space and are indicated thus: [...]. Longer cuts are indicated by textual summaries, also in square brackets.*

Émile; or, a New System of Education

Book I (Kenrick I, pp.1–84)

All things are good as their Creator made them, but every thing degenerates in the hands of man. By human art is our native soil compelled to nourish exotic[1] plants, and one tree to bear the fruits of another.[2] Improving man makes a general confusion of elements, climates, and seasons: he mutilates his dogs, his horses, and his slaves: he defaces, he confounds every thing, as if

---

[1] i.e. foreign, like the potato. [eds]

[2] i.e. by grafting. [eds]

he delighted in nothing but monsters and deformity. He is not content with any thing in its natural state, not even with his own species. His very offspring must be trained up for him, like a horse in the manège,[3] and [be] taught to grow, after his own fancy, like a tree in his garden.

Without this, indeed, in the present state of things, matters would be still worse than they are, for mankind cannot be civilized by halves. Should a man, in a state of society, be given up, from the cradle, to his own notions and conduct, he would certainly turn out the most preposterous of human beings. The influence of prejudice, authority, necessity, example, and of all those social institutions in which we are immersed, would stifle nature in him, and substitute nothing in her place. She would resemble a shrub, growing by accident in the highway, which would soon be destroyed by the casual injuries it must receive from the frequent passenger.[4]

It is to the tender and provident mother[5] I address myself, who is prudent enough to leave the beaten road, and seeks to preserve this rising shrub from the shocks of human prejudice. Cultivate, water the young plant before it die; so shall its fruit be hereafter delicious to your taste. Erect an early fence around the disposition of your child: another may mark out its position, but it remains with you only[6] to raise the barrier.

Plants are formed by culture, and men by education. If a man should come into the world in full growth and vigour, his bulk and strength would be useless, till he should have learnt how to exert them: they would be even prejudicial to him, as they would prevent others from thinking it needful to lend him any assistance;[7] and thus, left to himself, he would perish of want before he had discovered his needs. We lament the state of infancy, without reflecting that the human race must have been extinct, had not man been first a child.

---

[3] i.e. riding school. [eds]

[4] i.e. passerby. [eds]

[5] The early part of education is the most important, and belongs incontestably to the province of the females. If the Author of nature had designed it for the males, he would doubtless have furnished them with milk, for the nourishment of their children. In every treatise on education, therefore, it is proper more peculiarly to address the women; and that, not only because they are better adapted both by nature and custom for this sphere, and exert a greater influence within it, but also because they are more interested in the success of it. Widows are left generally, in a great degree at the mercy of their children, when they sensibly feel the good or ill effects of the manner in which they educated them. The laws, calculated less for persons than property, because their object is peace and not virtue, have not given sufficient authority to mothers. Their relation to a child, however, is more certain than that of fathers; their duties more painful and laborious, and their discharge of those duties more essential to the peace and good government of a family: nay, it is usual for them also to have a stronger attachment to their children. There are occasions, on which, if a son should want the respect due to his father, he might be, in some measure, excused; but if, on any occasion whatever, a child should prove so unnatural as to forfeit his respect to a mother, to her who bore him in her womb, who nourished him with her milk, who, for whole years, gave up her own ease to contribute to his, who had no cares but for him; should not justice hasten to smother the infamous wretch, as a monster unworthy to breathe a moment longer? It is said, that mothers spoil their children. In this, without doubt, they are wrong: but, perhaps, less wrong than you who corrupt them. A mother is desirous that her child should be pleased and happy; she desires he should be so at once; and so far she is right: if she be mistaken in the means of making him so, she should be better informed. The ambition, avarice, insolence, and mistaken foresight of fathers, their negligence and cruel insensibility, are an hundred times more destructive to children, than the blind fondness of mothers. It will be necessary, however, to explain the sense in which I use the term of mother; which is hereafter done. [Rousseau]

[6] i.e. with you alone. [eds]

[7] For, being in external appearance like themselves, ignorant of speech as well as destitute of those ideas it might express, he would be incapable to make them understand the need in which he stood of their assistance; nor would anything in his appearance suggest it to the spectator. [Rousseau]

We are born weak, we have need of help; we are born destitute of every thing, we stand in need of assistance; we are born stupid, we have need of understanding. All that we are not possessed of at our birth, and which we require when grown up, is bestowed on us by education.

This education we receive from nature, from men, or from things. The internal development of our organs and faculties is the education of nature: the uses we are taught to make of that development, constitute the education given us by men; and in the acquisitions made by our own experience, and the objects that surround us, consists our education from things.

We are formed, therefore, by three kinds of masters. The pupil, in whom the effects of their different lessons are contradictory, is badly educated, and can never be consistent with himself. Only he, in whom they are perfectly consonant, and always tend to the same point, hath attained the end of a complete education. His life and actions demonstrate this, and that he alone is well brought up.

Of these three different kinds of education, that of nature depends not on ourselves; and but in a certain degree that of things: the third, which belongs to men, is that only[8] we have in our power; and even of this we are masters only in imagination; for who can flatter himself he will be able entirely to govern the discourse and actions of those who are about[9] a child?

No sooner, then, doth education become an art, or profession, than it is almost impossible it should succeed, as the concurrent circumstances necessary to its success are not to be depended on. All that can be done, with our utmost solicitude, is to approach as near as possible the end we aim at, attributing it to good fortune if it be attained.

If it be asked, what is this end? it may be answered, that of nature, which has been already proved. For, since the concurrence of the three kinds of education is necessary to their perfection, it is by that one, which is entirely independent of us, that we must regulate the two others. But perhaps this word, Nature, may appear vague and equivocal; let us therefore endeavour to give it a precise and determinate meaning.

Nature, it has been said, is only habit.[10] But to what purpose is this said? Are there not habits, which are contracted only upon compulsion, and which can never suppress the tendency of nature? Such is, for example, the habitual growth of plants, restrained from pursuing their vertical direction. Take off the restraint, and it is true, they preserve the inclination they have been compelled to take: but, you will find, the rise of the sap has not on that account changed its primitive direction; and if the plant continues to vegetate, its future growth will still be upwards.

It is the same with the inclinations and dispositions of mankind. While we remain in exactly the same situation in which they were acquired, we may retain even the most unnatural habits; but as soon as circumstances change, the force of habit ceases, and that of nature exerts itself. Education itself is certainly nothing but habit: but are there not persons in whom the impressions they received in education are effaced? Are there not others again, that retain them? Whence arises this difference? If it be pretended[11] that by nature is only meant habits conformable to nature, we may be spared such absurd questions.

We are born capable of sensibility,[12] and from our birth are variously affected by the different objects that surround us. We no sooner

---

[8] i.e. the only one that. [eds]

[9] i.e. who surround and look after. [eds]

[10] It is probable that Rousseau had in mind here a play by Voltaire, *Fanaticism or the Prophet Mohammed* (act IV, sc.I) in which the following line occurs: 'Nature is, to my eyes, no more than habit'. [eds]

[11] i.e. claimed or argued. [eds]

[12] i.e. of feeling, of forming sense-impressions. See Introduction to Part E Studies for a discussion of this term, *Studies* II. [eds]

acquire, if I may so express myself, a conscious- ness of our sensations, than we are disposed to avoid or pursue, the objects producing them, firstly in proportion as they are agreeable or dis- pleasing: We next learn to approve or dislike them, according to the convenient or incon- venient relation that subsists between ourselves and such objects; and lastly, according to the judgment we form of their consistency with those ideas, which reason gives us of happiness or perfection. These dispositions extend and confirm themselves, in proportion as we become more susceptible[13] and enlightened: but, subject to the restraint of custom, they are more or less distorted by our opinions. Before they have taken this tincture of habit, they are what I call the dispositions of our nature.

It is to these original dispositions, there- fore, we should on every occasion recur: this might also be effected, if our three kinds of edu- cation were merely different. But what can be done, when they are directly opposite, and totally contradictory? when, instead of educating a man for himself, he must be educated for others? Their concurrent action is here destroyed; reduced to the dilemma of acting in opposition to nature, or to the institutions of society, we must chuse either to form the man or the citizen; for to do both at once is impossible.

Every particular society, when it is confined and its members well united, alienates itself from the general one of mankind. A true patriot is inhospitable to foreigners: they are mere men, and appear to have no relation to him.[14] This inconvenience is inevitable, but it is not great. The most essential point is a man's being

beneficent and useful to those among whom he lives. The inhabitants of Sparta, when abroad, were ambitious, covetous, and unjust; but disin- terestedness, equity, and concord reigned within their walls. Be ever mistrustful of those cosmop- olites, who deduce from books the far-fetched and extensive obligations of universal benevo- lence, while they neglect to discharge their actual duties towards those who are about them. A philosopher of this stamp affects to have a regard for the Tartars, by way of excuse for his having none for his neighbours. Natural man is every thing to himself: he is a numerical unit, an absolute integer,[15] that bears no relation but to himself or his species. Civilized man is only a relative unit, the numerator of a fraction, that depends on its denominator, and whose value consists in its relation to the integral body of society. The best political institutions are those which are best calculated to divest mankind of their natural inclinations, to deprive them of an absolute, by giving them a relative, existence, and incorporating distinct individuals in one common whole. In this way the individual no longer regards himself as one but as part of the whole, and enjoys only a shared or common con- sciousness. A citizen of Rome was neither Caius or Lucius; he was a Roman; nay, he even loved his country, exclusive of its relation to himself. Regulus[16] pretended himself[17] a Carthaginian, as being become[18] the property of his masters. In that character he refused to take his seat in the Roman senate, till a Carthaginian commanded him. He was filled with indignation at the remonstrances made to save his life, and returned triumphant to perish in the midst of

---

[13] 'Susceptible' here translates the French word *sensible*, which could mean 'sensitive' or 'of keen emotions'. [eds]

[14] Thus the wars of republics are more cruel than those of monarchies. But if the wars of kings are less cruel, their peace is terrible; better be their foe than their subject. [Rousseau]

[15] i.e. a whole number; a full, independent entity. [eds]

[16] Roman general of the third century BC, renowned for his loyalty to Rome. Captured by the Carthaginians during the first Punic war, he was sent to Rome, on oath, to negotiate an exchange of prisoners. He dissuaded the Senate from agreeing to this and was tortured to death on his return to Carthage. [eds]

[17] i.e. claimed that he was. Throughout this text, the word 'pretend' and its derived forms (for example, 'pretension') should be understood as meaning 'claim', 'allege', etc. [eds]

[18] i.e. as he had become the property of his (Carthaginian) masters. [eds]

tortures. This appears to me, indeed, to have but little relation to men with whom we are at present acquainted. [...]

A woman of Sparta, having five sons in the army, and being in hourly expectation to hear of a battle, a messenger at length arrived, of whom she, trembling, asked the news. Your five sons, said he, are killed – 'Vile slave, who asked you of my sons?' – 'But we have gained the victory,' continued he. This was enough; the heroic mother ran to the temple, and gave thanks to the gods. This woman was a true citizen.

Those who would have man, in the bosom of society, retain the primitive sentiments of nature, know not what they want. Ever contradicting himself, and wavering between his duty and inclination, he would neither be the man nor the citizen; he would be good for nothing either to himself or to others. Like men of the present times, the Englishman, the Frenchman, the *bourgeois*,[19] he would be in reality nothing at all.

To be something, to be consistent with one's self, and always the same individual, our words and actions should agree; we should be always determined in the part we ought to take; we should take it with an high hand, and persevere. If such a prodigy could be found, we might then know whether he be a man or a citizen, or how he can so manage as to be, at once, both the one and the other.

From these elements, which are necessarily opposed to each other, arise two contrary forms of institution; the one public and general, the other domestic and particular.

[Rousseau offers his views on public education or the 'public institution'as outlined by Plato. Plato's *Republic* is described as 'the finest treatise on education that ever was written.']

The public institution exists not, nor can it exist, any longer; for where there is no country there can be no citizens. Those two words, country and citizen, ought no longer to find a place in modern languages. I could give my reasons for it; which, however, I omit, as not immediately relative to[20] my subject.

It must be observed, I do not esteem, as public institutions, those ridiculous establishments that go by the name of colleges.[21] I regard just as little the education acquired by an intercourse with the world, because that experience, aiming at two contrary ends, falls short of both. It is only calculated to make men deceitful, appearing always to interest themselves in the good of others, and being never interested in any thing but what relates to their own. As these pretensions are, also, become general, there is no one deceived by them; so that it is only so much pains thrown away.

From these contradictions arises that which we constantly experience in ourselves. Impelled by nature and custom contrary ways, and forced to yield in a degree to both impulses, we take a route in the mean direction of both,[22] that leads us neither to the end of one or the other. Thus held in suspense, and wavering, during the whole course of our lives, we end our days without being able to render ourselves consistent, and without ever being good for any thing to ourselves or others.

---

[19] A modern translation of 'bourgeois' might be 'a person of the middle classes'. However, in the eighteenth century, bourgeois was commonly referred to the inhabitant of a particular town or city (English 'burgher' or 'burgess'), who enjoyed certain privileges. The term might be applied, for example, to the members of the Swiss oligarchy discussed in the Broadcast Notes to TV14. [eds]

[20] i.e. related to, relevant to. [eds]

[21] There are, indeed, professors, both in the academy of Geneva and in the university of Paris, for whom I have the greatest love and esteem, and think them very capable of instructing youth, were they not tied down to established customs. I would advise one of them to publish the project he has formed of a reformation therein. Perhaps an attempt may, some time or other, be made, to remove the evil, when it is seen to be not without remedy. [Rousseau] The term collège was applied to schools or institutions of higher education. Some of these were run by religious orders and others were incorporated into universities. When the Jesuits were expelled from France in 1762, most of their colleges passed into the hands of the universities; others came under the direction of other religious communities. [eds].

[22] i.e. the middle way between the two. [eds]

There remains then only a private education, or that of nature. But of what use to others, it may be said, would a man be, educated only for himself? Perhaps, if the two-fold object proposed could be reduced to a single one, in taking from man his contradictory motives of action, we should remove a great obstacle to his happiness. To judge of this it would be necessary to see him quite formed; to have observed his inclinations and propensities, have traced their progress, and attended them throughout; in a word, to be made acquainted with the natural man. I flatter myself the reader will have made some advance in these researches, after having perused this treatise.

In order to form this extraordinary man, let us consider first what we have to do. Much, doubtless, depends on preventing any thing from being done. When the wind is only against us, we have nothing to do but steer close and shape our course to windward: but in a strong current, if we would not lose ground, we must drop anchor. Take care, young pilot, that your cable does not veer, your anchor drag and your ship drive,[23] before you are aware.

According to the order of society, in which the respective places of individuals are fixed, every one ought to be educated for that which he is to fill. A man formed for one place, if taken out of it, would be fit for no other, and consequently good for nothing. In this state, education is useful only as[24] fortune seconds the intentions of parents; in every other case it would be hurtful to the pupil, were it only on account of the prejudices it might instil. In Egypt, where the son was obliged to follow the occupation or profession of his father, education had at least a determinate end; but among us, where social rank alone is permanent, and aims of the persons within each rank continually changing; a father would not know whether, in bringing up his child to his own profession, he might be doing him good or ill.

According to the order of nature, all men being equal, their common vocation is the profession of humanity; and whoever is well educated to discharge the duties of a man, cannot be badly prepared to fill up any of those offices that have a relation to him. It matters little to me whether my pupil be designed for the army, the bar, or the pulpit. Nature has destined us to the offices of human life, antecedent to the destination of[25] our parents concerning the part we are to act in society. To live is the profession I would teach him. When I have done with him, it is true, he will be neither a lawyer, a soldier, nor a divine. Let him first be a man; he will as the occasion arises become any thing that a man ought to be, as well as any other person whatever. In vain will fortune remove him from one rank to another, as she pleases, he will be always found in his rightful place.

Our chief study is that of human life; the good and evil of which he that is best able to support,[26] is, in my opinion, the best educated: and hence it follows that true education consists less in precept than action. We begin to instruct ourselves as we begin to live: our education commencing with our being, and our first preceptor the nurse. [...]

We must therefore generalise our views, and consider our pupil as man in the abstract; as exposed to all the various accidents of human life. If men were born inseparably attached to the soil of one country, if one season lasted the whole year, if individuals were incapable of changing their situation in life, the educational customs already established would be in some respects commendable: a child brought up to, and never removed from, one certain station, could not be exposed to the inconveniences of another. But, considering the instability of human affairs, with that restless and bustling spirit of our times which turns every thing upside down, in every new generation; can any method of education be more absurd than that of bringing up a child, as if he

---

[23] i.e. drift out of control. [eds]

[24] i.e. insofar as. [eds]

[25] i.e. before the destination intended for us by. [eds]

[26] i.e. bear, withstand. [eds]

were never to set his foot out of his nursery, or was to be perpetually surrounded by attendants? If the helpless creature takes but one step on the ground, or descends one step of the stairs, he is infallibly ruined. This will not teach him to bear pain, it will teach him to feel it.

In general, little more is thought of in the education of a child than to preserve his being. This is not enough: he ought to learn how to preserve himself when he is grown up to manhood; to support the shocks of fortune, to bear riches or poverty, and to live, if occasion require, either amidst mountains of ice in Greenland, or on the burning rocks of Malta. You may take what precaution you will to preserve his life; he must inevitably die; and though his death may not be justly charged to your solicitude, your pains will be in a great measure ill-judged. It is less needful to preserve your child from death than to teach him how to live. To live is not merely to breathe; it is to act, to make a proper use of our organs, our senses, our faculties, and of all those parts of the human frame which contribute to the consciousness of our existence. The man who has lived most, is not he who hath survived the greatest number of years, but he who has experienced most of life. A man may be buried at an hundred years of age who died in his cradle. Such a one would have been a gainer by dying young, at least he would have lived in our sense of the word, till the time of his decease.

All our wisdom consists in servile prejudice; all our customs are nothing but subjection, confinement and restraint. Civilised man is born, lives, and dies in slavery:[27] at his birth he is bound up in swaddling cloaths, and at his death nailed down in his coffin. As long as he wears the appearance of the human form, he is confined by our institutions.

It is said, some midwives pretend, in moulding the heads of new-born infants, to give them a more proper form; and their pretensions are admitted.[28] Strange infatuation! Our heads are very ill constructed by the Author of our being; we are therefore to have them new-modeled on the outside by the midwives, and within by the philosophers! The Carribeans [*sic*] are a much happier people.

> 'With us, an infant no sooner leaves the womb of its mother, and has hardly enjoyed the liberty of moving and stretching its limbs, than it is clapped again into confinement. It is swathed,[29] its head fixed, its legs stretched out at full length, and its arms placed streight down by the side of its body. In this manner it is bound tight with cloaths and bandages, so that it cannot stir a limb; indeed, it is fortunate if the poor thing be not so muffled up as to be unable to breathe; or if so much precaution be taken to lay it on its side, in order that the fluid excretions voided at the mouth may descend of themselves; for the helpless infant is not at liberty to turn its head to facilitate their discharge.'[30]

A new-born infant requires to be at liberty to move and stretch its limbs, to shake off that numbness in which, moulded together in a heap, they have remained so long. They are stretched out it is true, but they are prevented from moving: even the head itself is rendered immoveable by stay-bands:[31] so that one would imagine the nurses were afraid the poor creature should have the appearance of being alive.

---

[27] Compare the opening sentence of Rousseau's *Social Contract*: 'Man was born free and everywhere he is in chains'. [eds]

[28] i.e. their claims are accepted, agreed to. [eds]

[29] i.e. wrapped in swaddling bands. [eds]

[30] Buffon, *Natural History*, T.iv, p.190, 12°. [Kenrick]

[31] These bands were intended to hold the infant's head in a position that the infant would not choke on his/her own vomit. [eds]

Hence the impulsive force[32] of those internal parts of the body disposed to increase[33] finds an insurmountable obstacle to the necessary movements. The infant is continually making fruitless efforts, which waste its powers or retard their progress. More compressed, more confined, and less at ease in its swaddling cloaths than in its mother's womb, I see not what it has gained by its birth.

This state of inaction and constraint, in which the limbs of infants are confined, cannot fail to prevent the free circulation of the blood and secretion of the humours,[34] to hinder the child's growth and strength, and alter his natural constitution. In countries where no such extravagant precautions are taken, the people are tall, robust and well proportioned: whereas, on the contrary, those, where infants are thus treated, swarm with hunch-backed, crooked-legged, lame, rickety, and deformed persons of every kind. Lest their bodies should not grow distorted from their being at liberty to move freely, we are always in haste to distort them effectually by putting them into a press. We voluntarily deprive them of the use of their limbs, for fear they should by accident hurt or maim themselves.

May not such a cruel restraint have an effect upon their disposition, as well as upon their temperament? Their first sensations are those of uneasiness and pain; they find an obstacle opposed to every motion they are inclined to; more unhappy than a criminal in chains, they are continually making vain efforts, till their patience is exhausted, and they vent their anxiety in cries.

Do you say the first language of children is tears? I believe it: you thwart them from their birth: the first presents you bestow on them, are chains; the first treatment they receive at your hands, is torture. Their voice being all that is left them free, is it a wonder they should make use of it to vent their complaints? They cry because you hurt them; and, I doubt not, if you were bound and bolstered up in the same manner, but you would cry still louder than they.

Whence comes this irrational, this unnatural custom? Ever since mothers have taken upon them to despise their principal obligation, and give up the nursing of their own children, it has been necessary to commit them to the care of women hired for that purpose; who, thus become the temporary mothers of a stranger's children, without the ties of nature, have studied only to save themselves trouble. An infant, whose arms and legs are at liberty, must be continually watched; but when it is fast bound, it may be thrown into any corner, without troubling yourself about its cries. Provided there are no other proofs of the nurse's negligence, if the child break not a leg or an arm, what signifies to her whether it die, or remain a cripple the rest of its life? Its limbs are preserved at the expence of its whole body, and whatever may happen, the nurse is excused.

Do those polite mothers,[35] who, disengaged from the trouble of children, indulge themselves in the amusements of the town, know the treatment their harmless infants may, at the same time, receive in the country? How often is the little innocent, when its nurse is in the least hurry, hung up on a peg, like a bundle of clouts,[36] there to remain crucified, till other business be leisurely dispatched? Such children as have been found in this situation, have been observed to be always purple in the face; the stomach, being violently compressed, preventing the circulation of the blood and forcing it into the head; in the mean while the poor little creatures were supposed to be very patient, because they had not the power to cry. I know not precisely how long a child may remain alive in such a situation, but I imagine it cannot be a great while. This, however, I think, is one of the greatest conveniences of swaddling cloaths.

---

[32] i.e. the drive. [eds]

[33] i.e. with a natural disposition to grow. [eds]

[34] Bodily fluids (blood, phlegm, choler, melancholy) which, according to Hippocratic tradition, determined a person's physical and mental qualities. [eds]

[35] i.e. mothers free to move about in polite society. [eds]

[36] i.e. cloths. [eds]

It is pretended that children unswathed would be subject to various accidents, from their restlessness, destructive to the perfect conformation of their limbs. This is one of the futile arguments of our false reasoning, and which has never been confirmed by experience. Of the multitude of children that, among people more rational than we, are nursed without laying any restraint on the motion of their limbs, we shall not find one that wounds or maims itself: they are incapable of moving with sufficient force to hurt themselves; and if their limbs ever get into a wrong situation, the uneasiness they feel soon induces them to change it.

We have not as yet taken it into our heads to swathe[37] puppies or kittens; do we see any great inconvenience those animals labour under from our negligence? Infants, you will say, are more heavy: I grant it: but if they are more heavy, they are also proportionably feeble. They are hardly able to move, much less to maim themselves: nay if you lay them on their backs, they must perish in that position, like the tortoise, not having the power to turn themselves.

Not content with having ceased to suckle their children, the women of these times have acquired a reluctance to their production:[38] indeed the one is a natural consequence of the other. No sooner does the situation of being a mother become burthensome, than means are presently found to get rid of it entirely: a fruitless beginning only is aimed at, that it may be continually repeated: and thus the attraction which nature designed should promote the multiplication of our species operates to its destruction. This practice, added to the other causes of depopulation, forebodes the approaching fate of Europe. The sciences, arts, philosophy and manners it[39] gives birth to, will not fail to reduce it ere long to a desert. It will be peopled only by wild beasts; and in this will not have greatly changed its inhabitants.

I have frequently observed the little artifices of some new married women, who affect to be thought desirous of nursing their own children; and perceive they know very well how to get themselves solicited to give up this whim. I have observed how artfully the husband, the physician, and particularly the mother has been brought to interfere. A husband that would dare to consent that his wife should nurse her child, would be esteemed an abandoned wretch; an assassin that wanted to get rid of her. Ye prudent husbands, sacrifice, therefore, your paternal affection to domestic quiet; thinking yourselves happy that there are to be found, in the country, wives more continent than your own. And still more happy may you be deemed, if the time, which yours gain by these means is not bestowed on others as well as on yourselves.

The duties of women are by no means equivocal; but it is disputed whether, under the present contempt for them, it may not be the same thing to a child, if it be nourished by the milk of its mother or of any other person? This question should be determined by the physicians, who generally resolve it as the women would have them:[40] and, indeed, I really think it may be better for a child to be nourished by the milk of an healthy nurse, than of a diseased or an ill-conditioned mother, if there be any new evil to fear from her constitution.

But is the question answered by a physical solution only? Has a child less need of a mother's tenderness than of her breast? Other women, nay brutes, might afford it the milk which she refuses; but the solicitude, the tenderness of a mother cannot be supplied. She who suckles the child of another instead of her own, must be a bad mother; how then can it be expected she should make a good nurse? She may, it is true, become so, in time, but slowly, and as habit alters nature; in the mean while, the neglected child would have time enough to perish before his nurse had acquired a maternal affection for it.

---

[37] i.e. swaddle. [eds]

[38] Many contemporary commentators were worried by what they perceived as a trend towards depopulation. For Rousseau, population growth was the sign of a healthy government. [eds]

[39] i.e. Europe. [eds]

[40] The league between the women and the doctors has always struck me as one of the oddest things in Paris. The doctors' reputation depends on the women, and by means of the doctors the women get their own way. It is easy to see what qualifications a doctor requires in Paris if he is to succeed. [Rousseau]

There results even from this possible advantage an inconvenience, which is of itself sufficient to deter a woman of any sensibility[41] from having her children nursed by others: and this is that of a stranger's partaking with, or alienating from her the rights of a mother; of seeing her child love another woman as well, or better than herself; of perceiving the affection it retains for its natural parent, a matter of favour, and that for its adopted one a duty: for where I find the obligations of a mother duly discharged, I certainly ought to look for the attachment of the child.

The method usually taken to remove this inconvenience, is to inspire children with a contempt for their nurses, by treating them as real servants. When their business is done, the child is taken away, or the nurse dismissed, who is afterwards so ill received that she is soon disgusted with coming to see her nursery. At the end of a year or two, the child sees and knows her no more: but his mother, who imagines herself substituted in her place, and endeavours to repair her negligence by her cruelty, is mistaken. Instead of making an affectionate son of an unnatural nurse child, she only excites his ingratitude; and teaches him one day to despise her who gave him life, as he already despises her who nursed him with her milk.

How earnestly might I insist on this point, were it not so discouraging to expatiate in vain on useful subjects! More depends on it, by much, than is generally imagined. Would you have mankind return all to their natural duties, begin with mothers of families; you will be astonished at the change this will produce. Almost every kind of depravation[42] flows successively from this source; the moral order of things is broken; and the natural, quite subverted in our hearts: home is less chearful and engaging; the affecting sight of a rising family no more attaches the husband, nor attracts the eyes of a stranger: the mother is less truly respectable, whose children are not about her; families are no longer places of residence; habit no longer enforces the ties of blood; there are no fathers, nor mothers, children, brethren nor sisters; they hardly know, so how should they love, each other? Each cares for no one but himself; and when home affords only a melancholy solitude, it is natural for us to seek diversion elsewhere.

But should mothers again condescend to nurse their children, manners would reform themselves, the sentiments of nature would revive in our hearts; the state would be re-peopled; this principal point, this alone, would re-unite every thing. A taste for the charms of a domestic life is the best antidote against corruption of manners. The noise and bustle of children, which is generally thought troublesome, becomes hence agreeable; it is these that render parents more necessary, more dear, to each other, and strengthen the ties of conjugal affection. When a family is all lively and animated, domestic concerns afford the most delightful occupation to a woman, and the most agreeable amusement to a man. Hence, from the correction of this one abuse, will presently result a general reformation; nature will soon reassume[43] all its rights. Let wives but once again become mothers, and the men will presently[44] again become fathers and husbands.

Superfluous talk! even their disgust at the pleasures of the world will never bring them back to their duty. Wives have ceased to be mothers; they will not, they even have no desire to be such. Nay, tho' they should desire it, they can hardly effect it: as at present a contrary custom is established, every one desirous of being a mother, must stand in opposition to all that come near her, united in league against an example, which one party hath not set, and the other is unwilling to follow.

There are indeed some young persons to be found of a good natural disposition, who, despising the tyranny of mode and the clamours of their sex, venture to discharge with a virtuous intrepidity, the most delightful obligation nature

---

[41] i.e. feeling or sensitivity. [eds]

[42] i.e. depravity. [eds]

[43] i.e. again take possession of. [eds]

[44] i.e. straightaway. [eds]

can impose. May their number be augmented by the influence of that happiness which is destined for those who engage in so pleasing a task. I will venture, and that on the authority of the most obvious reasonings, and on observations that I have never seen disputed, to promise such worthy mothers, a real and constant attachment on the part of their husbands, a truly filial affection on that of their children, the esteem and respect of the public, happy delivery, speedy restoration to constant and vigorous health, and after all, the pleasure to see their daughters follow their example and see that example commended to others.

Where there is no mother, there can be no child. The obligations incumbent on both are reciprocal, and if they are neglected on one side they will hardly be fulfilled on the other. The child should love its mother before it is sensible[45] of it as a duty. If the ties of blood be not strengthened by habit and cultivation, they will be suppressed in their infancy, and the heart will perish, if I may so express myself, before it is born. Thus the very first steps which are taken with us are foreign to nature.

The obvious paths of nature are also forsaken, in a different manner, when, instead of neglecting the duties of a mother, a woman carries them to excess; when she makes an idol of her child; increases and nourishes its weakness, by preventing its sense of it, and as if she should emancipate him from the laws of nature, prevents every approach of pain or distress; without thinking that, for the sake of preserving him at present, from a few trifling inconveniences, she is accumulating on his head a distant load of accidents and misfortunes; without thinking that it is a barbarous precaution to enervate and indulge the child at the expence of the man.

Thetis,[46] says the fable, in order to render her son invulnerable, plunged him into the waters of Styx.[47] This is an expressive and beautiful allegory. The cruel mothers I am speaking of act directly contrary: by plunging their children

in softness, they render them more tender and vulnerable; they lay open, as it were, their nerves to every species of afflicting sensations, to which they will certainly fall a prey, as they grow up.

Observe nature, and follow the track she has delineated. She continually exercises her children, and fortifies their constitution by difficulties of every kind; inuring them betimes to grief and pain. In cutting their teeth, they experience the fever; griping colics throw them into convulsions; the hooping cough suffocates, and worms torment, them; surfeits corrupt their blood; and the various fermentations their humours are subject to, cover them with dangerous eruptions. Almost the whole period of childhood is sickness and danger; half the children that are born, dying before they are eight years old. In passing thro' these hardships the child gathers strength and fortitude, and, as soon as he is capable of living, the principle of life becomes less precarious.

This is the rule of nature. Why should you act contrary to it? Don't you see, that by endeavouring to correct her work, you spoil it and prevent the execution of her designs? Act you from without as she does within: this, according to you, would increase the danger; on the contrary, it will avert and lessen it. Experience shews that children, delicately educated, die in a greater proportion than others. Provided you do not make them exert themselves beyond their powers, less risk is run by exercising, than indulging them in ease. Inure them, therefore, by degrees, to those inconveniences they must one day suffer. Harden their bodies to the intemperance of the seasons, climates, and elements; to hunger, thirst and fatigue; in a word, dip them in the waters of Styx. Before the body hath acquired a settled habit, we may give it any we please, without danger; but when it is once arrived to its full growth and consistence, every alteration is hazardous. A child will bear those vicissitudes which to a man would be insupportable: the soft and pliant fibres[48] of the

---

[45] i.e. aware. [eds]

[46] Greek goddess of the sea and mother of Achilles (see note 69 below). [eds]

[47] The icy river of Hades or Hell, the waters of which bestowed invulnerability on those plunged into them. [eds]

[48] Filaments of which membranes and muscles are composed. [eds]

former readily yield to impression; those of the latter are more rigid, and are reduced only by violence to recede from the forms they have assumed. We may, therefore, bring up a child robust and hearty, without endangering either its life or health; and tho' even some risk were run in this respect, it would not afford sufficient cause of hesitation. Since they are risks inseparable from human life, can we do better than to run them during that period of it, wherein we take them at the least disadvantage?

The life of a child becomes the more valuable, as he advances in years. To the value of his person, must be added the cost and pains attending his education: to the loss of life, also, may be annexed his own sense and apprehensions of death. We should therefore, particularly direct our views to the future in his present preservation; we ought to arm him against the evils of youth, before he arrives at that period: for if the value of his life increases till he attain the age in which it is useful, what a folly is it to protect him from a few evils, in his infancy, to multiply his sufferings when he comes to years of discretion? Can such be the instructions of a master of his profession?

Man is born to suffer in every stage of his existence. Even self-preservation is attended with some degree of pain. Happy are we, who in our infancy know only physical evils! Evils much less cruel, much less terrible than others, and more seldom capable of reconciling us to death. Men never destroy themselves to get rid of the gout; the anguish of the mind only is productive of despair. We lament the state of infants, whereas it is our own that is most to be lamented. Our greatest evils are derived from ourselves.

A child, as soon as it is born, begins to cry; great part of its earliest infancy being spent in tears. Sometimes we dance it about and sooth[e] it; at others threaten and beat it, in order to make it silent. We always either do that which is pleasing to the child, or exact of it what pleases ourselves; either submitting to its whims, or obliging it to submit to ours. There is no medium,[49] it must either command or obey.

Hence the first ideas it acquires, are those of tyranny and servitude. Before it can speak it learns to command, and before it can act, it is taught obedience; nay sometimes it is punished before it be conscious of a fault, at least before it can commit one. Thus it is we early instil into their tender hearts, those passions which we afterwards impute to nature; and, after having taken the pains to make them vicious, complain that we found them so.

In this manner a child passes six or seven years, under the care of the women; the constant victim of their caprices and his own. After he has learnt of them what they usually teach, that is, after they have burthened his memory with words without meaning, and things of no consequence; after they have corrupted his natural disposition by the passions they have implanted, this factitious[50] being is turned over to the care of a preceptor,[51] who proceeds in the development of those artificial buds already formed; teaching him every thing except the knowledge of himself, how to make the best of himself, the business of human life, and the attainment of happiness. So that when this slavish and tyrannical infant, replete with science and deprived of sense, equally debilitated both in body and mind, comes at length to enter on the world, it is no wonder that the display he makes of his folly, vanity and vice, should cause us to lament the misery and perverseness of human nature. We are, however, mistaken: such is the man made by our own caprices; that of nature is differently constituted.

Are you desirous of preserving his original form? Begin to preserve it as soon as he comes into the world. Make yourself master of him as soon as he is born, nor quit him afterwards till he grows up to manhood: without this you will never perfectly succeed. As his mother is his only true nurse, so is his father his only true preceptor. Let them mutually agree in the ordering of their duties as well as in their method: let their child pass from the hands of one to the other. He will be better educated by a judicious father, tho' of confined talents, than by the most able

---

[49] i.e. no middle way. [eds]

[50] i.e. fabricated. artificial. [eds]

[51] i.e. tutor. [eds]

master in the world: for zeal will better supply the place of abilities, than abilities make up for the want of zeal.

But it will be said, men have other business, employments, duties – Duties! Surely those of a father are of the highest importance![52] We need not be surprized, however, if the man, whose wife disdains to nourish the fruit of their union, should in like manner disdain to cultivate and improve it. There is no picture in the world more delightful than that of a family; a single feature wanting, nevertheless, spoils the whole. If the mother be of too puny a constitution for a nurse, the father has too much business on his hands for a preceptor. Their children sent from home, and dispersed in boarding schools, convents, and colleges, carry elsewhere their family regards; or rather contract the habit of being attached to nothing. Brothers and sisters hardly know each other; but, when on any occasion assembled, behave to each other as politely, and with as much distant ceremony, as strangers. When intimacy between relations no longer subsists, the pleasures of life no longer depend on family society, but are sought for in the corruption of manners. Where is there a man so blind as not to see clearly the connection of these things?

A father, in begetting and providing for his children, hath in that discharged but a third part of his obligations. He owes a Being to his species, social Beings to society, and citizens to the state. Every man, who is capable of paying this triple debt, and refuses, is in that respect criminal; and perhaps is more so when he pays it by halves. He who is incapable of performing the duties of a father, has no right to be one. Neither poverty nor business, nor personal

importance can dispense with parents nursing, and educating their children. Readers, you may believe me, when I take upon me to assure every parent, who is indued with sensibility,[53] and neglects these sacred obligations, that he will long live to repent it in the bitterness of his sorrow, and never be comforted.[54]

But what step doth a wealthy parent take? this master of a family, so very much engaged as to be obliged to give up the education of his children? He pays another person, to discharge those obligations which are laid on himself. Venal soul! Dost thou think thou canst purchase thy son another father with money? Deceive not thyself; it is not a master thou givest him but a servant, who will soon make him as servile as himself.

Much has been said, and written, on the qualifications of a good governor. The first that I should inquire of him, and which would include a great many others, is that he should not be venal. There are some professions so noble that they cannot be practised for hire, without shewing the professor unworthy of them: such is the profession of arms, and such that of a tutor. To whom, then, shall I entrust the education of my child? – I have already told you; to yourself. But I am incapable –. Are you indeed incapable? Make then a friend. I see no other resource.

What a sublime idea do I entertain of a complete tutor! In fact, to be able to form the man, one ought either to be his father, or something more than man, one's self. Yet such is the office you carelessly confer on the merest mercenaries.

The more I reflect on this subject, the more I perceive new difficulties arise. It is necessary the governor should have been educated for his

---

[52] When we read, in Plutarch, that Cato himself, the censor, who governed in Rome, with so much glory, brought up his son from the cradle, and that with so much assiduity that he would quit every business to be present when the nurse, that is to say, the mother, washed and rubbed him; when we read in Suetonius, that Augustus, master of the world he had conquered, and over which he reigned, taught his grand-children to write, to swim, to comprehend the elements of science, and had them constantly about him; we, that are grown so much wiser, cannot help laughing at the insignificant good people of those days, who amused themselves with such trifles, too confined, doubtless, in their abilities to be equal to the important affairs of the great men of the present times. [Rousseau]

[53] i.e. sense and feeling. [eds]

[54] There is some evidence that Rousseau was thinking here of the abandonment of his own children. See *The Confessions*, Penguin Books, 1988, p.516, p.321–2 and, in particular, p.549. [eds]

pupil, that his domestics should have been educated for their master, that every one who comes near him should have received the same impressions which they are to communicate to him; and thus education on education becomes necessary no body knows how far. How can a child be properly educated by one who has not been properly educated himself?

But where is such an extraordinary mortal to be found? I confess I am ignorant. In these abject times, who knows what degree of virtue the human mind may attain? Yet suppose this prodigy found. It is in examining what he ought to do, that we shall see what he ought to be. I can venture to pronounce beforehand, however, that the father who is the most sensible of[55] the value of a good governor will be the first to do without one; as he will find it more difficult to procure one, than to become such himself. Or is he desirous, in such a case, to make a friend? Let him educate his child to that end; he will then have no need to seek one elsewhere, and nature will have already done half his work.

A certain personage, of whom I knew nothing more than his elevated station, once made me a proposal to educate his son. In this, he doubtless did me great honour: so far, however, from being offended at my refusal, he ought to commend my discretion. Had I accepted his offer, and my method proved wrong, his son's education would have been spoiled; and if it proved right, it had been still so much the worse. The son would have renounced the titles of his father, he would have had no inclination to be a prince.

I am too sensible of the importance of a preceptor's duty, I feel too much my own incapacity, ever to accept of such an employ, from any person whatever; even the motives of friendship itself affording to me additional reasons to refuse it. I imagine, indeed, that after having read this book, few will be disposed to make me such an offer; and I must beg of those who are, not to take the trouble of a fruitless application. I made formerly a sufficient essay[56] in this business to

convince me I am not fit for it,[57] and even my situation would excuse me were my talents equal to it. I thought it incumbent on me to make this public declaration, to satisfy those, who do not appear to think so respectfully of me, as to believe my resolutions on this head sincere.

But, tho' I hold myself incapacitate to undertake the most useful part of this arduous task, I shall venture to attempt that which is the most easy: To follow the example of many others, I shall not set my hand to the work, but to the pen; and instead of doing it myself, endeavour to advise others, what ought to be done.

In attempts of this kind, their authors, generally very easy about the consistency of a theory they are not concerned to put in practice, lay down, without a scruple, a number of fine precepts impossible to be followed; and for want of sufficient details and examples of their application, render even those which are practicable useless.

I have, therefore, in this work made choice of an imaginary pupil, and have taken the liberty to suppose myself of a proper age, in health, and possessed of the requisite knowledge and abilities, to undertake his education, to conduct him from the time of his birth till, grown up to maturity, he may stand in need of no other guide than himself. This method appears to me useful, in preventing an author, diffident of himself, from running into chimeras: for, when he deviates from the ordinary practice, he has only to try his method on the pupil; and he will soon see, or the reader will see for him, whether he follows the natural progress of infancy and the natural growth of the human heart.

This is what I have endeavoured to do, amidst the various difficulties that presented themselves. That I might not needlessly swell the size of my book, I have contented myself, however, with simply laying down those principles, of which every one, at first sight, must acknowledge the truth. As to those which require proof; I have applied them all either to my Émile, or other examples, and have shown by the most

---

[55] i.e. well aware of, alert to. [eds]

[56] i.e. attempt. [eds]

[57] Rousseau had acted as tutor to the sons of M. Mably for a short, unsuccessful period, (*The Confessions*, p.253). [eds]

circumstantial[58] applications, in what manner my theory may be reduced to practice: such, at least, is the plan I have laid down: it remains with the reader to decide how far I have executed my design.

Agreeable to this sketch of my plan, I speak but little, at first setting out, of Emile; because, my first maxims of education, altho' contrary to those generally established, are so self-evident, that it is not easy for persons of common sense to refuse their assent to them. But, in proportion as I advance, my pupil, brought up very different from yours, is no longer an ordinary youth; but requires a regimen peculiar to himself. He appears then more frequently in the scene; and, toward the latter end of my tuition, I lose view of him not a moment, till he has, whatever he may say, no longer occasion for my assistance.

I shall not here expatiate on the qualifications of a complete tutor; I suppose them,[59] and, at the same time, suppose myself possessed of them all. In the perusal of the work, the reader will see how liberal I have been to myself.

I shall here observe only, in contradiction to the common opinion, that, the governor of a child should be young, even as young as possible, consistent with his having attained necessary discretion and sagacity. I would have him be himself a child, that he might become the companion of his pupil, and gain his confidence by partaking of his amusements. There are not things in common enough between infancy and manhood, to form a solid attachment at so great a distance. Children sometimes caress old men, but they never love them.

It is generally required that a governor should have already educated one pupil. This is too much: the same man can provide but one education. If a first be necessary to qualify him for the second, what right had he to engage in that first?

From longer experience he may know better how to act, but he will be no longer capable of action. Whoever has filled that station well enough to be sensible of its difficulties, will not be disposed to enter on it a second time; and if he has but ill acquitted himself the first time, it is a bad recommendation for the second.

It is a very different thing, I own, to follow a young man up and down for four years, and to conduct him for five and twenty. You give your son a tutor, when he is already formed; I would have him have had a governor before he was born.

Your preceptor may change his pupil every five years; mine can have but one. You make a distinction between a preceptor and a governor: another folly! Do you distinguish between the pupil and the scholar? There is but one science to be taught children; and that is, the duties of man. This is, besides, a science of itself, and whatever Xenophon[60] has said of the education of the Persians, is not to be divided. I should rather also denominate a master in it a governor, than a preceptor; because it is less his province to instruct than conduct: it is not his business to lay down precepts, but to teach his pupil to discover them.

If so much care is to be taken in the choice of a governor, it should be surely permitted him on the other hand to chuse his pupil, particularly in a case where a model for imitation is proposed. This choice cannot be directed either by the genius or character of the child, which can only be known when the task of educating him is completed, whereas I adopt him before he is born. Nay, were I capable in this respect to make a choice, I should fix on an ordinary capacity, such therefore I suppose that of my pupil. Common men alone are the objects of education; and theirs only should serve as an example to the rest of their species. The others educate themselves, no matter what is offered to them.

The soil[61] is not a matter of indifference in the cultivation of mankind: they are not all such as they might have been if born in temperate climates. The disadvantage is visible in either extreme. A man is not planted like a tree, in any

---

[58] i.e. detailed. [eds]

[59] i.e. assume them to be understood. [eds]

[60] Athenian historian, philosopher, general, and follower of Socrates, *c*. 430–355 BC. [eds]

[61] i.e. immediate or native environment. [eds]

country, to grow there continually, but is frequently changing his place; and he who removes from one extreme to the other, is obliged to go twice as far to arrive at the same point, as he who sets out from a line drawn between both.

If the inhabitant of a temperate clime visits successively both extremes, his advantages are further evident: for although he should undergo the same modification as one that should pass from one extreme to the other, yet he would depart each way, the less by half from his natural constitution. Thus a French-man may live in Guinea or in Lapland; but a Negro would not live so well at Torneo;[62] nor a Samoyed[63] at Benin.[64] It appears, also, that the organization of the brain is less perfect in the two extremes. Neither the negroes nor the Laplanders have the natural understanding of Europeans. If, therefore, my pupil must be an inhabitant of the earth, I would select him from those of a temperate zone; from the French, for instance, in preference to all others.

As we go northwards, we find men consume a great deal upon an ungrateful soil; towards the south, they consume little on a fertile one. Hence arises a new distinction; the one being thereby rendered laborious and the other contemplative. Society presents us, on one spot, with a picture of this distinction, in that between the poor and the rich. The former reside on the ungrateful soil, and the latter on the plentiful one.

The poor stand in no need of education, that of their station is confined, and they cannot attain any other. On the contrary, the education of those who are in a wealthy station, is that which is the least adapted to their own good or to the good of society. Moreover, all education adapted to the nature of things, ought to qualify a man for all the conditions of life; now it is certainly less reasonable to educate the poor for a high station, than the rich for a low one; for, in proportion to the number of both, there are

much fewer poor persons who become rich, than there are rich persons who become poor. Our pupil, therefore, shall be rich; thus we are sure, at least, of forming one man the more; a poor one may become a man of himself.

It is for the same reason, I shall not be sorry that Emile should be, also, of noble birth: as we are sure of snatching one victim from the absurdities of prejudice.[65]

Emile is an orphan. It is to no purpose he should have a father or mother. As I charge myself with their obligations, I succeed to their rights and authority. He ought, indeed, to honour his parents; but all his complacence[66] is due to me. This is the first, or rather the only condition I make with him.

To this I should add, what is only a consequence of it, that we are never to part but by mutual consent. This is an essential article, and I would even have both the governor and pupil look upon each other as inseparable, and the fortunes of each as common to both. For as soon as they regard, tho' at a great distance, their future separation; as soon as they foresee the moment, when they are to become strangers to each other, they begin to be so already: each forms his separate views, and both, taken up with the prospect of what may happen after their parting, continue together against their inclination. The pupil looks upon the tutor only as the badge and scourge of childhood; while the latter regards the former as an inconvenient burthen, of which he should be glad to be lightened: thus they sigh, in concert, for the moment in which they shall see themselves rid of each other; and as there can be no real attachment between them, the one is as careless as the other is intractable.

But when they regard themselves, as formed to spend their days together, it is of the utmost consequence to both to endear themselves to each other; and this of itself is sufficient

---

[62] A town in Lapland. [eds]

[63] Race of Siberian mongols. [eds]

[64] City in present-day Nigeria. [eds]

[65] Class prejudice, presumably. [eds]

[66] i.e. complaisance, obedience. [eds]

to create a reciprocal esteem. The pupil will not be ashamed to be conducted, in his infancy, by the friend he is to accompany, when grown up: on the other hand, the governor cannot but interest himself in the cultivation of the plant of which he is to reap the fruit; while in adding to the merit of his pupil he is laying up a fund, by which he is to profit in his old age.

This preliminary contract supposes[67] that from an happy delivery, a well-shaped, vigorous and healthy child will be received. A father has no choice, and therefore ought to give no preference to any of the children God has given him; they are all equally his children, and are entitled to the same care and tenderness. Whether they are maimed or perfect, sickly or robust, each of them is a sacred deposit, of which he is to give an account to him of whom he received it, marriage being a contract made with nature as well as between the parties.

But whoever lays himself under an obligation which nature has not imposed, ought to be well assured of the means to discharge it; otherwise he will thereby render himself accountable for what is out of his power to perform. Whoever undertakes the tuition of an infirm and valetudinary infant, converts his office of governor into that of an attendant on the sick; he will lose that time, in preserving an useless life, which was intended to increase its value; he will be exposed himself to the mortification of seeing himself, one day, reproached, by a weeping mother, for the death of her son, whom he hath long and assiduously kept alive.

I would not take charge of a sickly child, though I were sure it would live to be fourscore. I would not be troubled with a pupil always useless to himself and to others, whose only concern would be self-preservation, and the weakness of whose body would prevent the cultivation of his mind. What should I be doing, in vainly bestowing all my time and pains on such an object, but adding to the loss of society, be depriving it of the services of two men instead of one? Let any one else take charge of his infirmities, I consent, and approve his charity; but my talent lies not

that way: I could never teach a child to live, who should be in continual apprehensions of dying.

The body should be vigorous, to act in obedience to the mind: a good servant should be robust and strong. I know intemperance will inflame the passions; that in time it will also wear away the body; mortification and abstinence, too, produce the same effect from a different cause. The more feeble a body is, the greater influence it has over the mind; the stronger it is, the more obedient is it to its commands. The sensual passions all lodge in effeminate bodies; they are excited by so much the more, in proportion as they are incapable of gratification.

A debilitated body enervates the mind. Hence the influence of physic,[68] an art more destructive to mankind than all the evils it pretends to cure. I know not, for my part, of what malady we are cured by the physicians, but I know many fatal ones which they inflict on us; such are cowardice, pusillanimity, credulity, and the fear of death: if they cure the body of pain, they deprive the soul of fortitude. What end doth it answer to society, that they keep a parcel of rotten carcases on their legs? It is *men* the community wants, and those we never see come out of their hands.

It is however the present mode to take physic; and it must be so. It is a pretty amusement for idle people that have nothing to do, and not knowing how to bestow their time otherwise, throw it away in self-preservation. Had they been so unfortunate as to have been born immortal, they would have been the most miserable of beings. A life, which they would not be under the continual apprehension of losing, would be to them of no value. Physicians pay their court to such persons, by frightening them, and affording them daily the only pleasure they are susceptible of; that of hearing they are in danger, and yet not quite dead.

I have no design to enlarge here on the futility of physic; my present purpose being only to consider it in a moral light. I cannot, however, forbear observing, that mankind use the same sophistry, in regard to the use of medicine, as

---

[67] i.e. takes for granted, assumes. [eds]

[68] i.e. the practice of medicine. 'Physic' which translates the French *médicine* could, like the French term, refer to either the practical science of medicine or to potions, prescriptions in bottles. Rousseau is disillusioned with both. [eds]

they do with respect to their search after truth. They suppose always that, when a physician treats a patient who recovers, he has cured him; and that, when they have gone through a disquisition concerning the truth, they have found it. They do not see that we ought to put in the balance, against one cure effected by physic, the deaths of an hundred patients it has killed; or that we should oppose to the utility of one boasted truth, the mischief of a thousand errors fallen into by making the discovery. The science which enlightens, and the physic that cures, are doubtless very useful: but the pretended science that misleads, and the physic that kills, are as certainly destructive. Teach us therefore to distinguish between them. This is precisely the point in question. Could we teach our vain curiosity not to thirst after truth, we should never be the dupes of falsehood: could we be satisfied to bear the maladies to which nature denies a cure, we should never die by the hands of the physician. Self-denial in these two instances is prudent; men would be evidently gainers by such abstinence and submission. I do not pretend to deny that physic may be useful to some few particular persons, but I affirm it to be destructive to the human race in general.

It may be replied, as it constantly is, the fault lies in the physician, and not in the science of medicine, which is otherwise infallible. Well, well, be it so: take care, however, the physic be never accompanied by the doctor: for as sure as ever they come together, there will be an hundred times more to fear, from the blunders of the artist, than to hope for, from the efficacy of the art.

This deceitful science, calculated more to affect the mind than the body, is not more useful to one than to the other; it cures us less of sickness than it kills us with terror. It does not so much keep death at a distance, as it anticipates his horrors. It wears us out, instead of prolonging our lives; and though it could be said to prolong the life of individuals, it would be still to the prejudice of our species; since it renders us less serviceable to society, by the regimen it imposes, and the constant solicitude it lays us

under. It is to our knowledge of danger that we are indebted for our fears: the man who should think himself invulnerable would be afraid of nothing. By arming Achilles[69] against danger, the poet had deprived his character of all the merit of his valour: any one in such circumstances might have been an Achilles too.

Do you seek men of true courage? Look for them where there are no physicians, where men are ignorant of the consequence of diseases, and where they are never apprehensive of death. Man, by nature, is formed to suffer with patience, and die in peace. It is the physicians with their prescriptions, the philosophers with their precepts, and the priests with their prayers and exhortations, that have debased the heart of man, and made him ignorant how to die.

Let me have a pupil, therefore, who will have no occasion for any of these gentry, or I shall reject him. I am unwilling that other people should spoil my work: I will have the education of him entirely myself, or not take any further trouble about him. The sagacious Mr Locke, who had spent part of his life in the study of medicine, earnestly advises us, never to give children physic by way of precaution or for slight indispositions. I will go farther, and declare, as I never call in the physician for myself, so I will never trouble him on the account of Emile; unless, indeed, his life be in evident danger; and then the doctor cannot do more than kill him.

I know very well the physician will not fail to take advantage of that delay. If the child dies, he was called in too late; had he been sent for sooner – – if he recovers, it is then the physician who saved him. Be it so. I am content the doctor should triumph, on condition he is never sent for till the patient be at the last extremity.

For want of knowing the way to get cured, a child should learn to know how to be sick; this art will supply the want of the other, and often succeed a great deal better: this is one of the arts of nature. When a brute animal is sick, it suffers in silence and keeps itself still; and yet we do not see that brutes are more sickly than men. How many persons have impatience, disquietude, apprehension,   and   particularly   medicines,

---

[69] Homeric hero and son of Thetis. See above, p.181 where Rousseau uses this myth to support a contrary point. Achilles' heel, the only part of his body not to be dipped in the Styx, was wounded by a poisoned arrow at the siege of Troy. [eds]

destroyed, whom their diseases would have spared, and whom time alone would have cured? Will it be objected that brute animals, living in a manner conformable to nature, ought to be less subject to diseases? This is the very point I aim at. I would bring up my pupil precisely in the same manner; from which he would doubtless deduce the same advantages.

The only useful part of medicine is the Hygiene. This, however, is rather a virtue than a science. Temperance and exercise are the two best physicians in the world. Exercise whets the appetite, and temperance prevents the abuse of it.

To know what kind of regimen is the most salutary, we need only enquire, what is that of those people, who enjoy the greatest share of health, are the most robust, and live the longest? If the arts of medicine are found, from general observation not to confer better health or longer life; the very proof of their being useless shows them to be hurtful, as so much time, so many persons and things are taken up thereby to no purpose. Not only the time mispent in the preservation of life, is lost from its enjoyment, it should be deducted also from its duration: but when the time is employed in tormenting us, it is still worse than the mere annihilation of it; it gives a negative quantity, and if we calculate justly, should be taken from the future duration of our lives. A man who lives ten years without physicians, lives more for himself and others than he who survives, as their patient, for thirty. Having experienced both, I conceive myself peculiarly authorised to determine this point.

Such are my reasons for making choice only of a robust and healthy pupil, and the principles on which I should preserve him so. I shall not go about to prove the utility of manual labour, and those bodily exercises, which serve to strengthen the constitution and preserve health: this is a point which nobody disputes: instances of longevity are almost all of them found among persons accustomed to exercise, and who have undergone the greatest labour and fatigue.[70] I shall be as far from entering into a tedious detail of the methods I shall take to effect this end. It will be seen that they necessarily enter into the practical part of my plan, so that this intimation will be sufficient, without farther explanation.

Our wants commence with our lives. The new-born infant must be provided with a nurse. If its mother consent to take upon herself that office, it is well. Directions for her behaviour will be given her in writing: for this advantage has its inconvenience, and keeps the governor at a little more distance from his pupil. But it is to be presumed the good of the child, and the esteem she must have for him to whom she would commit so important a charge, will render the mother attentive to the directions and advice of its master: this presumed, we are certain that every thing she does, will be better done by her than by any one else. If it must have an hired nurse, we must begin with making a good choice.

One of the misfortunes attending the rich, is their being universally imposed on. Is it to be wondered at, then, they should know so little how to judge of mankind? Their own wealth serves to corrupt them; and, by a just retaliation, they are the first who feel the defects of the only advantage they are acquainted with. Every thing about them is done wrong, but what they do themselves, and this is hardly any thing at all. Is the choice of a nurse the point in question; they apply to the *accoucheur*.[71] The consequence of this is, that she is the best nurse who has made him the greatest bribe. I shall not consult a man midwife, therefore, in the choice of a nurse for Emile; but shall take care to chuse one myself. I

---

[70] I cannot help citing the following instance, on the authority of the English Newspapers, as it affords so much room for reflection on this subject. One Patrick O'Neil, born in the year 1647, married his seventh wife in 1760. He served in the dragoons in the 17th year of the reign of Charles II and in different corps till 1740, when he obtained his discharge. He had made all the campaigns of King William and the Duke of Marlborough. This extraordinary person never drank anything stronger than small beer, and lived upon vegetables and never has eaten meat except on a few occasions when he made a feast for his relations. His custom was to rise with the sun, and go to bed when it set; except on such urgent occasions as prevented. He is at present in his one hundred and thirtieth year; he is healthy, his hearing is good and he walks without a stick. Notwithstanding his great age, he is hardly ever unemployed, and every Sunday goes to his parish church, accompanied by his children, grandchildren, and great grandchildren. [Rousseau]

[71] Doctor or male mid-wife who has delivered the baby. [eds]

may not reason on this head, perhaps, so scientifically and eloquently as a professed chirurgeon;[72] but this I am certain of, I shall be more sincere, and my zeal will be less apt to mislead me, than his avarice.

There is no great mystery in this choice; the rules for it are well known; but I conceive a little more regard should be had to the age of the nurse's milk, as well as to its quality. New milk is altogether thin and waterish; it is required, indeed, to be in a manner purgative, in order to carry off the remains of the *meconium*[73] thickened in the intestines of the newborn infant. By degrees the milk acquires consistence, and furnishes a more solid aliment[74] to the child as it becomes more able to digest it. It is not without design, surely, that, among the females of every species of animals, nature thus varies the consistence of their milk according to the age of the infant.

A child newly born, therefore, requires a nurse newly delivered. This, I know, has its inconvenience; but as soon as ever we depart from the natural order of things, we find inconveniences in every attempt to do right. The only commodious expedient is to do wrong; and that is generally preferred.

A nurse should have a good heart as well as good health: the intemperature[75] of the passions will alter her milk, as well as that of the humours; add to this, that to regard the matter only in a physical light, is to take a view but of half the object. A nurse may be a very bad one, and yet her milk may be good: a good disposition is as essential as a good constitution. If we take a vicious woman, I don't say the child will contract her vices, but I say it will suffer by them. Is it not incumbent on her to be careful, obliging, and cleanly, as well as to suckle it? If she be

gormandizing and intemperate, she will soon spoil her milk; if she be negligent or passionate, what will become of the poor little wretch that lies at her mercy, and can neither defend itself nor complain? Persons of vicious dispositions are not at all adapted for any laudable employment whatever.

The choice of a nurse is of so much the greater consequence, as a child ought to have no other governess, in the same manner as he ought to have no other preceptor[76] than his governor. Such was the custom of the ancients, who, though less pretenders to reason,[77] were more rational than we. With them, the nurses who once undertook the education of children of their own sex, never left them afterwards: and hence we see the reason why, in their theatrical pieces, the confident[78] is generally a nurse. It is impossible that a child, who passes successfully through so many hands, should ever be well brought up. At every change, he will naturally make secret comparisons, which tend to diminish his respect for those who superintend his education and consequently their authority over him. If he should once come to think there are grown persons, who have no more sense than children, all the authority of age is lost, and his education spoiled. A child should know no other superiors than its father and mother, or, in default of them, its nurse and governor: even these are too many by one; but this participation is inevitable, and the only way to remedy its defects, is that they should so act in concert as to be only one, respecting him.

It is requisite that a nurse should live a little better than ordinary, and take more substantial aliment; but not that she should entirely vary her regimen. A sudden and total change, even though from bad to good, is always dangerous to

---

[72] i.e. surgeon. [eds]

[73] A somewhat technical term, i.e. for the first faeces of an infant. [eds]

[74] i.e. food. [eds]

[75] i.e. abnormality, or severe imbalance. [eds]

[76] i.e. tutor. [eds]

[77] i.e. less willing to claim to be rational. [eds]

[78] i.e. confidante. [eds]

health: and if her ordinary manner of living preserve her health and constitution, why should she be made to change it?

The peasants eat less animal food and more vegetables than our women in town; a regimen which is rather favourable than otherwise to them and their children. When they are engaged to suckle those of the upper classes, they are, however, obliged to vary their aliment, from the notion that meat soups, and broths, afford a better chyle[79] and greater plenty of milk. I am not at all of this opinion, and have experience on my side, which informs us that children thus nourished are more subject to the gripes and worms than others.

Nor is this to be wondered at, since animal substances, when putrefied, are covered with worms, in a manner never experienced in the substance of vegetables. Now, the milk, as it is prepared in the animal body, becomes a vegetable substance;[80] as may be demonstrated by analization;[81] it turns readily to acids, and so far from affording the least appearance of a volatile alcali,[82] as animal substances do, it yields, like plants, an essential neutral salt.

The milk of those who live chiefly on vegetables, is more sweet and salutary than that of carnivorous females. Formed out of substances of a similar nature to its own, it keeps longer, as it is less subject to putrefaction. And with respect to its quantity, every one knows that farinaceous[83] foods increase the quantity of blood more than meat; and why not therefore that of the milk? I cannot believe that a child, who is not weaned too soon, or should be weaned only with vegetable nutriment, and whose nurse also should live entirely on vegetables, would ever be subject to worms.

Vegetable aliment may possibly make the milk more apt to turn sour; but I am very far from regarding sour milk as unwholesome nutriment. There are people in some countries who have no other, and yet are in good health: the whole apparatus of absorbent alcali[84] is, to me, indeed, a piece of quackery.

There are some constitutions with which milk does not at all agree; nor will any absorbent reconcile it to the stomach, while others digest it very well without absorbents. Much inconvenience has been apprehended from the milk's turning to curds; this is an idle apprehension, because it is well known the milk always curdles in the stomach. Hence it is that it becomes an aliment solid enough to nourish infants and other animals; whereas, if it remained fluid, it would pass off, and afford them no nourishment at all.[85] We may cook up milk in what form soever we please; mix it with a thousand absorbents, it will be all to no purpose; whoever takes milk into the stomach will infallibly digest cheese. The stomach, indeed, is particularly calculated to curdle milk; it is in the stomach of a calf that rennet is made.

---

[79] Now understood to be a white milky fluid formed by the action of pancreatic juice and bile on chyme (food converted by gastric secretion into acid pulp). Rousseau's own understanding of the term was probably much less precise. [eds]

[80] Women eat bread, vegetables, and milk diets: the females of the canine and feline species, feed on the same; she-wolves eat grass. Hence they derive vegetable juices for their milk: it remains to be examined, what is the milk of those animals, which absolutely cannot receive nourishment from any thing but meat; if there are any such, which I much doubt. [Rousseau]

[81] i.e. chemical analysis. [eds]

[82] i.e. alkaline substance. [eds]

[83] i.e. starchy. [eds]

[84] Substances which neutralize strong acids, in this case also liable to rapid evaporation. [eds]

[85] Although the juices contributing to our nourishment are all liquid, it is yet necessary they should be compressed from solid aliments. A working man, who should live only upon broths, would soon be emaciated. He would be supported much better on milk, because it curdles, and assumes solidity in the stomach. [Rousseau]

I am of opinion therefore, that, instead of changing the ordinary diet of nurses, it is sufficient only to increase its quantity, and take care it be the best of its kind. It is not from the nature of the aliment that vegetable foods are difficult to digest. It is their high seasoning only that makes them unwholesome. Reform your kitchen; throw aside your roux and oil; let not your butter, salt, or milk-meats, come near the fire; let not your vegetables, boiled or stewed, have any seasoning, till they come hot to table: this kind of diet will then, instead of disturbing the nurse, furnish her with milk in abundance, and of the best quality.[86] Can it be supposed that a vegetable diet should be the best adapted for a child, and animal food for its nurse? There is an evident contradiction in the notion.

It is particularly in their earliest years, that the constitutions of children are affected by the ambient air. It penetrates through the pores of their soft and delicate skin, acts powerfully on their growing bodies, and makes such impressions as are never after effaced. I should not advise, therefore, the taking a woman from the country, to shut her up in a close nursery in town, there to bring up my child. I should rather it should go to breathe the fresh air of some open village, than the stinking atmosphere of a city. It should adopt the situation of its new mother, dwell beneath her rustic cottage, and its governor should follow it. The reader will please to remember that its governor is not a hireling, but the friend of its father, 'Well, but,' it may be said, 'what if no such friend can be met with? what if such a removal be inconvenient? what if all this you are advising be impracticable? What is to be done then?' – I have already told you; act as you do: you will need no counsel to advise you to do that.

Mankind were not formed to be heaped together in ant-hills, but to spread over the face of the earth, to cultivate it. The more they assemble together, the more they corrupt one another. The infirmity of the body, and the depravity of the mind, are both the inevitable effect of their too numerous concourse. Man is of all animals, the least adapted to live in herds. If men flocked together like sheep, they would all perish in a short time. Their breath is destructive to their fellow-creatures; nor is it less so in a literal than a figurative sense.

Cities are the graves that swallow up the human species. At the end of a few generations, races perish or degenerate; so that they require to be constantly recruited and regenerated from the country. Send then your children, to regenerate themselves, if I may so express myself, in the country; and to recover in the open fields, that vigour which is lost in the unwholesome air of populous cities. It is customary for pregnant women, who are in the country, to hasten their return to town, in order to lie in: they ought to take the contrary method; particularly those who intend to nurse their own children. They would have less to regret than they imagine; and, in a situation better adapted to their species, with the pleasures inseparably attached to the discharge of their natural duties, they would soon lose all taste for such as have no relation to nature.

As soon as the child is born, it is washed with warm water, usually mixed with wine. This addition of wine appears to me little necessary. As no fluid in its natural state is in fermentation, it is hardly to be thought the use of an artificial liquor needful to our preservation.

For the same reason, the precaution of warming the water may as well be dispensed with; and, in fact, among many different people, their children are taken, immediately after their birth, and bathed in the river or the sea, without farther ceremony. But ours, enervated before they are born by the softness of their parents, bring into the world with them constitutions already spoilt, and which will not bear to be submitted immediately to those trials which are necessary to restore them. It is by degrees only they are to be restored to their native vigour. Follow, then, at first, the established custom, and depart from it by degrees. Children should be frequently washed; their unavoidable uncleanliness sufficiently indicates the necessity of it. If they are only wiped their skin will be injured. But as they gain strength, diminish, by degrees, the warmth of the water, till you come, at length, to wash them, winter and summer, with it quite cold, or even freezing. As, in order not to expose

---

[86] Those who are desirous of seeing the advantages and inconveniences of the Pythagorean (vegetarian) regimen considered at length, may consult the tracts of the Dr Cocchi and of his opponent Dr Bianchi, on this important subject. [Rousseau]

them to danger, this diminution must be slow, gradual and insensible, a thermometer may be made use of, to measure the degree of heat or cold exactly.

This custom of bathing, once begun, ought never to be left off, but to be continued during life. I consider it, not only in respect to cleanliness and present health, but also as a salutary precaution; rendering the texture of the fibres more pliant and apt to yield, without effort or danger, to the impressions of the various degrees of heat and cold. For this reason, I would have my pupil, as he grows up, accustom himself to bathe in water, of all the different degrees of cold and heat, from the utmost tolerable degree of heat to the same of cold, making use of both alternately. Thus by habituating himself to support the different temperatures of water, which, being a denser fluid, touches the body in more points, and affects us more powerfully, he would become almost insensible to the changes in the temperature of the air.

I would not have a child, also, the moment he is at liberty to breathe, by being freed from one incumbrance, be laid under others still more restrictive. No stay-bands,[87] no rollers,[88] no swaddling clothes; but blankets, loose and large enough to leave all its limbs at liberty; neither so heavy as to lay a restraint on its motion, nor so warm as to prevent its feeling the impressions of the air.[89] Place it in a roomy cradle,[90] well lined, where it may roll and tumble about at ease, and without danger. When it hath gathered sufficient strength, let it crawl on its hands and knees about the nursery; let it use and stretch its little limbs, and you will see it daily grow stronger. Compare it with a child of the same age, wrapt up in swaddling clothes, and you will be astonished at the difference of their progress.[91]

Great opposition is doubtless to be expected on the part of the nurses, to whom a child, well bolstered up in swaddling clothes, will certainly give less trouble, than one, whose legs and arms being at liberty, must be constantly watched. Add to this, that, its uncleanliness being more apparent in an open dress, its clothes would oftener want shifting;[92] and, after all, custom is an argument which in some countries is impossible to be refuted, to the satisfaction of the vulgar of every rank.

---

[87] i.e. bandages intended to hold the child's head on its side, to prevent suffocation by vomiting. [eds]

[88] i.e. bandages which strapped the arms alongside the body. [eds]

[89] Children are stifled, in great cities, in consequence of their being kept indoors and in thick cloathing. Those who have the care of them being ignorant, that the cold air, so far from hurting them, braces up their fibres and strengthens them; and that hot air relaxes, gives them a fever, and kills them. [Rousseau]

[90] I say, a cradle, to make use of a common word, for want of a better: otherwise I am well persuaded children have no occasion for rocking, and that this custom is often hurtful. [Rousseau]

[91] 'The ancient Peruvians, in loosely swathing their children, left their arms at full liberty. When they threw aside this dress they placed them at freedom in a little hollow, dug in the earth and lined with cloths. Here their children, the lower part of their bodies in the hollow, had their arms quite loose, and could move their heads and bend their bodies, without running the risk of falling or hurting themselves. As soon as they were able to stand, the nipple was shewn them at a distance, and thus they were enticed to learn to walk. The young negroes are often in a situation, in which it is with much more difficulty they come at the breast: they cling round the hip of the mother with the knees and feet, and by that means stick so close, that they stand in no need of being supported, while they reach the breast with their hands, and thus continue to suck, without letting go their hold, or danger of falling, notwithstanding the various motions of the mother, who all the while is employed in her usual labour. These children begin to walk at the end of the second month, or rather to shuffle along on their hands and knees; an exercise that gives them ever afterwards a facility of running almost as swift in that manner as on their feet.' [Buffon, *Natural History*, T.iv. p.192.]

To these examples M. Buffon might have added that of the English, among whom the extravagant and barbarous custom of swaddling is daily losing ground. I could, indeed, fill twenty pages with quotations, if it were necessary to support what I have advanced, by the evidence of facts. [Rousseau]

[92] i.e. changing. [eds]

Never go about, therefore, to convince nurses. Lay on them your commands; see them executed, and spare no pains to make them as easy as possible in the execution. Why should you not partake of the trouble? In common nurseries, the physical part of education only is regarded: provided the child lives, and does not perish, all is well; nothing more is regarded. But according to my system, wherein the care of a child's education commences with its being, the infant becomes at his birth the disciple, not indeed directly of his governor, but of nature. The governor does nothing more than study her[93] superior precepts, and endeavour to prevent them from being thrown away. It is his province to have an eye over, to observe and attend his pupil; to watch as diligently the first dawning of his feeble understanding, as the Mahometans[94] look for the rising of the new moon.

We are born with a capacity for acquiring knowledge; but without knowing any thing. The soul, confined in half-formed and imperfect organs, possesses not even the sense of its own existence. The movements and cries of a new-born infant, are effects purely mechanical, void of sense or will.

Let us suppose a child, at its birth, possessed of the strength and stature of a man; taken from his mother's womb, as one may say, armed at all points, like Pallas issuing from the brain of Jove: this adult infant would be a perfect ideot,[95] an automaton, an immoveable and almost insensible statue. He would see nothing, understand nothing, know nothing; nay he would not be able to turn his eyes toward the object he might have occasion to see. He would not only be incapable of perceiving external objects, he would not be able to perceive them in the respective organs of perception: colours would not appear to be painted on the retina, sounds would seem not to strike on the ear, the bodies in contact with him would not appear to touch his own; nay he would not be sensible of his having any body at all. The feeling of his hands would seem to exist in the brain; all his sensations would be generalized into one; he would seem to exist only in the common *sensorium*;[96] he would have but one idea; i.e. that of a *self*, in which all his feelings would be absorbed; and this idea, or rather this sentiment, would constitute the only difference between such a supposed being and a common child.

This being, also, thus formed on a sudden, would be as little capable of standing on his legs: it would require a long time for him to learn how to keep his body in equilibrio. Perhaps he would not even attempt it, and you would see this tall robust animal fixed in one place like a stock or a stone, or crawling and tumbling about like a puppy.

He would perceive uneasiness[97] occasioned by his wants, without knowing what he wanted, or dreaming of any means to gratify them. There is no immediate communication between the muscles of the stomach and those of the legs, and arms, that, supposing him ravenous with hunger and surrounded with victuals, would make him take one step to approach, or reach out his hand to lay hold of them: so that, his body having none of the natural propensities to growth, nor any of those constant emotions which actuate children on that account, he would die of hunger before he would move to seek any thing for his subsistence. If we reflect ever so little on the order and progress of our acquirements,[98] we shall not be able to deny that man must nearly have been in such a situation of primitive ignorance and stupidity, before experience or his fellow creatures taught him anything.

---

[93] i.e. nature's. [eds]

[94] i.e. Muslims, followers of Islam. (Muslims themselves do not accept the label 'Mohammedans' derived by false analogy from 'Christians'.) [eds]

[95] i.e. person totally self-absorbed, unaware of the world outside. [eds]

[96] 'Sensorium commune' – a kind of repository of physical sensations. [eds]

[97] i.e. experience discomfort. [eds]

[98] i.e. acquired faculties. [eds]

The point, therefore, is known, or may be known, from which we all set out to arrive at common understanding: but who is there can tell how distant is the other extremity of the line? Every one advances more or less according to his genius, taste, necessities, talents, zeal, and the opportunities afforded him. I know of no philosopher who hath been rash enough to prescribe the limits of our knowledge, and to say, Thus far, O man, shalt thou go, and no farther. We are ignorant of the extent of the human capacity, nor hath any one as yet measured the utmost possible distance between that of one man and another. Where is the mind so base as never to have been elevated by this reflection? Where is the man, who does not sometimes say, in the pride of his heart, 'How many men have I already surpassed! How many men may I not yet overtake! Why should my equal go farther than myself?'

I say it again; the education of a man commences at his birth: before he can speak, before he can understand he is already instructed. Experience is the forerunner of precept; the moment he knows the features of his nurse, he may be said to have acquired considerable knowledge. Trace the progress of the most ignorant of mortals, from his birth to the present hour, and you will be astonished at the knowledge he has acquired. If we divide all human science into two parts, the one consisting of that which is common to all men, and the other of what is peculiar to the learned, the latter will appear insignificant and trifling in comparison with the other. But we think nothing of general acquisitions,[99] because they are made insensibly,[100] and even before we arrive at the age of reason; knowledge becomes conspicuous only in its difference on comparison; just as in working algebraic equations, common quantities are struck out and stand for nothing.

Even brutes themselves have their acquirements. They have organs of sense, and must learn to make use of them; they have wants which they must learn to provide for; they must learn to eat, to walk, and to fly. Quadrupeds are not capacitated to walk merely because their legs are able to support them: as soon as they are brought forth, the first essays they make are very hobbling and uncertain. A singing bird, escaped from the cage in which it was bred, will not know how to fly, because it has never flown. Sensible[101] and animated beings owe every thing to instruction. If trees and plants had a progressive locomotion,[102] they must have been endued[103] with senses and have acquired knowledge, otherwise their species would have been soon extinct.

The first sensations of children are those which are merely affecting; they perceive nothing for some time but pleasure and pain. Being unable to walk about, or lay hold of any thing, they require a good deal of time to form to themselves by degrees, those representative sensations, which make objects appear to have an external existence. In the mean time, and while such objects are extending themselves, retreating as it were, from the eye, and assuming forms and dimensions, the return of the affecting sensations begins to submit to the influence of habit: the eyes of children are turned constantly toward the light, and, if it come from one side, they imperceptibly take that direction; so that care should always be taken to set them facing the light, lest they should become squint-eyed, or accustom themselves to look crosswise. They should, also, be early accustomed to the absence of light, otherwise they will be apt to cry when they find themselves in the dark. Sleep and nutriment, when too exactly proportioned, become necessary to them at the end of stated intervals, and after a time their propensities thereto arise not from physical necessity but

---

[99] i.e. of the general skills and abilities we have acquired. [eds]

[100] i.e. without our being aware of it. [eds]

[101] i.e. capable of sensation. [eds]

[102] i.e. an ability to move from place to place. [eds]

[103] i.e. endowed. [eds]

habit, or rather, habit produces an additional necessity to those of nature: this must, by all means, be prevented.

The only habit in which a child should be indulged, is that of contracting none; he should not be carried on one arm more than the other; we should not accustom him to present his right hand oftener than his left, or to make use of one more than the other; he should not be used to eat, sleep, or do any thing, at stated hours, or not to be left alone whether in the day or night. Prepare early for his enjoyment of liberty, and the exercise of his natural abilities, by leaving him in full possession of them unrestrained by artificial habits, and by putting him in a situation to be always master of himself, and to do whatever his resolution prompts him, as soon as he is able to form one.

As soon as a child begins to distinguish objects, a proper choice should be made in those which are presented to it. Every new object is naturally interesting to a child: it finds itself so weak and feeble that it is fearful of every thing it is not acquainted with: but familiarity which renders objects unaffecting destroys this timidity. We see children educated in neat houses, where cobwebs are carefully swept away, are always afraid of spiders, and retain the same disgust for them, as they grow up: whereas I never knew a peasant, either man or woman, afraid of a spider.

Why should not the education of a child, therefore, begin before it can speak or understand, since even the choice of objects, presented to its view, is sufficient to render it either timid or courageous? I would have them habituated to new objects, to ugly, disgustful[104] and uncommon animals; beginning with them, however, at a distance, and letting them approach by degrees; or till, being used to see others handle them, they will venture to handle them themselves. If a child, during his infancy, hath been used to regard toads, serpents or crayfish with indifference, he will look without horror, as he grows up, on any animal whatever. No object is frightful to such as are daily accustomed to frightful objects.

All children are terrified at a mask. I would begin to reconcile Emile to masks, by shewing him first an agreeable one. Somebody should afterwards put it on, at the sight of which I would laugh, the company should laugh, and the child would then laugh with the rest. By degrees, I would use[105] him to others less agreeable; and lastly, to the most hideous and frightful. By artful management, he will thus be brought to laugh, and he as much pleased with the last as the first; I should not be afraid he would ever after be terrified at a mask.

[...]

To accustom Émile to the report of firearms, I would first make a flash in the pan of a pistol; the sudden light of which would give him pleasure. I would then repeat it, with a larger prime: after being some time used to this, I would put a small charge into the barrel, without ramming it; and after that a greater, and so on, till I had brought him, by degrees, to hear with indifference the report of musquetry, bombs, cannon, and even the most terrible explosions.

I have remarked that children are seldom afraid of thunder, unless the claps are excessively loud and really hurt the drum of the ear. They have otherwise no such fear, till they have learnt that it is sometimes hurtful and even mortal. The fears thus instilled by reason should be eradicated by habit: while, by slow and artful means, both children and men would acquire intrepidity and be afraid of nothing.

In a state of infancy, wherein the memory and imagination are as yet inactive, a child is attentive to nothing but what actually affects his senses with pain or pleasure. His sensations being thus the original materials of his ideas, to regulate the order in which he meets these sensations, is to prepare his memory to present them, hereafter, in the same order, to his understanding: but as while so young he is only capable of attending to his sensations, it is sufficient at first, to make him sensible of the connection between these sensations, and the objects that excite them. He is curious to touch and handle everything he sees; he should be indulged in the

---

[104] i.e. offensive. [eds]

[105] i.e. accustom. [eds]

gratification of this curiosity; it suggests to him a very necessary course of experiments. Hence it is he must learn to feel heat and cold, the hardness, softness, and weight of bodies; to judge of their magnitude, figure,[106] and other sensible[107] qualities, by looking, touching,[108] hearing, and particularly by comparing the sight with the touch, and judging, by means of the eye, of the sensation which would be acquired by the fingers.

It is by motion only that we discover any thing to exist out of ourselves; and it is by our own motion that we acquire the idea of extension.[109] It is because a child has no such idea, that it will stretch out its hand, in the same manner, to lay hold of an object within its reach, or at an hundred yards distance. This effort appears to you only a token of command, an order to the object to come to him, or to you to fetch it; but it is in fact no such thing. It is made, because the objects which a child first perceives to exist in the brain, and afterwards in the eye, appear now to exist at arm's length; and he has no conception of any extension beyond his reach. Care should be taken, therefore, to walk him about often, to have him carried about from one place to another, where he chuses to go, in order to give him just ideas of change of place, and teach him to judge of distances. When he begins, however, once to know these, your method must be changed, and you must let him go, or carry him, only where you please; not where he pleases: for when his senses no longer deceive him in this respect, the efforts I have been speaking of change their cause. This change is so remarkable that it may require some explanation.

The uneasiness occasioned by our wants, is expressed by signs, when the assistance of others is required to relieve them. Hence the cries of infants. They are almost perpetually in tears: and indeed so they must be. As all their sensations are of the affecting kind, when these are agreeable they enjoy them in silence; but, when painful, they naturally express themselves in their own language, and demand relief. Now while they are awake they seldom are in a state of indifference; they are generally asleep, or some how or other affected with sensations.

All modes of speech are the factitious[110] productions of art. It has been long a subject of enquiry, whether there existed in nature an universal language. Without doubt there does, and this is what children speak before they can talk any other. This language, indeed, doth not consist of articulate words, but is emphatic, sonorous, and intelligible. The use of the invented modes of speech, hath made us neglect this so much as even quite to forget it. Let us study the wants and efforts of children, and we shall soon learn it again. Nurses are our masters in this language; they understand every thing said by their respective children: they make replies and hold connected dialogues with them; and, though they themselves make use of words, those words are perfectly needless: the child comprehends not the sense of the word, but the accent[111] with which it is pronounced.

To the language of the tongue, we may also add that of gesture, equally expressive. By gesture I do not mean any motion of the feeble hands of such young children; the gesture of infants lies in the muscles of their face. It is astonishing to see such strength of expression in their half formed physiognomies: their features are continually varying, with inconceivable rapidity of transition. You will see smiles, fears, desires, take place on their countenances, and vanish like lightning; at every change a new face appearing in an instant.

---

[106] i.e. shape. [eds]

[107] i.e. perceptible by the senses. [eds]

[108] The sense of smelling is that which comes the latest to perfection, in children. They appear not to be sensible of either good or ill scents, till they are two or three years old. They seem to have in this respect the same indifference, or rather insensibility, which is remarked in many other animals. [Rousseau]

[109] i.e. the idea of space and distance. [eds]

[110] i.e. artificial. [eds]

[111] i.e. intonation. [eds]

The muscles of their faces are certainly more mobile than ours. On the other hand, their dull and languid eyes hardly speak at all. Such a species of expression indeed is adapted to an age whose wants are merely corporeal; the expression of our sensations consists in grimace and the distortion of our features; that of our sentiments lies in our eyes.

As man, in his first stage of life, is a wretched and helpless being, so his first mode of expression is that of tears and complaint. An infant is sensible of his wants, and incapable of satisfying them; he therefore implores the assistance of those about him, by his cries. If he be hungry or have thirst, he cries; if too cold or too hot, if he want to move, or to be held still, he cries: if he want to sleep or to be danced about, he has no other method to express himself but by crying.

The less he is in a situation to help himself, the more frequently he requires assistance, to vary his circumstances or position. He has but one kind of language, because he knows, in fact, but one kind of inconvenience: in the present imperfection of his organs, he is incapable of distinguishing their different impressions; all the different causes of his uneasiness form but one sensation of pain.

Thus from the tears of children, which one is apt to think so little worthy of attention, arises the first sense of the relation which man bears to the objects that surround him: here is forged the first link of that extensive chain which forms the social order.

When a child cries it is evidently uneasy, it hath some want that requires to be satisfied; we look, we examine what it is, find it out and relieve it. If this be not the case, and the cause of uneasiness cannot be found, its tears continue to flow, and it begins to grow outrageous: we sooth[e] it, to make it quiet, rock it or endeavour to sing it asleep: if this does not succeed, we grow impatient and threaten it; nay sometimes the brutal nurse will beat the poor innocent in these circumstances. Strange lessons these, surely, at our first entrance into life!

I shall never forget that I once saw a crying child thus beaten by its nurse; on which it became immediately silent, and, as I thought, intimidated. I reflected upon this occasion, what a servile mind this will be, on which nothing will operate but rigour. I was, however, deceived; the little wretch was almost suffocated with choler; it lost its breath, and I saw it grow black in the face. In a moment after it set up the most piercing cries; expressing all the signs of resentment, fury and despair, adapted to its age. I was even apprehensive it would expire under the violence of its agitation. This example alone would have convinced me, if I could ever have doubted it, of an innate sense of right and wrong being implanted in the human heart. I am very certain, had a burning coal fallen by accident on the hand of the child, it would have been less agitated than by this slight blow, given with a manifest intention to hurt it.

This disposition in children to passion, and excessive anger, requires very nice management. Boerhaave[112] thinks the diseases of children should be ranked, for the most part, in the class of convulsions; because their heads being proportionably larger, and the nervous system more extended than in adults, their nerves are more susceptible of irritation. Be careful, therefore, to keep them from servants, who are continually teizing,[113] and provoking them; such servants are infinitely more fatal to children than the intemperature of the air or the seasons. While infants are crossed only by the resistance of things, and not by persons, they will never grow fractious nor passionate. This is one reason why the children of common people, being more free and independent, are for the most part less infirm, and delicate in their constitutions, and more robust than those of others, who, by pretending to educate them better, are perpetually contradicting them. It must, however, be remembered that there is a very wide difference between acting always in obedience to, or humouring, a child, and not contradicting it.

Tears are the petitions of young children; if they be not looked upon as such, they will soon

---

[112] Dutch doctor and botanist, 1668–1738, who influenced many of the ideas in Book 1 of Émile. [eds]

[113] i.e. teasing. [eds]

become commands: infants would begin by praying our assistance, and go on to command our service. Thus from their own weakness, whence at first arises the sense of their dependence, follows the notion of domineering and command. This idea, however, is less excited by their wants than by our assiduities; and here we begin to perceive those moral effects, whose immediate cause doth not exist in nature. At the same time, we see how necessary it is, to discover the secret motives of the cries of children even in their earliest infancy.

When a child sometimes holds out its hand, without speaking, it thinks to reach the object, because it cannot estimate the distance of it: it is here only mistaken: but when in reaching out his hand, it cries, or manifests other signs of impatience, it is not deceived in the distance of the object, but is either commanding it to approach or you to fetch it. In the first case, therefore, it is proper to undeceive the child, by carrying it gently toward the object, and in the last not to appear to mind it; but the louder it cries the less notice to take of it. It is of consequence to check children betimes,[114] in usurping the command over persons, who are not in their power; or over things, which cannot hear them. For the latter reason, it is better, when a child desires any thing that may be proper to give him, to carry him to the object, than to bring the object to the child: as, by this means, he deduces a conclusion adapted to his tender years, and which there is no other way of suggesting to him.

The Abbé de St. Pierre[115] calls men great children; we may with equal propriety give a turn to the expression, and call children little men. These propositions are true, as maxims; tho' as principles they require explanation: but when Hobbes calls a vicious man a robust child, he is guilty of an absolute contradiction. All vice takes its rise from weakness; an infant is vicious only because he is weak; give him power and you make him good; an all-powerful Being could never do any ill. Of all the attributes ascribed to an omnipotent Deity, that of goodness appears to be the most essential to his existence. We cannot conceive him to exist without it. Among all the people who entertained notions of good and evil principles, the evil one was constantly supposed inferior to the good; without which their whole system had been to the last degree absurd. Compare this with the profession of faith of the Savoyard priest later in this book.[116]

Reason only teaches us to know good from evil. Conscience, which excites us to love the one and hate the other, altho' independent of reason, cannot discover one from the other without it. Before we come to be capable of reasoning, we do good and ill without knowing it: and there is no morality in our actions, tho' there may be, and frequently is, in our sentiments concerning the actions of others relative to us. A child will often put things into disorder, will break every-thing it comes near, will grasp a sparrow, as it would a stone, and kill it, without knowing what it is doing.

And why? A philosopher will presently account for it, from the vices inherent in our nature; the pride, the thirst of power, the self-love, and the wickedness of man: a sense of its weakness, he will add, makes the child eager to perform actions of strength, and to experience its own power. But, in answer to this, look upon that infirm and decayed old man, brought back by the revolutions of human life to the weakness of infancy: he not only remains peaceable and quiet in himself, but is desirous every thing about him should be so too. The least change of situation is troublesome to him, and he is pleased with an universal calm. How should the same imbecility joined with the same passions, produce such different effects in the two ages, if the original cause were not changed? And where are we to seek for this diversity of causes, unless in the physical constitution of the two individuals? The active principle, common to both, expands and unfolds itself in one, and contracts and closes itself in the other: in the one it tends to form, in the other to be destroyed; in the one it tends to life, and in the other to death. The drooping activity of the vital principle is concentrated in the heart of age; in that of infancy it overflows and diffuses itself: in the excess of its vivacity, a child seems to have life enough to animate every thing around it. Whether it makes or mars, it is

---

[114] i.e. at an early opportunity. [eds]

[115] French writer, 1658–1748. [eds]

[116] See below, p.205. [eds]

all one to a child, provided the situation of things be changed; as every change necessarily implies action. If it seem to have a propensity to destroy things, it is not from a vicious principle; but because the action, necessary to make or compose anything, is tedious and slow, whereas that of spoiling and breaking things to pieces, being quicker, agrees better with its natural alertness and vivacity.

At the same time, however, that the author of nature hath given to children this active principle, he hath taken care to prevent its being hurtful, by giving them as little strength in proportion to indulge it. But no sooner are they misled to conceive the persons about them as instruments which they themselves are to put in action, than they make use of them to assist their weakness in pursuing their inclinations. Hence it is they become importunate, tyrannical, imperious, mischievous and intractable; a progress that doth not arise from a natural spirit of domineering, but is the effect of wrong education: for it requires no great experience to perceive how agreeable it is to act by means of others, and to have occasion only to speak in order to put the world in motion.

As it grows up, a child acquires strength, and becomes less active and restless; it contracts its powers more within itself. The body and soul, if I may so say, keep each other in equilibrio; and nature requires no greater quantity of motion than is necessary to our preservation. But the desire of command doth not cease with the motives that gave rise to it; the notion of superiority is flattering to self-love, and is increased by habit: thus caprice succeeds to necessity, and the force of prejudice and opinion takes root in the mind.

The principle once known, we see clearly the track, wherein we begin to deviate from nature: let us enquire then, what must be done, in order to prevent our going astray.

So far from being endued with superfluous abilities, children have at first hardly sufficient for the purposes nature requires; it is requisite therefore to leave them at full liberty to employ those she hath given them, and which they cannot abuse: this is my first maxim.

It is our duty to assist them, and supply their deficences, whether of body or mind, in every circumstance of physical necessity: second maxim.

Every assistance afforded them should be confined to real utility, without administering any thing to the indulgence of their caprice or unreasonable humours; for they will never be capricious unless thro' neglect, or in some particular circumstance depending on their constitution: third maxim.

The meaning of their language and signs ought to be carefully studied, in order to be able to distinguish, in an age when they know not how to dissemble, between those inclinations that arise immediately from nature, and what are only fantastical: fourth maxim.

The design and tendency of these rules are, to give children more real liberty and less command; to leave them more to do of themselves than to require of others. Thus by being early accustomed to confine their desires to their abilities, they will be little affected with the want of what is out of their power.

Here we have new, and very important, reason for leaving body and limbs at full liberty; with this precaution, however, that we remove them from the danger of falling down, and put every thing out of their reach whereby they may wound or hurt themselves.

It cannot be doubted that an infant, whose body and arms are at liberty, will cry less than another bolstered up in swaddling clothes. The child, who is liable to suffer none but physical inconveniences, will cry only when it feels pain; which is a great advantage in its education; for then we are certain to know when it stands in real want of assistance, and this should be afforded it, if possible, immediately. But if it be out of our power to relieve it, we should take no notice, nor make any fruitless attempts to quiet it: kisses and caresses will not cure its cholic; yet it will remember the methods taken to sooth[e] it, and when it once knows how to employ you at its pleasure, it is become your master, and all is over.

Being less restrained in their efforts to move, children would cry less; if we were less importuned with their tears, it would require less trouble to quiet them; threatened and soothed more seldom, they would become less timid and obstinate, and would retain more of their natural temper and disposition. It is less from letting children cry unnoticed, than from striving to appease them, that they get ruptures:[117] my proof of this is: that those which are most neglected are

---

[117] i.e. hernias. [eds]

the least subject to those accidents. I am far, however, from recommending that children should, for this reason, be neglected: on the contrary, I would have so much care taken of them as to anticipate their wants, and not that their cries should give the first notice of them. Neither would I, at the same time, have a nurse be over solicitous about trifles. Why should they think it mischievous to cry when they see their tears bring so many advantages? When children come to be sensible[118] of the great value you set on their silence, they will take care you shall not have too much of it. They will, at length, set so great a value on it themselves, as to prevent your being able to obtain any; and it is then that, by dint of continual crying without success, they strain, exhaust, and sometimes destroy themselves.

The long fits of crying in a child, who is neither confined, sick, nor in real want of any thing, are only fits of habit and obstinacy. They are not to be attributed to nature but to the nurse, who, from not knowing how to bear such importunity, only increases it, without reflecting that, in making the child quiet to-day, she is only encouraging it to cry the more tomorrow.

The only way to cure, or prevent, this habit, is to take no notice of a child in such circumstances. Nobody cares, not even children, to take fruitless pains. They may for a while persevere in their trials; but, if you have more patience than they have obstinacy, they will be disgusted at the experiment, and repeat it no more. This is the method to prevent their tears, and to use them to cry[119] only when they are really in pain.

When they are possessed of these fits of caprice and obstinacy, a certain way to quiet them is, to divert their attention by some agreeable and striking object, that may make them forget their motive for crying. Most nurses excel in practising this expedient; and, if artfully managed, it is very useful: but it is of the utmost consequence that a child should not perceive this intention of diverting him, but that he should amuse himself without seeing that we are thinking of him: in this respect, however, all nurses are very inexpert.

Children are in general weaned too early. The proper season is indicated by the cutting of their teeth, an operation which is usually very sharp and painful. At this time, by a mechanical instinct, they carry every thing, which is put into their hands, up to their mouths to chew upon. In order to facilitate this task, therefore, the child is usually provided with hard objects such as ivory, or a wolf's tooth, to rub against its gums. I am of opinion, however, this doth not answer the end proposed. The rubbing of hard bodies in this case against the gums, so far from softening, must make them hard and callous; rendering the teeth still more difficult to cut, and the pain more acute and lasting. Let us follow the traces of instinct. We don't see the young of the canine species, in cutting their teeth, ever gnaw flints, iron or bones; but always wood, leather, rags or other soft substances, which tear to pieces, or yield to the impression of their teeth.

But simplicity is banished from every thing, even from our treatment of the most simple of animals, an helpless infant. It must have bells of silver and gold, and corals, crystals and rattles of all sorts and prices. What a useless and destructive apparatus! I would have nothing of all this. No bells, no corals, for my child; but little natural twigs taken from the tree, with their leaves and fruit, the dried heads of poppies, in which it might hear the seeds rattle, a stick of liquorish which it might suck and chew; these would amuse it as well as any such magnificent toys, and would not use it to the luxurious parade of wealth or distinction.

It is generally acknowledged that milk meats or puddings, made of raw flour, are not a very wholesome nutriment, boiled milk and crude meal never agreeing well with the stomach. In puddings the flour is less baked than in bread, besides that it has not been fermented: panada, or bread puddings, as also those made of the best rice, I should think much preferable. But if children must absolutely have flour puddings, it is proper the flour should be baked a little beforehand. We make, in my country, a very agreeable and wholesome soup, with

---

[118] i.e. aware. [eds]

[119] i.e. accustom them to crying. [eds]

meal thus prepared. Meat broths and other spoon meats of that kind, are also an indifferent aliment; which should be used but sparingly. It is necessary that children should accustom themselves early to chew; this is the true way to facilitate the cutting their teeth: and hence, when they begin to swallow, the saliva, mixed with their aliment, promotes digestion.

I would therefore use them, betimes,[120] to chew dried fruits and crusts of bread. I would give them dried bread and biscuits, like the Piedmont bread known in the locality as 'grisses',[121] to play with; by softening which in their mouths, they would sometimes swallow part of them: thus they would cut their teeth easily, and wean themselves almost imperceptibly. Infants born and brought up in the country, have generally a very good digestion, and require no other trouble in weaning.

Children are accustomed to listen to sounds from their birth: we not only talk to them before they can understand the meaning of what is said; but before they can mimic the sounds repeated in their hearing. Their organs of speech, as yet in a state of incapacity, are brought by slow degrees to the imitation of sounds; and, indeed, we are not well assured, that these make as distinct impressions on their organs of hearing as on ours. I do not disapprove the nurse's amusing her child with singing, and other very sprightly and chearful notes; but I am absolutely against her stunning it perpetually, with a confused heap of useless words, on which the child comprehends nothing but the tone in which they are spoken. The first words repeated in the hearing of an infant should be few, easy and distinct: they should also be repeated often, and be only such as serve to express sensible objects;[122] which may, at the same time, be pointed out to its view. Our unhappy readiness to content our selves with words we do not understand, takes place earlier than may be imagined. The school boy listens to the gabbling master of his class, with the same

stupid attention, as he did to the prattle of his nurse. Hence it appears to me to be a very useful mode of instruction to bring up children to hear nothing of it. (Kenrick I, pp.1–76)

[Rousseau goes on to discuss in detail the development of a child's speech. He speaks in defence of regional accents and is opposed to excessive correction of children's speech. He is confident that country children, who have to shout to make themselves heard in the open fields, develop clearer speech than children encouraged to whisper to their governesses in town nurseries – another example of the unnatural practices springing from city life. Children must be encouraged only to use words they understand.]

The first development of the several organs and faculties of a child, occur nearly all at once. He begins to talk, to eat, to walk, almost at the same time. This may be properly called the first epoch of human life. Before this period, he is little better than he was in the womb of his mother; he has no sentiments, no ideas, nay hardly any sensations; he is even insensible of his own existence:

Vivit, et est vitæ nescius ipse suæ.[123]

Ovid. *Tristes* 1,3,12.
(Kenrick I, p.84)
End of the first book.

Book II (Kenrick I, pp.85–280)

[In the following extract from Book 2, Rousseau explains how children learn about the world from experience gained through their senses, in accordance with the epistemological principles of Locke. Furthermore, they only learn when motivated. Emile's tutor sets out to educate his sense of sight and improve his physical fitness at the same time:]

In walking out with my young sluggard after dinner, I would sometimes put a couple of cakes, such as he should be most fond of, in my

---

[120] i.e. accustom them at the earliest opportunity. [eds]

[121] A kind of crumbly bread in the Savoie region. [eds]

[122] i.e. to indicate objects which can be seen or touched. [eds]

[123] He lives but has no consciousness of his own life. [eds]

pocket; we would each of us eat one,[124] and return contentedly home. One day he saw that I had taken out three cakes with me. As he could very easily eat half a dozen, he soon dispatched his own, and asked me for the third. No, said I, I can eat it very well myself, or we will divide it; or, stay, we had better let those two little boys, there, run a race for it. I called them to us, showed them the cake, and proposed the terms. The boys desired no better conditions; and the cake was accordingly placed on a great stone which served for the goal. The distance being marked, we went to sit down: at the signal given, the racers set off; the victor seizing the cake, and devouring it without mercy, before the face of the vanquished and the spectators.

This amusement was certainly of more value than the cake, but he did not take to it, and this first essay produced nothing. I was neither offended nor impatient; the education of children is a profession in which we must study how to lose time, in order to gain it. We continued our walks as usual; often taking three cakes, sometimes four; and giving from time to time one, and sometimes two, to the racers. If the prize were not considerable, those who disputed it, would not be ambitious of obtaining it; the winner, therefore, was always highly commended and caressed, as having done something extraordinary. To diversify the scene, and render it more interesting, I made the course longer, and admitted several candidates. They had hardly entered the lists, before the passengers[125] stopped to look at them; animating them, as they ran, with acclamations, shouting and clapping of hands; at the same time, I saw my little gentleman, every now and then, eagerly take part with one or the other of the runners, rising up and crying out when one was getting before another. These afforded to him the amusement of the Olympic games.

The runners, however, were sometimes guilty of foul play; they laid hold of each other, tumbled one another down, or threw flints in their way, to cut their feet. This furnished me with a just pretext to separate them, and make them run from different places equally distant from the goal. The reason of this precaution will appear presently;[126] for this important affair must be treated circumstantially.[127]

Being so frequently mortified at seeing his favourite cakes thus devoured by others before his eyes, my young gentleman at length began to suspect, that to run well is of some use; and seeing that he had two legs as well as other boys, he began in secret to make some trials of his abilities. I took care to seem not to observe him, but found that my stratagem took.[128] After some time he began to think himself equal to the enterprize; and, as I foresaw, affected to importune me for the remaining cake. I, of course, refused him; on which he seemed to take pet,[129] and said, 'Well, Sir, lay it down on the stone; mark the distance, and we will see who wins it.' Mighty good! I replied ironically; can so fine a gentleman as you run? You will only whet your appetite, and get nothing to eat. Piqued at my raillery, however, he exerted his strength, and bore off the prize; which was the more easy for him to do, as I had made the course but short, and had taken care to exclude one or two of the best runners. It is readily to be conceived that my point thus gained, it was not difficult for me to keep him up to this exercise. Indeed he acquired, in a short time, so

---

[124] The Reader will easily understand these walks are meant to be taken in the country. The public walks of great cities are destructive to children of both sexes. It is there they imbibe the principles of vanity, and a desire of being admired. It is at the Luxembourg, the Tuilleries, and particularly in the gardens of the Palais-Royal, that the young people in Paris go to learn these foppish and impertinent airs, which render them so ridiculous, and make them so much hissed at and so detestable in every part of Europe. [Rousseau]

[125] i.e. passers-by. [eds]

[126] i.e. at once. [eds]

[127] i.e. in some detail. [eds]

[128] i.e. worked. [eds]

[129] i.e. he made out that he was put out. [eds]

great an inclination for it, that, without partiality, he was able to beat almost all his companions, be the course as long as it pleased me.

This advantage gained, was productive of another which I did not think of: when he won the prize but seldom, he used to eat it up alone, as did the others; but being accustomed to win it often, he became generous and let the vanquished partake of it. This circumstance furnished me with a moral observation, and taught me the true principle of generosity.

By continuing to make my little runners set out from different places at one time, I contrived the distances, without his perceiving it, to be unequal; so that one having farther to run than another, had a visible disadvantage: but; tho' I left my disciple to his own choice, he knew not how to profit by this inequality. Without troubling himself about the distance, he always preferred the smoothest ground; so that, foreseeing his choice, I could make him win or lose the cake at pleasure; this piece of address[130] answered more ends also than one. As my design, however, was that he should perceive the difference in question, I endeavoured to make him sensible of it; but, however indolent at other times, he was so animated in his diversion, and distrusted me so little, that I had all the trouble in the world to make him perceive I tricked him. At length, nevertheless, in spite of his inattention, I gained my point; and he reproached me accordingly for the deception. To this I replied, by asking him, what right he had to complain?

'If I give you a cake, have not I a right to make my own conditions? Who obliges you to run? Did I promise to make your distances all equal? Have not you, besides, always your choice? Take the shortest; who will hinder you? Don't you see that I favoured you in this matter, and that the difference you complain of, is to your advantage, if you know how to make use of it?' All this was very plain; my young gentleman understood it; and, in order to make a proper choice, looked

more narrowly after the distances prescribed. He set out with measuring each by the number of steps: this method, however, he found slow and defective. Besides I took it into my head to diversify and increase their number, on the same day; the amusement of running thus becoming a kind of passion; it was with regret that he lost time in measuring the several distances, which should have been employed in running the race. The vivacity of infancy ill agrees with such delays; he learned, therefore, to see better, and to estimate distances by his eye. It was then easy to extend and develop his taste for this. In a word, after repeated trials for some months, and correcting a few of his mistakes, I succeeded so well in thus teaching him to measure by his eye, that when I placed an imaginary cake on any object, he knew its distance as well by looking at it, as if he had measured it with a chain.

As the judgment is more inseparably attached to the sight than to any other of the senses, it requires a great deal of time to learn to see: a long time is requisite for us, to compare the sensations of the sight with those of the touch; in order to habituate the former of those senses to make a faithful report of figures[131] and distances. The most penetrating sight in the world can give us no idea of extension, without the touch, or a sense of progressive motion. The whole universe must appear to an oyster but as a single point; nor would it seem otherwise, were that oyster animated by an human soul. It is only by means of walking about, touching, counting, and taking the dimensions of objects, that we learn to judge of them: but if we accustom ourselves always to measure them, the sense confiding on the instrument,[132] acquires no accuracy to estimate without it. Neither is it proper for a child to pass immediately from the mensuration of objects to estimate them; he should begin to estimate by parts, what he cannot comprehend all together; comparing such imaginary divisions to aliquot[133] parts of admeasurement: these again

---

[130] i.e. skill. [eds]

[131] i.e. shapes. [eds]

[132] i.e. the eyesight by coming to rely on the instrument. [eds]

[133] Part contained by the whole an integral number of times. In this case, a fixed unit of measurement into which the total distance divides exactly. [eds]

he should learn to apply by the sight only, and not by the hand. I would have him, however, confirm his operations at first, by taking afterwards the real admeasurement: in order to correct his errors, and that, if any false appearance remained in the sense, he might be able to rectify it by his judgment. There are natural measures, which are nearly the same in all places; such are the step of a man, the extent of his arms, his height, & c.[134] When a child wants to estimate the height of a room, his preceptor may serve him as a measuring rod; when he would estimate the height of a steeple, he may measure it by the height of an house. If he would know how many leagues he has travelled, let him reckon on hours he has been in going; which will serve him very well, particularly if you give him no assistance in any of these things, but let him discover them all himself.

It is impossible to judge accurately of the dimensions of bodies, unless we learn also to know their figures,[135] and even to imitate those figures; for this imitation is founded on nothing else but the rules of perspective, and we cannot estimate the extension of bodies by their appearance, unless we have some knowledge of those rules. Children, being great imitators, all attempt to design;[136] I would have my pupil cultivate that art; not for the sake of the art itself, but only to give him a good eye and a supple hand. It is to be observed, indeed, in general, that it is of little consequence whether he be expert at any of the exercises he partakes of, provided he acquires that perspicacity and agility, which they are calculated to teach him. I shall take particular care, therefore, he shall have no drawing-master, who will only teach him to imitate imitations, and design after designs. I would have him have no other master than nature; no other model than the objects themselves. He should have before his eyes the original itself, and not the paper representing it: thus he should design an house from a house, a tree from a tree, a man from a man, that he might be accustomed to observe minutely and accurately the appearances of bodies, and not take false and artificial imitations for true and genuine. I would

even discourage him from endeavouring to trace any thing from memory, till, by frequent and repeated observations, its figure should be strongly imprinted on his imagination; lest he should otherwise, by substituting some fantastic image instead of the real one, lose the knowledge of proportion, and a taste for the genuine beauties of nature. (Kenrick I, pp.232–8.)

Book IV (Kenrick II, pp.110–216 and III, pp.1–222)

The Profession of Faith of a Savoyard Priest

[In a sub-section of Book IV of *Émile*, Rousseau explains how, 30 years earlier, he had been offered spiritual guidance by a Savoyard priest. This story, a mixture of treatise, fiction and autobiography, is offered as a blueprint for Émile's religious education. He describes how he met the priest at sunrise at a location overlooking the Po valley and the Alps. The priest began by praising conscience (the 'immortal voice of heaven', 'an innate principle of justice and virtue' which 'follows the order of nature') and recommended it as a guide to all in matters of faith. He explained how he was suspended from Church duties following a breach of the chastity law and found himself in a position where he had to redefine his faith. Philosophy only served to 'multiply the doubts that tormented him' and he chose instead the 'inner light' as his guide. He found materialist philosophy unsatisfactory as it denied the existence of a non-material soul: according to materialists everything, including mind, soul and God, could be explained in terms of the operations of physical matter. He set out to prove that man does possess a non-material soul and a will which can influence his actions, independently of physical or physiological influences. The priest went on to reject the materialist view that matter can cause its own motion and that the universe is the result of chance combinations of physical matter. It must have been set in motion initially by a 'prime

---

[134] etc. [eds]

[135] i.e. shapes. [eds]

[136] i.e. draw. [eds]

mover', a supra-material will or intelligence, i.e. God: matter cannot, of itself, act to create motion:]

The first causes of motion do not exist in matter; bodies receive from and communicate motion to each other, but they cannot originally produce it. The more I observe the action and reaction of the powers of nature acting on each other, the more I am convinced that they are merely effects, and that we must ever recur to some volition as the first cause; for to suppose there is a progression of causes to infinity, is to suppose there is no first cause at all. In a word, every motion, that is not produced by some other, must be the effect of a spontaneous, voluntary act: inanimate bodies have no action but motion; and there can be no real action without volition. Such is my first principle. I believe, therefore, that a *Will* gives motion to the universe, and animates all nature. This is my first article of faith. (Kenrick III, pp.32–3.)

[In the following extract he puts forward the deist argument (the argument from design) that, as matter in motion appears to follow fixed laws, its prime mover (i.e. God) must be an intelligent being.]

If from matter being put in motion I discover the existence of a *Will*, as the first active cause, this matter, being subjected to certain regular laws of motion, suggests also to me intelligence: This is my second article of faith. To act, to compare, to prefer, are the operations of an active thinking being; such a being, therefore, exists. Do you proceed to ask me, where I discover its existence? I answer, not only in the revolutions of the celestial bodies; not only in the sun which gives us light; not only in myself; but in the flocks that feed on the plain, in the birds that fly in the air, in the stone that falls to the ground, and in the leaf blown by the wind.

I am enabled to judge of the order of things, although ignorant of their purpose; because, to be able to form such a judgment, it is sufficient for me to compare the several parts of the visible universe with each other, to study their mutual concurrence, their reciprocal relations, and to observe the general result of

the whole. I am ignorant why the universe exists, but I am enabled, nevertheless, to see how it is modified; I cannot fail to perceive that intimate connection, by which the several beings it is composed of, afford each other mutual assistance. I resemble, in this respect, a man who sees the inside of a watch, for the first time, and is captivated with the beauty of the work, although he is ignorant of its use and has never seen its face. I know not, he may say, what this machine is good for, but I see that each part is made to fit some other; I admire the artist for every part of his performance, and am certain that all these wheels act thus in concert to some common end which is impossible for me to see.

But let us compare the partial and particular ends, the means whereby they are effected, and their constant relations of every kind; then let us appeal to our innate sense of conviction; what man in his senses can refuse to acquiesce in such testimony? To what unprejudiced view does not the visible arrangement of the universe display the supreme intelligence of its author? How much sophistry does it not require, to disavow the harmony of created beings, and that admirable order in which all the parts of the system concur to the preservation of each other? You may talk to me as much as you please, of combinations and chances;[137] what end will it answer to reduce me to silence, if you cannot persuade me into the truth of what you advance? and how will you divest me of that involuntary sentiment, which continually contradicts you? If organised bodies are fortuitously combined in a thousand ways, before they assume settled and constant forms; if at first there are formed stomachs without mouths, feet without heads, hands without arms, and imperfect organs of every kind, which have perished for want of the necessary faculties of self-preservation; how comes it that none of these imperfect essays have engaged our attention? Why hath nature, at length, confined herself to laws to which she was not at first subjected? I confess that I ought not to be surprised that any possible thing should happen, when the rarity of the event is compensated by the number of chances that might bring it about. And yet if any one was to tell me that a

---

[137] Rousseau is here attacking the view, shared by some materialists, that the universe is the product of chance combinations of physical matter. According to this view the human form as we know it is the result of a series of mutations. [eds]

number of printers types, jumbled promiscuously together, had disposed themselves in the order of the letters composing the Æneid,[138] I certainly should not deign to take one step to verify or disprove such a story. It may be said, I forgot the number of chances; but pray how many must I suppose to render such a combination in any degree probable? I, who see only one chance for this combination to occur, fortuitously and an infinite number against it, must conclude that it is rather the effect of design. Add to this, that the product of these combinations must be always of the same nature with the combined elements: hence life and organization never can result from a blind concourse of atoms; nor will the chymist,[139] with all his art in compounds, ever find sensation and thought at the bottom of his crucible.[140] (Kenrick III, pp.36–8)

[The priest (a vehicle for Rousseau's own views) 'feels the existence of God: He cannot be analysed in any rational way and His qualities can only be deduced from observation of the natural world'.]

I believe, therefore, that the world is governed by a wise and powerful Will. I see it, or rather I feel it; and this is of importance for me to know. But is the world eternal or is it created? Are things derived from one self-existent principle? or are there two, or more? and what is their essence? Of all this I know nothing, nor do I see that it is of any consequence I should. In proportion as such knowledge may become interesting,[141] I will endeavour to acquire it: but, farther than this, I give up all such idle disquisitions, which serve only to make me discontented with myself, are useless in practice, and above my understanding.

You will remember, however, that I am not dictating my sentiments to you; but only displaying what they are. Whether matter be eternal or only created, whether it have a passive principle or not, certain it is that the whole universe is one design, and sufficiently displays one intelligent agent: for I see no part of this system that is not under regulation, or that does not concur to one and the same end; viz. that of preserving the present established order of things. That Being, whose will is his deed, whose principle of action is in himself, that Being, in a word, whatever it be, that gives motion to all the parts of the universe and governs all things, I call GOD. To this term I annex the ideas of intelligence, power and will, which I have collected from the order of things; and to these I add that of goodness, which is a necessary consequence of their union: but I am not at all the wiser concerning the essence of the Being to which I give these attributes. He remains at an equal distance from my senses and my understanding: the more I think of him, the more I am confounded; I know of a certainty that he exists, and that his existence is independent of any of his creatures. I know also that my existence is dependent on his, and that every thing I know is in the same situation with myself. I perceive the Deity in all his works, I feel him within me, and behold him in every object around me: but, I no sooner endeavour to contemplate what he is in himself; I no sooner enquire where he is, and what is his substance, than he eludes the strongest efforts of my imagination; and my bewildered understanding is convinced of its own weakness.

For this reason I shall never take upon me to argue about the nature of God, farther than I am obliged to it by the relation he appears to stand in to myself. There is so great a temerity in such disquisitions, that a wise man will never enter on them without trembling, and being

---

[138] Epic poem by Virgil, written 29–19 BC. [eds]

[139] i.e. chemist. [eds]

[140] It would be incredible, if we had not proof of it, that human extravagance could be carried to such a pitch. Amatus Lusitanus assures us, that he had seen in a phial a little man, about an inch long, which Julius Camillus, like another Prometheus, had generated by his skill in alchymy. Paracelsius in his treatise *De natura rerum*, [*The Nature of Things*. eds] gives the process of making these Mannikins and maintains, that Pygmies, Fauns, Satyrs and Nymphs, were engendered by chymistry. There wants nothing more, in my opinion, to establish the possibility of these facts, than to prove that the organical materials can resist fire, and that the component moleculae may preserve themselves alive in the intense heat of a reverberatory furnace. [Rousseau]

[141] Important to him. [eds]

fully assured of his incapacity to proceed far on so sublime a subject: for it is less injurious to the Deity to entertain no ideas of him at all, than to harbour those which are depreciating and unjust. (Kenrick III, pp.40–2)

[He goes on to argue that any confusion or disorder in the world is the work of man rather than of Nature or God. But man's intelligence and conscience are proof that he is not merely the plaything of physical and material needs and processes. His will is 'independent of his senses'. Man can use his will to refuse evil and restore the world to its natural order.]

The principle of all action lies in the will of a free being; we can go no farther, in search of its source. It is not the word liberty that has no signification; it is that of necessity. To suppose any act or effect, which is not derived from an active principle, is indeed to suppose effects without a cause and to reason in a vicious circle. Either there is no first impulse, or every first impulse can have no prior cause; nor can there be any such thing as will, without liberty. Man is, therefore, a free agent, and as such animated by an immaterial substance: this is my third article of faith. From these three first you may easily deduce all the rest, without my continuing to number them.

If man be an active and free being, he acts of himself; none of his spontaneous actions, therefore, enter into the general system of Providence, nor can be imputed to it. Providence doth not contrive the evil, which is the consequence of man's abusing the liberty his Creator gave him: it only doth not prevent it, either because the evil, which so impotent a being is capable of doing, is beneath its notice, or because it cannot prevent it, without laying a restraint upon his liberty, and causing a greater evil, by debasing his nature. Providence hath left man at liberty, not that he should do evil, but good, by choice. It hath capacitated him to make such choice, in making a proper use of the faculties it hath bestowed on him: his powers, however, are at the same time so limited and confined, that the abuse he makes of his liberty is not of importance enough to disturb the general order of the universe. The evil done by man, falls upon his own head, without making any change in the system of the world, without hindering the human species from being preserved, in spite of themselves. To complain, therefore, that God doth not prevent man from

doing evil, is in fact to complain that he hath given a superior excellence to human nature; that he hath ennobled our actions, by annexing to them the merit of virtue. The highest enjoyment is that of being contented with ourselves. It is in order to deserve this contentment that we are placed here on earth, and endowed with liberty; that we are tempted by our passions, and restrained by conscience. What could Omnipotence itself do more in our favour? Could it have established a contradiction in our nature, or have allotted a reward for well-doing, to a being incapable of doing ill? Is it necessary, in order to prevent man from being wicked, to reduce all his faculties to a simple instinct, and make him a mere brute? No, never can I reproach thee, God of my soul, for making me in thine own image, that I might be free, good, and happy, like my Maker! (Kenrick III, pp.50–2)

[Many evils, such as the 'apprehensions and miseries' engendered by medicine, are man-made and constitute an 'outrage' to the laws of nature. Natural evils, like physical pain, have a useful function: pain alerts us to the need for a remedy.]

Enquire no longer, man, who is the author of evil: behold him in yourself. There exists no other evil in nature than what you either do or suffer, and you are equally the author of both. A general evil could exist only in disorder; but, in the system of nature, I see an established order, which is never disturbed. Particular evil exists only in the sentiment of the suffering being; and this sentiment is not given to man by nature, but is of his own acquisition. Pain and sorrow have but little hold on those, who unaccustomed to reflection, have neither memory nor foresight. Take away our fatal progress, take away our errors and our vices, take away, in short, everything that is the work of men, and all the rest is good. (Kenrick III, pp.53–4.)

[He declares his faith in the goodness of God and in the existence of an immaterial soul capable of eternal life.]

But what is that life? Is the soul immortal in its own nature? My limited comprehension is incapable of conceiving any thing that is unlimited. Whatever we call infinite, is beyond my conception. What can I deny, or affirm, what arguments can I employ on a subject I cannot conceive? I believe that the soul survives the body so long as is necessary for the maintenance of order; but who knows that this will be for ever? I can readily conceive how material bodies wear away, and are destroyed by the separation of their parts; but I cannot conceive a like dissolution of a thinking being; and hence, as I cannot imagine how it can die, I presume it cannot die at all. This presumption, also, being consolatory, and not unreasonable, why should I be fearful to indulge it? (Kenrick III, pp.56–7)

[Hell and divine retribution, however, happen in this life rather than in the next. Rousseau rejects the value of prayers to God which ask for the order of nature to be altered. Underlining the importance of the 'internal sentiment' of conscience in morality and religion, the priest goes on to answer the charge that he has, so far, spoken of 'natural religion' rather than of revealed or organised religion. He distinguishes between the 'ceremonials of religion' and 'religion itself'. Man has tampered too much with forms of worship. Doctrines and miracles have developed and multiplied in order to bolster one another and remain highly suspect. Religion should be studied in the lives of men and in the 'book of nature' rather than in printed books. There follows an attack on the dogmatism and intolerance generated by established religions and on the harm done by the concepts of a severe God and divine grace. Revelation is an inadequate basis for faith and the truth of the Gospel is suspect. Moral duties should have precedence over the duties dictated by any particular sect. Despite this attack on revealed religion, however, the priest concludes that the latter has done less harm than unbelief. The following is taken from a footnote to the main text.]

The contending parties reciprocally attack each other with so many sophisms, that it would be a rash enterprize to undertake to explode them all. It is enough to note some of them as they occur. One of the most common among the partisans of philosophy is, to contrast an imaginary people, supposed to be all good philosophers, with another people all bad Christians; as if it were more easy to make a people true philosophers than good Christians. I know not whether, among individuals, one be more easily met with than the other; but this I know, that when we speak of a whole people, we must suppose that they would as much abuse a philosophy without religion, as ours abuses a religion without philosophy; and this consideration seems to me to make a great difference in the question.

Bayle[142] has proved very acutely, that fanaticism is more pernicious than atheism; and this is not to be disputed; but he neglected to observe, what is nevertheless true, that fanaticism, tho' sanguinary[143] and cruel, is a great and animating passion, that it elevates the heart of man, and makes him look down with contempt on death; that it is a prodigious spring of action, and requires only to be duly regulated in order to produce the most sublime virtues; whereas, on the contrary, irreligion, and a reasoning, philosophical spirit in general, attaches us to life, enervates and debases the soul; concentrating all our passions in degrading self-interest, in the meanness of the human self, and thus sapping by degrees the foundations of society; for selfish interests have so little in common that it will never outweigh their differences.

If atheism be less sanguinary, it is less out of a love to peace than from an indifference to virtue: let the world go how it will it little concerns these pretended[144] sages, provided they can loll at ease in their closets. Their principles do not excite them to slaughter mankind; but they prevent them from adding to their number, by corrupting the manners which tend to their increase, by detaching themselves from their species, and reducing all their affections to a selfish egotism, as fatal to population as to virtue. The indifference of the philosopher resembles the tranquillity of a state under a despotic government; it is the tranquillity of death, and more destructive than war itself.

Thus fanaticism, though more fatal in its immediate effects, than what is now called the philosophic spirit, is much less so in its remoter consequences. Moreover it is an easy matter to shew fine maxims in books, but the question is

---

[142] French writer (1647–1706) and author of *Historical and Critical Dictionary.* Compare the *Encyclopédie* article 14 in *Texts,* I, p.28. [eds]

[143] i.e. bloody. [eds]

[144] i.e. self-proclaimed. [eds]

this: are they faithful to an expressed doctrine; do they flow clearly from it? This has not been clearly proved so far. It remains to be seen whether philosophy, safely enthroned, could yield authority over the vanity, self-interest, ambition and lesser passions of man, and if it could practise this sweet humanity of which it boasts, pen in hand.

Philosophy, on its own principles, cannot be productive of any virtue, which does not flow from religion, and religion is productive of many virtues to which philosophy is a stranger.

As to practice, it is another thing, and remains to be examined. There is no man who practises in every particular the duties of his religion, when he has one; that is true; the greater part of mankind have hardly any religion at all, and practise nothing of what little they have; this also is very true: but after all, some people have religion, and practise it at least in part; and it is incontestible, that motives of religion prevent them often from falling into vice, and excite to virtuous and commendable actions, which they had not[145] performed but for such motives.

Let a monk deny that money was entrusted to him; what does this prove but that a block-head had trusted in him? If Pascal[146] himself had done it, this would have proved Pascal a hyp-ocrite; nothing more – But a monk! – Well, and what then? Are those who make a traffic of religion the truly religious? The crimes of the clergy by no means prove that religion is useless, but that few persons are religious. (Kenrick III, pp.125–7.)

Book V (Kenrick IV, pp.1–260)

[In Book V Rousseau outlines an educational programme for women, as Émile can only fulfil his moral and social duties, if he has the support of a virtuous wife. Sophie is first introduced in the book as an abstract construct: the ideal model, the perfect partner to be sought by Émile. Later, however, the novel takes over from the treatise: she becomes a character in the story

of Émile's life. The rest of the book deals with their courtship, marriage and life together as patrons of the rural poor.]

Sophie or Woman

Sophie should be such a woman as Émile is a man; that is, she should possess every thing requisite in the constitution of the species and sex, to fill her place in the physical and moral order of things. To know whether she be so qualified, we shall enter first on an examination into the various instances of conformity and dif-ference between her sex and ours.

In every thing, which does not regard the sex, woman is the same as man; she has the same organs, the same necessities, the same faculties: the corporeal machine is constructed in the same manner, its component parts are alike, their operation the same, and the figure similar in both. In whatever light we regard them, they differ from each other only in degree.

On the other hand, in every thing immedi-ately respecting sex, the woman differs entirely from the man; each is the complement of the other; the difficulty of comparing them together, lying in our inability to determine what are those particulars in the constitution of each that immediately relate to the sex. From their com-parative anatomy, and even from simple inspec-tion, we perceive some general distinctions between them, that do not appear to relate to sex; and yet there can be no doubt they do, although we are not capable of tracing their modes of relation to it. Indeed we know not how far the difference of sex may extend. All that we know, of a certainty, is, that whatever is common to both is characteristic of their species; and that every thing in which they differ, is distinctive of their sex. Under this two-fold consideration we find so much resemblance and dissimilitude, that it appears even miraculous, that nature should form two beings so much alike, and, at the same time, so very different.

This difference and similitude must necessarily have an influence over their moral character: such an influence is, indeed, obvious, and perfectly agreeable to experience; clearly

---

[145] Would not have. [eds]

[146] French mathematician, physicist, philosopher and writer, 1623–62. He became a Jansenist convert and his unfinished *Thoughts* contain an apology for the Christian religion. He was an advocate of asceticism. [eds.]

demonstrating the vanity of the disputes that have been held concerning the superiority or equality of the sexes; as if, in answering the different ends for which nature designed them, both were not more perfect than they would be in more nearly resembling each other. In those particulars which are common to both, they are equal; and as to those wherein they differ, no comparison is to be made between them. A perfect man and complete woman should no more resemble each other in mind than in feature; nor does perfection admit of more or less.[147]

In the union of the sexes, both pursue one common object, but not in the same manner. From their diversity, in this particular, arises the first determinate difference between the moral relations of each. The one should be active and strong, the other passive and weak: it is necessary the one should have both the power and the will; it suffices that the other should make little resistance.

This principle being established, it follows, that woman is expressly formed to please the man. If the obligation be reciprocal also, and the man ought to please in his turn, it is not so immediately necessary: his great merit lies in his power, and he pleases merely because he is strong. This, I must confess, is not one of the refined maxims of love; it is, however, one of the laws of nature, prior to love itself.

If woman be formed to please and to be subjected to man, it is her place, doubtless, to render herself agreeable to him, instead of provoking his anger. Her violence lies in her charms: it is by means of these she should urge him to the exertion of those powers which nature hath given him. The most successful method of exciting these powers is to render such exertion necessary by her resistance; as, in that case, self-love is added to desire, and the one triumphs in the victory which the other obliged him to acquire. Hence arise the various modes of attack and defence between the sexes, the boldness of one sex, and the timidity of the other, and, in a word, that bashfulness and modesty with which nature hath armed the weak, in order to subdue the strong.

Can it ever be thought that she[148] hath dictated indifferently the same advances to one as the other, and that the first to form desires should be also the first to display them? What a strange mistake in judgment must be such a conclusion! Their intercourse being productive of consequences so very different to each, can it be natural for both to engage in the mutual conflict with the same readiness and intrepidity? Is it not very evident that, from their unequal shares in the encounter, if reserve did not impose on one the same moderation as nature imposes on the other, the consequence would soon be fatal to both, and that the human race would be brought to destruction by the very means established by nature for its preservation? Considering the easy influence of women over men's senses, and how readily they can affect even the remains of an almost exhausted constitution, it is plain, that if there were an unhappy climate on earth, whence philosophy had banished all female reserve, the men, subjected to the tyranny of the women, would be soon sacrificed to their charms; particularly in hot countries, where are born more women than men, the latter would all be hurried presently to their graves, without any possibility of helping themselves.

That the females of animals have not the same modesty and reserve, makes nothing against my argument; as their desires are not, like those of women, left without restriction. In the latter, their reserve supplies the place of a physical restraint; while the former have no desires but what arise from physical necessity. This being satisfied, their desire ceases: they no longer repulse the male in appearance,[149] but in reality; acting contrary to the daughter of Augustus,[150] they receive no more passengers on board when the vessel hath compleated its cargo.

---

[147] i.e. perfection is absolute, not relative. [eds]

[148] i.e. nature. [eds]

[149] I have already remarked, that coquetries and an affected aversion to the males, are common to almost all females, even animals, and that even when they are most disposed to admit their caresses. One must have paid no attention to their ploys to doubt of this. [Rousseau]

[150] Julia, the daughter of Augustus, was banished for sexual excess. [eds]

Even when they are salacious, their time is short, and presently[151] over: instinct urges them on, and instinct restrains them. What substitute could be found for this negative instinct in women, if you deprive them of modesty? To expect that they should have no inclination towards the man, is to expect men to be good for nothing.

The supreme Being intended in every case to do honour to the human species. In leaving the desires of man unlimited, he gave him, at the same time, the law for their regulation, in order that he might be free and command himself: in delivering him to immoderate passions, he gave him also reason with which to restrain them: in leaving the passions of woman also unrestrained, he gave her modesty to restrain them. To these he hath further added an actual recompence for the regular use of their respective faculties; to wit, the delight which is taken in right conduct, when such is made the standard of our actions. All this appears to me more than equivalent to instinct in brutes.

Whether the female, therefore, of our species, be inclined to share and gratify the desires of the male or not, she is by nature constantly coy, and betrays a seeming reluctance to yield to his embraces. She does not resist or defend herself, however, always with the same resolution, nor of course with the same success. In order that the assailant should be victorious, it is necessary that the assailed should permit or direct the attack: for of how many artful means is not the latter possessed to compel the former to exert himself? The most free and delightful of all actions admits not of any real violence; both nature and reason are against it; nature, in that she hath provided the weakest party with sufficient force to make an effectual resistance, when she pleases; and reason, in that real violence, on such an occasion, is not only the most brutal of all actions, but the most contrary to its end and design; both because that, by such means, the man declares war against his companion, and thus authorises her to stand up in defence of her person and liberty, even at the hazard of the life of the aggressor; and also because that the woman is the only proper judge of her own situation, and that a child would have no father, if every man were at liberty to usurp the rights of a husband.

Hence we deduce a third consequence from the different constitutions of the sexes; which is, that the strongest should be master in appearance, and be dependent in fact on the weakest; and that not from any frivolous practice of gallantry or vanity of protectorship, but from an invariable law of nature, which, furnishing woman with greater facility to excite desires than she has given man to satisfy them, makes the latter dependent on the good pleasure of the former, and compels him to endeavour to please in his turn, in order to obtain her consent that he should be strongest. On these occasions, the most delightful circumstance a man finds in his victory is, to doubt whether it was the woman's weakness that yielded to his superior strength, or whether her inclinations spoke in his favour: the females are also generally artful enough to leave this matter in doubt. The understanding of women answers, in this respect, perfectly to their constitution: so far from being ashamed of their weakness, they glory in it: their tender muscles make no resistance; they affect to be incapable of lifting the smallest burthens, and would blush to be thought robust and strong. To what purpose is all this? Not merely for the sake of appearing delicate, but through an artful precaution: it is thus they provide an excuse beforehand, and a right to be feeble when they think it expedient.

The progress of our knowledge, increased by our vices, hath made the opinion of the moderns on this head very different from that of the ancients: and we hardly ever hear talk of rapes as they are become so little necessary, and are no longer credited:[152] [153] whereas they were very common in the earliest ages of the Greeks and Hebrews, because such notions were agreeable

---

[151] i.e. quickly. [eds]

[152] i.e. believed. [eds]

[153] There may happen, however, to be such a disproportion in the strength and age of the parties, as to admit of an actual rape; but as I am here treating of the relative state of the sexes in the common course of nature, I do not suppose any such disproportion. [Rousseau]

to the simplicity of nature, and are such as experienced libertinism only can eradicate. If we have fewer instances, however, in modern times of such acts of violence, it certainly is not because men are less licentious, but because they have less credulity; such a complaint as would have persuaded the simple people of former times, would, in ours, be disregarded with a smile: silence is now held to be the wisest course. There is a law recorded in Deuteronomy,[154] by which a young woman, when debauched, was condemned to suffer with her seducer, in case the crime was committed within the city: but if it happened in the field, or other unfrequented place, the ravisher was punished alone: *For* says the law, *the damsel cried, and there was none to save her.* This favourable interpretation, doubtless, taught the young women to take care not to be surprized in places that were frequented.

The effect of this change of opinion on manners is very perceptible. Modern gallantry is one of its consequences. The men, finding that their pleasures depended more on the goodwill of the fair sex than they at first imagined, cultivated the art of captivating them by a complaisance which has found its reward.

Thus we see how the physical insensibly[155] leads us to the moral, and in what manner the grosser union of the sexes gave rise, by degrees, to the more refined rules and softer maxims of love. The great influence of the women, therefore, is not owing to the voluntary submission of the men, but to the will of nature: they were possessed of it before they appeared to be so: that very Hercules [156] who proposed to violate the fifty daughters of Thespius [157] was, nevertheless, compelled to wield the distaff by Omphale;[158] and

Samson himself, strong as he was, was no match for Dalilah.[159] This power of the fair sex cannot be taken from them, even when they abuse it: if ever they could lose their influence, they would, undoubtedly, have lost it long ago.

There is no parity between man and woman as to the consequences of their sex. The male is such only at certain momentary intervals: the female feels the consequences of her sex all her life, at least during youth, and, in order to answer the purposes of it, requires first a suitable constitution. She requires next careful management in her pregnancy, repose in child-bed, ease and a sedentary life during the time of suckling her children, and, to bring them up, such patience, zeal, and affection, as nothing can disgust.[160] She serves as the means of their connection with their father: it is she alone who makes him love them, and gives him the confidence to call them his own. What tenderness and solicitude ought she not to be possessed of, in order to maintain the peace and unity of a whole family! Add to this, that her good qualities should not be the effects of virtue, but of taste and inclination, without which the human species would soon be extinct.

The relative duties of the two sexes do not require an equally rigorous observance in both. When women complain, however, of this partiality as unjust, they are in the wrong: this inequality is not of human institution; at least, it is not the effect of prejudice, but of reason. It certainly belongs to that party which nature hath more immediately intrusted with the care of children, to be answerable for that charge to the other. Neither of them, indeed, is permitted to violate their mutual engagements. Every faithless

---

[154] Deuteronomy, 22, 23–7. [eds]

[155] i.e. imperceptibly. [eds]

[156] Roman demi-god. [eds]

[157] Legend recounts that Hercules hid in the house of King Thespius while waiting to kill a ferocious lion, and lay in a single night with his host's fifty daughters. [eds]

[158] Hercules was obliged to spend a year as slave to Omphale, queen of Lydia, as his punishment for carrying off the Pythia's tripod from Delphi. [eds]

[159] See Judges 14–16. [eds]

[160] i.e. as nothing can make her lose her taste for bringing up her children. [eds]

husband, who deprives his wife of the only compensation for the severer duties of her sex, being guilty of cruelty and injustice. A faithless woman, however, does still more: she dissolves the union of her family, and breaks through all the ties of nature; in giving to a man children which are not of his begetting, she betrays both, and adds perfidy to infidelity. Such an action is naturally productive of the worst of crimes and disorders. If there be a situation in life truly horrid, it is that of an unhappy father, who, placing no confidence in his wife, cannot indulge himself in the most delightful sentiments of the heart; who doubts, while he is embracing his child, whether it is not the offspring of another, the pledge of his dishonour, and the usurper of the rights of his real children. What a scene doth a family in such a case present to us! Nothing but a community of secret enemies, whom a guilty woman arms one against the other, by compelling them to pretences of reciprocal affection.

It is not only of consequence, therefore, that a woman should be faithful to her husband, but also that he should think her so. It is requisite for her to be modest, circumspect, and reserved, and that she should bear, in the sight of others, as well as in her own conscience, the testimony of her virtue. If it be necessary for a father to love his children, it is first necessary for him to esteem their mother. Such are the reasons which place even the preservation of appearances among the number of female duties, and render their honour and reputation no less indispensible than chastity. From these principles is derived not only a moral difference in the sexes but a new motive of obligation and convenience, which prescribes peculiarly to women the most scrupulous circumspection in their manners, conduct, and behaviour. To maintain indiscriminately that the sexes are equal, and that their reciprocal duties and obligations are the same, is to indulge ourselves in idle declamations unworthy of a serious answer.

It is certainly a very superficial manner of reasoning, that of bringing exceptions as proofs to invalidate general laws so well founded. Women, you say, do not always bear children. That is true; their sex is, nevertheless, destined by nature to that end. What! because there are an hundred great cities in the world, where the women, leading a licentious life, have few children, do you pretend that women are naturally barren? What would become of all your populous towns, if the country districts, where the women live in great chastity and simplicity, did not compensate for the sterility of your town ladies? A woman who hath borne but four or five children, would, in many provinces, be far from being esteemed a fruitful breeder.[161] In a word, it is to no purpose that some particular women bear but few children; women in general are not the less formed by nature to become mothers; and is it not by general laws, that nature and manners operate to that end?

But were the intervals between the pregnancy of women so long as is supposed, is it possible for them to change so suddenly their manner of living, without hazard of life or health? Can a woman be one day a nurse and the next a soldier? Can she vary her temperament and inclination as the chameleon doth its colours? Is it practicable to pass, at once, from the secure inclosure of a cloister, and the business of domestic concerns, to brave the inclemencies of the weather, the labours, the fatigues, and the horrors of war? Can a woman be one day timid,[162] the next courageous; this hour delicate, and the next robust? If we see the young men of Paris hardly able to support the profession of arms, how can it be imagined, that women, whose faces were never exposed to the sun, and who hardly know how to walk, should support it, after having spent fifty years in softness and indolence? Can they take up this severe, laborious employment, at an age when the men usually lay it down?

---

[161] Were it not so, the species must necessarily perish; its preservation requiring that every woman, taking one with another, should produce nearly four children: for of all the children that are born, almost the half die before the mothers can have any more; two, therefore, must remain, to represent the father and mother. The propagation of the species, in great cities, is far from being in this proportion. [Rousseau]

[162] The timidity of women is another natural instinct given them to prevent the double danger they run during pregnancy. [Rousseau]

There are some countries, I must own, where the women undergo but little pain in child-birth, and nurse their offspring with very little trouble. In those countries, however the men go about in all seasons half-naked, strike down wild beasts, carry their canoes as they would a knap-sack, go seven or eight hundred leagues to hunt, sleep on the bare ground in the open air, support incredible fatigues, and pass many days together without eating. Where the women are hardy and robust, the men are much more so; and when the men grow soft and effeminate, the women become tender and feeble: so that both changing equally, the difference between them remains the same.

Plato, I know, in his Republic, prescribes to women the same exercises as the men. Having deprived his government of particular families,[163] and being ignorant where to place women, he was reduced to the necessity of making them men. This great genius had such powers of combination and foresight, that he could foresee such objections to his own system as no else would ever have thought of: he has but ill resolved, however, some that have been actually made. I do not speak of that pretended community of women, with which he hath been so often reproached: a proof that those who reproached him had never read his performance. What I mean is, the promiscuous[164] employment of both sexes in the same kinds of business and amusements, which could not fail of producing the most intolerable abuses. I speak of that subversion of the order of things, when the most delightful of all natural sentiments are sacrificed to artificial sentiments, which cannot exist without the former; as if the bonds of society could be formed independent of nature; as if the affection we bear to our families was not the source of our allegiance to the state; as if it was not on account of our little country, our own family, that we attach ourselves to the greater; and as if the good son, the good husband, and the good father, did not constitute the good citizen.

It being once demonstrated that man and woman are not, nor ought to be, constituted alike in temperament and character, it follows of course that they should not be educated in the same manner. In pursuing the directions of nature, they ought indeed to act in concert, but they should not be engaged in the same employments: the end of their pursuits should be the same; but the means they should take to accomplish them, and of consequence, their tastes and inclinations, should be different. Having endeavoured to lay down the principles of a natural education for a man, let us trace, in the same manner, the methods to form a woman answerable to him.

Are you desirous of being always directed aright? Observe constantly the indications of nature. Whatever is characteristic of the sex, should be regarded as a circumstance peculiarly established by her.[165] You are always complaining that women have certain defects and failings from which men are free; your vanity deceives you: such, indeed, would be defects and failings in you, but they are essential qualities in them, and things would be much worse without them. You may prevent these pretended defects from growing worse; but you ought to take great care not entirely to remove them.

The women, again, on their part, are constantly crying out, that we educate them to be vain and coquettish; that we constantly entertain them with puerilities, in order to maintain our authority over them; and attribute to us the failings for which we reproach them. What a ridiculous accusation! How long is it that the men have troubled themselves about the education of the women? What hinders mothers from bringing up their daughters just as they please? There are, to be sure, no colleges and academies for girls: a sad misfortune truly! Would to God there were none also for boys; they would be more sensibly and virtuously educated than they are. Who, ye mothers, compels your daughters to throw away their time in trifles? to spend half their lives, after your example, at the toilette?[166]

---

[163] The nuclear family does not exist in the Republic. See Republic Book V. [eds]

[164] i.e. without distinction or discrimination. [eds]

[165] i.e. nature. [eds]

[166] i.e. dressing-table. [eds]

Who hinders you from instructing, or causing them to be instructed in the manner you chuse? Is it our fault that they charm us when they are pretty, that we are seduced by their affected airs, that the arts they learn of you attract and flatter us, that we love to see them becomingly dressed, and that we permit them to prepare at leisure those arms with which they subdue us to their pleasure? Educate them, if you think proper, like the men; we shall readily consent to it. The more they resemble our sex, the less power will they have over us; and when they once become like ourselves, we shall then be truly their masters.

The qualities common to both sexes are not equally allotted to each; though taken all together they are equal in both: the woman is more perfect as a woman, and less as a man. In every case where she makes use of her own privileges, she has the advantage over us; but where she would usurp ours, she becomes inferior. The only reply to be made to this general truth, is by bringing exceptions to it; the method of argumentation constantly used by the superficial partizans of the fair sex.

To cultivate in women, therefore, the qualifications of the men, and neglect those which are peculiar to the sex, would be acting to their prejudice: they see this very well, and are too artful to become the dupes of such conduct: they endeavour, indeed, to usurp our advantages, but they take care not to give up their own. By these means, however, it happens that, not being capable of both, because they are incompatible, they fail of attaining the perfection of their own sex, as well as of ours, and lose half their merit. Let not the sensible mother, then, think of educating her daughter as a good man, in contradiction to nature; but as a virtuous woman; and she may be assured it will be much better both for her child and herself.

It does not hence follow, however, that she ought to be educated in perfect ignorance, and confined merely to domestic concerns. Would a man make a servant of his companion, and deprive himself of the greatest pleasure of society? To make her the more submissive, would

he prevent her from feeling or knowledge?[167] would he reduce her to a mere automaton? Surely not! Nature hath dictated otherwise, in giving the sex such refined and agreeable talents: on the contrary, she[168] hath formed them for thought, for judgment, for love, and knowledge. They should bestow as much care on their understandings, therefore, as on their persons, and add the charms of the one to the other, in order to supply their own want of strength, and to direct ours. They should doubtless learn many things, but only those which it is proper for them to know.

Whether I consider the peculiar destination of the sex, observe their inclinations, or remark their duties, all things equally concur to point out the peculiar method of education best adapted to them. Woman and man were made for each other; but their mutual dependence is not the same. The men depend on the women, only on account of their desires; the women on the men, both on account of their desires and their necessities: we could subsist better without them than they without us. Their very subsistance and rank in life depend on our will, and the estimation in which we hold them, their charms, their merit and their virtues. By the law of nature itself, both women and children lie at the mercy of the judgement of men: it is not enough they should be really estimable, it is requisite they should be actually esteemed; it is not enough they should be beautiful, it is requisite their charms should please; it is not enough they should be prudent, it is necessary they should be acknowledged as such: their glory lies not only in their conduct, but in their reputation; and it is impossible for any, who consents to be accounted infamous, to be ever virtuous. A man, secure in his own good conduct, depends only on himself, and may brave the public opinion: but a woman, in behaving well, performs but half her duty; as what is thought of her, is as important to her, as what she really is. It follows hence, that the system of a woman's education should, in this respect, be directly contrary to that of ours. Opinion is the grave of virtue among the men; but its throne among the women.

---

[167] In his *Confessions* (p.392) Rousseau regrets that he did not invest more time in the education of Thérèse Levasseur, his mistress-housekeeper and, eventually, wife. [eds]

[168] i.e. nature. [eds]

On the good constitution of mothers depends originally that of their children; on the care of the women depends the earliest education of men; on the women also depend our manners, our passions, our tastes, our pleasures, and even our happiness itself. For this reason, the education of the women should be always relative to the men. To please, to be useful to us, to make us love and esteem them, to educate us when young, and take care of us when grown up, to advise, to console us, to render our lives easy and agreeable; these are the duties of women at all times, and what they should be taught in their infancy. So long as we fail to recur to this principle, we run wide of the mark, and all the precepts which are given them contribute neither to their happiness nor our own.

But although every woman is, and ought to be, desirous of rendering herself pleasing to the men, there is a wide difference between the desire of being agreeable to a man of merit, a man truly amiable in himself, and the desire of captivating those affected pretty fellows, who are a disgrace to their own sex, as well as to that which they imitate. Neither nature nor reason induce a woman to admire those qualities in a man which resemble her own, nor is her copying their manners by any means the way to captivate their affections.

Whenever she throws aside, therefore, the reserved and modest behaviour of the female, to assume the pert airs of the masculine fop, she renounces, instead of pursuing, the vocation of her sex, and gives up those rights she means to usurp: she may think, indeed, she could not otherwise be pleasing to the men; but she is greatly mistaken. Fools only admire fools; and the desire of captivating such characters, is a sufficient indication of the taste of such as attempt it. Were there no frivolous and effeminate men, such women would make them; and the follies of the former would be more owing to the latter than are now those of the women to the men. The woman who loves real men, and is desirous of pleasing them, will take her measures accordingly. Woman is by her situation a coquette; but her coquetry changes its form and object according to her

views: let us regulate these views, therefore, by those of nature, and women will be properly educated.

Girls are, from their earliest infancy, fond of dress. Not content with being pretty, they are desirous of being thought so; we see, by all their little airs, that this thought engages their attention: and they are hardly capable of understanding what is said to them, before they are to be governed by talking to them of what people will think of their behaviour. The same motive, however indiscreetly made use of with boys, has not the same effect: provided they are left to pursue their amusements at pleasure, they care very little what people think of them. Time and pains are necessary to subject boys to this motive.

Whencesoever girls derive this first lesson, it is a very good one. As the body is born, in a manner, before the soul, our first concern should be to cultivate the former; this order is common to both sexes, but the object of that cultivation is different. In the one sex, it is the development of corporeal powers; in the other, that of personal charms: not that either the quality of strength or beauty ought to be confined exclusively to one sex; but only that the order of importance of both qualities is in that respect reversed. Women certainly require as much strength as to enable them to move and act gracefully, and men as much address[169] as to qualify them to act with ease.

From the extreme effeminacy of the women arises that of the men. Women ought not to be robust like them, but for them, in order that the men born of them should be robust also. In this respect, convents, where the boarders are coarsly dieted, but take much exercise in the gardens and open air, are preferable to home, where daughters are usually more nicely[170] fed and tenderly treated: here they are always either flattered or rebuked, and sitting under the eye of their mother in a close apartment, hardly ever venture to rise up, walk about, talk or breathe; they are not a moment at liberty, to play, run, romp about and make a noise, agreeable to the natural petulance of their age. They are always treated at home with excessive indulgence, or

---

[169] i.e. skill. [eds]

[170] i.e. with greater discrimination. [eds]

ill-judged severity; never according to the dictates of reason. Thus it is we spoil the persons and the hearts of youth.

Among the Spartans, the girls used[171] themselves to military exercises, as well as the boys, not indeed to go to fight, but in order to be capable of bearing children able to undergo the fatigues of war. Not that I approve of their practice in this particular; it is not necessary for the women to carry a musket and learn the Prussian exercise, in order to be capable of bearing robust children; what I would infer from this instance is, that the Greeks well understood the business of education. The young females appeared often in public, not mixing promiscuously[172] among the boys, but in select companies of their own sex. There was hardly a single festival, sacrifice, or public ceremony, at which the daughters of the principal citizens did not make their appearance, crowned with chaplets of flowers, singing hymns, dancing with their baskets of oblations in their hands; and presenting to the depraved sense of the Greeks, a spectacle delightful in itself, and proper to counteract the bad effects of their indecent gymnastics. But whatever impressions this custom might make on the hearts of the men, it was an excellent one, as well to form the constitution of the fair sex, by agreeable, moderate, and salutary[173] exercise, as to refine their taste, by cherishing in them a continual desire to please, without exposing them to a corruption of manners.

No sooner, however, were their females married, than they were secluded from public view, and shut up in their houses; their future concern relating entirely to the management of their families. Such is the manner of life which both nature and reason prescribe to this sex; and hence it was, that the Spartan mothers gave birth to the most healthy, robust, and well-made men in the world. Notwithstanding the dissolute character of some of the Grecian islands,[174] it is certain that the women of no people on earth, not excepting even the Romans, were at once more prudent and amiable and able to unite morals and beauty than those of ancient Greece.

It is well known, that a loose and easy dress contributes much to give both sexes those fine proportions of body, that are observable in their statues, and which serve as models to our present artists; nature being too much disfigured among us to afford them any such. The Greeks knew nothing of those Gothic[175] shackles, that multiplicity of ligatures and bandages, with which our bodies are compressed. The women were ignorant of the use of whalebone stays, by which ours distort their shape, instead of displaying it. I cannot but conceive, that this practice, carried to so great an excess as it is in England, must in time degenerate the species; and I will maintain it to be an instance of wretched taste. Can it be a pleasing sight to behold a woman, cut in two in the middle, as it were, like a wasp? On the contrary, it is as shocking to the eye, as it is painful to the imagination. A fine shape, like the limbs, hath its due size and proportion, a diminution of which is certainly a defect. Such a deformity also would be striking in a naked figure; wherefore, then, should it be esteemed a beauty in one that is dressed?

I dare not be too explicit as to those reasons the women have for persisting to gird themselves up in this manner: a falling breast, a rising belly, &c. are, I confess, disagreeable enough in a young woman of twenty; but these are no longer shocking when a woman is turned of thirty; and as we must be at all times and in spite of ourselves whatever pleases nature; as there is no deceiving the eye of man; such defects at any age are less displeasing than the ridiculous affectation of a little miss of forty.

Every thing that confines, and lays nature under a restraint, is an instance of bad taste: this is as true in regard to the ornaments of the body

---

[171] i.e. accustomed. [eds]

[172] i.e. without restraint. [eds]

[173] i.e. health-giving. [eds]

[174] Lesbos, for example. The Greeks themselves did not regard Lesbos as dissolute, however. [eds]

[175] i.e. not classical, not simple in line and manner, over-elaborate. [eds]

as to the embellishments of the mind. Life, health, reason, and convenience, ought to be taken first into consideration: gracefulness cannot subsist without ease; delicacy is not debility, nor must a woman be sick in order to please. Infirmity and sickness may excite our pity: but desire and pleasure require the bloom and vigour of health.

Children of both sexes have a great many amusements in common; and so they ought; have they not also many such when they are grown up? Each sex hath also its peculiar[176] taste to distinguish in this particular.[177] Boys love sports of noise and activity; to beat the drum, to whip the top, and to drag about their little carts: girls, on the other hand, are fonder of things of shew and ornament; such as mirrors, trinkets, finery and dolls: the doll is the peculiar amusement of the females; from whence we see their taste plainly adapted to their destination. The physical part of the art of pleasing lies in dress; and this is all which children are capacitated to cultivate of that art.

You shall see a little girl spend whole days about her waxen baby; be perpetually changing its clothes, dress and undress it an hundred times, and be for ever studying new combinations of ornament; well or ill-sorted, it is no matter: her fingers want dexterity, and her taste is not yet formed; but her inclinations are sufficiently evident. While thus occupied to eternity, her time slips insensibly away; she forgets even her meals, and has more appetite to dress than to food. You will say, perhaps, that she dresses up her baby, and not herself. Doubtless, it is her baby she sees, and not herself: she can do nothing as yet about her own person, she is not fully grown, she has no talent or strength, she is as yet nothing; all her concerns center in her doll, and in the management of this it is that she displays all her coquetry. This, however, will not be always the case; the time approaches when she will take the same pleasure in ornamenting herself.

Here then we see a primary propensity firmly established, which you need only to pursue and regulate. The little creature will doubtless be very desirous to know how to dress up her doll, to make its sleeve knots, its tippets, its flounces, its head-dress, &c. She is obliged to have so much recourse to the people about her, for their assistance in these articles, that it would be much more agreeable to her to owe them all to her own industry. Hence we have a good reason for the first lessons that are usually taught these young females: in which we do not appear to be setting them a task, but obliging them, by instructing them in what is immediately useful to themselves. And, in fact, almost all of them learn with reluctance to read and write; but very readily apply themselves to the use of their needles. They imagine themselves already grown up, and think with pleasure that such qualifications will enable them to decorate themselves.

The first path being laid open, it is very easy to pursue it: sewing, embroidery, and lace-making follow of course: tapestry, indeed, is not so much their taste. Household furniture is too far removed from their present thoughts; it does not immediately relate to their persons, but is rendered interesting by other considerations. The working of tapestry is an amusement for grown women; girls never take much pleasure in it.

Their voluntary progress in these employments may be easily extended to the art of drawing, which is by no means indifferent to such as would dress themselves with taste and elegance. I would not have girls, however, apply themselves to draw landscapes, and still less to history-pieces and figures. Foliage, fruits, flowers, drapery, and whatever may tend to enable them to give an elegance to dress, or to design themselves a pattern for embroidery, when they meet with none to their taste, are sufficient. If, in general, it behoves men to confine their studies to useful knowledge, this is still more necessary for the women; because the lives of the latter, tho' less laborious, yet requiring greater assiduity, will not permit them to cultivate any talent, to the neglect of their duty.

Whatever may be sometimes said in raillery, good sense is equally the property of both sexes. Girls in general are more docile than boys, and, indeed, we ought to use more authority over

---

[176] i.e. its own particular. [eds]

[177] i.e. in this matter of amusements. [eds]

them, as I observe hereafter; but it does not thence follow, that we should require them to do any thing, of which they do not see the utility: it is the art of a mother to shew them the usefulness of whatever they are set to do; and this is by so much the more easy, as the understanding ripens much sooner in girls than boys. This rule frees their sex, as well as ours, not only from those indolent and useless studies, which answer no good purpose, nor even render those who cultivate them the more agreeable to others; but also all those whose utility is not adapted to their present age, nor perceptible in a future one. If I am against compelling boys to learn to read,[178] it is with still greater reason that I oppose using any such compulsion with girls, at least till they are well instructed in the utility of reading: the manner, however, in which this utility is usually inculcated, is much better adapted to our own notions of things than to theirs. And, after all, where is the necessity for a girl's learning to read and write so early? does she so soon take on herself the management of a family? I am afraid there are but few who do not make rather a bad use than a good one of this fatal science;[179] and I am certain they have all so much curiosity as to learn it without compulsion, whenever they have leisure and opportunity. Perhaps they ought to learn arithmetic, in preference to every thing else; for nothing can appear more useful at any time of life, requires longer practice, nor gives so great an opportunity for error, than the keeping accounts. If a little girl should have no means of obtaining cherries or sugar-plums, but by resolving a question in arithmetic, I will answer for it she would soon learn to calculate for them.

I once knew a young person who learned to write before she learned to read, and began to write with her needle before she could use a pen. At first, indeed, she took it into her head, to make no other letter than the O. This letter she was constantly making of all sizes, some inside others, and always drawn backwards. Unluckily, one day she was intent on this employment, she happened to see herself in the looking-glass; when, taking a dislike to the constrained attitude in which she sat while writing, she threw away her pen, like another Pallas,[180] and determined against making the O any more. Her brother was also equally averse to writing: it was the discomfort, however, and not the air it gave him, that most disgusted him. A method was soon taken with the sister to bring her back to her writing: being very nice, and not a little vain, she did not chuse that her sisters should wear any of her linen; for this reason they used to be marked, a circumstance which was now wilfully neglected: it became necessary for her, therefore, to mark them herself; which she speedily effected; and by that method, it will be readily conceived, soon learned to write.

Let there be propriety[181] in all the injunctions you lay upon young girls, but take care always to impose on them something to learn or to do. Indolence and indocility are two of the most dangerous ill qualities they are subject to, and what they are the most seldom cured of, when they have once contracted them. Girls ought to be active and diligent; nor is that all; they should also be early subjected to restraint. This misfortune, if it really be one, is inseparable from the sex; nor do they ever throw it off but to suffer more cruel evils. They must be subject, all their lives, to the most constant and severe restraint, which is that of decorum: it is, therefore, necessary to accustom them early to such confinement, that it may not afterwards cost them too dear; and to the suppression of their caprices, that they may the more readily submit to the will of others. If, indeed, they are fond of being always at work, they should be sometimes compelled to lay it aside. Dissipation, levity and inconstancy are faults that readily spring up from their first propensities, when corrupted or perverted by too much indulgence. To prevent this abuse, we should learn them, above all things, to lay a due restraint on themselves. The life of a modest woman is reduced by our absurd

---

[178] In Book II of *Émile* Rousseau asserts that 'reading is the curse of childhood'. [eds]

[179] i.e. skill. [eds]

[180] Presumably warrior-like, in the manner of Pallas Athene. [eds]

[181] i.e. sense, justification, fitness. [eds]

institutions, to a perpetual conflict with herself: not but it is just that this sex should partake of the sufferings which arise from those evils it hath caused us. (Kenrick IV, pp.4–29.)

[Rousseau addresses the problem of mother-daughter relationships and the importance of balancing a girl's enjoyment with serious occupations, in order to discourage caprice.]

There results from this habitual restraint a tractableness which the women have occasion for during their whole lives, as they constantly remain either under subjection to the men, or to the opinions of mankind; and are never permitted to set themselves above those opinions. The first and most important qualification in a woman is sweetness of temper: formed to obey a being so imperfect as man, often full of vices, and always full of faults, she ought to learn betimes[182] even to suffer injustice, and to bear the insults of a husband without complaint: it is not for his sake, but her own, that she should be of a mild disposition. The perverseness and ill-nature of women only serve to aggravate their own misfortunes, and the misconduct of their husbands; men might plainly perceive that such are not the arms by which women gain the superiority. Heaven did not bestow on them the powers of insinuation and persuasion to make them perverse and morose; it did not constitute them feeble to make them imperious; it did not give them so soft and agreeable a voice to vent abuse, nor features so delicate and lovely to be disfigured with anger. When they give way to rage, therefore, they forget themselves: for, though they may often have reason to complain, they are always in the wrong to scold. Each sex should preserve its peculiar tone and manner; a meek husband may make a wife impertinent; but mildness of disposition on the woman's side will always bring a man back to reason, at least if he be not absolutely a brute, and will sooner or later triumph over him.

Daughters should be always submissive; their mothers, however, should not be inexorable. To make a young person tractable, she ought not to be rendered stupid. On the contrary, I should not be displeased at her being permitted to use some art, not to elude punishment in case of disobedience, but to exempt herself from the necessity of obeying. It is not necessary to make her dependence burthensome, but only to let her feel it. Subtility is a talent natural to the sex; and, as I am persuaded, all our natural inclinations are right and good in themselves, I am of opinion this should be cultivated as well as the others: it is requisite for us only to prevent its abuse.

I appeal, for the truth of this remark, to every fair and candid observer. I would not have the examination, however, confined to the women themselves; it is possible that our narrow scheme of educating them may have cramped their genius: but let us observe the children of both sexes. If we compare little girls, newly-born so to speak, with boys of the same age, the latter will be found extremely dull and stupid in comparison of the former, or I am greatly mistaken. Of this I will take the liberty to give an example, attended with the greatest degree of puerile simplicity.

It is very common to forbid children asking for any thing at table; always thinking it requisite to lay them under some needless injunction; as if what they asked for were not easily granted or refused them,[183] without our making a poor child uneasy between desire and expectation. Every body hath heard of the address[184] of the little boy, who, being thus prohibited to ask, and seeing himself neglected, petitioned only for a little salt. It is here certain that he incurred, in some measure, the penalty of disobedience in asking directly for salt, and by so doing indirectly for meat; the neglect of him, however was so cruel, that, though he had more openly transgressed this absurd law, and said in plain terms, I am hungry, I can hardly think any body could have found in their hearts to have punished him. But the method which I saw a little girl, of six years old, once take to gain her point, on a like occasion, was still more subtle and artful. Her

---

[182] i.e. at the earliest opportunity. [eds]

[183] A child will always be importunate when it finds its interest in it: but it will never ask twice for the same thing, if the first denial is always irrevocable. [Rousseau]

[184] i.e. skilful ruse. [eds]

situation was also more nice[185] and critical; for being not only strictly forbidden to ask, either directly or indirectly, her disobedience would have been more unpardonable, as she had been already helped from every dish on the table except one, of which she was extremely fond; and this had been forgotten.

To effect a reparation of this neglect, therefore, without being charged with disobedience, she began to number the dishes on the table, pointing to each, and saying, This I have eat of, and that I have eat of; at the same time making a remarkable pause, and passing over in silence that which she had not tasted; which some body taking notice of, and saying, And this; have you not eaten of this too? Oh ! no, replied the little epicure, very modestly, not yet. Compare these instances: the latter shews the finesse and cunning of a girl, the former that of a boy.

Whatever is, is right: nor can any general rule in nature be wrong. The superiority of address peculiar to the female sex, is a very equitable indemnification for their inferiority in point of strength: without this, woman would not be the companion of man; but his slave: it is by her superior art and ingenuity that she preserves her equality, and governs him while she affects to obey. Woman has every thing against her, as well our faults, as her own timidity and weakness; she has nothing in her favour, but her subtility and her beauty. Is it not very reasonable, therefore, she could cultivate both? Beauty, indeed, is not very general; it is liable to be destroyed by accident, it loses its power by habit, and its existence by time. Woman's best resource is in her intellectual talents; by which, however, I do not mean those which are usually so much admired in the gay world,[186] and contribute nothing to her happiness; but such as are adapted to her situation, and enable her to profit even by our advantage.

It is hardly to be conceived how useful this address in the women is to ourselves; how much it adds to our social pleasures, restrains the petulance of children, corrects the brutality of husbands, and preserves that order in a family, which would without it be entirely destroyed. That artful and wicked women sometimes make a bad use of this address, is very certain; but what will not vice abuse? Let us not destroy the instruments of our happiness, because the wicked sometimes make use of them to our prejudice.

Dress may make a woman fine, but personal charms only make her please.[187] Our clothes are not ourselves: they often disfigure and are unbecoming, because they are too remarkable:[188] and those which most distinguish the wearer, are often such as are least remarkable in themselves. The usual method of educating girls is, in this respect, quite absurd: they are promised fine clothes, &c. by way of rewards, and are taught to admire affected modes of dress. "How beautiful she is!", people respond when they are finely dressed; whereas they ought to be given to understand, that so much care to deck them out is bestowed on them only to hide their defects, and that the real triumph of beauty lies in the display of its native charms. A fondness for fashions is thus a proof of bad taste, as the person and features do not change with the mode; what is becoming or unbecoming at one time, must therefore be always so.

Should I see a young lady strutting about and priding herself in her fine clothes, and seem uneasy about what people would think of her figure, thus disguised, should I say, These ornaments make her too fine; it is a pity; do you think she is handsome enough to wear plainer clothes? to look well without this stomacher[189] or that aigrette?[190] She herself would very probably be the first to wish them laid aside, that I might

---

[185] i.e. delicate; requiring tact or discrimination. [eds]

[186] i.e. in the world of fashionable society. [eds]

[187] i.e. only her personal charms make her agreeable

[188] i.e. noticeable. [eds]

[189] Covering worn under the lacing of a bodice. [eds]

[190] A plume or sprig of jewels. [eds]

judge: this is the occasion on which to offer praise, if there is occasion to do so. I should never pay her so many compliments as when she might happen to be plainly dressed. Were she once taught to regard dress as a supplement only to the charms of her person, and as a tacit confession that they stood in need of such assistance, she would be no longer proud of dress, but humbled by it; so that should any body say, How beautiful she is, when tricked out finer than ordinary, instead of being elated by the compliment, she would be apt to blush for shame.

There are indeed some persons, who require the assistance of dress to render them agreeable: there are none, however, that can require their apparel to be rich and tawdry. Such dresses are owing to the pride of rank, and not to personal vanity; being merely the effect of prejudice. Genuine coquetry is sometimes affectedly elegant, but never affectedly rich: Juno was more superbly attired than Venus. *As you could not make her beautiful, you have made her fine,* said Apelles,[191] one day, to a wretched painter, who had drawn a picture of Helen, with very rich drapery. In fact, I have always observed, that the most pompous dresses have been worn by ordinary women: there cannot be a more absurd piece of vanity than this. Furnish a girl, that hath taste enough to despise the fashion, with ribbands, gauze, muslin and flowers; and she will presently dress her head, without diamonds, pompons or lace,[192] in a manner infinitely more agreeable than if she had employed all the brilliant trumpery of La Duchapt.[193]

As what is once becoming, is always so, and it is expedient to appear ever as agreeable as possible, those women who are good judges of dress, make choice of what is becoming, and keep to it: by which means, they are also less busied about their apparel than such as are perpetually changing. A true regard to dress requires not the labours of the toilette; young ladies have seldom that elaborate apparatus; their lessons and work take up too much of their time, and yet they are in general as nicely dressed (the article of rouge excepted) as their mamas, and often in much better taste. We are mistaken concerning the abuse of the toilette; it is owing more to listlessness and disgust[194] than to vanity. A woman of fashion, who spends six hours at her toilette, is not ignorant that she is no better dressed than another, who might spend only half an hour: but the hours thus spent are so much deducted from the killing length of time, under which we labour; and it is thought more adviseable to amuse ourselves with decorating our own persons, than to remain discontented with every thing about us. Without the toilette, how would it be possible to fill up the hours between twelve at noon and nine in the evening? A woman of fashion, in assembling her women about her on this occasion, amuses herself not a little in teizing[195] them; this is something: by this method also she avoids a disagreeable *tête à tête* with her husband, whom she sees at no other time; this is still more: then come in the tradesmen, the fine gentlemen, the fine writers, with their verses, songs, and pamphlets; these things could never be so commodiously brought together without the toilette. The only real advantage of the toilette, however, is the pretext for a lady's displaying her charms a little more than when she is full drest: but this advantage is not so considerable as is generally imagined. Scruple not to bestow on women the education proper for their sex; bring them up to love the occupations peculiar to it, to be modest, and to employ themselves in the management of family concerns; the parade of the toilette will then fall into neglect of itself, and the women will only be dressed in a better taste.

---

[191] Greek painter, 4th to early 3rd century BC. [eds]

[192] Women, whose complexions are so fair that they have no occasion for lace, give great offence, nevertheless, to others, if they do not wear it. It is almost always the ugly people who set fashions; which the handsome ones are, notwithstanding, foolish enough to follow. [Rousseau]

[193] A famous Parisian dressmaker. [eds]

[194] i.e. boredom. [eds]

[195] i.e. teasing. [eds]

The first thing which young persons observe, as they grow up, is, that all these foreign aids of dress are still insufficient, if they have no charms in their own persons. Beauty cannot be acquired by dress, and coquetry is an art not so early and speedily attained. While girls are yet young, however, they are in a capacity to study agreeable gesture, a pleasing modulation of voice, an easy carriage and behaviour; as well as to take the advantage of gracefully adapting their looks and attitudes to time, place, and occasion. Their voice extends its range, gains firmness and resonance, their arms become plumper, their walk more assured and they learn that, in whatever manner they are dressed, there are means of making themselves noticed. Their application, therefore, should not be solely confined to the arts of industry and the needle, when they come to display other talents, whose utility is already apparent.

I know some persons are so severe, that they would not have girls taught singing, dancing, nor any of the agreeable arts.[196] This seems to me, however, very absurd and ridiculous. Pray, on whom would they have these talents bestowed? On the boys? Do these accomplishments best become the men or the women? They will answer, perhaps, that they become neither: that profane songs are criminal: that dancing is the invention of the devil: and that girls ought to have no other amusement than their sampler and their prayers. Strange amusements, truly, for a girl of ten years of age! For my part, I am somewhat afraid that these little saints, in consequence of being thus compelled to spend their childhood in praying to God, will be tempted to spend their youth in very different employment; and that they will endeavour to make up, when they are married, for the time they will conceive they lost before hand. It is, in my opinion, necessary to pay a regard to their age as well as their sex: a little miss ought not, surely, to lead the life of her grandmother, but, on the contrary, to be indulged in her vivacity

and childish amusements; she should be permitted to sing, to dance, to play about as much as she pleases, and to enjoy all the innocent pleasures of her age: the time will come but too soon, when she must be more reserved, and put on a more constrained behaviour.

But may we not ask, if even the necessity of this change be real? Is this not also the effect of our prejudices? In subjecting modest women only to the more sad and melancholy duties of life, we banish from the marriage-state every thing that should render it agreeable to the men. Need we be astonished that the sad solemnity, which usually prevails at home, should send them to seek diversions abroad? Or that men should be so little inclined to embrace so disagreeable a state? Christianity, by carrying our duties to extremes, hath rendered them absurd and impracticable: by prohibiting songs, dancings, and other worldly amusements, to women, it makes them heavy, morose, factious, and insupportable in their houses. There is no other religion in the world, by which the duties of marriage are rendered so severe, nor is so sacred an engagement any where so much despised as among Christians. So much pains is taken to prevent the women from being amiable, that husbands are thereby rendered indifferent. I know very well that the latter are blameable in this; but I know also that it cannot be otherwise, as husbands, though Christians, are still men. For my part, I would have a young Englishwoman cultivate her agreeable talents, in order to please her future husband, with as much care and assiduity as a young Circassian[197] cultivates hers to fit her for the harem of an eastern bashaw.[198] It is said, that husbands, in general, give themselves little concern about such talents in their wives. I can very easily believe it, as, instead of their being employed in pleasing them, they can usually serve only as a bait to allure a parcel of impudent young fellows to dishonour them. But can you imagine that an amiable and prudent woman, possessed of such talents, and consecrating

---

[196] Dancing lessons were common in Paris but frowned upon by the Calvinist pastors of Rousseau's native Geneva. [eds]

[197] Member of a tribe from the Caucasus whose women were renowned for their fair skin and beauty and were said to be much in demand as slaves for Eastern harems. [eds]

[198] Form of pasha, grandee. [eds]

them to the amusement of her husband, would not greatly add to the happiness of his life, and prevent him, when leaving his closet with a mind fatigued with study, from going to seek recreation abroad? Are there no instances of happy families, so united, that each can furnish something in itself for their common amusement? And are not the confidence and familiarity subsisting between them, the innocence and sweetness of the pleasures they experience, infinitely superior to the riotous pleasures of public entertainments? (Kenrick IV, pp.31–40.)

[Rousseau goes on to discuss whether girls should be educated by masters or mistresses.]

The tongues of women are very voluble: they speak earlier, more readily and more agreeably than the men: they are accused also of speaking much more; but so it ought to be: and I should be very ready to convert this reproach into a compliment: their lips and eyes have the same activity, and for the same reason. A man speaks of what he knows, a woman of what pleases: the one requires knowledge, the other taste. The principal object of man's discourse should be what is useful, that of a woman's what is agreeable. There ought to be nothing in common between their different conversation but truth.

We ought not, therefore, to restrain the prattle of girls, in the same manner as we should that of boys, with that severe question, *To what purpose are you talking?* but by another, which is not less difficult to answer, *How will your discourse be received?* In infancy, while they are as yet incapable to discern good from evil or to judge anyone, they ought to observe, as a law, never to say any thing disagreeable to those whom they are speaking to. What will render the practice of this rule also the more difficult, is, that it must ever be subordinate to the former, of never speaking falsely or telling an untruth.

There are, indeed, many other difficulties attending the practice of this rule; but they belong to a more advanced age. At present, the only pains it will cost girls to be sincere, is to avoid at the same time being rude; and as rudeness is what they are naturally averse to, they may

be soon taught, by education, to avoid it. I have observed, from my experience in the world, that in general the politeness of the men is more officious,[199] and that of the women more obliging. The men appear more desirous to serve you, and the women to please you. It hence follows, that, notwithstanding our judgement of the character of women, their politeness is less insincere than ours: in them it is only a diffusion of their natural instinct. But when a man pretends to prefer my interest to his own, whatever demonstrations he may make to varnish over the falsehood, I am very certain it is one. It costs the women, therefore, no trouble to be polite; nor, of consequence, girls to become so. Their first lesson is inculcated by nature; art only seconds her designs, and determines the manner in which they are to be carried into execution. With regard to the politeness of women among each other, it is a different thing. They mix with it such an air of constraint, and are so cold in their civilities, that, as the restraint is mutual, they give themselves little trouble to hide it, and appear even sincere in their dissimulation, by never striving to conceal it. Not but that young females are sometimes frank and earnest in their friendships. At their age, chearfulness supplies the place of a good disposition, and, being satisfied with themselves, are satisfied with all the world. It is, however, certain that they salute and caress each other more heartily, and with a better grace, in the presence of the men; taking a pleasure, as it were, in whetting the desires of the latter, by tantalizing them with the shadow of those favours which they know so well how to make them envy.

If boys ought not to be indulged in asking indiscreet questions, much less should girls; whose curiosity, either satisfied or imprudently evaded, is of much greater consequence, on account of their penetration to foresee the mysteries which are concealed from them, and their address in discovering them.[200] But, without permitting them to ask questions, I would have them be continually interrogated themselves; and excited to prattle, in order to accustom them to a fluency of speech, to make them quick

---

[199] i.e. dutiful, zealous. [eds]

[200] i.e. their skill in uncovering them. [eds]

at reply, and to refine their wit and their tongue as much as possible, without danger. Such conversations being always accompanied with gaity, but managed with art and discretion, would be an amusement adapted to their years, and might be made the means of inculcating, in the innocent hearts of such young persons, the first, and perhaps the most useful lessons of morality they may ever receive; teaching them, under the appearance of pleasure and vanity, what are the qualities for which men truly hold them in esteem, and in what conflict the glory and happiness of a modest woman.

It is easy to be conceived, that if male children are not in a capacity to form any true notions of religion, those ideas must be greatly above the conception of the females: it is for this very reason, I would begin to speak to them the earlier on this subject; for if we were to wait till they were in a capacity to discuss methodically such profound questions, we should run a risk of never speaking to them on this subject as long as they lived. Reason in women is a practical reason, capacitating them artfully to discover the means of attaining a known end, but which would never enable them to discover that end itself. The social relations of the sexes are indeed truly admirable: from their union there results a moral person, of which women may be termed the eyes and man the hand, with this dependance on each other, that it is from the man that the woman is to learn what she is to see, and it is of the woman that man is to learn what he ought to do. If woman could recur to the first principles of things as well as man, and man was capacitated to enter into the *minutiae* as well as woman, always independent of each other, they would live in perpetual discord, and their union could not subsist. But in the present harmony which naturally subsists between them, their different faculties tend to one common end; it is difficult to say which of them conduces the most to it: each follows the impulse of the other; each is obedient, and both are masters.

As the conduct of a woman is subservient to the public opinion, her faith in matters of religion should for that very reason be subject to authority. Every daughter ought to be of the same religion as her mother, and every wife to be of the religion of her husband: for, though such religion should be false, that docility which induces the mother and daughter to submit to

the order of nature, takes away, in the sight of God, the criminality of their error. As they are not in a capacity to judge for themselves, they ought to abide by the decision of the fathers and husbands as confidently as by that of the church.

Women, being incapable of forming articles of faith for themselves, cannot confine them within the limits of evidence and reason; but permitting themselves to be led astray by a thousand foreign impulses, are always wide of the mark of truth. Always in extremes, they are either libertines or devotees: none of them being capable of uniting wisdom and piety. The origin of this evil is not only in the exaggerated character of their sex, but also in the ill regulated authority of our own: loose morals bring contempt upon this authority, the terrors of remorse render it tyrannical, and we do either too much or too little.

[...]

In order to teach religion to young girls, we ought, in the first place, never to make it an object of sadness or restraint, never to impose it as a task or a duty: of course we should never oblige them to get any thing by heart, not even their prayers. Content yourself with regularly performing your devotions in their presence, without ever requiring them, however, to join with you. Let your prayers be short, after the example of Jesus Christ. Repeat them with proper solemnity and reverence; remembering that when we require the attention of the supreme Being, we certainly ought ourselves to pay the utmost attention to what we say.

It is of less consequence that girls should be early, than that they should be fully and clearly, instructed in the articles of their religion, and particularly that they should be induced to take a delight in them. When you render them burthensome; when you represent God as always incensed at them; when you impose on them, in his name, a number of disagreeable duties, which they see you give yourself no trouble to discharge; what can they think but that learning their catechism, and praying to God, are the duties only of little girls, and therefore they long to grow up, in order to be exempted, as you appear to be, from such disagreeable injunctions? Example! It is example, without which nothing is to be done with children.

When you would explain to them the articles of their faith, let it be by direct instruction, and not in the way of question and answer. They ought never to reply otherwise than as they think; and not in terms dictated to them. All the answers in our catechisms are perverted: it is there the scholar who instructs the master: they are even so many falsehoods in the mouths of children, because they thus take on them to explain what they do not understand, and affirm what they are in no capacity to believe. Nay, I should be glad to find those among the most intelligent of mankind, who do not lie abominably in saying their catechism.

The first question that presents itself in our catechism is this; *Who made you, and brought you into the world?* To which the child, though she believes all the while it was her mother, answers without hesitation, *God.* The only thing she finds in all this is, a question she can hardly understand at all.

I could wish that some able person, who is well acquainted with the progress of the understanding in children, would write a proper catechism for them. It would be, perhaps, the most useful book that ever was penned; nor would it, in my opinion, be less to the honour of its author. This is very certain, that such a catechism, well executed, would very little resemble ours.

Such a design, however, would not be properly effected, unless the replies were such as a child might make to the questions proposed, without being verbally taught them. At the same time, it must be understood, that the child should find itself sometimes in a capacity to interrogate in its turn. To make the reader understand perfectly what I mean, it may not be improper to give something of a specimen: I perceive, indeed, the difficulty of it; but shall try, at least, to trace a slight sketch of what I propose on this head.

I conceive, then, to begin with the first question of our catechism, it should commence nearly thus:

Nurse. Do you remember, my dear, when your mama was a little girl?

Child. No.

Nurse. No! How so? You that have so good a memory!

Child. I was not then come into the world.

Nurse. Then you have not always lived?

Child. No.

Nurse. And shall you always live?

Child. Yes.

Nurse. Are you young or old?

Child. I am young.

Nurse. And your grand-mama, is she old or young?

Child. She is old.

Nurse. Was she ever young?

Child. Yes.

Nurse. And why is she not so still?

Child. Because she is grown old.

Nurse. Shall you grow old like her?

Child. I don't know.[201]

Nurse. Where are the robes you wore last year?

Child. They have been unpicked.

Nurse. And why unpicked?

Child. Because they were too little for me.

Nurse. And why were they too little for you?

Child. Because I am grown bigger.

Nurse. Shall you still grow bigger?

Child. Oh! yes.

Nurse. And what do great girls come to?

Child. They come to be women.

Nurse. And what do they become then?

Child. They become mothers.

Nurse. And what do mothers grow?

Child. They grow old.

---

[201] Wherever I have made the child answer, I don't know, should she give a different answer, we should distrust what she said, and make her carefully explain herself. [Rousseau]

Nurse. You, then, will grow old.

Child. Yes, when I shall be a mother.

Nurse. And what becomes of people when they are old?

Child. I don't know.

Nurse. Why, what is become of your grand-papa?

Child. He is dead.[202]

Nurse. And why did he die?

Child. Because he was old.

Nurse. You see then what becomes of people when they are old.

Child. Yes, they die.

Nurse. And you, when you grow old, must —

Child, interrupting her. Oh, no, nurse; I will not die.

Nurse. No body, child, is willing to die, and yet every body must.

Child. What! must my mama die too?

Nurse. Certainly, as well as every body else. Women grow old as well as men; and old age brings on death.

Child. What must one do to make it a long time before one grows old?

Nurse. Live prudently while one is young.

Child. Then I will be always prudent, nurse.

Nurse. So much the better; but after all, can you expect to live for ever?

Child. When I am grown very, very old —

Nurse. Well, what then?

Child. Why, when one is so very old, you say one must die.

Nurse. You, therefore, will die some time or other?

Child. Ah! yes.

Nurse. Who were they that lived before you?

Child. My father and mother.

Nurse. And who lived before them?

Child. Their father and mother.

Nurse. Who will live after you?

Child. My children.

Nurse. Who after them?

Child. Their children, &c.

In pursuing this method, we trace out, by sensible inductions, a beginning and end of the human race; that is to say, we come by degrees to a father and mother who had neither father nor mother, and to children that will have no children. It requires a long series of similar questions to prepare a child for understanding the first question in our common catechisms. Only then can we put the question and the child understand it. But to pass on from that to the second answer, which is in a manner a definition of the divine essence, what a transition! When will the intermediate space be filled up? *God is a spirit!* And what is a spirit? Shall I lead an infant into those metaphysical obscurities, from which men have taken so much pains to extricate themselves? It is not for a little girl to resolve such questions; it is even the utmost she can do, to ask them. In which case I should answer her very simply: You ask me what is God? That question is not easy to resolve. God is not to be seen, heard, or felt: he is to be known only by his works. To form a judgment of what he is, wait till you know what he hath done.

If our tenets are all equally true, they are not all, for that reason, of equal importance. It is very indifferent to the glory of God, that it should be known to us in every circumstance; but it is of great consequence to every member of society, that every man should know and discharge those obligations which are imposed on him by the laws of God respecting his neighbour and himself. These are what we ought constantly to teach each other; and are those in which fathers and mothers are bound, above all things, to instruct

---

[202] The child might make this answer, because she had heard it so said; but it would be necessary to see whether she entertained any clear idea of death; for this idea is not so simple, nor so much within the capacity of children as might be imagined. In the poem of Abel, there is given an example of the method that should be taken to communicate this idea to the minds of children. This charming piece breathes a delightful simplicity, which cannot be too much imitated in our conversations with children. [Rousseau]

their children. That a virgin should become the mother of her Creator, and give birth to God, or only to a man united to the divine nature; that the substance of the Father and of the Son should be the same, or only similar; that the Holy Ghost should proceed from one of these two, or both conjointly; I do not see that the solutions of these difficulties, however essential in appearance, are of any greater consequence to mankind, than it is to know what day of the moon we ought to celebrate Easter; whether we ought to tell[203] our beads, feast or fast, speak Latin or French in church, adorn the walls with images, say or hear mass, marry, or have no woman of one's own. Let every one think of these matters as he pleases, I know not that it is of any consequence to others; at least, I am sure it is of no consequence to me. But what I am, indeed, interested in, as well as every individual of the human species, is, that every one should know that there exists a supreme Arbiter over the destiny of all mankind, of whom we are all the children, who commands us all to be just, to love each other, to be benevolent, merciful, and to fulfil our engagements with the world, and even with our enemies, as well as with his; that the apparent happiness of this life is nothing; that there will be another life after this, in which the supreme Being will reward the good, and punish the wicked. These tenets, and others of the like import, are those, which it is incumbent on us to teach youth, and to espouse on all occasions among our fellow citizens. Whoever opposes such sentiments as these deserves undoubtedly to be punished, as a disturber of the peace, and an enemy to society. Whoever sets these aside, and would subject us to his own opinions, though he should purpose to arrive at the same point by different means, disturbs the peace also, in order to establish it in his own manner: he undertakes, with great presumption, to be the interpreter of the Deity, and exacts, in his name, the homage and respect of mankind; he erects himself, as far as he is able, into a Deity, or assumes the place of God. Such a one ought to be punished for his sacrilege, if not for his intolerance.

Disregard, therefore, all those mysterious tenets, which consist only of words without ideas; all those whimsical doctrines, which usurp the place of morals in those who adopt them, and serve rather to make men vain than virtuous. Confine your children ever within the narrow circle of those doctrines, which relate to morality. Let them be well persuaded that there is nothing necessary for them to know, but that which teaches them to act aright. Make not your daughters theologists nor disputants; teach them nothing about the things of heaven, but what relates to the cultivation of human prudence. Accustom them to think themselves always in the sight of the Deity: to reflect that he is constantly a witness of their actions, their thoughts, their pleasures; use[204] them to do good without ostentation, because it is pleasing to God; to suffer without murmuring, because he will recompence them, and, in short, to be, during every hour of their lives, such as they could wish to be in that hour when they shall all appear before him in judgment. Such is the true religion; such is that only which[205] is not capable of being abused, and admits neither of impiety nor fanaticism. Let others preach up a religion more sublime; for my part, I shall acknowledge none but this.

As for the rest, it is proper to observe, that till girls arrive at the age, when their enlightened reason or growing sentiment gives use to the dictates of conscience, they should be governed in their notions of good and evil entirely by the decisions of those who are about them. Whatever they are commanded to do, should be thought right, and what they are forbidden to do, wrong: they ought at present to know nothing farther than this: hence we see of how much greater importance it is, that we should be careful in the choice of persons to educate girls than we are of those who take the charge of boys. At length, however, the time will come when even girls will begin to judge for themselves, and when it will be necessary to diversify our plan of education.

I have, indeed, hitherto, perhaps, said too much. How low should we reduce the women, if we gave them no other laws than those of public

---

[203] i.e. count. [eds]

[204] i.e. accustom. [eds]

[205] i.e. and it is only such religion that.[eds]

opinion? Let us not so far disparage that sex, which governs and doth honour to ours, when we do not debase it. There exists, for the whole species, a rule prior to opinion. It is to the fixed and certain direction of that rule we should subject all others; it is the judge of prejudice itself, and it is only insofar as the esteem of men agrees with that rule that such esteem should have authority over us.

This rule is that of innate sentiment. I shall not repeat what I have already said on that subject: it is sufficient to observe here, that if these two rules do not concur in the education of women, it will be always defective. Sentiment, without regard to opinion, will not give them that delicacy of mind, which adds to virtue the approbation of the world; and a regard to opinion, without sentiment, will only make them false and deceitful, placing the appearances of virtue in the room of virtue itself.

It is of consequence to them, therefore, to cultivate a faculty which serves as an umpire between the two guides, preventing the mistakes of conscience, and correcting the errors of prejudice. This faculty is reason: but how many queries offer themselves at that word? Are women capable of solid reasoning? Is it of any use for them to cultivate their reason? Can they do it with any success? Is that cultivation expedient to the functions imposed on them? Is it compatible with that simplicity of manners which becomes the sex? The various methods of comprehending and resolving these questions, occasion us to give in to contrary extremes: some persons confining women to the business of knitting and needle work among their domestics, making them only upper servants of their husbands: while others, not content with confirming them in their own rights, excite them to usurp ours; for to permit them to be superior to us in those qualities which are more peculiar to[206] their own sex, and to make them our equals in the qualities common to both, what is this but to transfer to women that superiority which nature hath given their husbands?

The reasoning which leads a man to the knowledge of his various duties is not very complicated; that which directs a woman to the knowledge of her duties is still more simple.

That obedience and fidelity which she owes to her husband, that care and tenderness which is due to her children, are such natural and affecting consequences of her situation, that unless she is abandoned to an habitual depravity, she cannot revolt from those internal principles which influence her conduct; nor mistake her duty, while she retains that propensity which nature has implanted in her bosom.

I would not indiscriminately condemn the practice of confining a woman solely to the occupations of her sex, and leaving her in profound ignorance with respect to all other concerns: But in such case it is necessary that the public morals should be very pure and simple, or that her manner of living should be extremely retired. In large cities, and in the midst of licentious men, such a woman would be easily seduced; her virtue would, on many occasions, be merely accidental; but this philosophic age requires a virtue which is at all times a proof against temptation. A woman ought to be sensible, beforehand, what may be said to her, and in what light it becomes her to consider it.

Besides, being subject to the opinion of men, she should study to merit their esteem: and she ought to be particularly anxious to acquire that of her husband; she should not only endeavour to make him love her person, but engage him to approve her conduct; she ought, in the eyes of the world, to justify the choice he has made, and derive honour to her husband, in consequence of the respect which is paid to his wife. But how should she accomplish these ends, if she is a stranger to our institutions, if she is ignorant of our customs and rules of decorum, if she is not acquainted with the sources of human judgment, nor with the passions by which it is determined? When she becomes sensible that she must depend both on the dictates of her own conscience, and on the opinion of others, it is necessary that she should learn to compare these two rules of action, to reconcile them, and never to prefer the former but when they stand in opposition to each other. From hence she becomes a judge over her judges; she determines within herself when she ought to submit to them, and when she ought to reject their authority. Before she adopts or rejects their prejudices, she

---

[206] i.e. more characteristic of. [eds]

considers their weight; she learns to recur to their first source, to obviate them, and render them favourable to her principles: she is cautious never to incur censure, when her duty will allow her to avoid it. These purposes cannot be effected, without enlarging her mind, and cultivating her reason. (Kenrick IV, pp. 43–58)

[Rousseau goes on to describe model families he has visited, where master and mistress entertain guests successfully and politely. When meals are served, the mistresses of such households show tact and keen powers of observation which allow them to be sensitive to the needs of their guests and to make all feel welcome and appreciated.]

The same turn of mind which makes a woman of fashion excel in the art of entertaining company, makes a coquette expert in the art of amusing a number of admirers. It even requires a more exquisite discernment to excel in coquetry, than in politeness; for if a well-bred woman behaves politely to every one, she has done all that is required of her; but a coquette would soon lose her dominion by such an awkward uniformity. By endeavouring to oblige all her lovers, she would offend them all. In company, an obliging behaviour to all never fails to please every one; as no one nicely[207] scrutinizes to whom the preference has been given: but in love, a favour which is not exclusive, is considered in the same light as a real injury. A man of sensibility, had rather a hundred times be the only person ill-treated, than to be caressed with the crowd; for the most mortifying circumstance is not to be distinguished. A woman, therefore, who would retain a number of lovers, should have the art to persuade every individual that she gives him the preference; and to persuade him into this opinion in the presence of all the rest, to whom she likewise insinuates the same persuasion in his presence.

Would you behold a man utterly embarrassed? place him between two women, with each of whom he has a secret connection, and then observe what a ridiculous appearance he will make. Place a woman under the same circumstances between two men (and the instance certainly is not more uncommon) you will be astonished with what address[208] she will delude each, and make them, in their turn, laugh at one another. But if this woman expressed the same confidence in each, and treated both with the same familiarity, how could they, for a moment, be duped by her artifice? By behaving equally to both, would she not discover[209] that both had equal pretensions to her? But how much more artfully does she conduct herself! Far from using them alike, she affects to make a distinction between them: she manages so skilfully, that he whom she flatters thinks it proceeds from affection; and that he whom she slights imagines that he is disregarded out of affectation. Thus each content with his lot, imagines her constantly attentive to him, while, in fact, she is wholly taken up with herself.

[...]

How is this art acquired, but by nice and constant observation, which every moment discovers to her what passes in mens [*sic*] bosoms, and enables her to apply to every secret feeling she observes, sufficient power to suspend or accelerate the emotion? Is this art to be learned? No: it is born with women; they are all mistresses of it, and the men never possess it to so high a degree. This is one of the distinguishing characteristics of the sex. A presence of mind, penetration, and acuteness of observation, constitute the science in which women excel; and the address with which they make their advantage of these excellencies is their peculiar talent.

This is the real case, and we have seen why it should be so. Is it said, that women are deceitful? They become false. Their proper talent is address, not deceit. If you attend to the natural propensities of their sex, you will find that, even while they utter untruths, they are not deceitful. Why do you consult their lips, when it is not through them that nature speaks. Examine their eyes, their complexion, their swelling bosoms, their timid air, their faint resistance: this is the language with which nature furnishes them. With their lips, they always say, No, as they ought;

---

[207] i.e. clearly. [eds]

[208] i.e. skill. [eds]

[209] i.e. reveal. [eds]

but they do not always pronounce that negative with the same accent;[210] and the accent never deceives you. Have not women the same desires with men, without having the same right to express them? Their lot would be very hard, if they could not intimate their lawful desires by a kind of language full as significant as that which they dare not utter. Must their modesty render them unhappy? Is it not necessary that they should have the art of indicating their inclinations, without expressing them? What skill is requisite to engage a man to ravish the favour, which they are ardent to grant? Of what consequence is it to them, to affect the hearts of men, without seeming to bestow a thought upon them? How beautifully expressive was the incident of Galatea's[211] apple, and her affected flight. What could she say more? Should she have declared to the shepherd following her among the willows, that she only ran away, with a view to be pursued? Had she said so, she had deceived herself; for in that case, she would not have engaged him to follow her. The more reserved a woman is, the more address she should be mistress of, even with her husband. I submit that by keeping coquetry within bounds it may become modest and true and one may derive from it a law of right conduct. (Kenrick IV, pp.60–62.)

[Rousseau goes on to attack those who undermine the virtue of modesty.]

Researches into abstract and speculative truths, the principles and axioms of sciences, in short, every thing which tends to generalize our ideas, is not the proper province of women; their studies should be relative to points of practice; it belongs to them to apply those principles which men have discovered; and it is their part to make observations, which direct men to the establishment of general principles. All the ideas of women, which have not an immediate tendency to points of duty, should be directed to the study of men, and to the attainment of those agreeable accomplishments which have taste for their object; for as to works of genius, they are beyond their capacity: neither have they sufficient precision or power of attention to succeed in sciences which require accuracy: and as to physical sciences, they belong to that sex which is most active, most inquisitive; who comprehend the greatest variety of objects; in short, they belong to those who have the strongest powers, and who exercise them most, to judge of the relations between sensible beings[212] and the laws of nature. A woman who is naturally weak, and does not conduct her observations far beyond herself, knows how to judge and make a proper estimate of those movements which she sets to work, in order to supplement her weakness; and these movements are the passions of men. The mechanism she employs is much more powerful than ours; for all her levers move the human heart. She must have the skill to incline us to do every thing which her sex will not enable her to do of herself, and which is necessary or agreeable to her; therefore she ought to study the mind of man thoroughly, not the mind of man in general, abstractedly, but the disposition of the men about her, the disposition of those men to whom she is subject, either by the laws of her country, or by the force of opinion. She should learn to penetrate into their real sentiments from their conversations, their actions, their looks and gestures. She should also have the art, by her own conversation, actions, looks, and gestures, to communicate those sentiments which are agreeable to them, without seeming to intend it. Men will argue more philosophically about the human heart; but women will read the heart of man better than they. It belongs to women, if I may be allowed the expression, to form an experimental morality, and to men to reduce the study of man to a system. Women have most wit, men have most genius; women observe, men reason; from the concurrence of both we derive the clearest light and the most perfect knowledge, which the human mind is, of itself, capable of attaining: in one word, from hence we acquire the most intimate acquaintance, both with ourselves and others, of which our nature is capable; and it is thus that art has a constant tendency to perfect those endowments which nature has bestowed. (Kenrick IV, pp. 65–7.)

---

[210] i.e. tone. [eds]

[211] Greek goddess of the sea, loved by the giant Polyphemus. Galatea preferred the shepherd Acis, who was eventually crushed under a rock by his rival Polyphemus. [eds]

[212] i.e. creatures with senses and feeling. [eds]

[He goes on to argue that young women should not be shielded too much from the world but that the virtue and sound judgment of women require careful nurturing in a city of pleasure like Paris. He dares to suggest that Protestant countries produce more family affection, more good wives and loving mothers than Catholic countries as convents encourage in girls a useless kind of coquetry. All great peoples have, like the Romans, revered women. Female virtue, particularly chastity, is essential to the health of a society. Girls should be educated in such virtues in a manner appropriate to their age and without resorting to bleak, austere lessons. At this point, Sophie is introduced.]

Sophie is a woman of family, and of a good disposition; she has a heart easily affected, and her exquisite sensibility sometimes gives her a sprightliness of imagination which is difficult to be controlled. Her understanding is less judicious than acute; her temper easy, but nevertheless unequal; her figure nothing extraordinary, but agreeable: she has a countenance which gives earnest of a soul, and does not deceive you. You may accost[213] her with indifference, but you cannot leave her without emotion. Others are endowed with good qualities in which she is deficient; others possess those, which she is mistress of, in greater perfection; but none have qualities better blended to form a complete character. She knows how to make her defects turn to her advantage; and if she was more perfect, she would be much less agreeable.

Sophie is not beautiful; but when the men are near her, they neglect the handsome women, and the beauties are dissatisfied with themselves. She is scarce pretty at first sight, but the more you see her, the more lovely she appears; she improves by that which impairs others, and what she gains, she never loses. Many may boast finer eyes, a handsomer mouth, a more commanding figure; but no one can have a better turned shape, a fairer complexion, a whiter hand, a more delicate foot, a more benign aspect, a more moving countenance. Without dazzling, she engages, she charms, and no one can tell how.

Sophie loves dress, and understands it; her mother has no waiting woman but her; she has a fine taste in displaying herself to advantage, but she has an aversion to rich clothes. In her dress, you always see simplicity united with elegance; she is not fond of what glitters, but of what is becoming. She is a stranger to what colours are in fashion, but she knows exactly what suit her complexion. No young lady seems to have bestowed less thought about dress, and yet there is no one whose apparel is more studied; not a part of her attire is taken at random, and yet art is no where conspicuous. Her dress is extremely modest in appearance, and yet very coquettish in fact: she does not make a display of her charms, she conceals them; but in concealing them, she knows how to affect your imagination. Every one who sees her, will say, There is a modest and discreet girl; but while you are near her, your eyes and affections wander all over her person, so that you cannot withdraw them; and you would conclude, that every part of her dress, simple as it seems, was only put in its proper order, to be taken to pieces by the imagination.

Sophie has fine natural talents; she is conscious of them, and has not neglected them; but not having had it in her power to cultivate them with any extraordinary art, she contents herself with exercising her sweet voice in singing with justness and taste, and with using her little feet in walking gently and gracefully, and in making her compliments in every attitude without constraint or awkwardness. Nevertheless, she has had no singing-master but her father, no one to instruct her in dancing but her mother, and an organist in the neighbourhood has given her some lessons on the harpsicord, which she has improved by her own genius. At first she only thought of displaying her hand to advantage on those black keys; afterwards she found that the sharp tone of the harpsicord rendered her voice more mellow, till at length she acquired a sense of harmony. As she grew up, she became susceptible of the charms of expression, and to love music for itself. But it is rather her taste than her talent; she does not know [how] to decypher a single tune by the notes.

That in which Sophie excels most, and in which she has been most carefully instructed, is the proper occupation of her sex, but such as one would not think of, that is, cutting out and

---

[213] i.e. approach. [eds]

making up her clothes. There is not any kind of needle work in which she is not well skilled, and in which she does not take delight; but the work which she prefers to all others is making of lace, because there is no other which throws the person into such an agreeable attitude, and where the fingers are employed with more grace and activity. She has likewise applied herself to all the branches of house-keeping; she attends the kitchen and the pantry; she knows the price of goods, and is a judge of their quality; she understands keeping of accounts very well, and serves her mother by way of house steward. Being destined to become the mother of a family herself, in managing her father's house, she learns to take care of her own; she knows how to supply the duties of[214] the several domestics, and does it with chearfulness. No one can properly give orders about concerns of which they are ignorant: it is for this reason that her mother employs her thus. As for Sophie, she does not extend her views so far. Her principal duty is that of a daughter, and it is the only one at present which she thinks of fulfilling. Her sole view is to be serviceable to her mother, and to relieve her from part of her fatigue. It is true, nevertheless, that she does not perform all her duties with the same pleasure. For example, though she is a little epicure, she is not fond of cooking; she always finds something in it which offends her, and things are never sufficiently clean for her. Her delicacy in these points is extreme; and she has carried it to such excess, that it is become one of her defects: she had rather let the dinner fall into the fire, than soil her ruffle. She would never superintend the garden for the same reason, the soil appears to her too dirty, and as soon as she sees a dunghill, she imagines a disagreeable odour.

This failing arises from her mother's instructions. According to her, neatness is one of the principal perfections of a woman; a particular and indispensable duty enjoined by nature: there cannot be a more disgusting object that a slatternly woman, and a husband cannot be blamed for disliking her. She has so continually preached up this duty to her daughter from her very infancy; she has required so much neatness about her person, about her clothes, her apartment, her work, her toilet, that this attention, being grown into habit, takes up a great part of her time, and is always uppermost in every thing she does; so that with her, doing things well, is but a secondary concern; her principal concern is to do them neatly.

Nevertheless, the foible has not degenerated into a ridiculous effeminacy or vain affection: she does not admit any of the refinements of luxury. Nothing but plain water ever enters her apartment; she is a stranger to all perfumes but flowers, and her husband will never find any thing more fragrant than her breath. But the attention she bestows on her person, does not make her forget that her life should be devoted to more noble employment. She is not acquainted with, or she despises, that extravagant delicacy of person which sullies the mind. Sophie is more than neat, she is pure.

I have said that Sophie was a little epicure. She was so naturally, but by habit she is grown temperate, which habit is now become a confirmed virtue. It is not with girls as it is with boys, who may, to a certain degree, be governed by their voracious appetites. Such a propensity is of consequence to women, and is of too dangerous a nature not to be opposed. When Sophie was in her childhood, if she could get alone into her mother's closet, she never returned empty, for she was not proof against sugar-plumbs and sweetmeats. Her mother discovered her, reprimanded her, punished her, and made her fast. She persuaded her at last that sweetmeats spoiled the teeth, and that eating too much would spoil her figure. Thus Sophie corrected herself. As she grew up, she corrected her taste for other things, which diverted her from that grovelling appetite. In women as well as men, when once the heart is actuated, gluttony has no longer any ascendancy. Sophia has preserved a taste most suitable to her sex; she is fond of milk-meats, sweets, pastry, and little dainties, but scarce eats any meat; and she has never tasted wine or any strong liquors. Moreover, she eats very sparingly, her sex, not being so laborious[215]

---

[214] i.e. stand in for. [eds]

[215] i.e. not so physically hard-working. [eds]

as ours, has less need of refreshment. She knows what is good of the kind, and knows how to relish it; but she can also accept or dispense with what is not quite so nice, without being uneasy.

Sophie has an understanding which is agreeable without being brilliant, and solid without being profound; an understanding which no one takes particular notice of, because none observe her to have more or less than themselves. She has always the art of pleasing those who converse with her, though her conversation is not embellished according to the idea we form of an accomplished woman: for her ideas are not acquired by reading, but by conversing with her father and mother, by her own observations, and by the remarks she has made in the little company she has seen. Sophie has a natural gaiety; she was even a romp in her childhood: but her mother took care to restrain her giddiness by degrees, lest this should become a sudden necessity; she, therefore, became modest and reserved before it was requisite for her to be mistress of those qualities: and now that the time is come, it is easier for her to practise the habit she has contracted, than it would be for her to acquire it, without exposing the reason for such an alteration in her behaviour. It is pleasant to observe her sometimes give way to the vivacity of her youth, and then of a sudden recollect herself, become silent, look down, and blush. The intermediate space between childhood and womanhood should partake of the disposition of each.

Sophie has too exquisite a sensibility to be always even tempered; but she has too much gentleness to let her sensibility be troublesome to others; it is herself that she makes uneasy. If you say a word to vex her, she never pouts; but her heart swells, and she withdraws, in order to vent her tears. But if her father or mother call to her, in the midst of her weeping, and say but a single word, she endeavours, in an instant, to stifle her sobbing; she dries her eyes, and comes in smiling and cheerful.

Neither is Sophie altogether free from caprice. Her humour, when carried too far, degenerates into obstinacy, and then she is apt to forget herself: but give her time to recollect, and her manner of atoning for her foible renders it almost a merit. If she is punished, she is docile and submissive; and you may perceive that her shame arises not from the sense of correction, but of her fault. If you take not notice of her foibles, she never fails to correct them herself; but with so much ingenuity, and with such a good grace, that it is impossible to harbour any resentment against her. She would ask pardon of the meanest domestic, without being mortified by her humility; and when she is forgiven, the joy she discovers, and the caresses she bestows, shew from what a weight her tender heart is relieved. In a word, she patiently endures the injuries she receives, and is ready to repair those she undesignedly offers. Such is the amiable disposition of the sex, before we have corrupted it. Woman was formed to yield to man, and even to bear with his injustice. You will never bring boys to such submission. In them an inward sentiment swells and revolts against injustice. Nature did not form them to endure it.

> gravem
>
> Pelidae stomachum cedere nescii[216]

Sophie is religious, but her religion is simple and rational, burdened with few of the dogmas and less with the ceremonies of devotion; or rather, being a stranger to any essential point of practice, but morality, she entirely devotes her life to the service of God, by doing good. In all the instructions which her parents have given her on this subject, they have always accustomed her to a respectful submission, by saying to her, 'My dear, there are points of knowledge not suitable to your age: your husband will instruct you in good time.' In short, instead of holding long pious discourses, they have been content to make their own example serve her as lesson; and that example is deeply imprinted in her heart.

Sophie is enamoured of virtue; that love is become her reigning passion. She is fond of it, because there is nothing so lovely as virtue: she is fond of it, because virtue constitutes the glory of a woman; and a woman of virtue, in her estimation, is equal to an angel: she loves virtue as the only road to true felicity, and because she sees nothing but misery, misfortune, and ignominy, in the life of an abandoned woman. In a word, she loves

---

[216] 'the terrible anger of the Son of Peleus, who knows not how to yield' (Horace, *Odes* I, 6, 5–6). [eds]

virtue, as it is dear to her honoured father, to her worthy and affectionate mother. Not content with the happiness they derive from their own virtue, they wish for an increase of felicity from the virtues of their daughter; and her prime felicity consists in the hope of making them happy. These sentiments inspire her with an enthusiasm which exalts her mind, and keep all meaner propensities in subjection to so noble a passion. Sophie will be chaste and virtuous to her last breath: she has made the vow from the bottom of her heart: she made it at a time when she knew with what difficulty such vows are kept; when she would have revoked it if she had been the slave of her senses. (Kenrick IV, pp.80–8.)

[Rousseau proposes that marriage should be based on mutual attraction and there should not be too much disparity of intellect: but female wits and bluestockings are a 'scourge' to their families. Sophie is intelligent without calling attention to herself. She is pretty without being stunning. ('I think that great beauty is rather to be shunned than sought after in marriage.') Her timidity is seductive. She is angel and nurse to the poor people she visits. Her marriage with Émile gives rise to some musings on the subtle power relationships within marriage. *Émile* ends on a sentimental note, with the birth of Émile and Sophie's first child: Émile's tutor is asked to guide them through parenthood.]

Source: J–J. Rousseau (1779) *Emilius and Sophia: or, a New System of Education*, 4 vols, translated by W. Kenrick, London.

Mary Wollstonecraft

Prepared for the Course Team by
Susan Khin Zaw

Contents

Mary Wollstonecraft

The following thirteen extracts are taken from four works: Mary Wollstonecraft's Original Stories from Real Life *(first published 1788), A* Vindication of the Rights of Men *(first published 1790), and A* Vindication of the Rights of Woman *(first published 1792); and Edmund Burke's* Reflections on the Revolution in France *(first published 1790). The text of the Wollstonecraft extracts has been taken from volumes 4 and 5 of the 1989 edition of her complete works* (The Works of Mary Wollstonecraft, *edited by Janet Todd and Marilyn Butler, William Pickering, London, 1989); however indications of variant readings and pagination of eighteenth-century editions have been removed. Todd and Butler's explanatory footnotes to the text have been retained, and are indicated by the initials [TB] at the end of the note; editorial footnotes by the author of the Wollstonecraft study are similarly indicated by [eds]. Wollstonecraft's own footnotes to her text are indicated by [W]. The text of the Burke extract is from the Pelican edition of 1976 (Edmund Burke,* Reflections on the Revolution in France, *edited with an introduction by Conor Cruise O'Brien, Penguin Books, Harmondsworth 1968, reprinted 1973, 1976).*

The extracts are numbered and appear in the order in which they are set for reading in the Wollstonecraft study, not in chronological order of composition or publication. Page references to the editions used are given in each case. The extracts are in no sense epitomes or summaries of the works from which they are taken; a very small proportion of each work has been extracted, principally for reading in conjunction with the Wollstonecraft study. Wollstonecraft's Original Stories *is represented by one complete story, and its aftermath in the next, from a collection of 25 stories; her* Rights of Men *by about 1100 words from a pamphlet of about 25000 words, and her* Rights of Woman *by about 14000 words from a book of about 100,000 words. The extract from Burke is a not altogether typical passage of about 1700 words from a work of about 92000 words.*

Extract 1

Wollstonecraft, Rights of Woman

Contents

Chapter I
The rights and involved duties of mankind considered, p.15

Chapter II
The prevailing opinion of a sexual character discussed, p.32

Chapter III
The same subject continued, p.75

Chapter IV
Observations on the state of degradation to which woman is reduced by various causes, p.109

Chapter V
Animadversions on some of the writers who have rendered women objects of pity, bordering on contempt, p.170

Chapter VI
The effect which an early association of ideas has upon the character, p.259

Chapter VII
Modesty. – Comprehensively considered, and not as a sexual virtue, p.273

Chapter VIII
Morality undermined by sexual notions of the importance of a good reputation, p.298

Chapter IX
Of the pernicious effects which arise from the unnatural distinctions established in society, p.320

Chapter X
Parental affection, p.343

Chapter XI
Duty to parents, p.349

Chapter XII
On national education, p.361

Chapter XIII
Some instances of the folly which the ignorance of women generates; with concluding reflections on the moral improvement that a revolution in female manners might naturally be expected to produce, p.414

Source: Mary Wollstonecraft, *A Vindication of the Rights of Woman* (1792).

Extract 2

Wollstonecraft, **Rights of Woman**, *from Chapter I,
The rights and involved duties of mankind considered*

In the present state of society it appears necessary to go back to first principles in search of the most simple truths, and to dispute with some prevailing prejudice every inch of ground. To clear my way, I must be allowed to ask some plain questions, and the answers will probably appear as unequivocal as the axioms on which reasoning is built; though, when entangled with various motives of action, they are formally contradicted, either by the words or conduct of men.

In what does man's pre-eminence over the brute creation consist? The answer is as clear as that a half is less than the whole; in Reason.

What acquirement exalts one being above another? Virtue; we spontaneously reply.

For what purpose were the passions implanted? That man by struggling with them might attain a degree of knowledge denied to the brutes; whispers Experience.

Consequently the perfection of our nature and capability of happiness, must be estimated by the degree of reason, virtue, and knowledge, that distinguish the individual, and direct the laws which bind society: and that from the exercise of reason, knowledge and virtue naturally flow, is equally undeniable, if mankind be viewed collectively.

The rights and duties of man thus simplified, it seems almost impertinent to attempt to illustrate truths that appear so incontrovertible; yet such deeply rooted prejudices have clouded reason, and such spurious qualities have assumed the name of virtues, that it is necessary to pursue the course of reason as it has been perplexed and involved in error, by various adventitious circumstances, comparing the simple axiom with casual deviations. Men, in general, seem to employ their reason to justify prejudices, which they have imbibed, they can scarcely trace how, rather than to root them out. The mind must be strong that resolutely forms its own principles; for a kind of intellectual cowardice prevails which makes men shrink from the task, or only do it by halves. Yet the imperfect conclusions thus drawn, are frequently very plausible, because they are built on partial experience, on just, though narrow, views...

Source: Mary Wollstonecraft, 'A Vindication of the Rights of Woman', *Works*, vol.5, pp.81–2).

Extract 3

Wollstonecraft, **Rights of Woman**, *from Chapter II,
The prevailing opinion of a sexual character discussed*

To account for, and excuse the tyranny of man, many ingenious arguments have been brought forward to prove, that the two sexes, in the acquirement of virtue, ought to aim at attaining a very different character: or, to speak explicitly, women are not allowed to have sufficient strength of mind to acquire what really deserves the name of virtue. Yet it should seem, allowing them to have souls, that there is but one way appointed by Providence to lead *mankind* to either virtue or happiness.

If then women are not a swarm of ephemeron[1] triflers, why should they be kept in ignorance under the specious name of innocence? Men complain, and with reason, of the follies and caprices of our sex, when they do not keenly satirize our headstrong passions and grovelling vices. – Behold, I should answer, the natural effect of ignorance! The mind will ever be unstable that has only prejudices to rest on, and the current will run with destructive fury when there are no barriers to break its force. Women are told from their infancy, and taught by the example of their mothers, that a little knowledge of human weakness, justly termed cunning, softness of temper, *outward* obedience, and a scrupulous attention to a puerile kind of propriety, will obtain for them the protection of man; and should they be beautiful, every thing else is needless, for, at least, twenty years of their lives.

---

[1] Ephemeron: 'Insect which in the winged state lives only for a day' (Shorter OED). Wollstonecraft is using the noun adjectivally – cf. 'women have butterfly minds'. [eds]

Thus Milton describes our first frail mother; though when he tells us that women are formed for softness and sweet attractive grace, I cannot comprehend his meaning, unless, in the true Mahometan strain,[2] he meant to deprive us of souls, and insinuate that we were beings only designed by sweet attractive grace, and docile blind obedience, to gratify the senses of man when he can no longer soar on the wing of contemplation.[3]

How grossly do they insult us who thus advise us only to render ourselves gentle, domestic brutes! For instance, the winning softness so warmly, and frequently, recommended, that governs by obeying. What childish expression, and how insignificant is the being – can it be an immortal one? who will condescend to govern by such sinister methods! 'Certainly', says Lord Bacon, 'man is of kin to the beasts by his body; and if he be not of kin to God by his spirit, he is a base and ignoble creature!'[4] Men, indeed, appear to me to act in a very unphilosophical manner when they try to secure the good conduct of women by attempting to keep them always in a state of childhood …

Children, I grant, should be innocent; but when the epithet is applied to men, or women, it is but a civil term for weakness. For if it be allowed that women were destined by Providence to acquire human virtues, and by the exercise of their understandings, that stability of character which is the firmest ground to rest our future hopes upon, they must be permitted to turn to the fountain of light, and not forced to shape their course by the twinkling of a mere satellite. Milton, I grant, was of a very different opinion; for he only bends to the indefeasible right of beauty, though it would be difficult to render two passages which I now mean to contrast, consistent. But into similar inconsistencies are great men often led by their senses.

To whom thus Eve with *perfect beauty* adorn'd.
My Author and Disposer, what thou bidst
Unargued I obey; so God ordains;
God is *thy law, thou mine*: to know no more
Is Woman's *happiest* knowledge and her *praise*.[5]

These are exactly the arguments that I have used to children; but I have added, your reason is now gaining strength, and, till it arrives at some degree of maturity, you must look up to me for advice – then you ought to *think*, and only rely on God.

Yet in the following lines Milton seems to coincide with me; when he makes Adam thus expostulate with his Maker.

Hast thou not made me here thy substitute,
And these inferior far beneath me set?
Among *unequals* what society
Can sort, what harmony or true delight?
Which must be mutual, in proportion due
Giv'n and receiv'd; but in *disparity*
The one intense, the other still remiss
Cannot well suit with either, but soon prove
Tedious alike: of *fellowship* I speak
Such as I seek, fit to participate
All rational delight –[6]

In treating, therefore, of the manners of women, let us, disregarding sensual arguments, trace what we should endeavour to make them in order to co-operate, if the expression be not too bold, with the supreme Being.

By individual education, I mean, for the sense of the word is not precisely defined, such an attention to a child as will slowly sharpen the senses, form the temper, regulate the passions as they begin to ferment, and set the understanding to work before the body arrives at maturity; so that the man may only have to proceed, not to begin, the important task of learning to think and reason.

---

[2] A reference to the widespread Christian misconception that Islam denied that women had souls. [TB]

[3] *Paradise Lost* IV, 297–8: 'For contemplation he and valour formed/For softness she and sweet attractive grace', is quoted in James Fordyce, *Sermons to Young Women* (3rd corrected edition, 1766), XIII, p.221. [TB]

[4] Francis Bacon, *Essaies* (1606), XIV 'of Atheism', p.89. [TB]

[5] *Paradise Lost*, IV, 634–8; the emphasis is Wollstonecraft's. [TB]

[6] *Paradise Lost*, VIII, 381–92; the emphasis is Wollstonecraft's. [TB]

To prevent any misconstruction, I must add, that I do not believe that a private education[7] can work the wonders which some sanguine writers have attributed to it. Men and women must be educated, in a great degree, by the opinions and manners of the society they live in. In every age there has been a stream of popular opinion that has carried all before it, and given a family character, as it were, to the century. It may then fairly be inferred, that, till society be differently constituted, much cannot be expected from education. It is, however, sufficient for my present purpose to assert, that, whatever effect circumstances have on the abilities, every being may become virtuous by the exercise of its own reason; for if but one being was created with vicious inclinations, that is positively bad, what can save us from atheism? or if we worship a God, is not that God a devil?...

Consequently, the most perfect education, in my opinion, is such an exercise of the understanding as is best calculated to strengthen the body and form the heart. Or, in other words, to enable the individual to attain such habits of virtue as will render it independent. In fact, it is a farce to call any being virtuous whose virtues do not result from the exercise of its own reason. This was Rousseau's opinion respecting men:[8] I extend it to women, and confidently assert that they have been drawn out of their sphere by false refinement, and not by an endeavour to acquire masculine qualities. Still the regal homage which they receive is so intoxicating, that till the manners of the times are changed, and formed on more reasonable principles, it may be impossible to convince them that the illegitimate power, which they obtain, by degrading themselves, is a curse, and that they must return to nature and equality, if they wish to secure the placid satisfaction that unsophisticated affections impart. But for this epoch we must wait – wait,

perhaps, till kings and nobles, enlightened by reason, and, preferring the real dignity of man to childish state, throw off their gaudy hereditary trappings: and if then women do not resign the arbitrary power of beauty – they will prove that they have *less* mind than man.

I may be accused of arrogance; still I must declare what I firmly believe, that all the writers who have written on the subject of female education and manners from Rousseau to Dr Gregory,[9] have contributed to render women more artificial, weak characters, than they would otherwise have been; and, consequently, more useless members of society ...

Many are the causes that, in the present corrupt state of society, contribute to enslave women by cramping their understandings and sharpening their senses. One, perhaps, that silently does more mischief than all the rest, is their disregard of order.

To do every thing in an orderly manner, is a most important precept, which women, who, generally speaking, receive only a disorderly kind of education, seldom attend to with that degree of exactness that men, who from their infancy are broken into method, observe. This negligent kind of guess-work, for what other epithet can be used to point out the random exertions of a sort of instinctive common sense, never brought to the test of reason? prevents their generalizing matters of fact – so they do to-day, what they did yesterday, merely because they did it yesterday.

This contempt of the understanding in early life has more baneful consequences than is commonly supposed; for the little knowledge which women of strong minds attain, is, from various circumstances, of a more desultory kind than the knowledge of men, and it is acquired more by sheer observations on real life, than from comparing what has been individually observed with the results of experience generalized by

---

[7] By 'a private education', Wollstonecraft means an education at home rather than in schools. [eds]

[8] Rousseau, *Emilius and Sophia: or, a new system of education* (1762, 1763) trans. William Kenrick. See I, i, p.76: 'Reason only teaches us good from evil'; and 'The profession of faith of a Savoyard Priest', III, IV, pp.16–154. [TB] *Emilius and Sophia*, afterwards referred to by Todd and Butler as *Emilius*, is of course an early English translation of Rousseau's *Émile*. [eds]

[9] *Emilius*, Bk.V; John Gregory (1724–73), a Scottish professor of medicine, wrote *A Father's Legacy to his Daughters* (1774) which Wollstonecraft quoted extensively in *The Female Reader*. [TB]

speculation. Led by their dependent situation and domestic employments more into society, what they learn is rather by snatches; and as learning is with them, in general, only a secondary thing, they do not pursue any one branch with that persevering ardour necessary to give vigour to the faculties, and clearness to the judgement. In the present state of society, a little learning is required to support the character of a gentleman; and boys are obliged to submit to a few years of discipline. But in the education of women, the cultivation of the understanding is always subordinate to the acquirement of some corporeal accomplishment; even while enervated by confinement and false notions of modesty, the body is prevented from attaining that grace and beauty which relaxed half-formed limbs never exhibit. Besides, in youth their faculties are not brought forward by emulation; and having no serious scientific study, if they have natural sagacity it is turned too soon on life and manners. They dwell on effects, and modifications, without tracing them back to causes; and complicated rules to adjust behaviour are a weak substitute for simple principles.

As a proof that education gives this appearance of weakness to females, we may instance the example of military men, who are, like them, sent into the world before their minds have been stored with knowledge or fortified by principles. The consequences are similar; soldiers acquire a little superficial knowledge, snatched from the muddy current of conversation, and, from continually mixing with society, they gain, what is termed a knowledge of the world; and this acquaintance with manners and customs has frequently been confounded with a knowledge of the human heart. But can the crude fruit of casual observation, never brought to the test of judgement, formed by comparing speculation and experience, deserve such a distinction? Soldiers, as well as women, practise the minor virtues with punctilious politeness. Where is then the sexual difference, when the education has been the same? All the difference that I can discern, arises from the superior advantage of liberty, which enables the former to see more of life.

It is wandering from my present subject, perhaps, to make a political remark; but, as it was produced naturally by the train of my reflections, I shall not pass it silently over.

Standing armies can never consist of resolute, robust men; they may be well disciplined machines, but they will seldom contain men under the influence of strong passions, or with very vigorous faculties. And as for any depth of understanding, I will venture to affirm, that it is as rarely to be found in the army as amongst women; and the cause, I maintain, is the same. It may be further observed, that officers are also particularly attentive to their persons, fond of dancing, crowded rooms, adventures, and ridicule.[10] Like the *fair* sex, the business of their lives is gallantry. – They were taught to please, and they only live to please. Yet they do not lose their rank in the distinction of sexes, for they are still reckoned superior to women, though in what their superiority consists, beyond what I have just mentioned, it is difficult to discover.

The great misfortune is this, that they both acquire manners before morals, and a knowledge of life before they have, from reflection, any acquaintance with the grand ideal outline of human nature. The consequence is natural; satisfied with common nature, they become a prey to prejudices, and taking all their opinions on credit, they blindly submit to authority. So that if they have any sense, it is a kind of instinctive glance, that catches proportions, and decides with respect to manners; but fails when arguments are to be pursued below the surface, or opinions analysed.

May not the same remark be applied to women? Nay, the argument may be carried still further, for they are both thrown out of a useful station by the unnatural distinctions established in civilized life. Riches and hereditary honours have made cyphers of women to give consequence to the numerical figure;[11] and idleness has produced a mixture of gallantry and despotism into society, which leads the very men who are the slaves of their mistresses to tyrannize over their sisters, wives, and daughters. This is only keeping them in rank and file, it is true.

[10] Why should women be censured with petulant acrimony, because they seem to have passion for a scarlet coat? Has not education placed them more on a level with soldiers than any other class of men? [W]

[11] Women are compared to the zero after a number in a multiple of ten, e.g. 10, 120, 1230, etc. [eds]

Strengthen the female mind by enlarging it, and there will be an end to blind obedience; but, as blind obedience is ever sought for by power, tyrants and sensualists are in the right when they endeavour to keep women in the dark, because the former only want slaves, and the latter a plaything. The sensualist, indeed, has been the most dangerous of tyrants, and women have been duped by their lovers, as princes by their ministers, whilst dreaming that they reigned over them.

I now principally allude to Rousseau, for his character of Sophia is, undoubtedly, a captivating one, though it appears to me grossly unnatural;[12] however it is not the superstructure, but the foundation of her character, the principles on which her education was built, that I mean to attack; nay, warmly as I admire the genius of that able writer, whose opinions I shall often have occasion to cite, indignation always takes place of admiration, and the rigid frown of insulted virtue effaces the smile of complacency, which his eloquent periods are wont to raise, when I read his voluptuous reveries. Is this the man, who, in his ardour for virtue, would banish all the soft arts of peace, and almost carry us back to Spartan discipline? Is this the man who delights to paint the useful struggles of passion, the triumphs of good dispositions, and the heroic flights which carry the glowing soul out of itself? – How are these mighty sentiments lowered when he describes the pretty foot and enticing airs of his little favourite! But, for the present, I wave the subject, and, instead of severely reprehending the transient effusions of overweening sensibility, I shall only observe, that whoever has cast a benevolent eye on society, must often have been gratified by the sight of humble mutual love, not dignified by sentiment, nor strengthened by a union in intellectual pursuits. The domestic trifles of the day have

afforded matters for cheerful converse, and innocent caresses have softened toils which did not require great exercise of mind or stretch of thought: yet, has not the sight of this moderate felicity excited more tenderness than respect? An emotion similar to what we feel when children are playing, or animals sporting,[13] whilst the contemplation of the noble struggles of suffering merit has raised admiration, and carried our thoughts to that world where sensation will give place to reason.

Women are, therefore, to be considered either as moral beings, or so weak that they must be entirely subjected to the superior faculties of men.

Let us examine this question. Rousseau declares that a woman should never, for a moment, feel herself independent, that she should be governed by fear to exercise her *natural* cunning, and made a coquettish slave in order to render her a more alluring object of desire, a *sweeter* companion to man, whenever he chooses to relax himself. He carries the arguments, which he pretends to draw from the indications of nature, still further, and insinuates that truth and fortitude, the corner stones of all human virtue, should be cultivated with certain restrictions, because, with respect to the female character, obedience is the grand lesson which ought to be impressed with unrelenting rigour.[14]

What nonsense! when will a great man arise with sufficient strength of mind to puff away the fumes which pride and sensuality have thus spread over the subject! If women are by nature inferior to men, their virtues must be the same in quality, if not in degree, or virtue is a relative idea; consequently, their conduct should be founded on the same principles, and have the same aim.

Connected with man as daughters, wives, and mothers, their moral character may be

---

[12] See *Emilius*, Bk. V; Sophia is the 'idealized' submissive heroine. [TB]

[13] Similar feelings has Milton's pleasing picture of paradisiacal happiness ever raised in my mind; yet, instead of envying the lovely pair, I have, with conscious dignity, or Satanic pride, turned to hell for sublimer objects. [See *Paradise Lost*, Bk.IV.] [TB] In the same style, when viewing some noble monument of human art, I have traced the emanation of the Deity in the order I admired, till, descending from that giddy height, I have caught myself contemplating the grandest of all human sights; – for fancy quickly placed, in some solitary recess, an outcast of fortune, rising superior to passion and discontent. [W]

[14] See *Emilius*, Bk. IV, v, pp.31–3. [TB]

estimated by their manner of fulfilling those simple duties; but the end, the grand end of their exertions should be to unfold their own faculties and acquire the dignity of conscious virtue. They may try to render their road pleasant; but ought never to forget, in common with man, that life yields not the felicity which can satisfy an immortal soul. I do not mean to insinuate, that either sex should be so lost in abstract reflections or distant views, as to forget the affections and duties that lie before them, and are, in truth, the means appointed to produce the fruit of life; on the contrary, I would warmly recommend them, even while I assert, that they afford most satisfaction when they are considered in their true, sober light.

Probably the prevailing opinion, that woman was created for man, may have taken its rise from Moses's poetical story;[15] yet, as very few, it is presumed, who have bestowed any serious thought on the subject, ever supposed that Eve was, literally speaking, one of Adam's ribs, the deduction must be allowed to fall to the ground; or, only be so far admitted as it proves that man, from the remotest antiquity, found it convenient to exert his strength to subjugate his companion, and his invention to shew that she ought to have her neck bent under the yoke, because the whole creation was only created for his convenience or pleasure.

Let it not be concluded that I wish to invert the order of things; I have already granted, that, from the constitution of their bodies, men seem to be designed by Providence to attain a greater degree of virtue. I speak collectively of the whole sex; but I see not the shadow of a reason to conclude that their virtues should differ in respect to their nature. In fact, how can they, if virtue has only one eternal standard? I must therefore, if I reason consequentially, as strenuously maintain that they have the same simple direction, as that there is a God.

It follows then that cunning should not be opposed to wisdom, little cares to great exertions, nor insipid softness, varnished over with the name of gentleness, to that fortitude which grand views alone can inspire.

I shall be told that woman would then lose many of her peculiar graces, and the opinion of a well-known poet might be quoted to refute my unqualified assertion. For Pope has said, in the name of the whole male sex,

Yet ne'er so sure our passion to create,
As when she touch'd the brink of all we hate.[16]

In what light this sally places men and women, I shall leave to the judicious to determine; meanwhile I shall content myself with observing, that I cannot discover why, unless they are mortal, females should always be degraded by being made subservient to love or lust.

To speak disrespectfully of love is, I know, high treason against sentiment and fine feelings; but I wish to speak the simple language of truth, and rather to address the head than the heart. To endeavour to reason love out of the world, would be to out Quixote Cervantes, and equally offend against common sense; but an endeavour to restrain this tumultuous passion, and to prove that it should not be allowed to dethrone superior powers, or to usurp the sceptre which the understanding should ever coolly wield, appears less wild.

Youth is the season for love in both sexes; but in those days of thoughtless enjoyment provision should be made for the more important years of life, when reflection takes place of sensation. But Rousseau, and most of the male writers who have followed his steps, have warmly inculcated that the whole tendency of female education ought to be directed to one point: – to render them pleasing ...[17]

Love, the common passion, in which chance and sensation take place of choice and reason, is, in some degree, felt by the mass of mankind; for it is not necessary to speak, at present, of the emotions that rise above or sink below love. This passion, naturally increased by suspense and difficulties, draws the mind out of its accustomed state, and exalts the affections; but the security of marriage, allowing the fever of love to subside, a healthy temperature is thought insipid, only by those who have not sufficient intellect to substitute the calm tenderness

---

[15] Genesis 2: 18–22, Genesis is traditionally ascribed to Moses. [TB]

[16] Alexander Pope, *Of the characters of women: an epistle to a lady* (1735), ll.51-2. [TB]

[17] *Emilius*, Bk. IV, v, pp.19–20. [TB]

of friendship, the confidence of respect, instead of blind admiration, and the sensual emotions of fondness.

This is, must be, the course of nature – friendship or indifference inevitably succeeds love. – And this constitution seems perfectly to harmonize with the system of government which prevails in the moral world. Passions are spurs to action, and open the mind; but they sink into mere appetites, become a personal and momentary gratification, when the object is gained, and the satisfied mind rests in enjoyment. The man who had some virtue whilst he was struggling for a crown, often becomes a voluptuous tyrant when it graces his brow; and, when the lover is not lost in the husband, the dotard, a prey to childish caprices, and fond jealousies, neglects the serious duties of life, and the caresses which should excite confidence in his children are lavished on the overgrown child, his wife.

In order to fulfil the duties of life, and to be able to pursue with vigour the various employments which form the moral character, a master and mistress of a family ought not to continue to love each other with passion. I mean to say, that they ought not to indulge those emotions which disturb the order of society, and engross the thoughts that should be otherwise employed. The mind that has never been engrossed by one object wants vigour – if it can long be so, it is weak.

A mistaken education, a narrow, uncultivated mind, and many sexual prejudices, tend to make women more constant than men; but, for the present, I shall not touch on this branch of the subject. I will go still further, and advance, without dreaming of a paradox, that an unhappy marriage is often very advantageous to a family, and that the neglected wife is, in general, the best mother. And this would almost always be the consequence if the female mind were more enlarged: for, it seems to be the common dispensation of Providence, that what we gain in present enjoyment should be deducted from the treasure of life, experience; and that when we are gathering the flowers of the day and revelling in pleasure, the solid fruit of toil and wisdom should not be caught at the same time. The way lies before us, we must turn to the right or left; and he who will pass life away in bounding from one pleasure to another, must not complain if he acquire neither wisdom nor respectability of character ...

I love man as my fellow; but his scepter, real, or usurped, extends not to me, unless the reason of an individual demands my homage; and even then the submission is to reason, and not to man. In fact, the conduct of an accountable being must be regulated by the operations of its own reason; or on what foundation rests the throne of God?

It appears to me necessary to dwell on these obvious truths, because females have been insulated, as it were; and, while they have been stripped of the virtues that should clothe humanity, they have been decked with artificial graces that enable them to exercise a short-lived tyranny. Love, in their bosoms, taking place of every nobler passion, their sole ambition is to be fair, to raise emotion instead of inspiring respect; and this ignoble desire, like the servility in absolute monarchies, destroys all strength of character. Liberty is the mother of virtue, and if women be, by their very constitution, slaves, and not allowed to breathe the sharp invigorating air of freedom, they must ever languish like exotics, and be reckoned beautiful flaws in nature.

As to the argument respecting the subjection in which the sex has ever been held, it retorts on man. The many have always been enthralled by the few; and monsters, who scarcely have shewn any discernment of human excellence, have tyrannized over thousands of their fellow-creatures. Why have men of superior endowments submitted to such degradation? For, is it not universally acknowledged that kings, viewed collectively, have ever been inferior, in abilities and virtue, to the same number of men taken from the common mass of mankind – yet, have they not, and are they not still treated with a degree of reverence that is an insult to reason? China is not the only country where a living man has been made a God.[18] *Men* have submitted to

---

[18] Chinese emperors were considered to be divine cf. Gottfried Leibniz, *Novissima Sinica Historiam nostri temporis illustratura* (n.p., 1697), preface: 'Quis vero non miretur Monarcham tanti Imperii, qui pene humanum fastigium magnitudine excessit, et mortalis quidam Deus habetur.' *Translation*: Who indeed would not be amazed at the monarch of such an empire, who almost exceeds human condition in grandeur, and a mortal is considered to be a god. [TB]

superior strength to enjoy with impunity the pleasure of the moment – *women* have only done the same, and therefore till it is proved that the courtier, who servilely resigns the birthright of a man, is not a moral agent, it cannot be demonstrated that woman is essentially inferior to man because she has always been subjugated.

Brutal force has hitherto governed the world, and that the science of politics is in its infancy, is evident from philosophers scrupling to give the knowledge most useful to man that determinate distinction.

I shall not pursue this argument any further than to establish an obvious inference, that as sound politics diffuse liberty, mankind, including woman, will become more wise and virtuous.

Source: Mary Wollstonecraft: 'A Vindication of the Rights of Woman', *Works*, vol.5, pp.88–96, 99, 105–6).

Extract 4

Wollstonecraft, Rights of Woman, *from Chapter III, The same subject continued*

… Besides, if women be educated for dependence; that is, to act according to the will of another fallible being, and submit, right or wrong, to power, where are we to stop? Are they to be considered as vicegerents allowed to reign over a small domain, and answerable for their conduct to a higher tribunal, liable to error?

It will not be difficult to prove that such delegates will act like men subjected by fear, and make their children and servants endure their tyrannical oppression. As they submit without reason, they will, having no fixed rules to square their conduct by, be kind, or cruel, just as the whim of the moment directs; and we ought not to wonder if sometimes, galled by their heavy yoke, they take a malignant pleasure in resting it on weaker shoulders.

But, supposing a woman, trained up to obedience, be married to a sensible man, who directs her judgement without making her feel the servility of her subjection, to act with as much propriety by this reflected light as can be expected when reason is taken at second hand, yet she cannot ensure the life of her protector; he may die and leave her with a large family.

A double duty devolves on her; to educate them in the character of both father and mother; to form their principles and secure their property. But, alas! she has never thought, much less acted for herself. She has only learned to please[19] men, to depend gracefully on them; yet, encumbered with children, how is she to obtain another protector – a husband to supply the place of reason? A rational man, for we are not treading on romantic ground, though he may think her a pleasing docile creature, will not choose to marry a *family* for love, when the world contains many more pretty creatures. What is then to become of her? She either falls an easy prey to some mean fortune-hunter, who defrauds her children of their parental inheritance, and renders her miserable; or becomes the victim of discontent and blind indulgence. Unable to educate her sons, or

---

[19] 'In the union of the sexes, both pursue one common object, but none in the same manner. From their diversity in this particular, arises the first determinate difference between the moral relations of each. The one should be active and strong, the other passive and weak: it is necessary the one should have both the power and the will, and that the other should make little resistance.

This principle being established, it follows that woman is expressly formed to please the man: if the obligation be reciprocal also, and the man ought to please in his turn, it is not so immediately necessary: his great merit is in his power, and he pleases merely because he is strong. This, I must confess, is not one of the refined maxims of love; it is, however, one of the laws of nature, prior to love itself.

If woman be formed to please and be subjected to man, it is her place, doubtless, to render herself agreeable to him, instead of challenging his passion. The violence of his desires depends on her charms; it is by means of these she should urge him to the exertion of those powers which nature hath given him. The most successful method of exciting them, is, to render such exertion necessary by resistance; as, in that case, self-love is added to desire, and the one triumphs in the victory which the other is obliged to acquire. Hence arise the various modes of attack and defence between the sexes; the boldness of one sex and the timidity of the other; and, in a word, that bashfulness and modesty with which nature hath armed the weak, in order to subdue the strong.'

Rousseau's *Emilius*, (Bk. IV,v, pp.3-4). [TB]

I shall make no other comment on this ingenious passage, than just to observe, that it is the philosophy of lasciviousness. [W]

impress them with respect; for it is not a play on words to assert, that people are never respected, though filling an important station, who are not respectable; she pines under the anguish of unavailing impotent regret. The serpent's tooth enters into her very soul, and the vices of licentious youth bring her with sorrow, if not with poverty also, to the grave.[20]

This is not an overcharged picture; on the contrary, it is a very possible case, and something similar must have fallen under every attentive eye.

I have, however, taken it for granted, that she was well-disposed, though experience shews, that the blind may as easily be led into a ditch as along the beaten road. But supposing, no very improbable conjecture, that a being only taught to please must still find her happiness in pleasing; – what an example of folly, not to say vice, will she be to her innocent daughters! The mother will be lost in the coquette, and, instead of making friends of her daughters, view them with eyes askance, for they are rivals – rivals more cruel than any other, because they invite a comparison, and drive her from the throne of beauty, who has never thought of a seat on the bench of reason.

It does not require a lively pencil, or the discriminating outline of a caricature, to sketch the domestic miseries and petty vices which such a mistress of a family diffuses. Still she only acts as a woman ought to act, brought up according to Rousseau's system. She can never be reproached for being masculine, or turning out of her sphere; nay, she may observe another of his grand rules, and, cautiously preserving her reputation free from spot, be reckoned a good kind of woman. Yet in what respect can she be termed good? She abstains, it is true, without any

great struggle, from committing gross crimes; but how does she fulfil her duties? Duties! – in truth she has enough to think of to adorn her body and nurse a weak constitution.

With respect to religion, she never presumed to judge for herself; but conformed, as a dependent creature should, to the ceremonies of the church which she was brought up in, piously believing that wiser heads than her own have settled that business: – and not to doubt is her point of perfection. She therefore pays her tythe of mint and cummin[21] – and thanks her God that she is not as other women are.[22] These are the blessed effects of a good education! These the virtues of man's help-mate![23]

I must relieve myself by drawing a different picture.

Let fancy now present a woman with a tolerable understanding, for I do not wish to leave the line of mediocrity, whose constitution, strengthened by exercise, has allowed her body to acquire its full vigour; her mind, at the same time, gradually expanding itself to comprehend the moral duties of life, and in what human virtue and dignity consist.

Formed thus by the discharge of the relative duties of her station, she marries from affection, without losing sight of prudence, and looking beyond matrimonial felicity, she secures her husband's respect before it is necessary to exert mean arts to please him and feed a dying flame, which nature doomed to expire when the object became familiar, when friendship and forbearance take place of a more ardent affection. – This is the natural death of love, and domestic peace is not destroyed by struggles to prevent its extinction. I also suppose the husband to be virtuous; or she is still more in want of independent principles.

---

[20] Cf. *King Lear*, I, iv, 297–8: 'How sharper than a serpent's tooth it is To have a thankless child!' [TB]

[21] Cf. Matthew 23:23: 'Woe unto you, scribes and Pharisees, hypocrites! for ye pay tithe of mint and anise and cummin, and have omitted the weightier matters of the law, judgement, mercy and faith.' [TB]

[22] Cf. Luke 18:11: 'The Pharisee stood and prayed thus with himself, God, I thank thee, that I am not as other men are,' IV, v, p.128. [TB]

[23] 'O how lovely,' exclaims Rousseau, speaking of Sophia, 'is her ignorance! Happy is he who is destined to instruct her! She will never pretend to be the tutor of her husband, but will be content to be his pupil. Far from attempting to subject him to her taste, she will accommodate herself to his. She will be more estimable to him, than if she was learned: he will have a pleasure in instructing her.' Rousseau's *Emilius*. [W] *Emilius* Bk. IV, v, p.128. [TB].

Fate, however, breaks this tie. – She is left a widow, perhaps, without a sufficient provision; but she is not desolate! The pang of nature is felt; but after time has softened sorrow into melancholy resignation, her heart turns to her children with redoubled fondness, and anxious to provide for them, affection gives a sacred heroic cast to her maternal duties. She thinks that not only the eye[24] sees her virtuous efforts from whom all her comfort now must flow, and whose approbation is life; but her imagination, a little abstracted and exalted by grief, dwells on the fond hope that the eyes which her trembling hand closed,[25] may still see how she subdues every wayward passion to fulfil the double duty of being the father as well as the mother of her children. Raised to heroism by misfortunes, she represses the first faint dawning of a natural inclination, before it ripens into love, and in the bloom of life forgets her sex – forgets the pleasure of an awakening passion, which might again have been inspired and returned. She no longer thinks of pleasing, and conscious dignity prevents her from priding herself on account of the praise which her conduct demands. Her children have her love, and her brightest hopes are beyond the grave, where her imagination often strays.

I think I see her surrounded by her children, reaping the reward of her care. The intelligent eye meets hers, whilst health and innocence smile on their chubby cheeks, and as they grow up the cares of life are lessened by their grateful attention. She lives to see the virtues which she endeavoured to plant on principles, fixed into habits, to see her children attain a strength of character sufficient to enable them to endure adversity without forgetting their mother's example.

The task of life thus fulfilled, she calmly waits for the sleep of death, and rising from the grave, may say – Behold, thou gavest me a talent – and here are five talents[26] ...

Source: Mary Wollstonecraft: 'A Vindication of the Rights of Woman', **Works**, vol.5, pp.116–19.

Extract 5

Wollstonecraft, **Rights of Woman,** *from Chapter V, Animadversions on some of the writers who have rendered women objects of pity, bordering on contempt, Section V*

... The fact is, that men expect from education, what education cannot give. A sagacious parent or tutor may strengthen the body and sharpen the instruments by which the child is to gather knowledge; but the honey must be the reward of the individual's own industry. It is almost as absurd to attempt to make a youth wise by the experience of another, as to expect the body to grow strong by the exercise which is only talked of, or seen.[27] Many of those children whose conduct has been most narrowly watched, become the weakest men, because their instructors only instil certain notions into their minds, that have no other foundation than their authority; and if they be loved or respected, the mind is cramped in its exertions and wavering in its advances. The business of education in this case, is only to conduct the shooting tendrils to a proper pole; yet after laying precept upon precept, without allowing a child to acquire judgement itself, parents expect them to act in the same manner by this borrowed fallacious light, as if they had illuminated it themselves; and be, when they enter life, what their parents are at the close. They do not consider that the tree, and even the human body, does not strengthen its fibres till it has reached its full growth.

There appears to be something analogous in the mind. The senses and the imagination give a form to the character, during a childhood and youth; and the understanding, as life advances, gives firmness to the first fair purposes of sensibility – till virtue, arising rather from the clear conviction of reason than the impulse of the heart, morality is made to rest on a rock against which the storms of passion vainly beat.

---

[24] i.e. God's eye. [eds]

[25] i.e her dead husband's eyes. [eds]

[26] For the parable of the talents see Matthew 25:14–30. [TB]

[27] 'One sees nothing when one is content to contemplate only; it is necessary to act oneself to be able to see how others act.' Rousseau. [W]

I hope I shall not be misunderstood when I say, that religion will not have this condensing energy, unless it be founded on reason. If it be merely the refuge of weakness or wild fanaticism, and not a governing principle of conduct, drawn from self-knowledge, and a rational opinion respecting the attributes of God, what can it be expected to produce? The religion which consists in warming the affections, and exalting the imagination, is only the poetical part, and may afford the individual pleasure without rendering it a more moral being. It may be a substitute for worldly pursuits; yet narrow, instead of enlarging the heart: but virtue must be loved as in itself sublime and excellent, and not for the advantages it procures or the evils it averts, if any great degree of excellence be expected. Men will not become moral when they only build airy castles in a future world to compensate for the disappointments which they meet with in this; if they turn their thoughts from relative duties to religious reveries.

Source: Mary Wollstonecraft: 'A Vindication of the Rights of Woman', *Works*, vol.5, pp.183–4.

Extract 6

Wollstonecraft, **Rights of Woman**, *from Chapter V, Animadversions on some of the writers who have rendered women objects of pity, bordering on contempt, Section IV*

I do not mean to allude to all the writers who have written on the subject of female manners – it would, in fact, be only beating over the old ground, for they have, in general, written in the same strain; but attacking the boasted prerogative of man – the prerogative that may emphatically be called the iron sceptre of tyranny, the original sin of tyrants, I declare against all power built on prejudices, however hoary.

If the submission demanded be founded on justice – there is no appealing to a higher power – for God is Justice itself. Let us then, as children of the same parent, if not bastardized by being the younger born, reason together, and learn to submit to the authority of reason – when her voice is distinctly heard. But, if it be proved, that this throne of prerogative only rests on a chaotic mass of prejudices, that have no inherent principle of order to keep them together, or on an elephant, tortoise, or even the mighty shoulders of a son of the earth,[28] they may escape, who dare to brave the consequence, without any breach of duty, without sinning against the order of things.

Whilst reason raises man above the brutal herd, and death is big with promises, they alone are subject to blind authority who have no reliance on their own strength. They are free – who will be free! –[29]

The being who can govern itself has nothing to fear in life; but if any thing be dearer than its own respect, the price must be paid to the last farthing. Virtue, like every thing valuable, must be loved for herself alone; or she will not take up her abode with us. She will not impart that peace, 'which passeth understanding',[30] when she is merely made the stilts of reputation; and respected, with pharisaical exactness, because 'honesty is the best policy'.

That the plan of life which enables us to carry some knowledge and virtue into another world, is the one best calculated to ensure content in this, cannot be denied; yet few people act according to this principle, though it be universally allowed that it admits not of dispute. Present pleasure, or present power, carry before it these sober convictions; and it is for the day, not for life, that man bargains with happiness. How few! – how very few! have sufficient foresight, or resolution, to endure a small evil at the moment, to avoid a greater hereafter.

---

[28] According to ancient belief the world was a disc, surrounded by water, supported by a huge creature, either a tortoise or a mammoth; in Greek mythology Atlas supported the world on his shoulders. [TB]

[29] 'He is the free man, whom the *truth* makes free!' *Cowper.* [W] William Cowper, *The Task* (1785), v, l.733; the emphasis is Wollstonecraft's. [TB]

[30] Philippians 4:7: 'the peace of God, which passeth all understanding,'. [TB]

Woman in particular, whose virtue[31] is built on mutable prejudices, seldom attains to this greatness of mind; so that, becoming the slave of her own feelings, she is easily subjugated by those of others. Thus degraded, her reason, her misty reason! is employed rather to burnish than to snap her chains ...

Source: Mary Wollstonecraft, 'A Vindication of the Rights of Woman', *Works*, vol.5, pp.170–1.

Extract 7

Headnote

On November 4th 1789, Wollstonecraft's friend from Newington Green, the Welsh Unitarian minister Dr Richard Price, preached a sermon to the Society for Commemmorating the Revolution in Great Britain. The revolution commemmorated was the 'Glorious Revolution' of 1688, when the aristocracy and commons of England combined to replace an unpopular Catholic King with a Protestant one; and Price's sermon was largely concerned with political justice. At its close, he could not forbear referring enthusiastically to the events of that year in France, which he welcomed as the harbingers of another, equally glorious revolution. In response to a massive financial crisis, and to mounting and widespread pressure for reform, the French King had summoned the Estates-General, who had defied the king, converted themselves into a National Assembly, and set about reforming the constitution – with the reluctant consent of the King. A Declaration of the Rights of Men had been promulgated, laying down the principles of constitutional reform: the feudal privileges of the aristocracy had been abolished, and the Church had been dispossessed of its lands. In July, the Bastille had been stormed; in October, the King and Queen, suspected of conspiring against the National Assembly, had been extracted, with some loss of life, from their court at Versailles by an unruly mob and brought to Paris, where they remained confined in the Tuileries palace. There had thus been some widely-supported popular violence; nevertheless, without large-scale civil strife or major bloodshed, France appeared poised to dismantle the old political order of rule by an arbitrary monarch, and eager to construct a new one from first principles – the first principles being the ideas of natural equality and justice advocated by the *philosophes*. So in his conclusion Price says:

> What an eventful period is this! I am thankful that I have lived to it; and I could almost say, *Lord, now lettest thou thy servant depart in peace, for mine eyes have seen thy salvation.* I have lived to see a diffusion of knowledge, which has undermined superstition and error – I have lived to see the rights of man better understood than ever; and nations panting for liberty, which seemed to have lost the idea of it. – I have lived to see THIRTY MILLIONS of people, indignant and resolute, spurning at slavery, and demanding liberty with an irresistible voice; their king led in triumph, and an arbitrary monarch surrendering himself to his subjects. – After sharing in the benefits of one Revolution, I have been spared to be a witness to two other Revolutions, both glorious. – And now, methinks, I see the ardour for liberty catching and spreading; a general amendment beginning in human affairs; the dominion of kings changed for the dominion of laws, and the dominion of priests giving way to the dominion of reason and conscience.

When Price's sermon was published as *A Discourse on the Love of Our Country* (1789) these sentiments outraged the great orator and statesman Edmund Burke; and in the following year he published his *Reflections on the Revolution in France*, a vehement attack on Price and democratic politics. In the following extract, Burke responds to the passage from Price just quoted. Burke's book is written in the form of a (very long!) letter to a young French nobleman, a supporter of the Revolution, who had asked Burke for his opinion of it.

Edmund Burke, Reflections on the Revolution in France

In France you are now in the crisis of a revolution, and in the transit from one form of government to another – you cannot see that

---

[31] I mean to use a word that comprehends more than chastity the sexual virtue. [W]

character of men in the same situation in which we see it in this country. ... The worst of the politics of the revolution is this; they temper and harden the breast, in order to prepare it for the desperate strokes which are sometimes used in extreme occasions. ... This sort of people are so taken up with their theories about the rights of man, that they have totally forgot his nature. Without opening one new avenue to the understanding, they have succeeded in stopping up those that lead to the heart. They have perverted in themselves, and in those that attend to them, all the well-placed sympathies of the human breast...

I find a preacher of the gospel prophaning the beautiful and prophetic ejaculation, commonly called '*nunc dimittis*', made on the first presentation of our Saviour in the Temple, and applying it, with an inhuman and unnatural rapture, to the most horrid, atrocious, and afflicting spectacle, that perhaps ever was exhibited to the pity and indignation of mankind. This '*leading in triumph*', a thing in its best form unmanly and irreligious, which fills our preacher with such unhallowed transports, must shock, I believe, the moral taste of every well-born mind. Several English were the stupified and indignant spectators of that triumph. It was (unless we have been strangely deceived) a spectacle more resembling a procession of American savages, after some of their murders called victories, and leading into hovels hung round with scalps, their captives, overpowered with the scoffs and buffets of women as ferocious as themselves, much more than it resembled the triumphal pomp of a civilized martial nation...

This, my dear Sir, was not the triumph of France. I must believe that, as a nation, it overwhelmed you with shame and horror. I must believe that the National Assembly find themselves in a state of the greatest humiliation, in not being able to punish the authors of this triumph, or the actors in it; and that they are in a situation in which any enquiry they may make upon the subject, must be destitute even of the appearance of liberty or impartiality...

History will record, that on the morning of the 6th of October 1789, the king and queen of France, after a day of confusion, alarm, dismay, and slaughter, lay down, under the pledged security of public faith, to indulge nature in a few hours of respite, and troubled melancholy

repose. From this sleep the queen was first startled by the voice of the centinel at her door, who cried out to her, to save herself by flight – that this was the last proof of fidelity he could give – that they were upon him, and he was dead. Instantly he was cut down. A band of cruel ruffians and assassins, reeking with his blood, rushed into the chamber of the queen, and pierced with an hundred strokes of bayonets and poniards the bed, from whence this persecuted woman had but just time to fly almost naked, and through ways unknown to the murderers had escaped to seek refuge at the feet of a king and husband, not secure of his own life for a moment.

This king, to say no more of him, and this queen, and their infant children (who once would have been the pride and hope of a great and generous people) were then forced to abandon the sanctuary of the most splendid palace in the world, which they left swimming in blood, polluted by massacre, and strewed with scattered limbs and mutilated carcases. Thence they were conducted into the capital of their kingdom. Two had been selected from the unprovoked, unresisted, promiscuous slaughter, which was made of the gentlemen of birth and family who composed the king's body guard. These two gentlemen, with all the parade of an execution of justice, were cruelly and publickly dragged to the block, and beheaded in the great court of the palace. Their heads were stuck upon spears, and led the procession; whilst the royal captives who followed in the train were slowly moved along, amidst the horrid yells, and shrilling screams, and frantic dances, and infamous contumelies, and all the unutterable abominations of the furies of hell, in the abused shape of the vilest of women. After they had been made to taste, drop by drop, more than the bitterness of death, in the slow torture of a journey of twelve miles, protracted to six hours, they were, under a guard, composed of those very soldiers who had thus conducted them through this famous triumph, lodged in one of the old palaces of Paris, now converted into a Bastile for kings.

Is this a triumph to be consecrated at altars? to be commemorated with grateful thanksgiving? to be offered to the divine humanity with fervent prayer and ethusiastick ejaculation? ...

... I must think, that such treatment of any human creatures must be shocking to any but those who are made for accomplishing Revolutions. But I cannot stop here. Influenced by the inborn feelings of my nature, and not being illuminated by a single ray of this new-sprung modern light, I confess to you, Sir, that the exalted rank of the persons suffering, and particularly the sex, the beauty, and the amiable qualities of the descendant of so many kings and emperors, with the tender age of royal infants, insensible only through infancy and innocence of the cruel outrages to which their parents were exposed, instead of being a subject of exultation, adds not a little to my sensibility on that most melancholy occasion.

I hear that the august person, who was the principal object of our preacher's triumph, though he supported himself, felt much on that shameful occasion. As a man, it became him to feel for his wife and children, and the faithful guards of his person, that were massacred in cold blood about him; as a prince, it became him to feel for the strange and frightful transformation of his civilized subjects, and to be more grieved for them, than solicitous for himself. It derogates little from his fortitude, while it adds infinitely to the honour of his humanity. I am very sorry to say it, very sorry indeed, that such personages are in a situation in which it is not unbecoming in us to praise the virtues of the great.

I hear, and I rejoice to hear, that the great lady, the other object of the triumph, has borne that day (one is interested that beings made for suffering should suffer well) and that she bears all the succeeding days, that she bears the imprisonment of her husband, and her own captivity, and the exile of her friends, and the insulting adulation of addresses, and the whole weight of her accumulated wrongs, with a serene patience, in a manner suited to her rank and race, and becoming the offspring of a sovereign distinguished for her piety and her courage; that like her she has lofty sentiments; that she feels with the dignity of a Roman matron; that in the last extremity she will save herself from the last disgrace, and that if she must fall, she will fall by no ignoble hand.[32]

It is now sixteen or seventeen years since I saw the queen of France, then the dauphiness, at Versailles; and surely never lighted on this orb, which she hardly seemed to touch, a more delightful vision. I saw her just above the horizon, decorating and cheering the elevated sphere she just began to move in, – glittering like the morningstar, full of life, and splendor, and joy. Oh! What a revolution! and what an heart must I have, to contemplate without emotion that elevation and that fall! Little did I dream when she added titles of veneration to those of enthusiastic, distant, respectful love, that she should ever be obliged to carry the sharp antidote against disgrace[33] concealed in that bosom; little did I dream that I should have lived to see such disasters fallen upon her in a nation of gallant men, in a nation of men of honour and of cavaliers. I thought ten thousand swords must have leaped from their scabbards to avenge even a look that threatened her with insult – But the age of chivalry is gone – That of sophisters, oeconomists, and calculators, has succeeded; and the glory of Europe is extinguished for ever. Never, never more, shall we behold that generous loyalty to rank and sex, that proud submission, that dignified obedience, that subordination of the heart, which kept alive, even in servitude itself, the spirit of an exalted freedom. The unbought grace of life, the cheap defence of nations, the nurse of manly sentiment and heroic enterprize is gone! It is gone, that sensibility of principle, that chastity of honour, which felt a stain like a wound, which inspired courage whilst it mitigated ferocity, which ennobled whatever it touched, and under which vice itself lost half its evil, by losing all its grossness.

This mixed system of opinion and sentiment had its origin in the antient chivalry; and the principle, though varied in its appearance by the varying state of human affairs, subsisted and influenced through a long succession of generations, even to the time we live in...

But now all is to be changed. All the pleasing illusions, which made power gentle, and obedience liberal, which harmonized the different

---

[32] Burke implies that the Queen will commit suicide rather than submit to the dishonour of execution. In fact she did not. [eds]

[33] i.e. a dagger. [eds]

shades of life, and which, by a bland assimilation, incorporated into politics the sentiments which beautify and soften private society, are to be dissolved by this new conquering empire of light and reason. All the decent drapery of life is to be rudely torn off. All the super-added ideas, furnished from the wardrobe of a moral imagination, which the heart owns, and the understanding ratifies, as necessary to cover the defects of our naked shivering nature, and to raise it to dignity in our own estimation, are to be exploded as a ridiculous, absurd, and antiquated fashion.

On this scheme of things, a king is but a man; a queen is but a woman; a woman is but an animal; and an animal not of the highest order. All homage paid to the sex in general as such, and without distinct views, is to be regarded as romance and folly. Regicide, and parricide, and sacrilege, are but fictions of superstition, corrupting jurisprudence by destroying its simplicity. The murder of a king, or a queen, or a bishop, or a father, are only common homicide; and if the people are by any chance, or in any way gainers by it, a sort of homicide much the most pardonable, and into which we ought not to make too severe a scrutiny ...

Source: Edmund Burke, *Reflections on the Revolution in France*, pp.155–6, 159, 164–5, 167–70, 171.

Extract 8

Wollstonecraft, Rights of Men

... Knowing, however, the influence of a ruling passion, and how often it assumes the form of reason when there is much sensibility in the heart,[34] I respect an opponent, though he tenaciously maintains opinions in which I cannot coincide; but, if I once discover that many of those opinions are empty rhetorical flourishes, my respect is soon changed into that pity which borders on contempt; and the mock dignity and haughty stalk, only reminds me of the ass in the lion's skin.

A sentiment of this kind glanced across my mind when I read the following exclamation. 'Whilst the royal captives, who followed in the train, were slowly moved along, amidst the horrid yells, and shrilling screams, and frantic dances, and infamous contumelies, and all the unutterable abominations of the furies of hell, in the abused shape of the vilest of women.' Probably you mean women who gained a livelihood by selling vegetables or fish, who never had had any advantages of education; or their vices might have lost part of their abominable deformity, by losing part of their grossness. The queen of France – the great and small vulgar, claim our pity; they have almost insuperable obstacles to surmount in their progress towards true dignity of character; still I have such a plain downright understanding that I do not like to make a distinction without a difference. But it is not very extraordinary that *you*[35] should, for throughout your letter you frequently advert to a sentimental jargon, which has long been current in conversation, and even in books of morals, though it never received the *regal* stamp of reason. A kind of mysterious instinct is *supposed* to reside in the soul, that instantaneously discerns truth, without the tedious labour of ratiocination. This instinct, for I know not what other name to give it, has been termed *common sense*, and more frequently *sensibility*; and, by a kind of *indefeasible* right, it has been *supposed*, for rights of this kind are not easily proved, to reign paramount over the other faculties of the mind, and to be an authority from which there is no appeal...

It is to this instinct, without doubt, that you allude, when you talk of the 'moral constitution of the heart'. To it, I allow, for I consider it as a congregate of sensations and passions, *Poets* must apply, 'who have to deal with an audience not yet

---

[34] The psychological concept of the ruling passion originated in the theories of Bacon and Montaigne, who understood it as the source of self-control at the centre of the human personality; Pope, who most fully propounded the concept, treated it as the force that provides the individual with direction, stability, protection from chaos, which can be channelled towards either good or evil. In the scheme of providence its function is to differentiate the objectives of individuals so that the world's work can be accomplished. See Alexander Pope, *An Essay on Man* (1733–4), ll. 11.123–44; *On the Use of Riches, An Epistle to* (...) *Lord Bathurst* (1732), 1.154; *An Epistle to* (...) *Lord Visct. Cobham* (1733), 1.174 ff. [TB]

[35] i.e. Burke. [eds]

graduated in the school of the rights of men'.[36] They must, it is clear, often cloud the understanding, whilst they move the heart by a kind of mechanical spring; but that 'in the theatre the first intuitive glance'[37] of feeling should discriminate the form of truth, and see her fair proportion, I must beg leave to doubt. Sacred be the feelings of the heart! concentred in a glowing flame, they become the sun of life; and, without his invigorating impregnation, reason would probably lie in helpless inactivity, and never bring forth her only legitimate offspring – virtue. But to prove that virtue is really an acquisition of the individual, and not the blind impulse of unerring instinct, the bastard vice has often been begotten by the same father.

In what respect are we superior to the brute creation, if intellect is not allowed to be the guide of passion? Brutes hope and fear, love and hate; but, without a capacity to improve, a power of turning these passions to good or evil, they neither acquire virtue nor wisdom. – Why? Because the Creator has not given them reason.[38]

But the cultivation of reason is an arduous task, and men of lively fancy, finding it easier to follow the impulse of passion, endeavour to persuade themselves and others that it is most *natural*. And happy it is for those, who indolently let that heaven-lighted spark rest like the ancient lamps in sepulchres, that some virtuous habits, with which the reason of others shackled them, supplies its place. – Affection for parents, reverence for superiors or antiquity, notions of honour, or that worldly self-interest that shrewdly shews them that honesty is the best policy: all proceed from the reason for which they serve as substitutes; – but it is reason at second-hand.

Children are born ignorant, consequently innocent; the passions, are neither good nor evil dispositions, till they receive a direction, and either bound over the feeble barrier raised by a faint glimmering of unexercised reason, called conscience, or strengthen her wavering dictates till sound principles are deeply rooted, and able to cope with the headstrong passions that often assume her awful form. What moral purpose can be answered by extolling good dispositions, as they are called, when these good dispositions are described as instincts: for instinct moves in a direct line to its ultimate end, and asks not for guide or support. But if virtue is to be acquired by experience, or taught by example, reason, perfected by reflection, must be the director of the whole host of passions, which produce a fructifying heat, but no light, that you would exalt into her place. – She must hold the rudder, or, let the wind blow which way it list, the vessel will never advance smoothly to its destined port; for the time lost in tacking about would dreadfully impede its progress.[39]

Source: Mary Wollstonecraft, 'A Vindication of the Rights of Men', *Works*, vol. 5, 1790, pp.29–30, 31–2.

---

[36] Burke, *Reflections*, p.120: 'Poets, who have to deal with an audience not yet graduated in the school of the rights of men, and who must apply themselves to the moral constitution of the heart would not dare to produce such a triumph [the French Revolution] as a matter of exultation.' (Todd and Butler's page references to Burke's *Reflections* are to the original 1790 edition. [eds]) [TB]

[37] Burke, *Reflections*, p.121. [TB]

[38] I do not now mean to discuss the intricate subject of their mortality; reason may, perhaps, be given to them in the next stage of existence, if they are to mount in the scale of life, like men, by the medium of death. [W]

[39] Cf. Rousseau, *Émile, ou de l'Éducation* (1762), I, p.112: 'La raison seule nous apprend à connôitre le bien et le mal. La conscience qui nous fait aimer l'un et haïr l'autre, quoiqu' indépendant de la raison, ne peut donc se développer sans elle. Avant l'âge de raison nous faisons le bien et le mal sans le connôitre; et il n'y a point de moralité dans nos actions.' [*Translation*: Reason alone teaches us to know good and evil. Conscience therefore, which makes us love the one and hate the other, although independent of reason, cannot develop without it. Before reaching the age of reason, we do good and evil without knowing it; and there is absolutely no morality in our actions.], and Locke, *Some Thoughts Concerning Education* (1693), pp. 1–2: 'I think I may say, that of all the Men we meet with, Nine Parts of Ten are what they are, Good or Evil, useful or not, by their Education (…) I imagine the Minds of Children as easily turned this or that way, as Water it self;'. [TB]

Extract 9

Wollstonecraft, **Rights of Men**

… It may be confidently asserted that no man chooses evil, because it is evil; he only mistakes it for happiness, the good he seeks. And the desire of rectifying these mistakes, is the noble ambition of an enlightened understanding, the impulse of feelings that Philosophy invigorates. To endeavour to make unhappy men resigned to their fate, is the tender endeavour of short-sighted benevolence, of transient yearnings of humanity; but to labour to increase human happiness by extirpating error, is a masculine god-like affection. This remark may be carried still further. Men who possess uncommon sensibility, whose quick emotions shew how closely the eye and heart are connected, soon forget the most forcible sensations. Not tarrying long enough in the brain to be subject to reflection, the next sensations, of course, obliterate them. Memory, however, treasures up these proofs of native goodness; and the being who is not spurred on to any virtuous act, still thinks itself of consequence, and boasts of its feelings. Why? Because the sight of distress, or an affecting narrative, made its blood flow with more velocity, and the heart, literally speaking, beat with sympathetic emotion. We ought to beware of confounding mechanical instinctive sensations with emotions that reason deepens, and justly terms the feelings of *humanity*. This word discriminates the active exertions of virtue from the vague declamation of sensibility.

Source: Mary Wollstonecraft, 'A Vindication of the Rights of Men', *Works*, vol.5, p.53.

Extract 10

Wollstonecraft, **Original Stories**, *Chapter I*, The Treatment of Animals   The Ant   The Bee Goodness   The Lark's Nest   The Asses

One fine morning in spring, some time after Mary and Caroline were settled in their new abode, Mrs Mason proposed a walk before breakfast, a custom she wished to teach imperceptibly, by rendering it amusing.

The sun had scarcely dispelled the dew that hung on every blade of grass, and filled the half-shut flowers; every prospect smiled, and the freshness of the air conveyed the most pleasing

sensations to Mrs Mason's mind; but the children were regardless of the surrounding beauties; and ran eagerly after some insects to destroy them. Mrs Mason silently observed their cruel sports, without appearing to do it; but stepping suddenly out of the foot-path into the long grass, her buckle was caught in it, and striving to disentangle herself, she wet her feet; which the children knew she wished to avoid, as she had been lately sick. This circumstance roused their attention; and they forgot their amusement to enquire *why* she had left the path; and Mary could hardly restrain a laugh, when she was informed that it was to avoid treading on some snails that were creeping across the narrow footway. Surely, said Mary, you do not think there is any harm in killing a snail, or any of those nasty creatures that crawl on the ground? I hate them, and should scream if one was to find its way from my clothes to my neck! With great gravity, Mrs Mason asked how she dared to kill any thing, unless it were to prevent its hurting her? Then, resuming a smiling face, she said, Your education has been neglected, my child; as we walk along attend to what I say, and make the best answers you can; and do you, Caroline, join in the conversation.

You have already heard that God created the world, and every inhabitant of it. He is then called the Father of all creatures; and all are made to be happy , whom a good and wise God has created. He made those snails you despise, and caterpillars, and spiders; and when he made them, did not leave them to perish, but placed them where the food that is most proper to nourish them is easily found. They do not live long, but He who is their Father, as well as your's, directs them to deposit their eggs on the plants that are fit to support their young, when they are not able to get food for themselves. – And when such a great and wise Being has taken care to provide every thing necessary for the meanest creature, would you dare kill it, merely because it appears to you ugly? Mary began to be attentive, and quickly followed Mrs Mason's example, who allowed a caterpillar and a spider to creep on her hand. You find them, she rejoined, very harmless; but a great number would destroy our vegetables and fruit; so birds are permitted to eat them, as we feed on animals; and in spring there are always more than at any other season of the year, to furnish food for the young broods. – Half-convinced, Mary said, But worms are of little consequence in the world. Yet, replied Mrs Mason, God cares for them, and gives them every thing that is necessary to render their existence comfortable. You are often troublesome – I am stronger than you – yet I do not kill you.

Observe those ants; they have a little habitation in yonder hillock; they carry food to it for their young, and sleep very snug in it during the cold weather. The bees also have comfortable towns, and lay up a store of honey to support them when the flowers die, and snow covers the ground: and this forecast is as much the gift of God, as any quality you possess.

Do you know the meaning of the word Goodness? I see you are unwilling to answer. I will tell you. It is, first, to avoid hurting any thing; and then, to contrive to give as much pleasure as you can. If some insects are to be destroyed, to preserve my garden from desolation, I have it done in the quickest way. The domestic animals that I keep, I provide the best food for, and never suffer them to be tormented; and this caution arises from two motives: I wish to make them happy; and, as I love my fellow-creatures still better than the brute creation, I would not allow those that I have any influence over to grow habitually thoughtless and cruel, till they were unable to relish the greatest pleasure life affords, – that of resembling God, by doing good.

A lark now began to sing, as it soared aloft. The children watched its motions, listening to the artless melody. They wondered what it was thinking of – of its young family, they soon concluded; for it flew over the hedge, and drawing near, they heard the young ones chirp. Very soon both the old birds took their flight together, to look for food to satisfy the craving of the almost fledged young. An idle boy, who had borrowed a gun, fired at them – they fell; and before he could take up the wounded pair, he perceived Mrs Mason; and expecting a very severe reprimand, ran away. She and the little girls drew near, and found that one was not much hurt, but that the other, the cock, had one leg broken, and both its wings shattered; and its little eyes seemed starting out of their sockets, it was in such exquisite pain. The children turned away their eyes. Look at it, said Mrs Mason; do you not see that it suffers as much, and more than you did when you had the small-pox, when you were so tenderly nursed. Take up the hen; I will bind her wing together; perhaps it may heal. As to the cock, though I hate to kill any thing, I must put him out of pain; to leave him in his present state would be cruel; and avoiding an unpleasant sensation myself, I should allow the poor bird to die by inches, and call this treatment tenderness, when it would be selfishness or weakness. Saying so, she put her foot on the bird's head, turning her own another way.

They walked on; when Caroline remarked, that the nestlings, deprived of their parents, would now perish; and the mother began to flutter in her hand as they drew near the hedge; though the poor creature could not fly, yet she tried to do it. The girls, with one voice, begged Mrs Mason to let them take the nest, and provide food in a cage, and see if the mother could not contrive to hop about to feed them. The nest and the old mother was instantly in Mary's handkerchief. A little opening was left to admit air; and Caroline peeped into it every moment to see how they looked. I give you leave, said Mrs Mason, to take those birds, because an accident has rendered them helpless; if that had not been the case, they should not have been confined.

They had scarcely reached the next field, when they met another boy with a nest in his hand, and on a tree near him saw the mother, who, forgetting her natural timidity, followed the spoiler; and her intelligible tones of anguish reached the ears of the children, whose hearts now first felt the emotions of humanity. Caroline called him, and taking sixpence out of her little purse, offered to give it to him for the nest, if he would shew her where he had taken it from. The boy consented, and away ran Caroline to replace it, – crying all the way, how delighted the old bird will be to find her brood again. The pleasure that the parent-bird would feel was talked of till they came to a large common, and heard some young asses, at the door of an hovel, making a most dreadful noise. Mrs Mason had ordered the old ones to be confined, lest the young should suck before the necessary quantity had been saved for some sick people in her neighbourhood. But after they had given the usual quantity of milk, the thoughtless boy had left them still in confinement, and the young in vain implored the food nature designed for their particular support. Open the hatch, said Mrs Mason, the mothers have still enough left to satisfy their young. It was opened, and they saw them suck.

Now, said she, we will return to breakfast; give me your hands, my little girls, you have done good this morning, you have acted like rational creatures. Look, what a fine morning it is. Insects, birds, and animals, are all enjoying this sweet day. Thank God for permitting you to see it, and for giving you an understanding which teaches you that you ought, by doing good, to imitate Him. Other creatures only think of supporting themselves; but man is allowed to ennoble his nature, by cultivating his mind and enlarging his heart. He feels disinterested love; every part of the creation affords an exercise for virtue, and virtue is ever the truest source of pleasure.

Chapter II, The Treatment of Animals   The Difference between them and Man

After breakfast, Mrs Mason gave the children *Mrs Trimmer's Fabulous Histories;*[40] and the subject still turned on animals, and the wanton cruelty of those who treated them improperly. The little girls were eager to express their detestation, and requested that in future they might be allowed to feed the chickens. Mrs Mason complied with their request; only one condition was annexed to the permission, that they did it regularly. When you wait for your food, you learn patience, she added, and you can mention your wants; but those helpless creatures cannot complain. The country people frequently say, – How can you treat a poor dumb beast ill; and a stress is very properly laid on the word dumb; for dumb they appear to those who do not observe their looks and gestures; but God, who takes care of every thing, understands their language; and so did Caroline this morning, when she ran with such eagerness to re-place the nest which the thoughtless boy had stolen, heedless of her mother's agonizing cries!

Mary interrupted her, to ask, if insects and animals were not inferior to men? Certainly, answered Mrs Mason; and men are inferior to angels; yet we have reason to believe, that those exalted beings delighted to do us good. You have heard in a book, which I seldom permit you to read, because you are not of an age to understand it, that angels, when they sang glory to God on high, wished for peace on earth, as a proof of the good-will they felt towards men. And all the glad tidings that have been sent to men, angels have proclaimed: indeed, the word angel signifies a messenger. In order to please God, and our happiness depends upon pleasing him, we must do good. What we call virtue, may be thus explained: – we exercise every benevolent affection to enjoy comfort here, and to fit ourselves to be angels…

Source: Mary Wollstonecraft, 'Original Stories from Real Life', *Works*, vol.4, pp.367–71.

Extract 11

Wollstonecraft, Rights of Woman, *from Chapter IV, Observation on the state of degradation to which woman is reduced by various causes*

… women, in general, as well as the rich of both sexes, have acquired all the follies and vices of civilization, and missed the useful fruit. It is not necessary for me always to premise, that I speak of the condition of the whole sex, leaving exceptions out of the question. Their senses are inflamed, and their understandings neglected, consequently they become the prey of their senses, delicately termed sensibility, and are blown about by every momentary gust of feeling. Civilized women are, therefore, so weakened by false refinements, that, respecting morals, their condition is much below what it would be were they left in a state nearer to nature. Ever restless and anxious, their over exercised sensibility not only renders them uncomfortable themselves, but troublesome, to use a soft phrase, to others. All their thoughts turn on things calculated to excite emotion; and feeling, when they should reason, their conduct is unstable, and their opinions are wavering – not the wavering produced by deliberation or progressive views, but by contradictory emotions. By fits and starts they are warm in many pursuits; yet this warmth, never concentrated into perseverance, soon exhausts itself; exhaled by its own heat, or meeting with some other fleeting passion, to which reason has never given any specific gravity, neutrality ensues. Miserable indeed, must be that being whose cultivation of mind has only tended to inflame its passions! A distinction should be made between inflaming and strengthening them. The passions

---

[40] Sarah Trimmer, *Fabulous Histories, designed for the Instruction of Children, respecting their treatment of animals* (1786). [TB]

thus pampered, whilst the judgement is left unformed, what can be expected to ensue? – Undoubtedly, a mixture of madness and folly!

This observation should not be confined to the *fair* sex; however, at present, I only mean to apply it to them.

Novels, music, poetry, and gallantry, all tend to make women the creatures of sensation, and their character is thus formed in the mould of folly during the time they are acquiring accomplishments, the only improvement they are excited, by their station in society, to acquire. This overstretched sensibility naturally relaxes the other powers of the mind, and prevents intellect from attaining that sovereignty which it ought to attain to render a rational creature useful to others, and content with its own station: for the exercise of the understanding, as life advances, is the only method pointed out by nature to calm the passions...

It would be an endless task to trace the variety of meannesses, cares, and sorrows, into which women are plunged by the prevailing opinion, that they were created rather to feel than reason, and that all the power they obtain must be obtained by their charms and weakness:

'Fine by defect, and amiably weak!'[41]

And, made by this amiable weakness entirely dependent, excepting what they gain by illicit sway, on man, not only for protection, but advice, is it surprising that, neglecting the duties that reason alone points out, and shrinking from trials calculated to strengthen their minds, they only exert themselves to give their defects a graceful covering, which may serve to heighten their charms in the eye of the voluptuary, though it sink them below the scale of moral excellence?

Fragile in every sense of the word, they are obliged to look up to man for every comfort. In the most trifling dangers they cling to their support, with parasitical tenacity, piteously demanding succour; and their *natural* protector extends his arm, or lifts up his voice, to guard the lovely trembler – from what? Perhaps the frown of an old cow, or the jump of a mouse; a

rat, would be a serious danger. In the name of reason, and even common sense, what can save such beings from contempt; even though they be soft and fair?

These fears, when not affected, may produce some pretty attitudes; but they shew a degree of imbecility which degrades a rational creature in a way women are not aware of – for love and esteem are very distinct things.

I am fully persuaded that we should hear of none of these infantine airs, if girls were allowed to take sufficient exercise, and not confined in close rooms till their muscles are relaxed, and their powers of digestion destroyed. To carry the remark still further, if fear in girls, instead of being cherished, perhaps, created, were treated in the same manner as cowardice in boys, we should quickly see women with more dignified aspects. It is true, they could not then with equal propriety be termed the sweet flowers that smile in the walk of man; but they would be more respectable members of society, and discharge the important duties of life by the light of their own reason. 'Educate women like men,' says Rousseau, 'and the more they resemble our sex the less power will they have over us.'[42] This is the very point I aim at. I do not wish them to have power over men; but over themselves.

In the same strain have I heard men argue against instructing the poor; for many are the forms that aristocracy assumes. 'Teach them to read and write,' say they, 'and you take them out of the station assigned them by nature.' An eloquent Frenchman has answered them, I will borrow his sentiments. But they know not, when they make man a brute, that they may expect every instant to see him transformed into a ferocious beast. Without knowledge there can be no morality!

Ignorance is a frail base for virtue! Yet, that it is the condition for which woman was organized, has been insisted upon by the writers who have most vehemently argued in favour of the superiority of man; a superiority not in degree, but essence; though, to soften the argument, they have laboured to prove, with

---

[41] Pope, *Of the Characters of Women*, 1. 44: 'Fine by defect, and delicately weak.' [TB]

[42] *Emilius*, IV, v, p.17: 'Educate them, if you think proper, like the men; we shall readily consent to it. The more they resemble our sex, the less power will they have over us; and when they once become like ourselves, we shall then be truly their masters.' [TB]

chivalrous generosity, that the sexes ought not to be compared; man was made to reason, woman to feel: and that together, flesh and spirit, they make the most perfect whole, by blending happily reason and sensibility into one character.

And what is sensibility? 'Quickness of sensation; quickness of perception; delicacy.' Thus is it defined by Dr Johnson;[43] and the definition gives me no other idea than of the most exquisitely polished instinct. I discern not a trace of the image of God in either sensation or matter. Refined seventy times seven,[44] they are still material; intellect dwells not there; nor will fire ever make lead gold!

I come round to my old argument; if woman be allowed to have an immortal soul, she must have, as the employment of life, an understanding to improve. And when, to render the present state more complete, though every thing proves it to be but a fraction of a mighty sum, she is incited by present gratification to forget her grand destination, nature is counteracted, or she was born only to procreate and rot. Or, granting brutes, of every description, a soul, though not a reasonable one, the exercise of instinct and sensibility may be the step, which they are to take, in this life, towards the attainment of reason in the next; so that through all eternity they will lag behind man, who, why we cannot tell, had the power given him of attaining reason in his first mode of existence...

Source: Mary Wollstonecraft, 'A Vindication of the Rights of Woman', *Works*, vol.5, pp.129–30, 131–2.

Extract 12

Wollstonecraft, Rights of Woman, *from Chapter VIII, Morality undermined by sexual notions of the importance of a good reputation*

The leading principles which run through all my disquisitions, would render it unnecessary to enlarge on this subject, if a constant attention to keep the varnish of the character fresh, and in good condition, were not often inculcated as the sum total of female duty; if rules to regulate the behaviour, and to preserve the reputation, did not too frequently supersede moral obligations. But, with respect to reputation, the attention is confined to a single virtue – chastity. If the honour of a woman, as it is absurdly called, be safe, she may neglect every social duty; nay, ruin her family by gaming and extravagance; yet still present a shameless front – for truly she is an honourable woman!

Mrs Macaulay has justly observed, that 'there is but one fault which a woman of honour may not commit with impunity.[45] She then justly and humanely adds – 'This has given rise to the trite and foolish observation, that the first fault against chastity in woman has a radical power to deprave the character. But no such frail beings come out of the hands of nature. The human mind is built of nobler materials than to be easily corrupted; and with all their disadvantages of situation and education, women seldom become entirely abandoned till they are thrown into a state of desperation, by the venomous rancour of their own sex.'[46]

But, in proportion as this regard for the reputation of chastity is prized by women, it is despised by men: and the two extremes are equally destructive to morality.

Men are certainly more under the influence of their appetites than women; and their appetites are more depraved by unbridled indulgence and the fastidious contrivances of satiety. Luxury has introduced a refinement in eating, that destroys the constitution; and, a degree of gluttony which is so beastly, that a perception of seemliness of behaviour must be worn out...

The depravity of the appetite which brings the sexes together, has had a still more fatal effect. Nature must ever be the standard of taste, the gauge of appetite – yet how grossly is nature

---

[43] Johnson, *Dictionary*: 'Quickness of sensation. Quickness of perception.' [TB]

[44] Matthew 18: 21–22. [TB]

[45] Catharine Macaulay, *Letters on Education* (1790), p.210; 'let her only take care that she is not caught in a love intrigue, and she may lie, she may deceive, she may defame, she may ruin her family with gaming, and the peace of twenty others with her coquetry, and yet preserve both her reputation and her peace.' [TB]

[46] Macaulay, *Letters on Education*, p.212. [TB]

insulted by the voluptuary. Leaving the refinements of love out of the question; nature, by making the gratification of an appetite, in this respect, as well as every other, a natural and imperious law to preserve the species, exalts the appetite, and mixes a little mind and affection with a sensual gust. The feelings of a parent mingling with an instinct merely animal, give it dignity; and the man and woman often meeting on account of the child, a mutual interest and affection is excited by the exercise of a common sympathy. Women then having necessarily some duty to fulfil, more noble than to adorn their persons, would not contentedly be the slaves of casual lust; which is now the situation of a very considerable number who are, literally speaking, standing dishes to which every glutton may have access.

I may be told that great as this enormity is, it only affects a devoted[47] part of the sex – devoted for the salvation of the rest. But, false as every assertion might easily be proved, that recommends the sanctioning a small evil to produce a greater good; the mischief does not stop here, for the moral character, and peace of mind, of the chaster part of the sex, is undermined by the conduct of the very women to whom they allow no refuge from guilt: whom they inexorably consign to the exercise of arts that lure their husbands from them, debauch their sons, and force them, let not modest women start, to assume, in some degree, the same character themselves. For I will venture to assert, that all the causes of female weakness, as well as depravity, which I have already enlarged on, branch out of one grand cause – want of chastity in men.

This intemperance, so prevalent, depraves the appetite to such a degree, that a wanton stimulus is necessary to rouse it; but the parental design of nature is forgotten, and the mere person, and that for a moment, alone engrosses the thoughts. So voluptuous, indeed, often grows the lustful prowler, that he refines on female softness. Something more soft than woman is then sought for; till, in Italy and Portugal, men attend the levees of equivocal beings, to sigh for more than female languor.[48]

To satisfy this genus of men, women are made systematically voluptuous, and though they may not all carry their libertinism to the same height, yet this heartless intercourse with the sex, which they allow themselves, depraves both sexes, because the taste of men is vitiated; and women, of all classes, naturally square their behaviour to gratify the taste by which they obtain pleasure and power. Women becoming, consequently, weaker, in mind and body, than they ought to be, were one of the grand ends of their being taken into the account, that of bearing and nursing children, have not sufficient strength to discharge the first duty of a mother; and sacrificing to lasciviousness the parental affection, that ennobles instinct, either destroy the embryo in the womb, or cast it off when born. Nature in every thing demands respect, and those who violate her laws seldom violate them with impunity. The weak enervated women who particularly catch the attention of libertines, are unfit to be mothers, though they may conceive; so that the rich sensualist, who has rioted among women, spreading depravity and misery, when he wishes to perpetuate his name, receives from his wife only an half-formed being that inherits both its father's and mother's weakness.

Contrasting the humanity of the present age with the barbarism of antiquity, great stress has been laid on the savage custom of exposing the children whom their parents could not maintain; whilst the man of sensibility, who thus, perhaps, complains, by his promiscuous amours produces a most destructive barrenness and contagious flagitiousness of manners. Surely nature never intended that women, by satisfying an appetite, should frustrate the very purpose for which it was implanted?

I have before observed, that men ought to maintain the women whom they have seduced; this would be one means of reforming female manners, and stopping an abuse that has an equally fatal effect on population and morals. Another, no less obvious, would be to turn the

---

[47] devoted: set aside for this particular purpose, i.e. prostitution. [eds]

[48] According to Ned Ward, *A Compleat and Humourous Account of all the Remarkable Clubs and Societies in the Cities of London and Westminster* (1749), homosexual levees occurred in London. [TB]

attention of woman to the real virtue of chastity; for to little respect has that woman a claim, on the score of modesty, though her reputation may be white as the driven snow, who smiles on the libertine whilst she spurns the victims of his lawless appetites and their own folly.

Besides, she has a taint of the same folly, pure as she esteems herself, when she studiously adorns her person only to be seen by men, to excite respectful sighs, and all the idle homage of what is called innocent gallantry. Did women really respect virtue for its own sake, they would not seek for a compensation in vanity, for the self-denial which they are obliged to practise to preserve their reputation, nor would they associate with men who set reputation at defiance.

The two sexes mutually corrupt and improve each other. This I believe to be an indisputable truth, extending it to every virtue. Chastity, modesty, public spirit, and all the noble train of virtues, on which social virtue and happiness are built, should be understood and cultivated by all mankind, or they will be cultivated to little effect. And, instead of furnishing the vicious or idle with a pretext for violating some sacred duty, by terming it a sexual one, it would be wiser to shew that nature has not made any difference, for that the unchaste man doubly defeats the purpose of nature, by rendering women barren, and destroying his own constitution, though he avoids the shame that pursues the crime in the other sex. These are the physical consequences, the moral are still more alarming; for virtue is only a nominal distinction when the duties of citizens, husbands, wives, fathers, mothers, and directors of families, become merely the selfish ties of convenience.

Why then do philosophers look for public spirit? Public spirit must be nurtured by private virtue, or it will resemble the factitious sentiment which makes women careful to preserve their reputation, and men their honour. A sentiment that often exists unsupported by virtue, unsupported by that sublime morality which makes the habitual breach of one duty a breach of the whole moral law.

Mary Wollstonecraft, 'A Vindication of the Rights of Woman', *Works*, vol.5, pp.206–7, 208–10.

Extract 13

Wollstonecraft, **Rights of Woman**, *from Chapter VIII, Modesty – comprehensively considered, and not as a sexual virtue*

… in defining modesty, it appears to me equally proper to discriminate that purity of mind, which is the effect of chastity, from a simplicity of character that leads us to form a just opinion of ourselves, equally distant from vanity or presumption, though by no means incompatible with a lofty consciousness of our own dignity. Modesty, in the latter signification of the term, is, that soberness of mind which teaches a man not to think more highly of himself than he ought to think, and should be distinguished from humility, because humility is a kind of self-abasement…

Thus, discriminating modesty from humility in one case, I do not mean to confound it with bashfulness in the other. Bashfulness, in fact, is so distinct from modesty, that the most bashful lass, or raw country lout, often become the most impudent; for their bashfulness being merely the instinctive timidity of ignorance, custom soon changes it into assurance.[49]

The shameless behaviour of the prostitutes, who infest the streets of this metropolis, raising alternate emotions of pity and disgust, may serve

---

[49]   'Such is the country-maiden's fright,
When first a red-coat is in sight;
Behind the door she hides her face;
Next time at distance eyes the lace;
She now can all his terrors stand,
Nor from his squeeze withdraws her hand.
She plays familiar in his arms,
And ev'ry soldier hath his charms;
From tent to tent she spreads her flame;
For custom conquers fear and shame.'
(Gay [W] [John Gay, *Fables* (1727, no. xiii 'The Tame Stag') [TB]

to illustrate this remark. They trample on virgin bashfulness with a sort of bravado, and glorying in their shame, become more audaciously lewd than men, however depraved, to whom this sexual quality has not been gratuitously granted, ever appear to be. But these poor ignorant wretches never had any modesty to lose, when they consigned themselves to infamy; for modesty is a virtue, not a quality. No, they were only bashful, shamefaced innocents; and losing their innocence, their shame-facedness was rudely brushed off; a virtue would have left some vestiges in the mind, had it been sacrificed to passion, to make us respect the grand ruin.

Purity of mind, or that genuine delicacy, which is the only virtuous support of chastity, is near akin to that refinement of humanity, which never resides in any but cultivated minds. It is something nobler than innocence, it is the delicacy of reflection, and not the coyness of ignorance. The reserve of reason, which, like habitual cleanliness, is seldom seen in any great degree, unless the soul is active, may easily be distinguished from rustic shyness or wanton skittishness; and, so far from being incompatible with knowledge, it is its fairest fruit. What a gross idea of modesty had the writer of the following remark! 'The lady who asked the question whether women may be instructed in the modern system of botany, consistently with female delicacy? – was accused of ridiculous prudery: nevertheless, if she had proposed the question to me, I should certainly have answered – They cannot.'[50] Thus is the fair book of knowledge to be shut with an everlasting seal! On reading similar passages I have reverentially lifted up my eyes and heart to Him who liveth for ever and ever, and said, O my Father, hast Thou by the very constitution of her nature forbid Thy child to seek Thee in the fair forms of truth? And, can her soul be sullied by the knowledge that awfully calls her to Thee?

I have then philosophically pursued these reflections till I inferred that those women who have most improved their reason must have the most modesty – though a dignified sedateness of deportment may have succeeded the playful, bewitching bashfulness of youth. [51]

And thus have I argued. To render chastity the virtue from which unsophisticated modesty will naturally flow, the attention should be called away from employments which only exercise the sensibility; and the heart made to beat time to humanity, rather than to throb with love. The woman who has dedicated a considerable portion of her time to pursuits purely intellectual, and whose affections have been exercised by humane plans of usefulness, must have more purity of mind, as a natural consequence, than the ignorant beings whose time and thoughts have been occupied by gay pleasures or schemes to conquer hearts.[52] The regulation of the behaviour is not modesty, though those who study rules of decorum are, in general, termed modest women. Make the heart clean, let it expand and feel for all that is human, instead of being narrowed by selfish passions; and let the mind frequently contemplate subjects that exercise the understanding, without heating the imagination, and artless modesty will give the finishing touches to the picture.

She who can discern the dawn of immortality, in the streaks that shoot athwart the misty night of ignorance, promising a clearer day, will respect, as a sacred temple, the body that enshrines such an improvable soul. True love, likewise, spreads this kind of mysterious sanctity round the beloved object, making the lover

---

[50] John Berkenhout, *A Volume of Letters to his Son at University* (1790), xxxii, p.307. [TB]

[51] Modesty, is the graceful calm virtue of maturity; bashfulness, the charm of vivacious youth. [W]

[52] I have conversed, as man with man, with medical men, on anatomical subjects; and compared the proportions of the human body with artists – yet such modesty did I meet with, that I was never reminded by word or look of my sex, of the absurd rules which make modesty a pharisaical cloak of weakness. And I am persuaded that in the pursuit of knowledge women would never be insulted by sensible men, and rarely by men of any description, if they did not by mock modesty remind them that they were women: actuated by the same spirit as the Portugueze ladies, who would think their charms insulted, if, when left alone with a man, he did not, at least, attempt to be grossly familiar with their persons. Men are not always men in the company of women, nor would women always remember that they are women, if they were allowed to acquire more understanding. [W]

modest when in her presence.[53] So reserved is affection that, receiving or returning personal endearments, it wishes, not only to shun the human eye, as a kind of profanation; but to diffuse an encircling cloudy obscurity to shut out even the saucy sparkling sunbeams...

As a sex, women are more chaste than men, and as modesty is the effect of chastity, they may deserve to have this virtue ascribed to them in rather an appropriated sense; yet, I must be allowed to add an hesitating if: – for I doubt whether chastity will produce modesty, though it may propriety of conduct, when it is merely a respect for the opinion of the world,[54] and when coquetry and the love-lorn tales of novelists employ the thought. Nay, from experience, and reason, I should be led to expect to meet with more modesty amongst men than women, simply because men exercise their understandings more than women.

But, with respect to propriety of behaviour, excepting one class of females, women have evidently the advantage. What can be more disgusting than that impudent dross of gallantry thought so manly, which makes many men stare insultingly at every female they meet? Can it be termed respect for the sex? No, this loose behaviour shews such habitual depravity, such weakness of mind, that it is vain to expect much public or private virtue, till both men and women grow more modest – till men, curbing a sensual fondness for the sex, or an affection of manly assurance, more properly speaking, impudence, treat each other with respect – unless appetite or passion give the tone, peculiar to it, to their behaviour. I mean even personal respect – the modest respect of humanity, and fellow-feeling – not the libidinous mockery of gallantry, nor the insolent condescension of protectorship.

To carry the observation still further, modesty must heartily disclaim, and refuse to dwell with that debauchery of mind, which leads a man coolly to bring forward, without a blush, indecent allusions, or obscene witticisms, in the presence of a fellow creature; women are now out of the question, for then it is brutality. Respect for man, as man, is the foundation of every noble sentiment. How much more modest is the libertine who obeys the call of appetite or fancy, than the lewd joker who sets the table in a roar!

This is one of the many instances in which the sexual distinction respecting modesty has proved fatal to virtue and happiness...

In the same strain runs Rousseau's and Dr Gregory's advice respecting modesty, strangely miscalled! for they both desire a wife to leave it in doubt whether sensibility or weakness[55] led her to her husband's arms. The woman is immodest who can let the shadow of such a doubt remain in her husband's mind a moment.

But to state the subject in a different light. – The want of modesty, which I principally deplore as subversive of morality, arises from the state of warfare so strenuously supported by voluptuous men as the very essence of modesty, though, in fact, its bane; because it is a refinement on lust, that men fall into who have not sufficient virtue to relish the innocent pleasures of love. A man of delicacy carries his notions of modesty still further, for neither weakness nor sensibility will gratify him – he looks for affection.

Again; men boast of their triumphs over women, what do they boast of? Truly the creature of sensibility was surprised by her sensibility into folly – into vice;[56] and the dreadful reckoning falls heavily on her own weak head, when reason wakes...

But, if the sexes be really to live in a state of warfare, if nature have pointed it out, let them act nobly, or let pride whisper to them, that the victory is mean when they merely vanquish sensibility. The real conquest is that over affection not

---

[53] Male or female; for the world contains many modest men. [W]

[54] The immodest behaviour of many married women, who are nevertheless faithful to their husbands' beds, will illustrate this remark. [W]

[55] sensibility or weakness: sexual desire or inability to resist superior physical strength (i.e. submission to rape). Cf. the Présidente's yielding to Valmont in *Liaisons Dangereuses*. [eds]

[56] The poor moth fluttering round a candle, burns its wings. [W]

taken by surprise – when, like Heloisa, a woman gives up all the world, deliberately, for love. I do not now consider the wisdom or virtue of such a sacrifice, I only contend that it was a sacrifice to affection, and not merely to sensibility, though she had her share. – And I must be allowed to call her a modest woman, before I dismiss this part of the subject, by saying, that till men are more chaste women will be immodest. Where, indeed, could modest women find husbands from whom they would not continually turn with disgust? Modesty must be equally cultivated by both sexes, or it will ever remain a sickly hot-house plant, whilst the affectation of it, the fig leaf borrowed by wantonness, may give a zest to voluptuous enjoyments.

Men will probably still insist that woman ought to have more modesty than man; but it is not dispassionate reasoners who will most earnestly oppose my opinion. No, they are the men of fancy, the favourites of the sex, who outwardly respect and inwardly despise the weak creatures whom they thus sport with. They cannot submit to resign the highest sensual gratification, nor even to relish the epicurism of virtue – self-denial.

To take another view of the subject, confining my remarks to women.

The ridiculous falsities[57] which are told to children, from mistaken notions of modesty, tend very early to inflame their imaginations and set their little minds to work, respecting subjects, which nature never intended they should think of till the body arrived at some degree of maturity; then the passions naturally begin to take place of the senses, as instruments to unfold the understanding, and form the moral character.

In nurseries, and boarding-schools, I fear, girls are first spoiled; particularly in the latter. A number of girls sleep in the same room, and wash together. And, though I should be sorry to contaminate an innocent creature's mind by instilling false delicacy, or those indecent prudish notions, which early cautions respecting the other sex naturally engender, I should be very anxious to prevent their acquiring nasty, or immodest habits; and as many girls have learned very nasty tricks, from ignorant servants, the mixing them thus indiscriminately together, is very improper.

To say the truth women are, in general, too familiar with each other, which leads to that gross degree of familiarity that so frequently renders the marriage state unhappy. Why in the name of decency are sisters, female intimates, or ladies and their waiting-women, to be so grossly familiar as to forget the respect which one human creature owes to another? That squeamish delicacy which shrinks from the most disgusting offices when affection[58] or humanity leads us to watch at a sick pillow, is despicable. But, why women in health should be more familiar with each other than men are, when they boast of their superior delicacy, is a solecism in manners which I could never solve.

In order to preserve health and beauty, I should earnestly recommend frequent ablutions, to dignify my advice that it may not offend the fastidious ear; and, by example, girls ought to be taught to wash and dress alone, without any distinction of rank; and if custom should make them require some little assistance, let them not require it till that part of the business is over which ought never to be done before a fellow-creature; because it is an insult to the majesty of

---

[57] Children very early see cats with their kittens, birds with their young ones, etc. Why then are they not to be told that their mothers carry and nourish them in the same way? As there would then be no appearance of mystery they would never think of the subject more. Truth may always be told to children if it be told gravely; but it is the immodesty of affected modesty, that does all the mischief; and this smoke heats the imagination by vainly endeavouring to obscure certain objects. If, indeed, children could be kept entirely from improper company, we should never allude to any such subjects; but as this is impossible, it is best to tell them the truth, especially as such information, not interesting them, will make no impression on their imagination. [W]

[58] Affection would rather make one choose to perform these offices, to spare the delicacy of a friend, by still keeping a veil over them, for the personal helplessness, produced by sickness, is of an humbling nature. [W]

human nature. Not on the score of modesty, but decency; for the care which some modest women take, making at the same time a display of that care, not to let their legs be seen, is as childish as immodest.[59] ...

After the foregoing remarks, it is almost superfluous to add, that I consider all those feminine airs of maturity, which succeed bashfulness, to which truth is sacrificed, to secure the heart of a husband, or rather to force him to be still a lover when nature would, had she not been interrupted in her operations, have made love give place to friendship, as immodest. The tenderness which a man will feel for the mother of his children is an excellent substitute for the ardour of unsatisfied passion; but to prolong that ardour it is indelicate, not to say immodest, for women to feign an unnatural coldness of constitution. Women as well as men ought to have the common appetites and passions of their nature, they are only brutal when unchecked by reason: but the obligation to check them is the duty of mankind, not a sexual duty.[60]

Nature, in these respects, may safely be left to herself; let women only acquire knowledge and humanity, and love will teach them modesty.[61]

There is no need of falsehoods, disgusting as futile, for studied rules of behaviour only impose on shallow observers; a man of sense soon sees through, and despises the affectation...

Source: Mary Wollstonecraft, 'A Vindication of the Rights of Woman', *Works*, vol.5, pp.191, 192–7, 199–200.

---

[59] I remember to have met with a sentence, in a book of education, that made me smile. 'It would be needless to caution you against putting your hand, by chance, under your neckhandkerchief; for a modest woman never did so!' [W]

[60] Not a sexual duty: not a duty belonging to only one of the sexes. [eds]

[61] The behaviour of many newly married women has often disgusted me. They seem anxious never to let their husbands forget the privilege of marriage; and to find no pleasure in his society, unless he is acting the lover. Short, indeed, must be the reign of love, when the flame is thus constantly blown up, without its receiving any solid jewel! [W]

Denis Diderot
Salon of 1765

Prepared for the Course Team by John Greenwood and Linda Walsh

Contents

Denis Diderot
Salon of 1765

Denis Diderot (1713–84), one of the most prolific of the French philosophes, was the director and general editor of the Encyclopédie and contributed numerous articles to it. He was also a novelist and playwright and, when well into his forties, turned his talents to art criticism. In 1759 he was invited by Friedrich-Melchoir Grimm (1723–1807) to review the current Paris Salon exhibition for La Correspondance Littéraire, a private fortnightly journal with a small list of subscribers which included the Empress Catherine of Russia, the Queen of Sweden, the Grand-Duke of Tuscany and several German Princes. The journal provided the latest news of Parisian life and culture, and its private status meant that it escaped French royal censorship and the laws of libel. Diderot made full use of this freedom.

He reviewed each of the biennial Salon exhibitions from 1759 to 1771, and also those of 1775 and 1781. Although these Salons were not published in France until 1795, Diderot had extra copies made for his friends and thus ensured contemporary awareness of his writings.

When Diderot wrote the Salon of 1765 he was in the grip of the cult of sensibility which swept through French society, art and literature. Characteristic of this cult was the belief that ethical and aesthetic values were best detected and judged by the emotions. Many went further and felt that sensibility (a capacity for keenly felt and finely tuned emotional responses) was an essential prerequisite of personal virtue. In practice this meant that Diderot often blurred the distinction between art and morality. In the following appraisals of the art of Van Loo, Chardin, Vernet, Boucher, Greuze and others,

he relies on his own sensibility as a means of testing not only the intensity but also the ethical value of the emotions aroused by their paintings. He was not always consistent, however, in the criteria he adopted.

The following extracts represent approximately one-fifth of the complete Salon of 1765. Due to restrictions of space, entries on some artists are completely omitted and others are substantially edited. Page references at the head of an entry on an individual artist indicate the size of the unedited entry in the original text, while those at the foot of each entry indicate the specific pages from which extracts are drawn. In all, 42 artists exhibited 229 paintings that year. Sculptures and engravings also constituted an important part of the exhibition.

For information on the identification and location of the paintings discussed by Diderot we are indebted to the edition of the Salon de 1765 in the Oeuvres complètes de Diderot, Hermann, Paris, 1984 (vol. XIV, edited by E.M. Bukdahl, A. Lorenceau and G. May) and to E.M. Bukdahl in Diderot critique d'art, Rosenkilde et Bagger, Copenhagen, 1980.

Biographical details on the artists discussed by Diderot appear in alphabetical order in Appendix I. The relevant illustrations, where available, are in the Illustration Book. Sometimes a related sketch, engraving or drawing is available, where the actual painting discussed by Diderot has been lost.

All footnotes contained with these extracts are by the author of the corresponding study; references to plates are to the Illustration Book for this course.

Salon of 1765

To my friend Mr Grimm

   Non fumum ex fulgore, sed ex fumo dare lucem cogitat

   [His thinking does not result in smoke after the flashing fire, but in light emerging from the smoke]

   If I have any considered opinions on painting and sculpture, it is to you, my friend, that I owe them. At the Salon I would have followed the idle throng; like them I would have given a distracted superficial glance at the productions of our artists; with one word, I would have thrown a precious morsel into the fire or praised to the skies a mediocre work, approving or disdaining without considering the motives for my infatuation or disdain. It is the task which you have set

me which made me fix my eyes on the canvas, made me walk round the marble statue. I allowed time for an impression to come to me, to enter me. I opened my soul to their effects. I allowed myself to be penetrated by them. I weighed the verdict of the old man and the thought of the child, the judgement of the man of letters, the word of the man of the world and the talk of the ordinary people; and if I happen to wound the artist, it is often with the weapon he has sharpened himself. I questioned him and understood what was meant by drawing a fine line and being true to nature. I gained some conception of the magic of light and shade. I became acquainted with colour. I acquired a feeling for flesh and blood. When alone, I meditated on what I had seen and heard; and those terms such as art, unity, variety, contrast, symmetry, organisation, composition, characters, expression, so easy to say yet so vague in my mind, became circumscribed and fixed.

Oh my friend, those arts which have as their object the imitation of nature; arts which use words, such as eloquence and poetry; or sounds such as music; or colours and paint brush such as painting; or a chalk such as drawing; or chisel and clay such as sculpture; burin, stone and metals such as engraving; engraving wheel such as engraving semi-precious stones; punches, caulking chisel and graver, such as embossing; how long, painful and difficult they are.

Chardin appeared to doubt that there was a longer or more difficult education than that of a painter, not excepting that of the doctor, lawyer or Doctor of the Sorbonne.[1] 'At the age of seven or eight' he said, 'a chalk-holder is placed in our hand. We start to copy from examples: eyes, mouths, noses, ears then feet and hands. Our back has been bent over our portfolio for a long time, when we are put in front of a Hercules or a torso; and you would not believe the amounts of tears which have been shed over this satyr, this gladiator, this Venus de Medicis, this Antinous.[2] You can be sure that these masterpieces of the Greek artists would no longer arouse the jealousy of the teachers if they had been surrendered to the resentment of the pupils.[3] After passing arid days and lamp-lit nights in front of immobile, inanimate objects, we are presented with a living model and suddenly the work of all the preceding years seems to be reduced to nothing; we seem more embarrassed than the first time we took chalk in hand. We have to teach our eye to look at nature and how many people have never and will never see it! Our life was tormented by it. We were kept five to six years in front of the model and then we were abandoned to our genius, if we had any.

Talent is not decided in a single moment. A man does not have the frankness to admit his ineptitude after the first attempt. How many tries, some successful some unsuccessful! Precious years pass before that day of loathing, of weariness, of tedium comes. The pupil is nineteen to twenty years of age when the palette falls from his hands and he now has no status, no means and no morals; for it cannot be that a man should be continually looking upon nature in the nude and yet remain young and wise. What is he to do, what is he to become? He has to throw himself into one of those inferior conditions, whose door is open wide to misery, or die of hunger. He takes the first option; and with the exception of twenty or so who come here every two years to expose their work to the common herd, the others, unknown and perhaps less unfortunate, are wearing a breastplate on their chests in a drill-hall or sloping arms in a regiment or treading the boards in a theatre. That, I'm telling you, is the story of Belcourt, LeKain and Brisart who became bad actors in despair at being only mediocre artists.'

I shall describe the pictures to you and my description will be such that with a little imagination and taste you will visualise them in space and place the objects almost as we saw them on the canvas; and so that a sober assessment can be made of my censure or my praise, I shall finish my account of the exhibition with some thoughts on painting, sculpture, engraving and architecture.[4] Read me as you would an ancient author, with whom you overlook a pedestrian page for the sake of one good line.

It is true that my head is tired. The burden which I have been carrying for twenty years[5] has weighed me down so that I despair of ever standing upright. But however, remember my epigraph: *non fumum ex fulgore, sed ex fumo dare lucem.* Let me smoke for a moment and then we shall see.

---

[1] Faculty of Theology of the University of Paris.

[2] See *Illustration Book*, Pls 136, 137, 138.

[3] The meaning of the text is unclear here. The suggestion seems to be that the pupils would deface the masterpieces which would then no longer be so protectively regarded by their teachers.

[4] He later developed such thoughts in his *Essay on Painting*.

[5] i.e. work on the *Encyclopédie*.

The late Carle Van Loo (Seznec and Adhémar pp.60–75)

The Graces (Pl. 188)

A painting seven feet six inches high and six feet two inches wide.

Because these figures are touching, the artist has thought that they were adequately grouped. The eldest of the three sisters occupies the centre; her right hand is placed on the small of the back of the one to the left and her left arm is linked with the right arm of the one to the right. She is shown in a frontal view. The setting, if there is one, is in the country. We can see a cloud, coming down from the sky, passing behind the figures and spreading along the ground. The Grace to the left, whose face and back are two-thirds visible, has placed her left arm on the shoulder of the one in the middle and is holding a flask in her right hand. This one is the youngest. The second one, whose back is shown two thirds visible and her head in profile, has a rose in her left hand; as for the eldest, she has been given a sprig of myrtle[6] which she holds in her right hand. The site is strewn with a few flowers.

It is difficult to imagine a more lifeless composition, with the Graces more insipid, less buoyant, less pleasing. They have neither life, nor action, nor character. What are they doing there? I'd die if they really knew. They're exposing themselves. The poet[7] did not see them thus. It was Spring-time. The moon was shining brightly. New green growth covered the mountains. Streams murmured. Their silvery, sparkling waters could be heard and seen. The orb of the night rippled shimmering on their surface. The place was isolated and tranquil. They sang and danced on the soft grass of the prairie in the vicinity of a forest. I can see them and hear them. How sweet is their singing, how beautiful they are, how firm is their flesh! The tender light of the moon enhances still further the whiteness of their skin. How graceful and light are their movements! Old Pan is playing the flute. The young fauns at his side have pricked up their pointed ears. Their glowing eyes search out the most secret charms of the young dancers. What they see does not stop them regretting what is hidden from them by the variety of dance movements. The wood nymphs have drawn near. The water nymphs have looked out from amongst the reeds. Soon they will join in the games of the lovable sisters.

But let us return to Van Loo's Graces, who in no way measure up to those I leave. The one in the middle is stiff. You would say that she has been posed by Marcel.[8] Her head is too heavy. She can scarcely support it. And those little scraps of material which have been stuck round the buttocks of one and the top of the other's thighs, what makes them stay there? Only the bad taste of the artist and the bad manners of the people. They do not know that it's not a nude woman but a half-dressed women who is indecent. An indecently dressed woman could have a hat on her head, stockings on her legs and slippers on her feet. This calls to mind, the way in which Madam Hocquet made modest Venus into the least virtuous of creatures. One day she imagined that the goddess's lower hand was not hiding her private parts very well; so she had a plaster drape placed between that hand and the corresponding part of the statue, which immediately made her look like a woman who was towelling herself dry. Do you think, my friend, that Apelles[9] would have thought to put draperies even so big as a hand on any part of the body of the three Graces? Oh dear! from the time they came nude from the head of the old poet[10] to the time of Apelles, if any painter has seen them I swear to you that it isn't Van Loo.

---

[6] The rose and the myrtle were attributes of Venus and of the three Graces. The latter symbolized everlasting love while the former represented beauty and fragrance; the pricking of its thorns the wounds of love.

[7] See Horace, *Odes*, 1, iv.

[8] A fashionable dancing master.

[9] Greek painter of the fourth century BC

[10] Probably Hesiod, a Greek poet living *c.*700 BC. Nude figures of the Graces were popular with sculptors and painters from Hellenistic times: their nudity indicated their freedom from deceit. They appeared clothed in medieval art but naked again in much Renaissance art where they were symbolically associated with giving and receiving thanks; pleasure, chastity and pagan beauty.

The Graces of Van Loo are long and thin, especially as regards the upper part of the body. The cloud, which comes down from the right and spreads around their feet, doesn't make sense. For sweet, pliable natures like these, the touch is too firm, too heavy; and then all around is this lovely imaginary greenness which darkens and befogs them. There is no effect, no interest. A routine painting and drawing performance. A very inferior composition to that which he exhibited at the previous Salon and which he has discarded. Undoubtedly, since the Graces are sisters, there should be a family likeness; but do they have to have the same head?

But, having said all that, the worst of these three figures is better than the simpering affectations and red backsides of Boucher. It is at least flesh, even beautiful flesh, with a severe character which is yet less displeasing than dissolute habits and bad morals. If there is a manner here, it's a grand manner.

Susanna and the old men (Pl. 189)[11]

A picture seven feet six inches high and six feet two inches wide.

Susanna is seated in the centre of the canvas; she has just got out of her bath. Positioned between two old men, she is leaning towards the one on the left while exposing to the eyes of the one on the right her beautiful arm and shoulders, her back, one of her thighs and all of her head; that is, three quarters of her charms. Her head is thrown back. Her eyes, turned toward heaven, are appealing for help; her left arm is clutching the linen garments which cover the top of her thighs; her right hand is fending off and rebuffing the left arm of the old man who is on that side. What a beautiful figure! It has a fine position; her trouble and sadness are strongly expressed; she is drawn with great taste; the flesh tones are true, a beautiful colour and true to nature all over her neck, throat and knees. Her legs, her thighs, all her undulating limbs, could not be better placed. There is grace without harming the nobility; variety without any affected contrast. That part of the figure which is in half-tone has been executed very well. The white linen, spread along the thighs, is reflected admirably in the flesh; it's a mass of clarity, which does not destroy the effect of the flesh; a

difficult magic which demonstrates both the cleverness of the master and the vigour of his colouring.

The old man to the left is seen in profile. His left leg is bent and his right knee seems to be pressing against the lower part of Susanna's thigh. His left hand is tugging at the linen which covers her thighs and his right hand is inviting Susanna to yield. This old chap has the appearance of Henry IV, which type of head is a good choice, but more movement, action, desire, expression should have been added. It's a cold, heavy figure, offering nothing but a big, stiff garment, unvarying, without any folds, and under which nothing stands out. It's a sack with a head and two arms sticking out. Ample draperies were doubtless necessary; but not like these. The other old man is standing and is seen almost full face. He has pulled aside with his left hand all the veils which on his side were screening Susanna from him. He is still holding the veils he has pulled aside. His right hand and arm, extended in front of the woman, are making a threatening gesture, which also applies to his facial expression. This chap is colder still than the other one. If you covered up the rest of the canvas you would see in this figure no more than a Pharisee propounding some poser to Jesus Christ.

More warmth, more violence, more rage in the old men would have given an extraordinary interest to this innocent, beautiful woman, surrendered to the mercy of two old scoundrels. She herself would have had more terror resulting from this in her expression; for one thing involves the other. Passions on the canvas harmonise or clash like colours. There is in the whole a harmony of feelings as of tones. If the old men had been more urgent, the painter would have felt that the woman ought to be more frightened and soon her looks would have been making a very different appeal to heaven.

To the right we see a greyish stone structure. It is apparently a reservoir, a bathing place. In the foreground there is a channel from which a mean little trickle of water, in bad taste, squirts towards the right and breaks the silence. If the old men had really been in a frightful rage with Susanna showing a similar terror, I rather think

---

[11] This plate shows a counter proof engraving of a drawing based on this painting. 'Left' and 'right' orientations in the engraving do not therefore always agree with Diderot's account.

that the roar, the noise of a mass of water surging forward would have been a very creditable accessory.

But with these faults, this composition by Van Loo is still something beautiful. De Troye[12] has painted the same subject. There is scarcely a single painter whose imagination has not been struck with the subject[13] and whose paint brush it has not occupied; and I wager that Van Loo's picture can hold its own with anything that's been done. It is claimed that his Susanna has been academized; might it be that her action could indeed be somewhat affected, that her movements could be a little too measured for a violent situation? Or could it rather be that it sometimes happens that the model has been so well posed that this studio posture can be successfully transposed onto the canvas although it can be recognised as such? If there were a more violent action on the part of the old men, there could also be a more natural and truer action from Susanna. But I'm happy with her as she is. And if I were unfortunate enough to live in a palace, this piece might well pass from the artist's studio into my gallery.

Sketches for the Chapel of Saint Gregory, at the Invalides[14]

The sixth, (Pl. 190) in my opinion, is the finest. But there are only two figures; the saint who is dictating his homilies, and his secretary who is writing them down. The saint is seated, his elbow leaning on the table. He is dressed in surplice and rochet, a biretta[15] on his head. What a fine head! You don't know whether to feast your eyes on it or on the pose of the secretary, so simple, so natural, so true. You go from one to the other of these figures, always with the same pleasure. The nature, the truth, the solitude, the silence of this study, the soft and tender light which is shed upon it in the way which is most sympathetic to the scene, to the action, to the personages, all these things, my friend, are what makes this composition sublime, and something Boucher could never have conceived. This sketch is surprising. But tell me where this brute Van Loo found it; because he was a brute. He didn't know how to think, speak, write or read. Distrust those people who have their pockets full of good cheer and scatter it about at every opportunity. They haven't got the demon. They are not sad, sombre, melancholy and dumb. They are never awkward or stupid. The chaffinch, the lark, the linnet, the canary chatter and chirrup throughout the livelong day. When the sun goes down, they tuck their head under their wing, and off they go to sleep. It's then that the genius takes his lamp and lights it, and then that the solitary bird, wild and untameable, brown and sad of plumage, opens his throat and begins to sing making the woodland resound and melodiously breaking the silence and darkness of the night. (Seznec and Adhémar pp.62–6; 70–1)

Boucher (Seznec and Adhémar pp.75–82)

I do not know what to say about this man. The degradation of taste, of colour, of composition, of characters, of expression, of line has followed step by step the corruption of morals. What do you want this artist to throw on the canvas? What there is in his imagination. And what can there be in the imagination of a man who spends his life with the lowest type of prostitute? … I challenge you to find in any stretch of countryside one blade of grass as in his landscapes. And then there is a confusion of objects piled up one on top of the other, so out of place, so disparate, that it's less the picture of a man of sense than the dream of a fool …

---

[12] French painter, 1679–1752.

[13] The story, from the Old Testament Apocrypha, tells how Susanna, the wife of a prosperous Jew in Babylon during the Exile, was desired by two Elders of the community who plotted to seduce her as she bathed in the garden. Susanna spurned their attempts at blackmail and seduction. In Hebrew the name Susanna means a lily, the symbol of purity.

[14] Military hospital and church in Paris.

[15] Rochet: surplice-like vestment used chiefly by bishops and abbots.
    Biretta: square cap worn by Roman Catholic clerics.

I dare say that this man does not really know what grace is; I dare say that he has never known truth; I dare say that the ideas of delicacy, decency, innocence, simplicity have become almost completely unknown to him; I dare say that he has not for one instant seen nature, at least not that which is made to engage my soul, or yours, or that of a well-born child, or that of a sensitive woman; I dare say that he is devoid of taste. From an infinity of proofs of this that I could give, one will suffice; amongst the multitude of masculine and feminine forms that he has painted, I challenge anyone to find four suitable for bas-relief, still less for a statue. There are too many simpering airs and contrived expressions, too much mannerism and affectation for a severe art. It's useless him showing me nudes, I always see them wearing rouge, beauty spots, pompons and all the fripperies of their toilet …

Those fine, subtle analogies which call forth objects onto the canvas and bind them there by imperceptible threads, I swear he doesn't know what they are. All his compositions are an insupportable hubbub to the eyes. He's the deadliest enemy of silence that I know, he is so for the prettiest puppets in the world; he will come down to being an illuminator. Oh well!, my friend, at the very moment when Boucher ceases to be an artist he is nominated first painter to the king … When he paints children, he groups them well; but he always leaves them frolicking about on some clouds. In all this numerous family you will not find one taking part in some real-life activity, learning his lesson, reading, writing, picking oakum. They are all the 'storybook', idealised little bastards of Bacchus and Silenus.[16] Sculpture would find enough use for that kind of child on the outside of an antique vase. They are fat, chubby, plump. We'll see what happens when a skilled artist carves such forms into marble. In a word, take all the pictures of this man and you will scarcely find one to which you could not say as Fontenelle[17] said to the sonata: Sonata, what do you want from me? Picture, what do you want from me? Was there not a time when he was consumed with a desire to paint virgins? Very well, what were these virgins? Pretty little gossips. And his angels? Little licentious satyrs. And then there is in his landscapes such a greyness of colour and uniformity of tone that you could take his canvas, from a distance of two feet, to be a stretch of turf or a square bed of parsley. But he isn't a fool. He's a false good painter, as you can be a false fine wit. He does not have the true idea of art; he has only *concetti*.[18]

Jupiter transformed into Diana in order to surprise Callisto (Pl. 177 and Col. Pl. 24)[19]

An oval picture about two feet high and one and a half feet wide

In the centre we see Jupiter metamorphosed; he is in profile; he is leaning over Callisto's knees; with one hand he is trying to gently push aside her underclothes; that's the right hand. His left hand is fondling her chin. Now there's two hands well occupied. Callisto is painted full-face. She's feebly fending off the hand which is trying to disrobe her. Below this figure the painter has spread some drapery and a quiver. There are trees in the background. To the left a group of children are playing in mid-air; above this group is the eagle of Jupiter.

But do people in mythology have hands different from ours? Ah! La-Grenée,[20] what do you want me to think of this, when I see you side by side and I am struck by your bold colour, the beauty of your flesh tints and your fidelity to nature, which are visible throughout your composition. Feet, hands, arms, shoulders, throat,

---

[16] A Greek god and satyr respectively, associated with wine and drunkenness.

[17] French writer, 1657–1757.

[18] i.e. far-fetched, over-elaborated metaphors and similes.

[19] The painting discussed by Diderot is in a private collection in New York. Pl. 177 shows a black and white reproduction of this. A later version (Col. Pl. 24) is also included in your Illustration Book. The latter was intended as a tapestry design and shows signs of being partly the work of studio assistants. See E.M. Bukdahl, *Diderot, critique d'art*, Rosenkilde et Bagger, Copenhagen, 1980, p.260, n.18 and the Wallace Collection Catalogue of Pictures and Drawings, 1968, pp.36–7.

[20] Eighteenth-century artist (1724–1805) and co-exhibitor at the Salon of 1765.

neck, just, if you want, as you have kissed some-times, La-Grenée will let you have them. Not Boucher; for the past fifty years, my friend, there has scarcely been one painter who bases his work on a model; they just do the routine thing, and Boucher is one of them; these are his old fig-ures, turned and turned again. Hasn't he shown us a hundred times already both this Callisto and this Jupiter, and this tiger skin with which he is covered?

Angélique and Médor (Pl. 178)

Same form and size as the preceding picture

The two principal figures are placed on the right as you look at the picture. Angélique is sit-ting nonchalantly on the ground, with her back to the viewer, with the exception of a small part of her face which can just be glimpsed, and which gives her a bad-tempered appearance. On the same side but more in the background, Médor is standing, facing the viewer, his body bent and his hand stretching out towards the trunk of a tree, on which he is apparently writing the two lines of Quinault[21] , those two lines which Lulli[22] has set to music so well and which give rise to a display of all Roland's generosity of soul to make me weep when others laugh:

Angélique's heart is engaged;
      Médor has conquered it

Cupids are busy garlanding the tree. Médor is half covered with a tiger skin and his left hand is holding a hunting spear. Under Angélique imagine some drapery and a cushion; a cushion, my friend, which fits there as well as would the carpet of La Fontaine's[23] Nicaise;[24] there is also a quiver and some flowers. One fat Cupid is lying on his back on the ground and two others are playing in mid-air around the tree, confident of Médor's happiness; and then to the left there is landscape and trees.

The painter has been pleased to call this *Angélique and Médor*, but it could be whatever I choose. I defy anyone to show me what it is that characterises this scene and identifies the indi-viduals. Oh! dammit, he had only to go where the poet has led. How much more beautiful, noble, more picturesque, better chosen is the place of his adventure; a rustic cavern, a secluded spot, the haunt of shade and silence; there far from all annoyances, you can make a lover happy, not in open countryside, in the open air, on a cushion. Médor is engraving his own name and Angélique's on a mossy rock. There's no sense to it. A little composition for a boudoir; and then no feet, no hands, no truth, no colour and always parsley on the trees. Just look at Médor, especially his legs, or maybe don't look at him; those legs such as a small boy would paint, who has neither taste nor training. Angé-lique is a little tripe-seller. Oh! what a nasty word! Agreed; but that's what he's painted: a round, soft line with flabby flesh. This man only takes up the paint brush to show me breasts and buttocks. I don't mind seeing them; but I don't want to be shown them.

Four Pastorals

Two are oval, and the four are about fifteen inches high and thirteen inches wide

I am fair, I am good, I like nothing better than to praise. These four pieces form a little charming poem. Let us say that for once in his life the painter had a moment of rationality. A shepherd ties a letter to the neck of a pigeon: the pigeon flies off; a shepherdess receives the letter; she reads it to one of her friends; he is proposing a rendez-vous; she goes there and so does the shepherd.

1 (Pl. 179) The shepherd is sitting on a rocky outcrop to the left of the viewer; he has the pigeon on his knees; he is attaching the letter; his

---

[21] French poet, 1635–88, who collaborated with Lulli on *Roland and Armida*, performed in 1685.

[22] French composer and violinist, 1632–87.

[23] French seventeenth-century poet, writer of fables and short stories.

[24] Nicaise, in classical French, meant 'simpleton'. In La Fontaine's tale, this name was given to a naïve apprentice cloth merchant abandoned by his offended lover after he had suggested that they should delay their lovemaking in a wooded garden until he had brought a carpet to spread on the damp ground. See *Oeuvres de la Fontaine*, edited by H. Regnier, Hachette, Paris, 1889, tome 5e, pp.207–26.

crook and his dog behind him: he has at his feet a basket of flowers which he is perhaps going to offer to his shepherdess. Further to the left are more rocks. To the right is a grassy bank, a stream, some sheep. How sober and simple it is; only colour is lacking.

2 (Pl. 180)[25] On the left the carrier pigeon is arriving, the messenger bird; it's coming as fast as its wings can carry it. The shepherdess is standing, leaning with her hand against a tree in front of her, and sees it amongst the trees, her eyes are fixed on it; she appears to be consumed with impatience and desire; both her position and action are simple, natural, interesting and elegant. A dog is watching the arrival of the bird, his two front paws planted on a raised hummock, his head lifted towards the messenger, he is barking with joy and seems to be wagging his tail; he has been conceived with spirit. The action of the animal points to a little, long established romantic attachment. To the right, behind the shepherdess we can see her distaff on the ground, a basket of flowers and a little hat with a kerchief; a sheep is at her feet, even simpler and better composed. Only colour is lacking; the subject is so clear that the painter has not been able to obscure it with his details.

3 (Pl. 181) To the right we can see two young girls; the one in the foreground is reading the letter; her companion is behind her. The first is turning her back to me; that's bad, because the expression on her face could easily reflect her action. Her companion should have been given that position. The secret is shared in a solitary, out-of-the-way place, at the foot of a rustic stone structure, out of which a fountain rises, above which is a little Cupid in bas-relief. To the left there are nanny-goats, billy-goats and some sheep. This picture is less interesting than the preceding one and that's the fault of the artist. Moreover, this place was really the spot for the rendez-vous; it's the fountain of love. The colour is still false.

4 (Pl. 182) The rendez-vous. At the centre, towards the viewer's right, the shepherdess is sitting on the ground, a sheep by her side, a lamb on her knees, her shepherd is holding her gently in his arms and looking at her with passion. Above the shepherd, there is his dog tied up. Very good. To the left, a basket of flowers. To the right a snapped broken down tree. Very good again. In the background a hamlet, hut and the end of a house. It's here that the letter should have been read and the rendez-vous should have been at the fountain of Love. But, however it is, the whole is fine, delicate and well thought-out; these are four little eclogues in the style of Fontenelle.[26] Perhaps the manners of Theocritus[27] or those of Daphne and Chloe,[28] more simple, more naive, would have interested me more. My shepherds would have done all that these shepherds here do; but a moment before they would not have had any suspicion of what was happening, whereas these know in advance what is going to happen, and I don't like that idea, unless it is very clearly expressed. (Seznec and Adhémar, pp.75–8; 80–1)

Bachelier (Seznec and Adhémar, pp.104–8)

Pictures painted with new pastels prepared with oil.[29]

In one of these pictures a woman is seen leaning with her elbow on a table on which there are pens, ink and paper. She is giving a sealed letter to a standing female slave. The slave is in a mood, a bad mood, you understand, not the mood of a painter. She does not appear willing to obey her mistress. The mistress is looking a little sullen and the slave is looking very sullen.

M. Bachelier, leave your secret there and go and thank M. Chardin for having had the idea of hiding your picture so well, that nobody but me has seen it.

---

[25] Counterproof engravings of this and the other paintings in this series of pastorals are presented in the Illustration Book.

[26] French writer 1657–1757.

[27] Greek pastoral poet of the third century BC

[28] Figures from Greek mythology in the poetry of Ovid, Dante and Petrarch.

[29] No illustrations available.

It seems to me that when you take up the paint brush, you must have some idea, either strong, ingenious, delicate or striking and aim for some effect, some impression. Giving a person a letter to take is such a common action that it must definitely be enhanced by some particular circumstance or by superior execution. There are very few artists who have ideas and there is hardly one who can dispense with them. Oh yes, undoubtedly, Chardin can show a kitchen with a servant-girl, bending over a barrel or doing the washing up;[30] but notice how accurate the action of the servant is, how her dress delineates the upper part of her figure, and how the folds of this petticoat delineate all that is below. Notice the astonishing accuracy of all the kitchen utensils and the colour and harmony of all the little composition. There is no room for compromise; there must either be interesting ideas, an original subject or an astonishing fact: the best would be to unite striking thought and a pleasing execution. If he did not have a sublime technique, Chardin's subject matter would be miserable. Remember that, M. Bachelier. (Seznec and Adhémar, pp.107–8)

Chardin (Seznec and Adhémar, pp.111–114)

You come just in time, Chardin, to refresh my eyes which your colleague Challe[31] had mortally afflicted. Here you are again then, great magician, with your silent compositions! How eloquently they speak to the artist! How much they tell him about the imitation of nature, about the science of colour, about harmony! How the air circulates around these objects! The light of the sun does not better harmonise the disparities of the beings on which it shines. For this man there is scarcely any such thing as compatible and incompatible colours!

If it is true, as the philosophers tell us, that only our sensations are real; that perhaps neither the emptiness of space nor even the solidity of physical entities is anything in itself, as we appear to experience it; let them tell me, these philosophers, what difference there is for them, standing four feet from your pictures, between the creator and you.

Chardin is so true, so true, so harmonious, that although you see on the canvas only inanimate objects, vases, cups, bottles, bread, wine, water, grapes, fruit, pastries, he maintains his ground and even perhaps makes you desert the two beautiful Vernets alongside which he has not hesitated to place himself. It is, my friend, as in the world at large, where the presence of a man, of a horse or an animal does not destroy the effect of a rocky outcrop, of a tree, or stream. The stream, the tree, the outcrop are undoubtedly less interesting than the man, the woman, the horse, the animal, but they are equally true.

I must, my friend, tell you of an idea which has come to me, and which will not perhaps come again at another time; it is that this painting which is called *genre*[32] painting, should be that of old men or of those who are born old. It only demands study and patience. There is no verve; little of genius; scarcely any poetry; much technique and truth; and that's all. Now, you know that that time of life when we take up, what is usually called, the search for truth, philosophy, is precisely that time when our temples are greying and when we'd be hard put to write a romantic letter. Talking of these grey hairs, my friend, this morning I saw my head quite hoary, and I cried like Sophocles[33] when Socrates[34] asked him how his love affairs were going: *A domino agresti et furioso profugi.* I am escaping from a wild and furious master.

I'm just passing time chattering away to you here, all the more willingly so since I shall only say one word to you about Chardin; this is

---

[30] See *The Scullery Maid*, Col. Pl. 25.

[31] Eighteenth-century artist and co-exhibitor at the 1765 Salon.

[32] Diderot includes in this, from the context, still-life painting as well as genre subjects.

[33] Athenian tragic dramatist of the fifth century BC.

[34] Athenian philosopher, 469–399 BC.

it. Select a site like his; place on this site objects as I shall indicate to you and you can be sure that you will have seen his pictures.

He has painted *The attributes of the sciences, The attributes of the arts*, and similarly for *music, refreshments, fruits, animals*. There's very little to choose between them; they're all of the same perfection. I shall sketch them for you as quickly as I can.

The attributes of the sciences[35]

On a table covered with a reddish coloured cloth, we see, going I think from right to left, books standing on their fore-edge, a microscope, a hand bell, a globe half hidden by a curtain of green taffeta, a thermometer, a concave mirror on its stand, a lorgnette with its case, some rolled-up maps and the end of a telescope.

As far as the accuracy of form and colour goes, it's nature itself; the objects separate themselves from one another, protrude, are set back just as if they were real; nothing could be more harmonious; and no confusion despite the number of objects and the small space.

Attributes of the arts (Pl. 187)[36]

Here are books lying on their sides, an antique vase, drawings, hammers, chisels, rulers, compasses, a marble statue, paint brushes, palettes, and other similar objects. They are placed on a kind of balustrade. The statue is that of *The Fountain of Grenelle*, Bourchardon's[37] masterpiece. The same accuracy, the same colour, the same harmony.

The attributes of music (Col. Pl. 23)

The painter has spread out on a table covered with a reddish coloured cloth a host of different objects, distributed in a most natural

and picturesque manner; there is an erect lectern; in front of the lectern is a two-branched candlestick; behind it is a trumpet and a hunting horn, of which the bell can be seen above the lectern; there are some oboes, a mandola, some sheets of music displayed, the neck of a violin with its bow and some books standing on their fore-edge. If a living, evil, creature, such as a snake had been painted as accurately it would be frightening.

These three pictures are three feet ten inches broad by three feet ten inches high.

Refreshments[38]

Fruits and animals. Imagine a square structure of greyish stone, a kind of window with its sill and cornice. Throw a garland of big unripe grapes, with as much nobility and elegance as you can, along the cornice so that it hangs down on both sides. Within the window put a glass full of wine, a bottle, a newly cut loaf, other carafes cooling in a pottery container, an earthenware jug, radishes, fresh eggs, a salt cellar, two steaming cups of coffee, and there you will see Chardin's picture. This structure, built of broad plain stone, decorated with its garland of grapes, is of the greatest beauty. It's a model for the façade of the temple of Bacchus.

Companion piece to the preceding picture[39]

The same stone structure; around it a garland of big white muscatel grapes; within, peaches, plums, carafes of lemonade in a green-painted tin bucket, a lemon, peeled and cut in two, a basket of simnel cakes, a Masulipatan[40] handkerchief hanging down outside, a carafe of orgeat[41] with a half-full glass. What a lot of objects! What diversity of form and colour! And

---

[35] This painting is lost.

[36] The dimensions of this and the following painting have been altered since the eighteenth century. The original dimensions of both *The Attributes of the Arts* and of *The Attributes of Music* were 125cm x 125cm.

[37] French sculptor, 1698–1762. The statue represents an allegorical figure of Paris from Bouchardon's fountain in the Rue de Grenelle, considered his masterpiece. Chardin probably intended this as a tribute to the sculptor, who died in 1762.

[38] No illustration available.

[39] No illustration available.

[40] Ancient name of Bandar, an Indian port.

[41] Cooling drink made from barley or almonds and orange-flower water.

yet what harmony! what repose! The handkerchief is of an astonishing softness.

Third picture of refreshments, to be placed between the first two (Col. Pl. 26)

If it is true that a connoisseur must have at least one Chardin, he should get hold of this one. The artist is starting to grow old. He's done as well sometimes; never better. Hang a water bird up by one foot. On the slab beneath it imagine whole and broken biscuits, a glass bottle with a cork stopper and full of olives, a covered decorated Chinese tureen, a lemon, a serviette unfolded and casually arranged, a pie on a wooden chopping board and a glass half full of wine. Here we see that there are scarcely any unresponsive objects in nature and that the point is to represent them properly. The biscuits are yellow, the bottle is green, the serviette white, the wine red and this yellow, green, white and red, placed in opposition to each other, refresh the eye with a most perfect harmony. And do not believe that this harmony results from a feeble, gentle, overdone manner. Not at all; it's the firmest of touches. It's true that these objects do not change under the eyes of the artist. They will appear on the morrow just as he sees them today. With living nature it is not so. Only stone has the attribute of unchangeability.

A basket of grapes (Col. Pl. 27)

That describes the picture; just scatter around the basket a few separate grapes, a macaroon, a pear and two or three lady-apples;[42] you would think that a few separate grapes, a macaroon and isolated lady-apples would not be suitable for a picture either in form or colour; but just you see Chardin's picture.

A basket of plums[43]

Place on a stone bench a willow basket full of plums, with a worn bit of string as a handle, and dot around nuts, two or three cherries and a few small bunches of grapes.

This man is the leading colourist of the Salon, and perhaps one of the leading colourists of the painting world …

Chardin's technique is special. It has something in common with the rough[44] style, so that close up you don't know what it is, but as you back away the object gradually forms and ends up by being true to nature. Sometimes you find it almost equally pleasing from near or far. This man is as far above Greuze as the sky is above the earth, but only in this respect. His work is not mannered; and yet he has his own manner. But since he has a manner peculiar to him, it should be false in some circumstances, and it never is. Try to explain that to yourself, my friend. Do you know of a literary style suitable for all occasions? Chardin's painting *genre* is the easiest to master; but no living painter, not even Vernet, is as perfect in his own *genre*. (Seznec and Adhémar, pp.111–14)

Vernet (Seznec and Adhémar, pp. 120–3)

View of the port of Dieppe. The four parts of the day. Two views of the environs of Ogent-sur-Seine. A shipwreck. A landscape. Another shipwreck. A seascape at sunset. Seven small landscapes. Two more seascapes. A storm and several more pictures listed under the same number.

Twenty five pictures, my friend! Twenty five pictures? And what pictures! As fast as the Creator and as life-like as Nature. There's scarcely one of these compositions that a painter would not have done well to paint in the two years it's taken him to do them all. What incredible effects of light! What beautiful skies! What seas! What composition! What a prodigious variety of scenes! Here a child saved from the wreck is being carried on his father's shoulders; there a woman is stretched out dead on the shore and her husband is grief-stricken. The sea roars, the winds whistle, the thunder rumbles, the sombre pale light of the flashes of lightning pierces the clouds to reveal and mask the scene. You can hear the noise as the sides of a ship are staved in; her masts are down, her sails in ribbons: some people on the deck have their arms raised towards heaven; others have thrown themselves into the water. They have been dashed by the waves against near-by, foam-whitened rocks, where their blood has been mingled with the

---

[42] A type of small apple.

[43] This painting is in a private collection in Paris.

[44] The French text has '*la manière heurtée*', i.e. a sketchy, uneven manner.

foam. I can see some floating; I can see some on the point of disappearing into the maelstrom; I can see some striving to reach the shore, against which they will be dashed. The same variety of characters, actions and expressions is prevalent with the spectators; some are trembling and looking away; others are helping, others, stock-still, are looking on. Some have lit a fire in the lee of a rock; they are busy reviving a dying woman and I hope that they will succeed. Turn your eyes to another sea and you will see a flat calm with all its charms. Tranquil waters, smooth and smiling stretch from the shore to where the horizon blends with the sky, imperceptibly losing their transparency and imperceptibly lightening their surface. The vessels are stationary; the sailors and the passengers are all passing the time in ways which relieve their impatience. If it is morning, what light mists are rising! These straggling mists around natural objects, how they have refreshed and revived them! If it is evening, how the mountain tops are glistening! With what fine nuances are the skies coloured! How the clouds are passing, moving, with the waters as a depository for the tints of their colours! go in to the countryside, turn your eyes towards the vault of the heavens, observe the passing scene and you will swear that a piece of the great luminous canvas, lit by the sun, has been cut out and transposed onto the artist's easel; or cup your hand so as to make a funnel so that you can see only a small part of the great canvas, and you will swear that it's one of Vernet's pictures which has been taken from his easel and transposed into the sky. Although he is the most prolific of all our painters, he gives me less trouble than them all. It's impossible to describe his pictures; you have to see them. His nights are as moving as his days are beautiful; his ports are as beautiful as his imaginary landscapes are striking. Everything is equally marvellous, whether his brush is captive to the task of portraying a given natural object, or whether his muse, loosed from all shackles, is free and abandoned to its own devices; all is incomprehensible, whether he employs the orb of the day or of the night, natural light or artificial light to illuminate his pictures; everything is always harmonious, vigorous and wise, just like

those great poets, those rare men in whom judgement is so perfectly balanced by verve, that they are never either exaggerated or cold. His structures, his edifices, clothing, actions, men, animals, everything is true. Close-up, he's striking; at a distance, he's even more striking. Chardin and Vernet, my friend, are two great magicians. You would say of the latter that he starts by creating the countryside and that he has men, women and children in reserve to people his canvas, as you would people a colony; then he makes the weather for them, the sky, the time of year, happiness, misfortune, just as he pleases. It's like the Jupiter of Lucian,[45] who, tired of hearing human beings' pitiful cries, rises from table and says: 'Let it hail in Thrace' and immediately the trees are stripped bare, the harvests are ruined and the cottage thatch spoiled. 'Plague in Asia' and house doors are shut, streets are deserted and men flee. 'A volcano here' and the ground erupts beneath our feet, buildings fall, animals are terrified and the inhabitants of the towns leave for the country. 'A war there' and nations rush to arms and devour each other. 'Death in this place' and the old labourer dies from hunger at his door. Jupiter calls that governing the world, and he's wrong. Vernet calls that painting pictures, and he's right.

The port of Dieppe (Col. Pl. 30)

A great and immense composition. A light, argentine sky; a fine mass of buildings; a picturesque, striking view; a crowd of figures busy catching, cleaning and selling fish, working with and repairing nets, and similar occupations; natural and true-to-life actions; figures depicted vigorously and with a spirited touch; but, it must be said, not so vigorously nor with so spirited a touch as usual.

In the four parts of the day (Pls 162–165)

The most wonderful interplay of lights. I'm going to rush through these pieces, only mentioning the particular talent and the characteristic ability which distinguishes them. What will happen as a result? At the end you will realise that this artist has every talent and ability.

Two views of Nogent-sur-Seine (Pl. 166)

An excellent lesson for Le Prince,[46] whose compositions have been placed side by side with

---

[45] Greek writer of the second century BC.

[46] See below, p.288.

those of Vernet. He will not lose what he has and he will recognise what he is lacking. There is a great deal of spirit, lightness and life-likeness about the figures of Le Prince; but there is weakness, dryness, little effect. The other artist with his paint laid on thickly, is always firm, harmonious and overwhelms his neighbour. The distant views of Vernet are misty, his skies light: the same cannot be said of Le Prince. But he isn't without merit. The greater the distance between his pictures and Vernet's, the more he strengthens and improves; Vernet fades and dies away. This cruel side by side display is another nasty trick of the picture hanger.[47]

Two companion pieces, one a shipwreck, the other a landscape (Pl. 167)[48]

The landscape is charming; but the shipwreck is something quite different. But you must concentrate especially on the figures: the wind is terrible; men have difficulty standing upright. Look at that drowned woman who has just been pulled out of the water; and try not to feel the grief of her husband, if you can.

Another shipwreck by moonlight (Pl. 168)[49]

Have a good look at those men busy warming that unconscious woman by the fire which they have lit in the lee of a rock, and then say that you have seen one of the most interesting groups that it was possible to imagine; look how this touching scene is lit; how the arch catches the reddish glare of the fire; how the feeble pale light of the moon contrasts with the strong and red, sad and sombre light of the lighted fires. Not just any painter could get away with opposing phenomena as discordant as this and remain harmonious; not every painter has the ability not to be false to the two lights where they meet, as they blend and form a particular splendour.

… Vernet ranks with *Claude le Lorrain*[50] in the art of creating mists on canvas and he is infinitely superior to him in the invention of scenes, the drawing of figures, the variety of incidents

and all the rest. The first is nothing more or less than a great landscape artist; the other is a history painter, in my definition of the term. *Le Lorrain* chooses natural phenomena which are quite rare and for that reason more striking. Vernet's atmosphere is more everyday and for that reason easier to recognize. (Seznec and Adhémar, pp.120–3)

Baudouin (Seznec and Adhémar, pp.137–141)

A good lad, good-looking too, gentle and spirited, if a bit of a libertine. But what's that to me? My wife's past forty-five and he won't get near my daughter, neither him nor his compositions.

There were at the Salon a number of little pictures by Baudouin and all the young girls, after casually looking round several pictures, ended their tours at the place where *A peasant girl scolded by her mother* and *The Cherry picker* were on view. They had reserved all their attention for this section. There is a time in life when you would rather read a suggestive book than a good book and when you would rather stop in front of an obscene picture than a good picture. There are even old men who are punished for having had such continual debaucheries by the sterile taste that they have maintained for these things. Some of these old men, stick in hand, backs bent, glasses perched on their noses, totter along too to Baudouin's little indecencies.

The Empty Quiver (Pl. 183)[51]

In a little room set aside for pleasure, a boudoir, we see, nonchalantly sprawled on a chaise longue, a man-about-town disinclined to tax himself again; standing by the side of him, there is a young girl in her petticoat, with a ruffled air, who seems to be saying to him while attending to her make-up: *Is that as much as you know how to do?*

---

[47] i.e. Chardin.

[48] It is thought that the "shipwreck" to which Diderot here refers is Vernet's painting *The Storm* at the Hermitage Museum in Russia. We are only able to provide a related engraving.

[49] We reproduce an engraving of this painting which itself is lost.

[50] Seventeenth-century painter of poetic or classical landscapes.

[51] We reproduce an engraving take from this painting.

The Cherry picker (Pl. 184)

We see a big gardener's boy up a tree picking cherries. At the foot of the tree a young peasant girl is waiting to receive them in her apron: another young girl, sitting on the ground, is looking at the picker; between the one on the ground and the tree there is a grazing donkey loaded with panniers. The gardener's boy has thrown a handful of cherries into the girl's lap; just two are still in his hand, joined by the same stalk and hanging from his middle finger. A bad jest, a flat and coarse idea; but I'll give my opinion on all this at the end.

The girl scolded by her mother (Pl. 185)[52]

The scene is in a cellar. The girl and her boy-friend were on the point, on the very point … you can tell all by not telling anything … when her mother arrived just in time, just in time … That tells it all clearly. The mother is extremely angry; she's standing arms akimbo. Her daughter is on her feet, crying, and behind her is a nice pile of straw recently lain upon. She has not had time to straighten her bodice and her shawl, as is easily apparent. Beside her, half way up the cellar steps, we have the rear view of a big lad, beating a hasty retreat. From the position of his arms and hands, we are in no doubt which of his garments he's pulling up. Our lovers, moreover, knew how to do things. At the bottom of the stairs there is a barrel and on it are a loaf, fruit, a serviette and a bottle of wine.

This is most indecent; but you can go as far as that. I have a look, I smile, and I pass on.

Greuze made himself a painter, a preacher of righteousness; Baudouin, a painter, a preacher of unrighteousness. Greuze, a painter of the family, of decent people; Baudouin, a painter of petites-maisons[53] and libertines: but fortunately he has neither drawing ability, genius, or colouring ability and we have genius, drawing ability and colouring ability and we will be the stronger. Baudouin discussed with me the subject of a picture. He wanted to portray at the mid-wife's a prostitute who has just given birth

secretly and who in her poverty is being forced to abandon her child to the Foundlings Hospital. 'And why', I replied, 'don't you place the scene in a garret, and show a decent woman being forced for the same reason into the same action? That will be nicer, more touching, more decent. A garret will afford more scope to your talent than a mid-wife's hovel. When it involves no sacrifice on the part of art, isn't it better to portray virtue rather than vice? Your composition will inspire only a sterile pity; mine will inspire the same sentiment, but bearing fruit … ' 'Oh! that's too serious; besides, when it comes to models for prostitutes, I can find as many as I like.' 'So you want a happy subject?' 'Yes, and a bit smutty if possible. Because I don't deny that I like smut, and the public doesn't mind it.' 'Since you've got to have smut, you shall have it and still get your models from the rue Fromenteau.'[54] 'Quick, quick, tell me,' said he, rubbing his hands with glee. 'Just imagine,' I continued, 'a cab on its way between eleven and twelve noon to Saint-Denis. In the middle of the street of this name one of the braces of the cab snaps and the vehicle overturns: the door opens and a monk and three prostitutes get out. The monk starts to run away. The cabbie's little dog jumps down from beside his master, follows the monk, catches up with him and seizes his long habit in his teeth. Whilst the monk is struggling to free himself from the dog, the cabbie, not wanting to lose his fare, gets down from his box and goes to the monk. In the meantime one of the prostitutes is dealing with a bump that one of her companions has received on the forehead and the other, to whom the whole caper seems funny, all dishevelled as she is, with her hands on her hips, bursts out laughing. The shopkeepers, men and women, standing in their doorways join in the laughter and the street urchins who come running together shout at the monk: 'He's crapped in bed! He's crapped in bed!' 'That's excellent', said Baudouin 'it even has a bit of a moral in it. At least vice is punished. And who

---

[52] We reproduce an engraving taken from this painting.

[53] Places frequented by dandies and libertines.

[54] One of five streets named in an official edict dating from the time of Saint-Louis as a designated area for brothels. It was in the northern part of Paris, between the Palais Royal and the Seine. Diderot included a similar anecdote to the one he is about to recount in his novel, *Jacques le Fataliste*.

knows if that monk of my acquaintance to whom this very thing happened, would not recognise himself while making a tour of the Salon, and blush a little? And you know how difficult it is to make a monk blush.'

The mother scolding her daughter is the best of Baudouin's little pictures: it's drawn better than the others and quite prettily coloured; but still a bit greyish. The dejection of the man lying on the sofa, with the girl attending to her make-up isn't bad ... (Seznec and Adhemar pp.137–41).

Greuze (Seznec and Adhémar pp.144–60)

I am being perhaps a little long-winded; but if only you knew how much I'm enjoying myself while boring you: I'm just like any other old bore in the world. But then after all I have already described a hundred and ten pictures and judged thirty-one painters.

Here is your painter and mine, the first amongst us who has taken it upon himself to invest art with morals and to link events of which it would be easy to make a novel. He's a little vain, our painter: but his vanity is that of a child, it's the intoxication of talent. Take away from him this naivety which makes him say of his own work: 'Just look at that! Isn't that lovely!' and you will take away his verve, you will extinguish his fire, his genius will be eclipsed. I am much afraid that when he does become modest he will have reason for being so. Our good qualities, certain of them at least, are very much mixed up with our failings. Most decent women have a temper; great artists are a little deranged. Almost all loose women are generous; devout people, even sincere ones, are not averse to backbiting. It's difficult for a master who knows he's doing good, not to be a little despotic. I hate all these little servilities which show only a poverty stricken soul, but I don't hate great crimes; firstly because beautiful pictures and fine tragedies can be made from them and then because great and sublime actions and great crimes are characterised by the same energy. If one man wasn't capable of setting fire to a town, another man wouldn't be capable of leaping into a chasm to save himself ...

We have three clever painters, fertile and studious observers of nature, who begin and finish nothing without having recourse several times to a model. These three are La-Grenée, Greuze and Vernet. The second of these carries his talent everywhere in the press of humanity, into the churches, onto the markets, onto the avenues, into the houses, into the streets; as he goes he ceaselessly gathers actions, passions, characters, expressions. Chardin and he can talk very well about their talent; Chardin with coolness and composure, Greuze with warmth and enthusiasm. La Tour,[55] when talking to a small number, is also very good to hear.

There are a great number of pieces by Greuze, some mediocre, several good, many excellent; let us run through them.

The young girl crying over her dead bird (Col. Pl. 31)

What a pretty elegy! What a pretty poem! What a beautiful idyll Gessner[56] would make of it! It's the vignette of a piece by this poet. What a delightful picture! It is the most charming and perhaps the most interesting in the Salon. She is facing us; she is resting her head on her left hand: the dead bird is lying on the top of the cage, its head hanging down, its wings drooping, its feet in the air. What a natural posture she has! How beautiful her head is! What an elegant hair-style! How expressive her face is! She is profoundly sad; she is sunk in her misery, quite lost in it. What a pretty bier the cage makes! How graceful is the garland of greenery that surrounds it! Oh, what a beautiful hand! What a beautiful hand! What a lovely arm! Just look how accurate the details of those fingers are, those dimples, that softness, and how the pressure of the head on the delicate finger tips has given them a reddish hue. Note the charm of it all. If I had no respect for this child and her sorrow, I would approach this hand and kiss it. Everything about her is enchanting, including her attire. The scarf around her neck is so tastefully arranged! Note the lightness of its folds! When you see this piece, you say: *delightful!* If you stop there or if you come back to it, you cry *delightful!*

---

[55] French artist, 1704–88, celebrated for his pastel portraits.

[56] Swiss poet and painter, 1730–88.

delightful! Soon you find yourself talking to the child, consoling her. That is so true that this is what I remember saying to her at different times.

My child, your sorrow is very deep, very thoughtful! What does this dreamy, melancholy air mean? What! you're not crying for a bird! You are afflicted and in your affliction, you start to think. There now, my little one, open your heart to me: tell me the truth; is it really the death of this bird that's making you retreat so much and so sadly into yourself? ... You're lowering your eyes; you won't reply to me. You're about to burst into tears: I'm not your father; I am neither indiscreet nor stern ... Ah, I know what's happened; he loved you, he swore he did, he'd been doing so for a long time. He was suffering so much: how can you see someone you love suffering? ... Now let me continue, why are you trying to stop my mouth with your hand? That morning, unfortunately, your mother was absent. He came; you were alone; he was so handsome, so passionate, so tender, so charming! there was so much love in his eyes! so much truth in his expression! he said words that went straight to your soul, and when he said them he was at your knees; I can imagine that too. He was holding one of your hands; from time to time you felt hot tears drop onto it and trickle the length of your arms. Your mother had still not come back. This isn't your fault, it's your mother's ... But there, you are crying ... But I'm not telling you this to make you cry. And why cry? He has promised; he won't let you down in anything that he's promised. When a man has been fortunate enough to meet a charming girl like you, to attach himself to you, to please you, it's for all his life ... And my bird? ... You're smiling. (Ah! my friend, how beautiful she was! Ah! if only you'd seen her smile and cry). I continued. Very well! Your bird! If someone forgets herself, would she remember her bird? When the time for your mother to return arrived, the one whom you love went away. How happy he was, how content, how overcome! How difficult he found it to tear himself away from you! Well may you look at me like that! I know all about it. How many times did he get up and then sit down again! How many times did he say goodbye and stop where he was! How many times did he go out and come back! I've just seen him at his father's place: he has a charming gaiety, a

gaiety which they all share, without being able to deny it ... And my mother? ... Your mother? Scarcely was he gone and she came back: she found you in a dreamy mood as you were just now. That's how it happens every time. Your mother spoke to you and you didn't hear what she was saying: she told you to do one thing and you did another. Some tears pricked your eyelids; you held them back or you turned your head so as to furtively wipe them. Your mother became impatient with your dawdling; she scolded you which gave you the excuse to weep unrestrainedly and thus relieve your heart ... Shall I continue? I fear that what I am going to say will renew your pain. You want me to? ... Very well. Your kind mother was full of remorse for having spoken sharply to you; she approached you, she took your hands, she kissed you on the forehead and cheeks, which made you weep the more. Your head leaned forward to her, and you hid your face, which had begun to be suffused with colour, just like your face in the picture, in her bosom. How many tender things did your mother say to you, which simply made you feel bad. But all in vain your canary was singing, warning you, calling to you, beating his wings, complaining of your forgetfulness; you didn't see him, you didn't hear him: your thoughts were elsewhere. Neither his water nor his bird seed were replenished; and this morning the bird was no more ... You're still looking at me; is there still something more to be said? Ah! I understand; it is he who had given you that bird: oh well, he'll find another one, just as beautiful ... But that's still not all: your eyes are still fixed on me and full of sorrow; What is it then? Tell me; I'm no good at guessing ... The death of this bird might only be an omen! What would I do? What would become of me? If he broke his word ... What stupidity! Never fear, that won't happen, that can't happen ... But, my friend, aren't you laughing to hear a sane person amusing himself by consoling a child in a painting on the loss of her bird, on the loss of anything you please. But just look how beautiful she is! how interesting! I don't like to cause pain; yet in spite of that, it wouldn't worry me too much to be the cause of her pain.

The subject of this little poem is so subtle, that many people have not understood it; they have thought that this young girl was only crying for her canary. Greuze has already painted the same subject once;[57] in front of a cracked mirror he placed a tall girl dressed in white satin, absorbed in a profound melancholy. Don't you think that it would be as silly to attribute the tears of the young girl in this Salon to the loss of a bird as it would have been to attribute the melancholy of the young girl in the preceding Salon to her broken mirror? This child is crying for something else, I tell you. First, you heard her yourself, she admits this; and in any case her thoughtful sadness tells us as much. Such sorrow! at her age! and for a bird! ... But how old is she? What shall I reply; and what question have you put to me? Her head is that of a fifteen to sixteen year-old and her arm and hand that of an eighteen to nineteen year-old. It's a fault in this composition which is the more recognisable since the head is leaning against the hand, thus the one can be used as a measure of the other. If the hand were placed differently, you would not notice that it is a little too strong and forceful. The fact is, my friend, that the head has been taken from one model and the hand from another. For the rest, this hand is very accurate, very beautiful, most perfectly coloured and drawn. If you are prepared to overlook in this piece this slight imperfection, together with a rather purplish colour tone, this is a very beautiful painting. The head is well-lit and coloured with the most suitable colour that could be given to a blonde; perhaps we might have asked that it be a little more rounded out. The striped shawl is broad, light and has a beautiful transparency; the whole is vigorously depicted, without destroying the detailed finesse. This painter may have done as well but not better. This piece is oval and two feet high.

A little girl holding a wooden capuchin[58] (Pl. 169)

What truthfulness! What a variety of tones! Who has not seen those patches of red on children's faces when they are cold or having teething troubles? Those eyes swimming with tears, the little hands numb and frozen, the strands of fair hair straggling over the forehead,

all dishevelled; they're so light and lifelike you want to push them back under her bonnet. A headscarf of good thick material with appropriate tucks. A scarf of good thick material around the neck, arranged conventionally; a little capuchin, very stiff, very wooden, dressed very stiffly. M. Drouais,[59] come here. You see this child, that's flesh; you see this capuchin, that's plaster. As far as truthfulness and vigour of colour go, it's a little Rubens.

Portrait of Madam Greuze[60]

Here, my friend, there is something to show how much ambiguity remains in even the best picture. You see this beautiful overweight fishwife, her head thrown back, whose pale colour, headdress undone and disordered, and expression of mingled pain and pleasure, exhibit a paroxysm sweeter to experience than proper to paint? Well, that's the sketch, the study for the well-beloved mother. How can it be that here a character is decent and there it ceases to be so? Are accessories, circumstances necessary for us to be able to properly assess a person's features? Without these aids are they indeterminate? I think there must be something in that idea. This half-open mouth, these swimming eyes, this thrown-back posture, this swollen neck, this voluptuous mixture of pain and pleasure, make every decent woman in the place blush and lower her eyes. But side by side, there is the same posture, the same eyes, the same neck, the same mixture of passions and not one of those women remarks upon it. Besides, if women pass that piece quickly, men stop there a long time; I mean those who are connoisseurs, and those who, under pretext of being connoisseurs, come to enjoy a spectacle of acute sensuality and those who, like me, come to do both. On the forehead, and from the forehead to the cheeks and from the cheeks toward the throat, there are incredible tonal gradations; it teaches you to observe nature and reminds you of nature. You have to see the details of this swollen throat, not talk about it. It's absolutely wonderful, true and

---

[57] In *The Broken Mirror*, in which the broken mirror symbolised the loss of virginity.

[58] Franciscan friar.

[59] French portrait painter, 1727–75.

[60] Location unknown.

clever. You've never seen two contradictory expressions present at the same time and so clearly delineated. It's a *tour de force* which Rubens has not excelled at the Luxembourg Gallery,[61] where the painter has shown us on the queen's face both the pleasure at having brought a son into the world and traces of the painful state which preceded it.

Another portrait of Madame Greuze (Pl. 170)[62]

This painter is certainly in love with his wife, and I don't blame him. I loved her very much when I was young and when she was called Mademoiselle Babuti. She had a little bookshop on the Quai des Augustins; she was rosy-cheeked, white and innocent as the lily, as red as the rose. I went in with that keen, ardent foolish air that I had and I said to her: 'Miss, La Fontaine's stories and a Pétrone,[63] please' … 'Here they are, Sir. Do you want anything else?' 'Excuse me, Miss, but er … ' 'Please tell me … ' 'The Nun in a petticoat' 'Really, Sir, do you think we have, do you think we read nasty books like that?' 'Oh! oh! it's a nasty book is it? Miss, I didn't know … ' And then on another day when I passed by, she smiled at me and I smiled at her.

At the last Salon there was a *Portrait of Madame Greuze in pregnancy*; her interesting condition made you stop; the beautiful colouring and the accuracy of the details then dumbfounded you. This one isn't as beautiful. But, taken as a whole, it's graceful. It is well posed; the posture is voluptuous. Her two hands show an enchanting finesse of tone. But the left one isn't a whole; one finger is even broken, which detracts from it. The dog caressed by the beautiful hand is a spaniel with long black hair, its muzzle and paws flecked with fire. Its eyes are full of life. If you look at it for any length of time, you will hear it bark. The blond hairstyle is enough to make you call for the man who did it. I'd say the same about the rest of the clothing. The head has given difficulty both to the painter and the model; as we notice this fact, this is already a point against the artist. Parts of the forehead are too yellow. I know that women who

have had children do have such blemishes, but if you push the imitation of nature to the point of wanting to show them, then they must be toned down; there's a case there for a little embellishment, since it can be done without losing lifelikeness. But because these facial irregularities, by reason of their difficulties, make it possible for the artist to display his talent, it's rare that he refuses to do so. A reddish eye goes with these patches, which is accurate, but not pleasant. Her lips are flat. The pinched set of her mouth makes her look somewhat prim. That's really affected. If this affectation lies in the personality, so much the worse for the personality, the painter and the picture. Is this woman maliciously inciting her spaniel against someone? Her spiteful, prim look would then be less artificial but no less shocking. For the rest, the turn of her mouth, her eyes and all the other details are delightful; endless finesse of colour; the neck marvellously supports the head. Both its drawing and colouring are beautiful as it joins naturally with the shoulders. But as for the bust, I just couldn't look at it; and even at fifty, I'm partial to busts. The painter has painted his figure leaning forward, and by doing so, he seems to be saying to the spectator: See my wife's bust. I do see it, M. Greuze. Well, your wife has a slack and yellow bosom. If that's what it looks like, so much the worse for you, for her and for the picture. One day M. de la Martelière was coming down from his apartment when on the stairs he met a big lad who was going up to pay madame a visit. Madame de la Martelière had the most beautiful head in the world, and M. de la Martelière, watching the young rake go up to his wife, said between his teeth: 'Yes, yes, but wait till he sees her thighs'. Madame Greuze also has a very beautiful head and there will be nothing to prevent M. Greuze also muttering between his teeth some day: 'Yes, yes, but wait till he sees her bosom'. That will not happen; his wife has good sense. The yellow colour and the slackness of this bosom are Madame's fault, but the lack of transparency and the dullness are Monsieur's.

---

[61] In his *Birth of Louis XIII.*

[62] This is a preparatory drawing for the pastel work discussed by Diderot, which is now lost.

[63] Caius Petronius Arbiter, Latin writer of the first century AD

The well-beloved mother Sketch (Pl. 173)[64]

Sketches have commonly a fire which the finished picture lacks. It's the artist's moment of passion, pure verve, without any admixture of the finish which fore-thought gives to everything; it's the soul of the painter spread freely across the canvas. The pen of the poet, the pencil of the clever draughtsman seem to run and play. Rapid thought says it all with a single line. Now, the more vague the artistic expression, the more the imagination has free play. You must listen for what is expressed in vocal music. I can make a well made symphony say almost anything I want; and as I know better than anyone the way to really move me, by what I have experiences of my own heart, it is rare that the meaning I give to the sounds, matching my actual situation, serious, tender or happy, does not touch me more than another which would suit me less well. It's almost the same with a sketch and a picture. I see in the picture a thing settled and clear: how many things did I not guess at in the sketch which are scarcely hinted at in the finished picture.

The composition of *The well-beloved mother* is so natural, so simple, that it could make those who don't think much about these things believe that they could have conceived it, and that it wouldn't take much effort to do so. Just let me say to those kind of people: Yes, I do think that you would have spread all these children around this mother, and that you would have had them all caressing her. But you would have had one of them crying with vexation at not being singled out from the rest, and at that moment you would have introduced this man so gay, so happy to be the husband of this woman and so proud of being the father of so many children. You would have had him say: 'It's me who has done all this!' And you are quite sure that you would have thought to make the grandmother part of it: quite, quite sure, of course!

This is excellent, both as regards talent and as regard morals. It's a sermon on population increase and portrays very sympathetically the happiness and inestimable value of domestic peace. This says to every man who has any soul and any sense: 'Keep your family in comfort, have children by your wife, have as many as you can by her, have none apart from her and be assured that you will be happy at home'. (Seznec and Adhémar, pp.144–9; 150; 152–5)

Loutherbourg (Seznec and Adhémar, pp.165–71)

Here is a young artist who, by the accuracy of his animals, by the beauty of his settings, and of his country scenes, and by the freshness of his mountains begins his career by putting himself on a par with Berghem the elder and who, by the vigour of his paint strokes, by the harmony he brings between natural and artificial light and his other artistic qualities dares to challenge Vernet the Formidable.

Courage, young man; you have come farther than is permitted at your age. There is no need for you to know poverty, for you work quickly and your compositions are esteemed. You have a charming companion with whom you should stay. Don't leave your studio except to go and commune with nature. Live in the fields with her. Go and see sunrise and sunset, the tints of the clouds against the sky. Walk in the meadows amongst the herds. See the dewdrops shining on the grass. See the mists rising in the evening, spreading along the plain and gradually obscuring from your view the tops of the mountains. Rise from your bed very early, in spite of the charming young woman with whom you are sleeping. Anticipate the rising sun. See its disc obscured, the outline of its orb indistinct, and the great mass of its rays lost, dissipated, blotted out by the tremendously thick mist, which is only lightly tinged with red by the rising sun. Already the nebulous volume is starting to weaken under its own weight and is condensing onto the ground, wetting and soaking it, with the softened earth clinging to your feet. Turn your eyes to the summit of the mountains. There they are, beginning to pierce the misty ocean. Quicken your steps, speedily climb some nearby hill and from there contemplate the surface of this ocean gently wafting above the ground and revealing, as it subsides, the tops of steeples, the tips of trees, the ridges of houses, towns, villages, entire forests, all the natural scene flooded with the

---

[64] This illustration represents the finished painting.

light of the orb of the day. This orb has scarcely started out on its career; your charming companion still has her eyes closed. Soon one of her arms will start feeling for you at her side. Make haste to return to the conjugal tenderness calling you. The spectacle of animated nature awaits you. Take the paint brush which you have just dipped in light, water, mists; the different phenomena of which your head is full, and which only ask to escape from there and fly to the canvas. While you are occupied, during the scorching daylight hours in painting the freshness of the morning hours, heaven is preparing new phenomena for you. Light is weakening, clouds are scudding, separating, massing, the storm is brewing. Go and see the storm as it forms, bursts and abates, and then two years from now, let me find at the Salon the trees that it will have broken down, the streams that it will have turned into torrents, all the spectacle of its devastation, and let us be, my friend and I, once more terrified by it, one leaning against the other and our eyes fixed on your work.

> *A morning after rain*[65]
> *A storm breaking at sunset*

At the centre of the canvas, an old country house; near the house, cattle going to the fields and at the rear a herdsman on horseback who is taking them; to the left, rocks and a road leading between them. How beautifully lit the road is! To the right, a distant prospect, with a stretch of country. That is beautiful; beautiful light and a beautiful effect, but an effect difficult to appreciate if you have not lived in the country. You have to have seen that misty, greyish morning sky, that sadness in the atmosphere which presages still more bad weather for the rest of the day. You must recall that kind of wan, melancholy aspect which rain during the night has left on the fields and puts the traveller in a bad mood when at daybreak he gets up and goes, in his night shirt and cap, to open the shutter of the inn window to look at the weather and see what kind of day the sky is promising him.

Anyone who has not seen the sky darkening at the approach of a storm, the cattle returning from the fields, the clouds massing and a weak, reddish light lighting up the tops of the houses; anyone who has not seen the peasant shutting his cottage door and has not heard the house shutters being banged shut on all sides; anyone who has never felt the horror, the silence and the solitude of that sudden moment settle over a hamlet, will experience nothing at the onset of Loutherbourg's Storm.

In the first of these two pictures, I like the freshness and the setting; in the second I like the old country house and this half-hidden door that gives access … The clouds which presage the storm are heavy, thick, and look too much like a swirl of dust or smoke … Agreed. The reddish mist is crude … Agreed again, provided that you're not speaking of that which is covering the mill on the left. That is a sublime imitation of nature. The more I look at it, the less do I know the limits of art. When somebody has done that, I no longer know what to call impossible. (Seznec and Adhémar, pp.165–6; 169)

Le Prince (Seznec and Adhémar pp.171–80)

Russian pastoral (Pl. 174)

Remember, my friend, that I always leave well alone customs of which I know nothing. The artists will say of this picture all that they wish; but there is about it a darkness, a rest, a peace, a silence, an innocence which I find enchanting. It seems that the painter has here been helped by his own weakness. The simple subject demanded a light, gentle touch, which it has received; not a great deal of light, and there isn't a great deal. There is an old man who has ceased to play on his guitar so as to listen to a young shepherd playing on his pipe. The old man is sitting under a tree. I think he is blind, but if he is not, I wish he were. A young girl is standing beside him. The young boy is sitting on the ground, at some distance from the old man and the young girl. His pipe is in his mouth. His position, his character, his clothing are of a delightful simplicity, the head above all is charming. The listening attitudes of the old man and young girl are wonderful. The right side of the scene shows some rocks, at the foot of which some sheep are grazing. This composition goes straight to the soul. I feel at ease there. I'll lean against this tree, between the old man and his young girl for

---

[65] The location of these paintings is unknown.

as long as the young lad will play. When he has ceased to play and the old man has applied his fingers once more to his balalaika, I'll go and sit beside the young lad; and when night approaches, all three of us together will take the old man back to his hut. A picture that you can think about like that, that puts you in the scene and from which your soul receives a delicious sensation, is never a bad picture. You tell me: 'But it's weak in colour' … Agreed … 'But it's dark and monotonous' … Maybe; but it gets through to me, it makes me pause: and what use to me are your learned tonal gradations, your pure and correct drawing, the vigour of your colouring, the magic of your chiaroscuro, if your subject leaves me cold? Painting is the art of getting to the soul by way of the eyes. If the effect stops at the eyes, the painter is not half-way there. (Seznec and Adhémar, pp.173–4)

L'Épicié *(Seznec and Adhémar pp.181–6)*

Jesus Christ baptised by Saint John (Pl. 175)

Desperate to finish and get paid, these people don't know what they're doing. Down with the productions of the clock-watching artist, who's only interested in his salary! This artist has done like the other one,[66] made a solitary scene of his Baptism; and going by the nebulous, greyish tone in which he paints, you could call his figure arrangement simply a fortuitous, bizarre arrangement of clouds. On the right, in the background, we see three terrified apostles; terrified of what? There's nothing terrifying about a voice saying 'This is my beloved son'. This Saint John, his eyes turned toward heaven, is pouring water over the head of Christ without looking at what he's doing. And who brought along that big block of squared stone on which he's standing? You could say that it was essential to the ceremony, that a detached rocky outcrop, more natural and more picturesque, wouldn't have been as good. For what is a mason doing when he dresses a stone? He's taking away from it all irregularities. It's a symbol of education, which civilises us, takes away from a man the brutish, wild imprint of nature, makes us easy to get along with in life, and is completely insipid in a poem, or on canvas. And that soft, flexible,

smooth clothing; I hope you're not asking me to take that for a sheep's skin. You're right, that's what it is really, but so well looked after, so well cared for, so white, so well prepared, certainly not that of a man of the forests and the mountains. This Christ, towards the left, is emaciated, with his usual ignoble, beggarly appearance. Is it then impossible for us to free ourselves from this miserable character of tradition? I think not, the less so since we have two different characters for Christ. The Christ on the cross is different from the Christ in the midst of his apostles. To the left we have as usual in the centre of light, the holy, scrawny, dove; around it on one side, some cherubim; on the other side a group of angels. And then you have to see the colouring, the feet, the hands, the drawing, the flesh tones of all this.

But it seems to me that if the only reason that pictures are used to decorate the churches is to engrave on the popular memory the facts and actions of the heroes of religion and to increase the veneration of the people, it is not a matter of small concern whether they be good or bad. In my opinion a church artist is a kind of preacher, clearer, more striking, more intelligible, more on the level of the common man than the vicar or his curate. These two speak to the ears, which are often stopped. A picture speaks to the eyes, like the spectacle of nature which has taught us almost everything we know. I'd go further and say that I regard the iconoclasts and the scorners of processions, images, statues and all the external trappings of worship as gangsters in the pay of some philosopher weary of superstition; with this difference, that the underlings do a great deal more harm than their bosses. Once you suppress the tangible symbolism, the rest will soon be reduced to a metaphysical balderdash, which will take as many forms and fancies as there are heads to do it. Suppose for a moment that all men had become blind and I wager that before ten years were out, they'd be disputing and annihilating each other over the question of the form, the operation, and the colours of the most familiar objects in the universe. It's the same in religion; suppress every visual representation and all imagery and soon they will not understand each other and will be tearing each other to pieces over the

---

[66] i.e. Le Prince in his *Russian Baptism*

simplest articles of their faith. These absurd purists do not know the effect of external ceremonies on the common people; they've never seen our adoration of the Cross on Good Friday, the enthusiasm of the crowd for the Corpus Christi procession, an enthusiasm with which I myself am sometimes infected. I have never seen that long file of priests in sacerdotal garments, those young acolytes clothed in their white albs, with broad blue sashes around their waists and strewing flowers in front of the Holy Sacrament; that silent, religious crowd going before and after them; so many men prostrating themselves with their foreheads to the ground; I have never heard that grave and moving chant sung by the priests with the voices of an infinity of men, women, young girls and children making the affectionate responses, without being moved in my innermost being, without trembling with emotion, without tears coming to my eyes. There is something in it indescribably grand, sombre, solemn and melancholy. I knew a Protestant painter who had spent a long time in Rome and who confessed that he could never see, the Supreme Pontiff officiating in Saint Peters, in the midst of his cardinals and clergy without becoming a Catholic. He resumed his own religion at the door. But, they say, these images, these ceremonies lead to idolatory. It's amusing to see purveyors of lies fearing that a passion will increase their number. My friend, if we love truth better than the fine arts, let us pray God for the iconoclasts. (Seznec and Adhémar pp.183–6)

Amand (Seznec and Adhémar, pp.186–8)

Joseph sold by his brothers (Pl. 176)

Well, I've seen *Joseph sold by his brothers*. You choose, my friend; would you like a description of the picture or shall I tell you a story? ... 'But', you say, 'it seems to me that it isn't a bad composition.' Right enough. 'That big rocky slab on which they're counting out the price for the child fits quite well in the centre of the canvas.' Agreed. 'That merchant bending over the stone and the merchant behind are not bad as regards characterisation and dress.' I don't deny it. 'If Joseph is stiff, short, graceless, hasn't a good

colour, is expressionless, without interest, even a little dropsical in the legs, that's no reason for writing off the complete picture.' I wouldn't want to ... 'The group of brothers on one side and merchants on the other are even intelligently arranged.' That seems so to me too. 'The colour ... ' Oh, don't talk about the colour or the drawing; I close my eyes to those. But I can feel a deadly chill coming upon me in this most moving of subjects. Where did you get the idea that it was permissible to show me a scene like that without breaking my heart? Don't let's talk about this picture any more, I beg you: just to think about it upsets me.

Before finishing, I should like to say a word about a charming picture that will never perhaps be exhibited at the Salon. It's the New Year's gift from Madame de Grammont to M. de Choiseul. I have seen this picture. It's by Greuze.[67] You would not recognise either the genre or even perhaps the brush of the artist; but his spirit, his finesse are all there. Imagine a window looking onto a street. At the window is a green half-opened curtain; behind the curtain, a charming young girl is getting out of bed, not having had time to dress. She has just received a note from her lover. The lover is passing beneath the window and she blows him a kiss in passing. It's impossible to describe to you the voluptuousness of this figure. Her eyes and eyelids are loaded with it! The hand that's thrown the kiss, what a marvellous one! What physiognomy! What a mouth! What lips! What teeth! What a bust! You can see her bust, her entire bust, although it's covered with a light veil. Her left arm ... She's drunk, no she's not, she doesn't know what she's doing and I almost don't know what I'm writing ... Her left arm which she can no longer hold up, has dropped onto a bowl of flowers and broken them; the note has slipped from her hand; the tips of her fingers are resting on the window sill, which has governed their position. You have to see how loosely bent back they are; how broad and true this curtain is; what a beautiful form this bowl has; how well these flowers are painted, how nonchalantly thrown back this head is and how the auburn hair springs from the forehead and flesh. You have to see the delicacy of the curtain's shadow on the arm, the delicacy of the shadow of the fingers on the

---

[67] The painting is *The Kiss*, Pl. 172.

inside of the hand, and the shadows of this hand and this arm on the chest. How beautifully and delicately the forehead merges with the cheeks, the cheeks with the neck and the neck with the bosom! What a lovely hairstyle she has! How well proportioned this head is! How it stands out from the canvas; and the voluptuous softness so evident to the very tips of her fingers and which we can trace from there throughout all the rest of the figure. How this softness invades you, spreading itself through the veins of the onlooker, as he sees it spreading through the figure! This is a picture to turn a man's head, even yours, you who are so good. Good night my friend, Let them make of it what they will, but I'm going to sleep on it. That's all for the painters. We'll talk about the sculptors tomorrow.

Source: D. Diderot (1965–83edns) *Salons*, vol. II, edited by J. Seznec and J. Adhemar, Clarendon Press, Oxford; translated by John Greenwood.

Appendix

(COMPILED BY LINDA WALSH)

Biographical information on artists discussed by Diderot

Jacques-François Amand (?–1769)

Reçu[68] in 1767. Some of his drawings, exhibited in 1767, were included in the volumes of plates of the *Encyclopédie: The Carpentry Workshop* and *The Gilder's Workshop*. He died in March 1769, before the opening of the Salon that year.

Jean-Jacques Bachelier (1724–1806)

Bachelier was *agréé*[69] in 1750. He was received in 1752 as a painter of flowers and later, in 1763, as a history painter as well. He exhibited regularly at the Salons between 1751 and 1767, and again in 1791. In 1752 he was made Artistic Director of the Manufacture de Vincennes before its transfer to Sèvres and he eventually became Director of the Manufacture de Sèvres. He received important commissions and was a beneficiary of the Marquise de Pompadour. In 1765 he opened a free drawing school in Paris, which met with great success. In 1786 Bachelier became Director of the academy of Marseille. He is mainly known as a painter of flowers. However, he also executed hunting scenes, *trompe-l'oeil* and figures of animals. He was not successful as a history painter but is now believed to have excelled in the still-life genre. (See M. Faré, *La nature morte en France. Son histoire et son évolution du XVIIème et XVIIIème siècle*, Geneva, 1962.)

Baudouin (1723–69)

Son-in-law of Boucher; a painter of miniatures. *Agréé* in 1761.

François Boucher (1703–70)

Boucher first studied under his father, who designed patterns and made prints for embroidery. He then studied under the history painter, Lemoine, whose style he imitated closely. He went on to study under the engraver, Cars. His success brought him a commission to reproduce the works of Watteau, who influenced his figure style and the rococo rhythms of his designs. In 1723 his *Evilmerodach freeing Joachim* won him the first prize at the academy. His works, according to the custom of the day, were hung in the Place Dauphine along the route of the Corpus Christi procession. They helped to establish his reputation. His dream of perfecting his art in Italy was realised when he left for Rome with Carle Van Loo in 1727. During his stay there (until 1731, in which year he became an *agréé* of the Academy) he painted religious or historical subjects. But his *Venus ordering arms from Vulcan for Aeneas* established him as a painter of elegant mythologies. (In the same period he also worked on illustrations for the works of Molière and La Fontaine.) In 1734 he was admitted into the Academy on the strength of his reception piece, *Rinaldo and Armida*.

From this period onwards Boucher's art was very varied. He decorated interiors, furniture, ceramics (the latter at the famous Sèvres porcelain factory). From 1744 to 1748, as chief decorator to the Royal Academy of Music, he painted canvases generally on bucolic subjects. From 1740 he showed his canvases at the Salons and in 1745 he exhibited and successfully sold his drawings and red chalks. In 1752 the patronage of the Marquis de Marigny secured him a pension and lodgings at the Louvre. Three years later he succeeded Oudry as deputy inspector of the Gobelins (tapestry) Manufactory and, in 1765, he was appointed principal painter to the King.

From this moment, however, his renown, which had been established before he won this coveted title (the protection of Madame de Pompadour in particular had secured him a pension and a great number of official commissions) began to decline noticeably. A change in art fashion meant that the art of Greuze began to overshadow that of Boucher.

Jean-Baptiste-Siméon Chardin (1699–1779)

Pupil of the history painters Pierre-Jean Cazes and Noel-Nicolas Coypel, Chardin remained a painter of still lifes and, from the early 1730s

---

[68] i.e. received as a full member of the Academy.

[69] i.e. received into the Academy on a 'probationary' basis and given the responsibility of executing a particular work.

onwards, genre subjects. *Agréé* and *reçu* in 1728 and made Conseiller[70] in 1743, he took an active part in the life of the Academy – as treasurer from 1755, and *tapissier* (picture hanger) from 1761 to 1773. He exhibited at the Salon between 1737 and 1777. (For more information on Chardin see Philip Conisbee, *Chardin*, Phaidon, Oxford, 1986.)

Jean-Baptiste Greuze (1725–1805)

A skilful draughtsman, he first trained in Lyons and then in Paris, where he was an *agréé* in 1755. His travels in Italy with the Abbé Gougenot, between 1756 and 1759, had little direct effect on his art. On his return to Paris he made his reputation as a painter of realistic portraits and genre scenes. Although he exhibited at the Salon, 1755–69, he ceased to do so when the Academy failed to recognise him as a history painter. He exhibited instead at the Salon de la Correspondance, 1779–85, and in his studio. His versions of the modern moral subject, or elevated genre, were fashionable until the 1780s. (See Anita Brookner, *Greuze*, Elek, London, 1972.)

Nicolas-Bernard L'Épicié (1735–84)

Son of François-Bernard L'Épicié, engraver and Secretary to the Academy. He was a pupil of Carle Van Loo. He won the Prix de Rome in 1759. *Agréé* in 1764, he was *reçu* in 1769 as a history painter, becoming a Professor in 1780. He exhibited at the Salon, 1765–85. A history painter until the early 1770s, he devoted his last 10 years to genre work, reminiscent of Greuze and Chardin.

Philippe-Jacques de Loutherbourg (1740–1812)

Born in Strasbourg, he was in Paris from 1755, a pupil of Carle Van Loo and J.-G. Wille. He also frequented the studio of Francesco-Guiseppe Casanova, a painter of battles and landscapes, and was influenced by Vernet. *Agréé* 1763 and *reçu* 1767, he exhibited landscapes, battles, genre and shipwrecks at the Salon, 1763–79, to great critical acclaim. In 1771 he moved to London.

(See *Philippe-Jacques de Loutherbourg*, London (Iveagh Bequest, Kenwood), 1973 (exhibition catalogue by R. Joppien.)

Jean-Baptiste le Prince (1733–81)

Born in Metz, le Prince eventually became a pupil of Boucher. In 1758 he went to Russia for five years and worked in the Imperial Palace in Saint Petersburg. He travelled extensively in the country. *Agréé* in 1764, he was received the next year with his *Russian Baptism*. He exhibited regularly at the Salon, specializing in popular scenes and representations of daily life in Russia. He also painted many pastoral scenes in the style of Boucher.

Carle Van Loo (1705–65)

Carle Van Loo died before Diderot completed his *Salon of 1765*. He was one of the Van Loo brothers – part of a famous eighteenth-century artistic dynasty. He travelled in Italy and won the painter-laureate prize in Rome in 1724. He returned to Rome in 1727 with Boucher. He stayed in Turin until 1731 and decorated the palace of the King of Sardinia. He was admitted to the Academy in 1735, and in 1748 was put in charge of the Academy's aided pupils. Painter to the King in 1762 he achieved a considerable success despite his legendary lack of culture and his "stupidity". He worked on the Château de Bellevue, the church of Saint-Sulpice and, from 1746 to 1755, painted seven canvases for the church of Nôtre-Dame-des-Victoires.

Claude-Joseph Vernet (1714–89)

Trained at Avignon and Aix-en-Provence he established his reputation as a landscape and marine painter in Italy, 1734–53. *Agréé* in 1746 and *reçu* in 1753 as a marine painter, he became a Conseiller of the Academy in 1766. His most important commission was for the *Ports de France* series, executed 1754–65. He exhibited at the Salon 1746–89. (See *Claude-Joseph Vernet*, London (Iveagh Bequest, Kenwood) and Paris, 1976 (exhibition catalogue by P. Conisbee).

---

[70] i.e. member of the Central Council or Board.

Choderlos de Laclos
Discourse on the education of women

Prepared for the Course Team by
Stephanie Clennell

Contents

Choderlos de Laclos
Discourse on the education of women

In 1783 the Academy of Châlons-sur-Marne offered a prize for a discourse on: 'What are the best ways in which the education of women could be improved'. Laclos drafted a discourse on this subject, but did not submit it. The text was not published until 1904. Extracts from the discourse have been selected from the text in Choderlos de Laclos, Oeuvres complètes, *Bibliotheque de la Pléiade. Page references are to this edition.*

Laclos: Discourse on the question put by the Academy of Châlons-sur-Marne

What are the best ways in which the education of women could be improved?

Evil is without remedy when vices have become a part of normal social behaviour. (Seneca, Letter XXXIX)

1 March 1783

Extract from the Introduction

Women, come and listen to me. Let your curiosity for once be usefully employed and look at the advantages which nature has given you and which society has taken away from you. Come and learn how, born as man's companion, you have become his slave and how, having fallen into this abject state, you have managed to take pleasure in it, to look on it as your natural condition; how finally, more and more degraded by being so long accustomed to slavery, you have preferred vices, which corrupt but which are comfortable, to the more burdensome virtues of a free being worthy of respect. If this carefully drawn picture leaves you cold, if you can look at it without emotion, go back to your futile occupations. *The evil is without remedy, vices have become a part of normal social behaviour.* But if, when you hear the story of your misfortunes and your losses, you blush with shame and anger, if tears of indignation start to your eyes, if you burn with a noble desire to regain your advantages, to take full possession of your own lives, don't let yourselves be led astray any longer by false promises, don't expect any help from men who have brought about your misfortunes: they have neither the will nor the power to end them and how could they be willing to educate women before whom they would be forced to blush for shame? You must realize that there is no escape from slavery except by means of a great revolution. Is this revolution possible? Only you can say so, since it is dependent on your own resolution. Is it probable? I give no answer to this question; but until this revolution happens and as long as men control your fate I shall be justified in saying and shall find it easy to prove that *there is no way of improving the education of women.*

Wherever there is slavery education cannot exist; women are slaves in every society; so women in society cannot be educated. If the propositions of this syllogism are established, then the conclusion cannot be rejected. It follows from the definition of this word (slavery) that wherever there is slavery education cannot exist; the main function of education is to develop the faculties, the main function of slavery is to stifle them; the function of education is to direct those faculties which have been developed towards the good of society; the function of slavery is to make slaves enemies of society. If there could be any doubts about these firm principles we have only to apply them to liberty in order to remove them. Presumably it will not be denied that liberty is one of the faculties of women and this implies that liberty can be developed in slavery; and it also implies that liberty can be directed towards the good of society since the liberty of a slave would necessarily be an attack on the social pact based on slavery. One can only conclude from this general principle that without liberty there is no morality and without morality no education. (p.391–2)

Section II
Chapter I On women and the aims of this work (p.392)

......

A classical writer defined man as a two-footed animal without feathers; woman is the female of this animal. Not a woman disfigured by our institutions, but as she emerges from the hands of nature. Like other animals her function is to be born and reproduce and like them it is her nature to fear pain, which is a means of self-preservation, and to enjoy pleasure, which is a means of preservation of the species. Of these two means the first, as being less important, should be, and in fact is, subordinated to the second. After the age of childbearing nature seems to abandon individuals, their bodies function less well. Their feelings are dulled, both pleasure and pain seem to disappear; insensibility increases and we call this old age; total insensibility is death. The laws which nature has imposed on women are to survive and reproduce. So the natural impulses which are found in women are to provide for their own nourishment, to accept the advances of males, to feed the children which result from this and leave them only when they can manage without their care. Often our institutions stifle these impulses in women and nature never fails to punish them for it. Have women gained or lost from these institutions? ...

Chapter II The Natural Woman (p.393)

The natural woman is a being who is free and strong, as a man is; free, in having full use of her faculties; strong, in that her faculties match her needs. Is such a being happy? Probably so, and if, in our view, her happiness seems a paradox, if we think about it more carefully, we shall soon acknowledge the truth of it. Men have wanted to improve everything and they have corrupted everything; they have loaded themselves with chains, then have complained that they are weighed down by them; they have been mad and unjust in abandoning nature which made them happy, then they have slandered it by accusing it of the ills which they have caused by abandoning it.

Chapter III Childhood (p.393)

As soon as he is born man in society is tightly bound in swaddling clothes; it is as if his parents wanted to get him used to the lasting slavery which awaits him; in this constricted and painful state his mother pushes him aside and sends him away from her; she deprives him of a mother's warmth which is the very thing his weakness needs. She refuses him the milk which is meant to feed him. A child of nature is not treated in this way ... A natural woman is happier; nothing

deprives her, nothing separates her from the object of her affections; a few hours after giving birth, she goes to bath her child in a nearby stream, she bathes in it herself, then when she has dried herself on the grass she dries the child in its turn, not by chafing it by rubbing or exposing it to heat to dry it, but by putting it to her breast; there it finds both comforting warmth and the food it needs. Milk is the natural bond which unites mother and child. One needs to receive it, it is at least dangerous for the other to be deprived of it. It is a happy society which is based on mutual benefit. So the mother never wants to abandon her child ...

Now we ask, despite the ostentatious array of obstetricians, nurses, wet-nurses, governesses, which, the son of a prince or the child of nature, which of the two has been abandoned at birth?

Chapter VIII Reflexions on the preceding chapters (pp.409–10)

... At least we can use our imagination to look for what society does not offer us. Let us follow our inclination and create a woman who is perfectly happy at least as far as the human condition allows: she will be a woman, born of a tender mother, who has not been handed over at birth to a paid nurse; who, when she is older, will have been brought up by a teacher who is equally kind, sensible and enlightened and who, without ever being repressive or boring her by her lessons, will have given her all the knowledge which is useful and who will have kept her free from all prejudice; who, when she reaches the age of sexual maturity, will have found as her husband a man who is never dull, who is loving without being jealous, attentive without being importunate; who, when she becomes a mother in her turn, will have enjoyed the happiness of maternal love, without experiencing its constant anxiety, often followed by terrible despair; whose sound imagination will have seen her youth pass without regret; who will have been able to avoid illness and ridicule as she grows older; who finally will have been able to look on death without fear and will fall peacefully into her last sleep; who will be spared personal sorrows and will not have sorrows caused by others; whose fortune will be such that it provides amply for her needs, but does not distress her by being much more than she could want; who will live both without ambition and without fear; who, having fully enjoyed pleasure, will show philosophical stoicism in pain and privation. But isn't such a woman just an illusion? No, in every feature, only in different words, it is a faithful account of a woman in the state of nature ...

Section III (pp.434–8)

Reading is really a second stage of education which supplements what was lacking in the first stage. The aim of this first stage was to get us to the point of educating ourselves rather than actually to educate us. In a way it gave us the materials and the tools; it seldom undertook to show us how to use them and even less often to guide us in the work which it leaves us to do. Knowledge of this work can be derived only from experience; but personal experience is often costly and always lagging behind; so it is useful to profit from the experience of others. It is in books that this can be found.

There are only two ways of acquiring knowledge: observation and reflection. It is easy to judge how limited our knowledge would be, if we had only our own observations and reflections and those of people close to us. This is the case of those peoples whom we call savages. But books enable us to enjoy the observations and reflections of men of all times and of all places. Without perhaps having all that we need, we have even come to the point when it is at least certain that we have a superabundance. Hence the need to choose; hence the usefulness of a guide. We feel that this choice should be made according to the person's age, sex and social position. The intelligence and taste of the subject must be considered as well. Moral reactions are like physical ones: meat which is too strong will not suit weaker temperaments and what is consumed without pleasure is rarely profitable.

According to what we have been told, in this particular case we are dealing with a young person who has intelligence and a good appearance; whose rank and fortune enable her to live in the most distinguished company and even to have influence in it. These advantages seem to put her under more of an obligation than most to cultivate her reason, her heart and her mind. She should have reason so that she knows what is good; be good-hearted so that she wants to do good; and amiability so that she has the means to do it.

The help which she can get from reading to achieve these three aims will be given by moralists, historians and men of letters. From the moralists she will learn to know the passions, to direct them and, if need be, to control them: to appreciate what is beautiful, just and honest, to face or endure pain and sorrow with courage or resignation: to distinguish what comes to men from nature and what comes from human institutions: finally what one owes to one's self and what one owes to others. The effect of this reading on someone who is well-born must be a love of virtue amounting to enthusiasm and finding pleasure only in what is beautiful, just and honest; a great horror of vice; courage and a strict attitude to one's self; pity and an indulgent attitude to others; finally a wide knowledge of man and his duties.

It is only when ideas have been directed to how things should be that it becomes useful, and cannot be dangerous, to know how they are in fact. This knowledge is acquired through history. It is here that men can be seen as they have been affected by all forms of society: it is here that one sees different nations, and often the same nation, in turn elevated by enlightenment and virtue, or degraded by brutishness and vice, according to the stimulus which they get from religion, government, laws and customs: it is here that one can often point to the influence of a single man, for good or evil, on a whole people: it is here that one sees the irresistible power of time and truth: it is here too that the eloquence of facts presents a discussion of that great, still unresolved question, about knowing whether prejudices should be respected, and to what extent this respect is harmful or salutary: and finally it is here that an attentive reader will perhaps be convinced that in every great administration good is created alongside evil as often as evil alongside good: and that the wise course for empires is constantly to repair and almost never destroy.

We cannot read history without being convinced that public and private happiness depends solely upon the number, extent and soundness of ideas; and since it is only in the way in which they are expressed that these ideas become consistent and can be communicated, we become aware of the usefulness of style. We are aware that an idea not only has to be good, but also that it must be clearly expressed to be easily understood and attractively expressed in order to be generally adopted. It is in this spirit that the reading of literature should be begun.

It is particularly by studying poets and orators that we become aware that someone who wants to speak well must have some acquaintance with every field of knowledge. If we apply this principle to the particular case with which we are concerned, it follows that elementary books about every field of knowledge must be included in the library of a young person who wants to be attractive. In fact one of the best ways of making a good impression is to be able to talk to people in their own language. What makes many talented men avoid the company of women, even attractive women, is the impossibility of talking to them, or even talking in their presence, about subjects in which they are interested. It happens only too often that two people, potentially well suited to each other, a talented man and an attractive woman, part regretfully but irrevocably, because they have no common language.

Finally there is another kind of work which deals with moral issues, history and literature: that is travel books, novels and plays. This kind of reading is useful but has its dangers; we shall come back to it later, but we think that it is better, initially, to go in for it to a very limited extent, for fear that the attraction of this kind of reading may make all other kinds of reading unattractive and that its easy charm may encourage lazy and inattentive reading.

Now that we have given an overall view of what should be read we shall say something about the order to be followed; and we shall try to combine pleasure and usefulness. With this in mind we advise linking the different kinds of reading together by arranging them in epochs.

We think that it is a good thing to begin with the Greeks and Romans, because they have been our teachers in every field. Reading the Greek and Roman philosophers is one of the most useful and interesting things that one can do. It is in their writings that we find the principles behind those great and fine actions which made the glory of these two peoples and which stimulates such great interest in their history, which must be studied next. When Roman history is considered alongside Greek history, we can see it as a successor: for it is soon clear that the Greeks, already on the decline, were destined to be constantly subjugated and degraded. But the interest which this brilliant nation arouses creates a wish to know the starting point which led to such heights of splendour, and this wish arouses interest in more ancient peoples: as Greek mythology, adopted by the Romans too, also makes interesting the history of legendary times on which this mythology is based. So we think that reading should begin with this epoch. We only just say that it is enough to go through it fairly rapidly and that this superficial knowledge should be studied in more depth only by someone who has a particular bent for it.

After going further back into the past we come back to our plan and take up Roman history again by reading Plutarch's *Lives*. By finding there the great men of a nation about which we already know something we shall gain some knowledge of the great men of a nation which we shall then study; and it seems to us that this preliminary knowledge should increase interest in it, rather as one has a greater wish to travel in a country, if one has already had the chance of seeing some of its great men ...... then Greek and Roman literature will be studied. It goes without saying that in this field our work is limited to imitating them and to gaining credit for ourselves at times by equalling them. The same thing is true of those examples of their arts and architecture which have survived into our own time.

......

Section III (pp.439–41)

One cannot read history, especially modern history, without realising that it deals only with public events and men; the result is that there is nothing for readers which concerns their own habits and feelings and that very few of them can get rules of behaviour from it and no one can get a knowledge of men. It is novels which can make up for what is lacking in history and from this point of view they can be of great service. But here the choice must be rigorous in every respect. For when works of this kind are without talent, reason or morality, they are only too

---

[1] *Clarissa Harlowe* (1767–8) by Samuel Richardson (1689–1761).

effective in corrupting the taste, the mind and the heart. Perhaps there is not even one which a young person could read without any danger, unless she is guided in the way in which she looks at it. To quote only one example, we shall choose that masterpiece among novels: *Clarissa*.[1] Certainly one cannot fail to have a very high opinion of it and even to respect the heroine of this novel; and yet Clarissa committed almost the greatest fault which a girl could commit, since she escaped from her family home with her seducer. So one might fear that this example might reassure a young person as to the fear of contempt which is so rarely avoided after taking such a step, and, in this sense, this book may be dangerous. But if on the other hand one points out to the young person that Clarissa, who has all the natural advantages and possesses all the virtues, as a result of taking a single step against the wishes of her parents (taking her reply to Lovelace to the woodshed), a step which she might well think innocent and even reasonable: if, we say, one points out that from that moment she was inevitably drawn into all the misfortunes of which she eventually became the victim, then few books could be of more use. The same views apply to plays. J-J. Rousseau has pointed out the dangers of these, and d'Alembert their usefulness, and both have simply adopted a different point of view. So in this field almost everything depends on the skill of the guide or the sound mind of the person who is reading. If one of these two conditions is adequately met, one has only to remove from her novels or comedies which include details which are too lax and which in some way would spoil that fresh innocence which, even more than natural freshness, gives youth its real charm.

Up to this point the different nations which our young pupil will have studied have all been, as it were, civilised, with the same principles and a common tradition; but there are other peoples, equally civilised, or with more ancient civilisations, who have been known to us only for a few centuries and were entirely unknown to the ancient peoples whose history we have studied. The knowledge which we can well gain from these peoples who are so different from us makes for agreeable reading in the fresh view which it gives us, and is useful in showing the different changes which diverse institutions can make in men. Finally there is a multitude of peoples who

are little civilised, or not at all, of which accounts of travels have given us some kind of knowledge. There is some pleasure and some profit in a view of these cruder mores too. However, as in the case of novels and plays, a careful choice of this kind of reading has also to be made. Moreover, it seems to go hand in hand with the study of modern geography to which it adds considerable interest. One can include with the reading of novels, writing on travel, and plays, French literary works; these go little further back than the age of Louis XIV. Those of Italy and Spain go a little further back; in this field England is even more recent than France; and Germany is, as it were, just being born.

The care which has been taken to provide us with French translations of the best works written in all other languages means that a knowledge of foreign languages is much less important and is nowadays more a matter of interest than of use. However, since study of this kind contributes to the study of the native language, and since it is necessary to have a perfect command of this, we think that it is a good thing to learn another language; the choice can be made according to personal taste. We should advise Latin, rather than any other language, to a young person who has the good sense to prefer knowledge which she can use to the kind which would enable her to shine in company where it would seem ridiculous if she said anything in Latin. But if she does not feel up to it she will do better to learn Italian or English according to whether she prefers works of brilliant imagination and pleasing expression to those with solid reasoning and depth of feeling.

......

Section III (p. 443)

If the young person we are discussing now has the courage to undertake the work which we are suggesting, we think we can assure her that she will not only be better informed but also happier than most other women. We hope at the same time that she will have enough good sense not to show off her knowledge except to her closest friends and as it were in confidence. Finally we warn her that, in the rivalry of the social circle, to be well received in it she will need to show more simplicity, just as she will contribute more real worth.

Source: C. de Laclos (1783?), *Oeuvres complètes*, Bibliothèque de la Pléiade, Paris.

Kant: What is Enlightenment

Translated by
H.B. Nisbet

Kant: What is Enlightenment

Immanuel Kant was born on 22 April 1724 in Königsberg, son of a saddle-maker. Having been educated at the University in his home town, he eventually obtained the ill-paid academic post of Privatdozent there. Indeed, so low was his salary that he had to continue to supplement it by giving private tuition, a time-consuming activity he disliked greatly. Despite this, he completed a number of influential works and became a popular lecturer. As a result, other universities offered him chairs, and it was probably for this reason that he was finally offered the professorship of logic and metaphysics at Königsberg in 1770. Financially secure at last, he was able to concentrate on the revolutionary philosophical ideas which were germinating in his mind. After eleven years, he issued the first edition of his great work The Critique of Pure Reason (1781), followed within a decade by a stream of what are now philosophical classics, notably The Critique of Practical Reason (1788) and The Critique of

Judgement (1790). Kant is an example of a rare phenomenon in the history of thought, namely a world-class philosopher whose great creative phase began in late middle-age.

Outwardly, Kant's life appears dull: he never left Königsberg, never married, and with the aid of his servant Lampe, organized his days with invariant precision: the inhabitants of Königsberg could set their clocks by watching Kant pass by on his daily constitutional. Yet Kant was not a dull man: he was a genial and witty host, and on principle never talked philosophy to his dinner guests, of whom there were many. And as a philosopher, he is by common consent one of the greatest in the Western tradition, the only one fit to be mentioned in the same breath as Plato and Aristotle.

Late in life his mental powers collapsed. His last six years were a painful epilogue to what had gone before and he died, after a sad period of intermittent senility, on 12 February 1804.

An Answer to the Question: 'What is Enlightenment?'[1]

Enlightenment is man's emergence from his self-incurred immaturity. Immaturity is the inability to use one's own understanding without the guidance of another. This immaturity is *self-incurred* if its cause is not lack of understanding, but lack of resolution and courage to use it without the guidance of another. The motto of enlightenment is therefore: *Sapere aude!*[2] Have courage to use your *own* understanding!

Laziness and cowardice are the reasons why such a large proportion of men, even when nature has long emancipated them from alien guidance (*naturaliter maiorennes*),[3] nevertheless gladly remain immature for life. For the same

reasons, it is all too easy for others to set themselves up as their guardians. It is so convenient to be immature! If I have a book to have understanding in place of me, a spiritual adviser to have a conscience for me, a doctor to judge my diet for me, and so on, I need not make any efforts at all. I need not think, so long as I can pay; others will soon enough take the tiresome job over for me. The guardians who have kindly taken upon themselves the work of supervision will soon see to it that by far the largest part of mankind (including the entire fair sex) should consider the step forward to maturity not only as difficult but also as highly dangerous. Having

---

[1]   *Beantwortung der Frage: Was ist Aufklärung?*, AA VIII, 33–42. First published in *Berlinische Monatsschrift*, IV (12 December 1784), 481–94. There is a reference in the original edition of the *Berlinische Monatsschrift* to p.516 of the number of that journal published on 5 December 1783. This reference is to an essay by the Rev. Zöllner, 'Is it advisable to sanction marriage through religion?'. The relevant passage reads (in translation): '*What is Enlightenment?* The question, which is almost as important as the question *What is truth?*, should be answered before one begins to enlighten others. And yet I have never found it answered anywhere.' [N]

[2]   Literal translation: 'Dare to be wise'. Horace, *Epodes* 1,2,40. Cf. Elizabeth M. Wilkinson and L.A. Willoughby (eds and trs.), Friedrich Schiller, *On the Aesthetic Education of Man* (Oxford, 1967) LXXIV ff.; cf; also Franco Venturi, 'Was ist Aufklärung? Sapere Aude!', *Rivista Storica Italiana*, LXXI (1959), 119 ff. Venturi traces the use made of this quotation from Horace throughout the centuries. cf. also p.5. [N]

[3]   'Those who have come of age by virtue of nature.' [N]

first infatuated their domesticated animals, and carefully prevented the docile creatures from daring to take a single step without the leading-strings to which they are tied, they next show them the danger which threatens them if they try to walk unaided. Now this danger is not in fact so very great, for they would certainly learn to walk eventually after a few falls. But an example of this kind is intimidating, and usually frightens them off from further attempts.

Thus it is difficult for each separate individual to work his way out of the immaturity which has become almost second nature to him. He has even grown fond of it and is really incapable for the time being of using his own understanding, because he was never allowed to make the attempt. Dogmas and formulas, those mechanical instruments for rational use (or rather misue) of his natural endowments, are the ball and chain of his permanent immaturity. And if anyone did throw them off, he would still be uncertain about jumping over even the narrowest of trenches, for he would be unaccustomed to free movement of this kind. Thus only a few, by cultivating their own minds, have succeeded in freeing themselves from immaturity and in continuing boldly on their way.

There is more chance of an entire public enlightening itself. This is indeed almost inevitable, if only the public concerned is left in freedom. For there will always be a few who think for themselves, even among those appointed as guardians of the common mass. Such guardians, once they have themselves thrown off the yoke of immaturity, will disseminate the spirit of rational respect for personal value and for the duty of all men to think for themselves. The remarkable thing about this is that if the public which was previously put under this yoke by the guardians, is suitably stirred up by some of the latter who are incapable of enlightenment, it may subsequently compel the guardians themselves to remain under the yoke. For it is very harmful to propagate prejudices, because they finally avenge themselves on the very people who first encouraged them (or whose predecessors did so). Thus a public can only achieve enlightenment slowly. A revolution may well put an end to autocratic despotism and to rapacious or power-seeking oppression, but it will never produce a true reform in ways of thinking. Instead, new prejudices, like the ones they replaced, will serve as a leash to control the great unthinking mass.

For enlightenment of this kind, all that is needed is *freedom*. And the freedom in question is the most innocuous form of all – freedom to make *public use* of one's reason in all matters. But I hear on all sides the cry: *Don't argue!* The officer says: Don't argue, get on parade! The tax-official: Don't argue, pay! The clergyman: Don't argue, believe! (Only one ruler in the world says: *Argue* as much as you like and about whatever you like, *but obey*!)[4] All this means restrictions on freedom everywhere. But which sort of restriction prevents enlightenment, and which, instead of hindering it, can actually promote it? I reply: The *public* use of man's reason must always be free, and it alone can bring about enlightenment among men; the *private use* of reason may quite often be very narrowly restricted, however, without undue hindrance to the progress of enlightenment. But by the public use of one's own reason I mean that use which anyone may make of it *as a man of learning* addressing the entire *reading public*. What I term the private use of reason is that which a person may make of it in a particular *civil* post or office with which he is entrusted.

Now in some affairs which affect the interests of the commonwealth, we require a certain mechanism whereby some members of the commonwealth must behave purely passively, so that they may, by an artificial common agreement, be employed by the government for public ends (or at least deterred from vitiating them). It is, of course, impermissible to argue in such cases; obedience is imperative. But in so far as this or that individual who acts as part of the machine also considers himself as a member of a complete commonwealth or even of cosmopolitan society, and thence as a man of learning who may through his writings address a public in the truest sense of the word, he may indeed argue without harming the affairs in which he is employed for some of the time in a passive capacity. Thus it would be very harmful if an officer receiving an order from his superiors were to

---

[4]   The allusion is to Frederick II (the Great), King of Prussia (1740–86). [N]

quibble openly, while on duty, about the appropriateness or usefulness of the order in question. He must simply obey. But he cannot reasonably be banned from making observations as a man of learning on the errors in the military service, and from submitting these to his public for judgement. The citizen cannot refuse to pay the taxes imposed upon him; presumptuous criticisms of such taxes, where someone is called upon to pay them, may be punished as an outrage which could lead to general insubordination. Nonetheless, the same citizen does not contravene his civil obligations if, as a learned individual, he publicly voices his thoughts on the impropriety or even injustice of such fiscal measures. In the same way, a clergyman is bound to instruct his pupils and his congregation in accordance with the doctrines of the church he serves, for he was employed by it on that condition. But as a scholar, he is completely free as well as obliged to impart to the public all his carefully considered, well-intentioned thoughts on the mistaken aspects of those doctrines, and to offer suggestions for a better arrangement of religious and ecclesiastical affairs. And there is nothing in this which need trouble the conscience. For what he teaches in pursuit of his duties as an active servant of the church is presented by him as something which he is not empowered to teach at his own discretion, but which he is employed to expound in a prescribed manner and in someone else's name. He will say: Our church teaches this or that, and these are the arguments it uses. He then extracts as much practical value as possible for his congregation from precepts to which he would not himself subscribe with full conviction, but which he can nevertheless undertake to expound, since it is not in fact wholly impossible that they may contain truth. At all events, nothing opposed to the essence of religion is present in such doctrines. For if the clergyman thought he could find anything of this sort in them, he would not be able to carry out his official duties in good conscience, and would have to resign. Thus the use which someone employed as a teacher makes of his reason in the presence of his congregation is purely *private*, since a congregation, however large it is, is never any more than a domestic gathering. In view of this, he is not and cannot be free as a priest, since he is acting on a commission imposed from outside. Conversely, as a scholar addressing the real public

(i.e. the world at large) through his writings, the clergyman making *public use* of his reason enjoys unlimited freedom to use his own reason and to speak in his own person. For to maintain that the guardians of the people in spiritual matters should themselves be immature, is an absurdity which amounts to making absurdities permanent.

But should not a society of clergymen, for example an ecclesiastical synod or a venerable presbytery (as the Dutch call it), be entitled to commit itself by oath to a certain unalterable set of doctrines, in order to secure for all time a constant guardianship over each of its members, and through them over the people? I reply that this is quite impossible. A contract of this kind, concluded with a view to preventing all further enlightenment of mankind for ever, is absolutely null and void, even if it is ratified by the supreme power, by Imperial Diets and the most solemn peace treaties. One age cannot enter into an alliance on oath to put the next age in a position where it would be impossible for it to extend and correct its knowledge, particularly on such important matters, or to make any progress whatsoever in enlightenment. This would be a crime against human nature, whose original destiny lies precisely in such progress. Later generations are thus perfectly entitled to dismiss these agreements as unauthorized and criminal. To test whether any particular measure can be agreed upon as a law for a people, we need only ask whether a people could well impose such a law upon itself. This might well be possible for a specified short period as a means of introducing a certain order, pending, as it were, a better solution. This would also mean that each citizen, particularly the clergyman, would be given a free hand as a scholar to comment publicly, that is in his writings, on the inadequacies of current institutions. Meanwhile, the newly established order would continue to exist, until public insight into the nature of such matters had progressed and proved itself to the point where, by general consent (if not unanimously), a proposal could be submitted to the crown. This would seek to protect the congregations who had, for instance, agreed to alter their religious establishment in accordance with their own notions of what higher insight is, but it would not try to obstruct those who wanted to let things remain as before. But it is absolutely impermissible to agree, even for a single lifetime, to a permanent religious constitution which no-one might publicly question. For this would virtually nullify a phase in man's upward progress, thus making it fruitless and even detrimental to subsequent generations. A man may for his own person, and even then only for a limited period, postpone enlightening himself in matters he ought to know about. But to renounce such enlightenment completely, whether for his own person or even more so for later generations, means violating and trampling underfoot the sacred rights of mankind. But something which a people may not even impose upon itself can still less be imposed on it by a monarch; for his legislative authority depends precisely upon his uniting the collective will of the people in his own. So long as he sees to it that all true or imagined improvements are compatible with the civil order, he can otherwise leave his subjects to do whatever they find necessary for their salvation, which is none of his business. But it is his business to stop anyone forcibly hindering others from working as best they can to define and promote their salvation. It indeed detracts from his majesty if he interferes in these affairs by subjecting the writings in which his subjects attempt to clarify their religious ideas to governmental supervision. This applies if he does so acting upon his own exalted opinions – in which case he exposes himself to the reproach: *Caesar non est supra Grammaticos*[5] – but much more so if he demeans his high authority so far as to support the spiritual despotism of a few tyrants within his state against the rest of his subjects.

If it is now asked whether we at present live in an *enlightened* age, the answer is: No, but we do live in an age of *enlightenment*. As things are at present, we still have a long way to go before men as a whole can be in a position (or can even be put into a position) of using their own understanding confidently and well in religious matters, without outside guidance. But we do have distinct indications that the way is now being cleared for them to work freely in this direction, and that the obstacles to universal enlightenment, to man's emergence from his self-incurred

immaturity, are gradually becoming fewer. In this respect our age is the age of enlightenment, the century of *Frederick*.[6]

A prince who does not regard it as beneath him to say that he considers it his duty, in religious matters, not to prescribe anything to his people, but to allow them complete freedom, a prince who thus even declines to accept the presumptuous title of *tolerant*, is himself enlightened. He deserves to be praised by a grateful present and posterity as the man who first liberated mankind from immaturity (as far as government is concerned), and who left all men free to use their own reason in all matters of conscience. Under his rule, ecclesiastical dignitaries, notwithstanding their official duties, may in their capacity as scholars freely and publicly submit to the judgement of the world their verdicts and opinions, even if these deviate here and there from orthodox doctrine. This applies even more to all others who are not restricted by any official duties. This spirit of freedom is also spreading abroad, even where it has to struggle with outward obstacles imposed by governments which misunderstand their own function. For such governments can now witness a shining example of how freedom may exist without in the least jeopardizing public concord and the unity of the commonwealth. Men will of their own accord gradually work their way out of barbarism so long as artificial measures are not deliberately adopted to keep them in it.

I have portrayed *matters of religion* as the focal point of enlightenment, that is of man's emergence from his self-incurred immaturity. This is firstly because our rulers have no interest in assuming the role of guardians over their subjects so far as the arts and sciences are concerned, and secondly, because religious immaturity is the most pernicious and dishonourable variety of all. But the attitude of mind of a head of state who favours freedom in the arts and sciences extends even further, for he realizes that there is no danger even to his *legislation* if he allows his subjects to make *public* use of their own reason and to put before the public their thoughts on better ways of drawing up laws,

---

5   'Caesar is not above the grammarians.' [N]

6   Kant here refers, of course, to Frederick the Great. [N]

even if this entails forthright criticism of the current legislation. We have before us a brilliant example of this kind, in which no monarch has yet surpassed the one to whom we now pay tribute.

But only a ruler who is himself enlightened and has no fear of phantoms, yet who likewise has at hand a well-disciplined and numerous army to guarantee public security, may say what no republic would dare to say: *Argue as much as you like and about whatever you like, but obey!* This reveals to us a strange and unexpected pattern in human affairs (such as we shall always find if we consider them in the widest sense, in which nearly everything is paradoxical). A high degree of civil freedom seems advantageous to a people's *intellectual* freedom, yet it also sets up insuperable barriers to it. Conversely, a lesser degree of civil freedom gives intellectual freedom enough room to expand to its fullest extent. Thus once the germ on which nature has lavished most care –

man's inclination and vocation to *think freely* – has developed within this hard shell, it gradually reacts upon the mentality of the people, who thus gradually become increasingly able to *act freely*. Eventually, it even influences the principles of governments, which find that they can themselves profit by treating man, who is *more than a machine*,[7] in a manner appropriate to his dignity.*

Königsberg in Prussia, 30th September, 1784.

*I read today on the 30th September in Büsching's[8] *Wöchentliche Nachrichten* of 13th September a notice concerning this month's *Berlinische Monatsschrift*. The notice mentions Mendelssohn's[9] answer to the same question as that which I have answered. I have not yet seen this journal, otherwise I should have held back the above reflections. I let them stand only as a means of finding out by comparison how far the thoughts of two individuals may coincide by chance.[10]

Source: H. B. Nisbet, ' An Answer to the Question: "What is Enlightenment?", *Journal of European Studies. Literature and Ideas from renaissance to the present*, 1982, pp.77–95.

---

[7] This allusion amounts to a repudiation of Julien Offray de Lamettrie's (1709–51) materialism as expressed in *L'Homme Machine* (1748).

[8] Anton Friedrich Büsching (1724–93), professor in the University of Göttingen, theologian and leading geographer of the day, editor of *Wöchentliche Nachrichten von neuen Landkarten, geographischen, statistischen und historischen Büchern*. Kant's reference is to XII, 1784 (Berlin, 1785), 291.

[9] Moses Mendelssohn (1729–86), a leading philosopher of the German Enlightenment. The reference is to Mendelssohn's essay 'Uber die Frage: was heisst Aufklärung?' ('On the question: what is Enlightenment?'), *Berlinische Monatsschrift*, IV (9 September 1784), 193–200.

[10] This was a footnote in Kant's original article. [eds]